# The

## Amateur

# Democrat

# The
## Amateur
# Democrat

**CLUB POLITICS IN THREE CITIES**

## By James Q. Wilson

THE UNIVERSITY OF CHICAGO PRESS

CHICAGO & LONDON

*ISBN: 0-226-90099-1 (clothbound); 0-226-90100-9 (paperbound)*
THE UNIVERSITY OF CHICAGO PRESS, CHICAGO 60637
The University of Chicago Press, Ltd., London

**TO MY FATHER AND MOTHER**

# Preface, 1966

When I began work on this book in the summer of 1960, I thought of it as a lengthy essay on the nature of political motivation and the relationship between such motives and the way in which the institutions of a democratic society operate. What now appear as chapters on the various local reform and club movements were originally to be nothing more than footnotes or brief anecdotes illustrating the major themes of the essay. Obviously they grew into something a bit more pretentious, so much so that I have found it necessary to warn friends who have read it not to think of it as a study of certain party organizations (which it seems to be) but as a study of a certain political mentality (which it ought to be).

Over the past five years, a great deal has happened to the organizations and people here described. The Manhattan reformers have won several more victories in contests for local office, have been joined by vigorous reform movements in the other boroughs of New York City, and have supported their own candidate for mayor. The warfare between the California clubs and certain party leaders—especially Assembly Speaker Jesse Unruh—has intensified, becoming a pitched battle in the 1964 Democratic senatorial primary election. Many of the activists in the struggling Illinois clubs have abandoned club politics (in the face of hopeless odds) in favor of organizations directed toward certain substantive ends, especially civil rights.

These changes in organization, tactics, or status have not, however, represented a change in the political mentality with which I was primarily concerned. Indeed, in many ways that mentality has become more pervasive in American politics, though not necessarily as the result of the organizational efforts of the club movement. The amateur spirit—the belief that the proper motive for political action is a concern for the ends of politics, that participation in the management of the affairs of the party ought to be widespread and in accord with strictly democratic procedures, and that party leaders and elective officials ought to be directly responsive to the substantive goals of the party activists—is becoming commonplace in our cities and counties. The reform ideal is being realized even though the reformers themselves are not everywhere successful. In part this is the inevitable result of the growing education and civic awareness of the American voter, who increasingly is discontent with a politics of interest, of favoritism, of ethnic recognition, and of localistic concerns. Americans more and more are trained to think in terms of large issues, causes, and principles. Because professional politicians seem to avoid such matters and instead speak in vague generalities and offer muddy or non-existent choices, Americans are increasingly restless with the professional style in politics.

At the same time, other forces are injecting fundamental and deeply divisive issues into American politics. Foremost among these is civil rights; crime in the streets and public safety and morality are not far behind. Government itself, in seeking solutions for various social problems, has created new issues and new political instruments that both divide the community and call forth a high level of citizen participation in the effort to cope with these issues. Fluoridation, urban renewal, and the community action programs of the war on poverty have, along with civil rights, brought to local politics an intensity, a passion, and a degree of involvement with which our traditional political institutions are not accustomed to dealing. People see politics more and more in terms of fundamental issues, and at the same time fundamental issues are more and more being placed on the civic agenda. Small wonder that professional politicians seem bewildered or disorganized.

Ironically, the greatest victory of the amateur spirit in recent American politics occurred, not in the Democratic, but in the Republican party. Barry Goldwater won the 1964 Republican presidential nomination as the very embodiment of the amateur spirit. Deeply committed volunteers working at the grass-roots level captured local party organizations from the professionals and from the elective officials and, pyramiding their strength, took their party's national convention by storm. The candidate himself seemed more interested in principles than in victory; the men who surrounded him in his campaign were, to an extraordinary degree, intellectuals and amateur politicians who refused to listen to pleas from other party leaders, governors, and legislators for moderation and compromise. The leaders of the Goldwater campaign saw themselves as responsible to a set of ideas, to a man, and to a cause—not to an organization, a coalition, a heterogeneous party. The result, of course, was a disaster.

Comparing Goldwater Republicans with reform or club Democrats does some injustice to both, and I do not wish to push the analogy too far. As I hope this book makes clear, there are many varieties of the amateur Democrat, many of whom—after several years in office—have acquired a sense of responsibility and a willingness to bargain that is almost indistinguishable from that of the professional politicians whom, in many cases, they replaced. I meant the book to be an account of the political vision and methods of those in the Democratic party who display the amateur spirit, recognizing that not all reformers or club members are amateurs and not all amateurs are in the reform or club movement.

Because at least one group of clubs studied in the book was explicitly interested in the reform of local government, and because I had some critical things to say about those clubs, I am often asked, "Why are you against reform?" The question, of course, misses the point by a considerable margin, and in time I suppose I shall learn not to be irritated by it. This book is about the functions of political parties, and especially about the relationship between party leaders and party followers; it is *not* about municipal reform, good government, the honest ballot, or public policy. If I had foreseen the Goldwater nomination (who did?), this book would have been about the amateur Republican and would have said essentially the same things, but in connection with a man and a movement very different in philosophy and objectives from the activists in the Democratic clubs. I suppose then I would have been asked, by outraged Goldwater militants, why I was in favor of communism.

In rereading the last chapter of this book, I think I failed to distinguish as carefully as I should between what the clubs profess and what they have actually done. The club movement in all three cities has accomplished some desirable—or at least unobjectionable—ends. In New York, for example, the Democratic party for decades had been suffering from an acute case of political anemia created by a chronic failure to bring new blood into the organization. The party was superannuated; in a period when able young governors and senators were appearing in many states, New York was carrying on with relics from the days of Al Smith. Furthermore, many elements in the party—especially the liberal New York City Jewish voters—were almost completely unrepresented, even at the level of assembly district leader, to say nothing of the congressional delegation or the county leadership. Liberals, reformers, and even amateurs (the terms are not necessarily identical) ought to be represented in the party if the party is to have both the vitality and the breadth necessary to win elections and govern citizens. The reform movement changed much of this, and in many cases the change was for the better. Able young people at last found a way into political life; elderly Irish leaders in heavily Jewish districts were replaced with men more representative of the electorate.

The point of the last chapter is that the party as a whole cannot and should not be made over into the image of its newest and most articulate members, for the political institutions with which they feel comfortable are not the ones best suited to other elements of the party. Furthermore, party activists are almost never a cross-section of the electorate, even in their own districts, and it is to the electorate that the elective officials must ultimately be responsible. The only guarantee of such responsibility is a two-party system; internal party arrangements, designed to amplify the voices of the militants, can never be a substitute for party competition.

# Preface

This study of amateur politicians in the Democratic party is intended for several audiences. It is written first of all for citizens and amateur and professional politicians who are involved in or deeply concerned about the forces shaping the local structure of our political parties and curious about the relationship between these parties and the large cities in which they are found. Second, it is hoped that there will be something here of interest to those scholars who, along with the author, have long lamented the shortage of studies of local politics which were comparative in nature and thus not limited to the phenomenon of a single city. This book attempts to be as "comparative" as the maddeningly refractory nature of the data permits. Third, I have tried to organize and interpret my data in terms of a single more or less consistent conceptual framework which is based on a theory of formal organizations which Peter Clark and I have set forth in other publications. I hope the book will be found "theoretically relevant," although if I must choose, I prefer that it be found interesting.

Since several audiences were in mind, the book probably meets the needs of each very imperfectly. There is probably too much theory for the layman and not enough for the social scientist; the language is probably too dry and technical for the citizen but too ambiguous for the scholar. I have tried throughout to make all necessary compromises in favor of the citizen.

For those who are interested in such things, let me briefly describe the method of research. The bulk of the data was derived from interviews with the principal leaders in the amateur club movement in New York, Chicago, and Los Angeles, as well as with the most important of the professional politicians with whom the amateurs must deal. The interviewing took place in New York in the summers of 1960 and 1961, in Los Angeles in the winter of 1961, and in Chicago in the summer of 1961. After most of the interviewing was completed, a "case study" running from one to five chapters in length was written for each city, and copies circulated to most of the interviewees for their comments and corrections. These case studies embodied almost all the factual and interpretive material which later found its way into the book. After all the comments had been received, the first draft of the book was written following its present outline. The case studies were torn apart and assimilated into the present format. This meant, in effect, writing the book twice, once on a city-by-city basis and a second time on a comparative or analytical basis, but the extra effort was well worth it. Due to the pressure of deadlines and an unwillingness to ask my interviewees to give me an unreasonable portion of their time and effort, the final draft was *not* circulated among them for comments. Thus, even more than is usual, I must accept full responsibility for all errors of fact which appear in these pages.

All research was done before reapportionment was carried out in 1962. Thus, all references in the book to political boundaries (assembly or congressional district or ward lines) are to these boundaries as they stood in 1960.

I want to acknowledge gratefully the help of my two research assistants. Michael Rogin undertook most of the interviewing in Illinois, wrote the first draft of chapter iii, and contributed data and ideas which were used in many other chapters as well. Donald Rosenthal did much of the bibliographic research and labored through several mountains of statistical material to produce some of the few quantitative items which were found to be useful.

I am happy to acknowledge once again the debt I owe Professor Edward C. Banfield for the many fruitful ideas and comments he offered on several versions of the manuscript.

Other scholars also contributed significantly to improving this work. The case study on New York was read by Professors Wallace Sayre of Columbia, Bert Swanson of Hunter College, and Theodore Lowi of Cornell. Professor Bruce B. Mason of Arizona State University contributed substantially to chapter iii. Professor V. O. Key, Jr., of Harvard made many helpful comments on chapters i, ix, and xi. Many other persons read and advised on the case studies, but since they were also interviewees, and since their anonymity was one of the conditions under which I enlisted their aid, they cannot be thanked by name. I alone, of course, bear the sole responsibility for the final product.

Financial support for this study came from several sources. Most of the funds were provided by two grants from the Social Science Research Council of New York. Money for secretarial assistance in the early stages of writing was made available by the Social Science Research Committee of the University of Chicago and in the final stages by the Joint Center for Urban Studies of the Massachusetts Institute of Technology and Harvard University.

The Free Press of Glencoe kindly gave me permission to reprint some parts of chapters i and ii which I had earlier published in their book, *Urban Government*, edited by Edward C. Banfield, under the title, "Egghead Politics in Manhattan."

My wife undertook the herculean task of saving me from those violations of the elementary rules of grammar and style which I persist in committing in spite of her many years of trying to teach me how to write.

One final personal note. I am a member of the same generation and I come from the same educational background as many of the amateur Democrats I describe in the following pages. Like them, I was once lured into an amateur Democratic club in order to ring doorbells for Adlai Stevenson. That was several years ago, and my views on this kind of activity have changed considerably. But I have not forgotten the excitement of that introduction to local politics.

# Contents

# Tables

# Maps

# Abbreviations

CDC   California Democratic Council

CDV   New York Committee for Democratic Voters

DFI    Democratic Federation of Illinois

IVI    Independent Voters of Illinois

# 1 Introduction

Since the Second World War a new kind of politician has appeared in large numbers in several of the biggest American cities. Although they are nowhere in complete control of their parties, these new politicians have played a crucial part in the defeat of the boss of Tammany Hall and have contributed to the election of several important officials: a governor in California, a mayor in New York City, and a state's attorney in Chicago. Their ambitions extend far beyond these offices, however, for they intend to alter fundamentally the character of the American party system, and accordingly of all governing institutions.

The new politicians are known by several names. In California, they are referred to, most generally, as the "club movement" and more specifically as the "CDC"—the California Democratic Council. In New York City, they are called the "reformers" or sometimes the "Lehman group," after one of their chief sponsors, former Senator Herbert H. Lehman. In Illinois, one group is known as the "IVI"—the Independent Voters of Illinois, a local affiliate of the Americans for Democratic Action—while another wing is called the "DFI"—the Democratic Federation of Illinois. Wherever they are found and whatever their name, however, they display certain common characteristics, and it is with these general traits that this study is concerned.

Although the traits these new politicians have in common are easy to list, it is difficult to find a single word which will describe them adequately and distinguish them from the more conventional politicians found in large cities. That they are so distinguished can scarcely be doubted. In every community where they are found in large numbers, a keen antipathy inevitably develops between the new and the conventional politicians. The former accuse the latter of being at best "hacks" and "organization men" and at worst "bosses" and "machine leaders." The latter retort by describing the former as "dilettantes," "crackpots," "outsiders," and "hypocritical do-gooders." Most of the new politicians in the Democratic party are also liberals, but it is not their liberalism that is their chief distinguishing characteristic. They can be found in the Republican party as well, and there they are likely to be extremely conservative. What is necessary is a definition that distinguishes the new from other politicians but which is applicable equally to liberals and conservatives.

## The Nature of the Amateur

It is not his liberalism or his age, education, or class that sets the new politician apart and makes him worth studying. Rather, it is his outlook on politics, and the style of politics he practices. This is sensed by the politicians themselves; the conventional and the new politicians, in almost every case, find it hard to "understand" one another or to "get along," even in those cases in which their interests or policies happen to coincide. Although in New York the new politicians are called "reformers," their counterparts in Wisconsin or California are not reformers at all, for in these states they are not preoccupied with matters of reform. Nor, as we shall see, are they all "intellectuals" or "eggheads," although some of the new politicians are fond of describing themselves and their colleagues in these terms. Although no single word is completely satisfactory, the word which I will use in this study is "amateur."

By amateur is not meant a dabbler, a dilettante or an inept practitioner of some special skill; many amateur Democrats have a highly sophisticated understanding of practical politics and have proved their skills in the only way that matters—by winning at the polls. Similarly, a good many undoubted professionals—by which word I mean all non-amateurs—are hopelessly incompetent and have proved themselves so in the only way that matters.

Nor does amateur here mean a person who is in politics for fun or as an avocation, rather than for money or as a career. To be sure, most amateurs do get their incomes from sources other than politics and regard it as other than a career. But there are also many professionals, as the word will be used here, who do not make money from politics and who think of it mainly as a game. In Chicago, of course, most professional politicians do as a rule have public jobs or get some income from politics, but this is not the case everywhere. In California few professionals other than those holding elective office are supported mainly by politics, and even in Manhattan there are as many or more workers in Tammany clubs who do not have political jobs as there are those who do.

An amateur is one who finds politics *intrinsically* interesting because it expresses a conception of the public interest. The amateur politician sees the political world more in terms of ideas and principles than in terms of persons. Politics is the determination of public policy, and public policy ought to be set deliberately rather than as the accidental by-product of a struggle for personal and party advantage. Issues ought to be settled on their merits; compromises by which one issue is settled other than on its merits are sometimes necessary, but they are never desirable. If the arena in which the amateur acts is the city and the question at hand a limited one, his tendency is to endow the issue with generality—either by making it a national issue or by finding in it wider implications. The amateur takes the outcome of politics—the determination of policies and the choice of officials—seriously, in the sense that he feels a direct concern for what he thinks are the ends these policies serve and the qualities these officials possess. He is not oblivious to considerations of partisan or personal advantage in assessing the outcome but (in the pure case) he dwells on the relation of outcome to his conception, be it vague or specific, of the public weal. Although politics may have attractions as a game of skill, it is never simply that. The professional, on the other hand—even the "professional" who practices politics as a hobby rather than as a vocation—is preoccupied with the outcome of politics in terms of winning or losing. Politics, to him, consists of concrete questions and specific persons who must be dealt with in a manner that will "keep everybody happy" and thus minimize the possibility of defeat at the next election. The professional politician rarely broods about his function in society, the larger significance of the issues with which he deals, or the consistency of his procedures with some well-worked-out theory of democracy. Although he is not oblivious to the ends implied by political outcomes, he sees (or, since he is rarely given to theorizing, acts as if he sees) the good of society as the by-product of efforts that are aimed, not at producing the good society, but at gaining power and place for one's self and one's party.

The principal reward of politics to the amateur is the sense of having satisfied a felt obligation to "participate," and this satisfaction is greater the higher the value the amateur can attach to the ends which the outcomes of politics serve. The principal reward of the professional is to be found in the extrinsic satisfactions of participation—power, income, status, or the fun of the game. The ideal amateur has a "natural" response to politics; he sees each battle as a "crisis," and each victory as a triumph and each loss as a defeat for a cause. The professional tends, by contrast, to develop a certain detachment toward politics and a certain immunity to its excitement and its outcomes.[1]

The difficulty with this distinction is not only that it is somewhat overdrawn, but that its applicability tends to vary with

[1] A politician develops a professional attitude toward politics in the same way that a mortician develops a professional attitude toward death, a scholar a professional attitude toward knowledge, and a prostitute a professional attitude toward love. To be sure, in many professional politicians there is a streak of the amateur—i.e., there are some issues about which they are not indifferent and thus which they cannot use instrumentally. To this extent, the distinction I am making is an analytical one. But in most cases it is also a concrete distinction.

the rank of the politician. Anyone with even a casual familiarity with amateur club politics in the Democratic party will
object immediately that many so-called "amateurs," particularly those who seek elective office or who lead amateur clubs,
are obviously and deeply ambitious, power-seeking, or eager
for patronage in a way that is indistinguishable from the professional politician. This is true. Many, but not all, of the
amateurs with long experience and personal stakes in politics
acquire the habits and motives of the professional; indeed, it
is entirely possible that an amateur club movement could not
endure if there were not in it at least a few pseudo-amateurs
who had made politics a career and who had a careerist's detachment about or even contempt for the "meaning" of politics.

This consideration raises the question of what, if anything,
keeps all amateurs from either dropping out of politics or becoming professionals. If higher-ranking amateurs and professionals tend to become indistinguishable in motive, what keeps
them distinguishable in style and rhetoric? In the long run, of
course, it may well be that nothing keeps them apart; indeed,
the brief course of most reform movements in American politics suggests that the amateur spirit cannot endure permanently. Eventually, the amateur either loses interest or becomes a
professional and plays the game by professional rules. But in
the short run at least—and perhaps, with the amateur Democrats examined in this book, even in the long run—the sharp
distinction between amateur and professional is maintained by
the existence of amateur clubs.

The ultimate source of the amateur spirit is found in the
expectations of the followers, not in the motives of the leaders.
The amateur Democrats are not just a small caucus of notables
but a large movement with, by any party's standards, a numerous and active rank and file. This rank-and-file is organized
into neighborhood political clubs and it is these clubs which
provide the principal resources of the amateur political leader.
The need to maintain these clubs is the principal constraint
that moves amateur leaders, whatever their private motives,
to protect their "amateur standing" carefully. Whether or not

the leaders are amateurs, they must act as if they are in order to take advantage of the resources which the clubs can offer. The militantly amateur political club, like the militant religious sect, does not tolerate a professional leadership and is quick to detect and criticize those who reveal some relativity of attitude, detachment of spirit, or selfishness of ambition. One difference between an amateur and a professional political organization may parallel the difference between a sect and a church: in the former, the followers or communicants are more ardent than the leaders or clergy; in the latter, the reverse is true.[2]

Even among the amateur leaders, however, there are men and women who are genuinely disinterested; not all, or perhaps even most, amateur leaders are ambitious men clever at manipulating the slogans of reform or liberalism. Among the group which came of age politically after the Second World War, there were both ambitious opportunists and dedicated idealists. A major point of this analysis, however, is that, in certain areas and for certain largely fortuitous reasons, ambition was harnessed to idealism and both the opportunist and the visionary were led to play the same game. In these areas, a new generation of leaders saw that a challenge to established party rulers could be made by mobilizing the chronic discontent among certain members of the educated, urban middle class and directing it into primary election contests. To organize this discontent, one had to demonstrate that he was more concerned with issues and candidates than with personal success or organizational maintenance. This placed constraints on ambition. And, added to the ambitious, there were articulate men in leading positions in the clubs who genuinely cared neither for personal political success nor for perpetuating a party organization, and these men, by demonstrating their

[2] Everett C. Hughes, *Men and Their Work* (Glencoe: Free Press, 1958), p. 84. Compare Hughes's definition of "professional" (pp. 140–41) with that used here. Hughes is speaking of those who are professionals by virtue of "giving an esoteric service" as are doctors, lawyers, and the like. My distinction refers, not to the character of the service, but to the motives of the practitioners.

disinterested, idealistic, and even ascetic approach to politics could set the tone for the movement as a whole by providing standards against which all others could be judged.[3]

New political leadership in times of party crisis or organizational decay is frequently provided by young men who are politically "marginal"—who stand between two worlds, the old and the new, the ascendant and the dying, and who because of their unique position can create a new alliance which will perpetuate the political system. Typically they have a background which symbolizes different and even competing values in the community. For example, one might be an Irish Catholic with a Harvard education and an intellectual manner; another might be the liberal scion of a conservative, Main Line Philadelphia family; a third an able Jewish lawyer with a heavily Puerto Rican and Negro clientele; a fourth a respectable Italian businessman with close connections in the underworld. New groups can be brought into politics or new coalitions formed between formerly warring elements through the mediation of such marginal politicians. In some cases, however, circumstances are such that these men lead, not a new coalition which restores the political equilibrium under a modified version of the conventional rules, but instead a frontal assault on the very foundation of the old political system which requires a radical redistribution of power in the community. This can occur when the new leaders find themselves, usually for reasons beyond their control, in charge of an army of new entrants to politics—a group of idealistic amateurs who are a new force to be reckoned with. Being at the head of such an army places constraints on the leaders which often prevent them from negotiating a new alliance among professional politicians under the old rules; instead, the expectations of their

[3] Situations in which ascetics place constraints on men of power are not, of course, uncommon. The history of the Church is in part the history of modifications in policy (as, for example, on the question of priestly celibacy) adopted to forestall invidious comparisons by followers between Church leaders and ascetic critics. See Henry C. Lea, *The History of Sacerdotal Celibacy in the Christian Church* (New York: Russell & Russell, 1957), pp. 14–26.

amateur followers require them to challenge, not simply certain professionals, but the very concept of professionalism itself.

The source of these expectations which account for the behavior of the amateur seems to be found in a "political ethic" which has been characteristic of the Anglo-Saxon, Yankee Protestant middle class in the United States and which is profoundly different from the political ethic of the immigrant, the Eastern and Southern European workers, and perhaps from that of the lower classes generally. Richard Hofstadter has given an excellent description of these competing political ethics in his book, *The Age of Reform.* One ethic,

> founded upon the indigenous Yankee-Protestant political traditions, and upon middle-class life, assumed and demanded the constant, disinterested activity of the citizen in public affairs, argued that political life ought to be run, to a greater degree than it was, in accordance with general principles and abstract laws apart from and superior to personal needs, and expressed a common feeling that government should be in good part an effort to moralize the lives of individuals while economic life should be intimately related to the stimulation and development of individual character.
>
> [In contrast,] the other system, founded upon the European backgrounds of the immigrants, upon their unfamiliarity with independent political action, their familiarity with hierarchy and authority, and upon the urgent needs that so often grew out of their migration, took for granted that the political life of the individual would arise out of family needs, interpreted political and civic relations chiefly in terms of personal obligations, and placed strong personal loyalties above allegiance to abstract codes of laws and morals.[4]

The political ethic of the immigrant became, of course, the basis of the big-city political machine, while the ethic of the Yankee Protestant became the basis for civic reform and assaults on that machine. Today, powerful, city-wide machines of the old style are hard to find; Chicago may be the only

---

[4] *The Age of Reform* (New York: Vintage Books, 1960), p. 9.

important example remaining. But the ethic of the machine persists, in modified form, in the habits of professional politicians for whom the value of organization and leadership are indisputable, personal loyalties and commitments remain indispensable, and the lower-class basis of the big-city electorate is unchanging. Similarly, contemporary amateur politicians are critical of the naïveté of older reform efforts which sought to capture elective offices without first capturing the party organization. Nonetheless, the essence of the reform ethic persists: the desire to moralize public life, the effort to rationalize power with law, and the insistence that correct goals will be served only if goals are set and officials selected by correct procedures.

The political ethic of the followers of the professional politician places constraints on him entirely different from those placed on the amateur. He is not expected to reflect on theories of government, take positions on controversial and abstract problems of public policy, or help club members devise organizational procedures which will give them control over his behavior. He is expected to win elections and, by winning them, provide the stream of inducements which the followers require as a condition of their contributing time, effort, and money. In some professional political organizations, notably those found in Chicago, the inducements are primarily material—jobs, payoffs, and political income. Should a city's political system be such that these material incentives are not readily available in sufficient quantity to "take care" of everybody, then other, less tangible inducements must be used. In Manhattan, for example, Tammany clubs have become more and more vehicles for the expression of neighborhood, ethnic, or tribal solidarity and for social action among old acquaintances.

In such organizations, the extrinsic rewards of politics may be intangible, but they are by and large unrelated to issues, the ends of government, the abstract desirability of citizen participation, or the need for the "better element" to control the party. Rather, the intangible rewards of the professional arise from the prestige, sociability, and personal loyalties which politics can provide: being a "big man" to one's neighbors, placing voters under an obligation to one's self, expressing one's gratitude to a district leader from whom a favor was received, taking pride in the congratulations from the leader when one has "delivered" his district or precinct, or simply being able to meet regularly with one's neighbors and friends as one canvasses for votes or petition signatures and thus overcome loneliness or boredom. An amateur may derive some of these satisfactions also, but not in a club where there is not at least a verbal concern for issues and "reform"; the professional, on the other hand, gets more out of politics precisely in those clubs where no one upsets pleasant relations with issues and reforms. When an amateur club splits into factions, the issues at stake quickly become infused with ideology; when a professional club suffers from internal friction, it is in the nature of a family fight over ethnic claims, the division of patronage, or the conflict of personalities: in short, over the rupture of *personal* ties. For the amateur politician, personal ties are mediated through a nexus of general ideas; for the professional, they are direct. Thus, an essential aspect of an amateur's relation to politics is that he is what Robert K. Merton has called a "cosmopolitan"; the professional, on the other hand, is a "local."

A local, from whose ranks most professional politicians are drawn, is a person who is preoccupied with the local community to the exclusion of affairs outside his community.[5] He is "parochial," and has lived in his community for many years, knows many people and is anxious to know more, and defines power in terms of interpersonal influence based on a network of friendships. He joins organizations which are local in order to avail himself of contacts and in order to associate himself with the broadest, most widely accepted symbols of community integration. A cosmopolitan, on the other hand, is a person with minimal ties to the locality but a strong attach-

[5] Robert K. Merton, "Patterns of Influence; Local and Cosmopolitan Influentials," in *Social Theory and Social Structure* (rev. ed.; Glencoe: Free Press, 1957), pp. 387–420.

ment to "the Great Society" of national and international problems, ideas, movements, fashions, and culture. He is often a recent arrival to the community and, if it is small, anxious to move on to large cities which are themselves "cosmopolitan." He is selective in his friendships, seeks out other cosmopolitans, joins organizations which have a professional and civic flavor, and endeavors to be influential through the display of his *expertise* and special skills. His attachment is to symbols which are not widely shared but esoteric and which are, thus, often divisive rather than integrating for the community as a whole.

Professional politicians, even those who do not earn their living in politics, are usually drawn from the ranks of the locals. The local is a man who can himself symbolize the shared sentiments of the community rather than any special set of ends or virtues. The most successful local politician is able, as George H. Mead said, "to enter into the attitudes of the group and mediate between them by making his own experience universal, so that others can enter into this form of communication through him."[6] These qualities are uniquely those which enable a man to grasp the motives of others by entering imaginatively into their feelings, and, by understanding them, turning these motives to his own benefit. A cosmopolitan often lacks these qualities, for to him, action is or ought to be governed by general principles. If he should enter politics, as the club leaders have, he must rely on the force of his ideas and the worth of his principles to provide him with standing and insure his success. This is a very difficult undertaking, and this study will attempt to show the consequences of this style of politics among "cosmopolitan" amateurs.

Because the amateur is attracted to politics by principles, there is some overlap between those who are interested in a politics of principle and those who are, in a broad sense, intellectuals. But the overlap between the world of intellectuals and the world of club politics is not great, for although many

[6] George Herbert Mead, *Mind, Self, and Society* (Chicago: University of Chicago Press, 1934), p. 257.

amateur politicians, particularly in the Democratic party, are intellectual "consumers," few are intellectual "producers." As intellectual consumers, they may be engaged in disseminating cultural or intellectual products (as are teachers and journalists), in applying them (as are lawyers and physicians), or simply in enjoying them by having a style of life which is vaguely intellectual (as do people who collect books, recordings of serious music, and works of art).[7] There is, however, a striking shortage of intellectual producers such as creative scholars, artists, and writers. Few university professors of stature are found active in club politics, and serious writers are usually active in politics, if at all, at a different level (for example, as contributors to liberal or conservative periodicals). Amateur, club-based politics can be found in certain parts of the Republican party as well as in the Democratic, and here the overlap between intellectuals and amateur politicians is, one suspects, even less.

The relative absence of professors is a complex phenomenon. In part it is because, as in New York, professors do not live in great numbers in the central city. But there is little academic participation in amateur politics even where, as in Chicago, almost the entire faculty of the university lives in the center city in the area of greatest amateur club activity. And there participation has been declining rather than growing. In 1947, 39 per cent of the Board of Directors of the Independent Voters of Illinois (IVI) were educators; by 1961, less than 10 per cent were. In the same period, the proportion of educators among the rank-and-file members of the IVI in the Fifth Ward (the site of the University of Chicago) fell from about one-fourth to less than one-sixth. Of the eleven-man IVI Political Action Committee in 1961, the only academic was one student; of the thirteen IVI ward chairmen, the only academics were one student and one teacher.

[7] Edward A. Shils, "The Intellectuals and the Powers: Some Perspectives for Comparative Analysis," *Comparative Studies in Society and History,* I (October, 1958), 5–22; Seymour Martin Lipset, "American Intellectuals: Their Politics and Status," in *Political Man: The Social Bases of Politics* (Garden City, N.Y.: Doubleday & Co., 1960), p. 311.

In California Democratic clubs around the University of California at Los Angeles and the California Institute of Technology, university teachers are from time to time active as club officers or candidates for assemblyman or congressman, but such men are almost always younger, relatively unknown academics who often are engaged in politics as a kind of substitute for scholarly research and publication. Prominent and ambitious university personnel are rarely in amateur politics or noted as spokesmen on behalf of amateur political causes; those who are involved are usually neither prominent nor productive.

The club movement has attracted many kinds of people to it, and no single description will suffice for all, but to a great extent the principal shared characteristics are precisely those which support the description of them as cosmopolitan, intellectually oriented amateurs. For the most part, they are young, well-educated professional people, including a large number of women. In style of life, they are distinctly middle- and upper-middle class; in mood and outlook, they are products of the generation which came of age after the Second World War and particularly after the Korean conflict; in political beliefs, they are almost entirely among the liberals of the left. They bring to politics a concern for ideas and ideals.

In Manhattan, between one-half and three-fourths of the members of three clubs studied were under forty years of age.[8] Not only were they young, they were fairly recent arrivals to the city. Over three-fourths did not live in their present neighborhood before 1949, and between one-half and two-thirds did not live there before 1953. Many were raised in New York, but most had left home to attend a university

[8] These data about the composition of Manhattan club members are based on a mail survey of a random sample of the membership of three clubs undertaken in the summer of 1960. Because, as with all mail surveys, the proportion of responses is low, the reader should not rely on these figures for anything except an indication of the gross magnitudes involved. Personal observation and interviewing suggest that the general pattern revealed by the figures is correct.

and had only recently returned. Between two-thirds and three-fourths had not joined a political club before 1957.

In two of the three clubs examined, over half of the members were of Jewish background; on the other hand, there were very few Catholics, never more than 10 per cent of the total. Only in one club did the proportion of married people exceed one-third; the rest were single, separated, or divorced. Often those who were married were childless; although about 30 per cent of the members were married, only 10 per cent had a family. Most club members, at least the most active ones, appeared to be sufficiently young and lacking in extensive family or professional obligations so that a considerable amount of time and energy could be devoted to politics. Often husband and wife were both club members; presumably this reduced the problems which might result if one or the other were perennially absent on political tasks. The wives of volunteer politicians were not, unlike their Tammany counterparts, the kind of women who were likely to remain at home and raise children while husbands pre-empted all the diversions and excitement of political activity. Many of the married but childless women in reform politics were anxious not to let marriage and the demands of a husband's career compel them to give up their interests, "lose their personalities," or become absorbed by household duties.

Lawyers represented between one-tenth and one-sixth of the membership but a much higher percentage (in one case, half) of the officers and activists. Nearly a quarter of the members of two clubs were in what are described as the "communications" business—public relations, advertising, journalism, editing, publishing, radio, and television. There were often as many members from medicine (physicians, psychiatrists, nurses) as from law, a rather striking fact given the general beliefs about the reluctance of such persons to become associated with political or controversial causes. Business, service, and clerical occupations accounted for one-fourth to one-third of the membership.

The backgrounds of the officers show even greater similarities. Officers were far more likely to be male, married, Jewish, and lawyers. In 1960, there were 36 men and women nominated for office in the Lexington Democratic Club, the oldest of the reform organizations. Of these, 26 were men and 10 women. Of the 34 who had graduated from college 19 had attended the desirable schools of the Ivy League. The majority (20) had completed law school and were practicing law in New York City (mostly with firms in and around Wall Street). Most of the rest were in public relations, advertising, the theater, college teaching, radio and television, and so on. Of the five who were in other businesses, most were associated with investment houses. In many cases, these young professionals were academically distinguished: there were 16 instances of school honors, including five Phi Beta Kappa members, two teaching fellows, and at least two law review editors. Although no precise determination of ethnic background is available, a rough estimate based on family name suggests that there were about 20 or 21 Jewish and 15 or 16 non-Jewish candidates for office.

When another reform club, the Riverside Democrats, was organized in 1957, all eight of its officers were college graduates and seven had done graduate work in prestigious eastern universities such as Harvard, Yale, Columbia, and Princeton. Despite the fact that the Seventh Assembly District, in which the Riverside Club was organized, includes Morningside Heights and Columbia University, there were few academic personnel associated with the club. No officer and only one member of the nineteen-man board of directors was a university teacher.[9]

The ranks of the amateur politicians seem constantly to be replenished by new, young recruits as age, professional preoccupations, or family responsibilities cause older members to fall away. Many stay active in the movement only while they are still on the lower rungs of their career ladders. As a result, there is a high turnover of activists.

[9] These facts are from Robert Lekachman, "How We Beat the Machine," *Commentary*, April, 1958, p. 292.

Essentially the same kinds of people are found in club politics in California as in New York. The active members of eight clubs studied in Los Angeles County in early 1961 were similar to club members in Manhattan in most respects. Over half were under forty years of age, over 60 per cent had a college education or better, most were in professional occupations, and practically no one was Catholic while nearly half were Jewish in their religious background.[10] (But not in their current beliefs. A large number of respondents from a Jewish background took the trouble to write on their questionnaires that they were no longer believers.) Contrary to the observations of some who have interpreted the California club movement as an organization providing social contact and a sense of belonging for the rootless, newly arrived intelligentsia in this rapidly growing state,[11] the overwhelming bulk of club members who responded were, by California standards, old-time residents. Over 80 per cent had lived in the state ten years or more, and nearly half had lived there twenty or more. But there were some differences between New York and California as well. Among California club members there was a higher proportion of older people (over one-third were fifty-five years of age or older), a somewhat larger number were married and had children, and more had belonged to the clubs for a considerable period of time (many California clubs are much older than the reform clubs in Manhattan).

## The Function of Parties

Political parties perform, to some degree, at least three functions in a democratic government. They recruit candidates, mobilize voters, and assemble power within the formal

[10] These data are from a mail questionnaire distributed to all members attending a given meeting of eight different clubs. I would like to acknowledge the invaluable assistance of the Los Angeles County Democratic Central Committee in making this survey and in providing much of the manpower for it. The same limitations described in footnote 8 of this chapter apply to the data here.

[11] See Bernard Crick, "California's Democratic Clubs: A Revolt in the Suburbs," *Reporter*, May 31, 1956, pp. 35–39.

government. The first two functions are indispensable regardless of the precise nature of the political institutions; the third, on the other hand, varies with the extent to which elective officials have sufficient formal, legal power to operate the government. If legal power is badly fragmented among many independent elective officials and widely decentralized among many levels of government, the need for informal methods of assembling power becomes great. The political party is one, although by no means the only, mechanism for performing this task. If a single elective official has complete legal authority over all aspects of the government, then the need for informally assembling power is much less—ideally, zero. All three party functions will in some degree be performed differently by amateur as contrasted to professional politicians. In order better to understand the empirical differences between the amateur and the professional which will be set forth in the remainder of this book, it is helpful first to set forth the logic of their differing conceptions of the function of a political party.

The professional, for whom politics primarily has extrinsic rewards, is preoccupied with maintaining his position in party and elective offices. Winning is essential, although sometimes electoral victory must be subordinated to maintaining the party organization.[12] Candidates will be selected on the basis of their electoral appeal. A ticket will be constructed which maximizes this appeal by offering "representation" to candidates of important ethnic, religious, racial, and nationality groups and to important geographic regions and civil divisions. This is the "balanced" ticket. Since most voters support parties out of traditional allegiances, these traditional loyalties will be reinforced. Added to them will be appeals to "interests"—private advantage, sectional loyalties, and ethnic and nationality claims. Issues will be avoided except in the most general terms or if the party is confident that a majority supports its position. Should a contrary position on the same issue seem

---

[12] See James Q. Wilson, "The Economy of Patronage," *Journal of Political Economy*, LXIX (August, 1961), 369–80.

best suited for winning a majority at the next election, the party will try to change or at least mute its position. Votes will be mobilized not only by such appeals but also by personal contacts through precinct captains. These workers will appeal to the voter on the basis of party loyalty and personal friendship; sometimes material inducements (money, favors, jobs) will be offered. To the extent that the party can enable its candidates to win by providing them with these resources (loyalty to a party name, a balanced ticket, appeals to interests, and the efforts of party workers), it places them under an obligation to it. Re-election without party support would be costly (in terms of money, time, effort, obtaining support from new groups in exchange for commitments to programs, and so forth). Since the party enables the candidate, in effect, to economize, his behavior in office can be controlled to some extent by threatening not to re-slate him for office if he acts independently. In this way, and through the distribution of patronage and money, the party is able to assemble power in the government.

The amateur politician, on the other hand, would in the ideal situation prefer to recruit candidates on the basis of their commitment to a set of policies. Voters would be mobilized by appeals to some set of principles or goals. The party would be held together and linked to the voter by a shared conception of the public interest. A politics of principle would necessarily attach little value to—and indeed would criticize—appeals to private, group, or sectional interest. Private interests, which for the professional are the motive force of politics, the amateur would consider irrelevant, irrational, or immoral. The task of assembling power in the formal government would be met, not by using sanctions to discipline elective officials, but by electing to those posts candidates who were committed to the policies of the party and who would therefore act in concert, not from coercion, but out of conviction. Amateur politicians thus seek to alter fundamentally the way in which the functions of parties are carried out. Instead of serving as neutral agents which mobilize majorities for whatever candidates and programs seem best suited to capturing public fancy, the parties would become the sources of program and the agents of social change. They would control the behavior of public officials by internalized convictions rather than external threats and for the purpose of realizing certain social policies rather than of enhancing the party's prospects for retaining power in the next election.

As we will discover, few amateurs act completely in accord with the logic of their position and many professionals have modified their behavior to keep pace with a changing political situation. Because of the social mobility and economic affluence in America, resulting in a growing middle class which has assimilated older immigrant groups, more and more people have, in effect, abandoned the political ethic of the lower classes and adopted the ethic of the Yankees. Shrewd professional politicians, such as Mayor Richard J. Daley of Chicago, have adapted in part to this change by providing the image, if not the substance, of a politics of principle. They have sought out "blue ribbon" candidates and appealing civic causes with which to attract the votes of a growing middle class unresponsive to the inducements a patronage-fed precinct captain can offer. Banfield explains this in part by noting that between 1948 and 1956, the proportion of the total Democratic vote in Cook County cast by the "inner wards" of Chicago declined from 37 to 31 per cent while the proportion cast by that part of Cook County outside Chicago rose from 13 to 18 per cent.[13] This ecological change compelled city bosses to devote more resources to attracting that vote which cannot be won by conventional precinct-captain appeals.

There is an important relationship between the contrasting attitudes of amateurs and professionals to party politics on the one hand and competing theories of the function of government on the other. In effect, the amateur asserts that principles, rather than interest, ought to be both the end and motive of political action. Government should not only serve

[13] Edward C. Banfield, *Political Influence* (New York: Free Press of Glencoe, 1961), pp. 244–47.

desirable goals, but the power to attain them ought to be assembled by appealing to those ends. Politicians ought to work for certain ends, not because such action is expedient or self-serving, but because they are convinced of the intrinsic worth of those ends.

This approach stands in sharp contrast to the actions of professional politicians who behave as if they believed that politics, like other forms of human activity, only occurs when individuals can realize their private aims and maximize their self-interest. Public policies are the by-product of political self-seeking just as the distribution of goods and services is the by-product of economic self-seeking. In both cases, the incentive for individual action is not the same as the ends served by the system as a whole. The social function of human action is not the reason that action is undertaken.

The amateur politicians maintain, in effect, that the ends of government and the incentives for political action ought to be identical. Many economists, as Anthony Downs has pointed out, have tacitly agreed with this theory by assuming that the government ought to act to maximize a "social welfare function" and that it in fact will act in this way because the end is intrinsically desirable.[14] There is thus a general intellectual tradition which supports the view that government officials do or should act in a disinterested manner, as contrasted to businessmen and party bosses who act out of "selfish" motives.

A fundamental question which this study will raise is whether a democratic society is better served by a system in which the motives of politicians are identical with their social function or by a system in which motives and social function are

[14] Anthony Downs, *An Economic Theory of Democracy* (New York: Harper & Bros., 1957), pp. 280–86. Joseph Schumpeter is one of the few economists who saw this issue clearly and who realized the problem of failing to understand realistically the motives of public officials. He wrote that "it does not follow that the social meaning of a type of activity will necessarily provide the motive power, hence the explanation of the latter. If it does not, a theory that contents itself with an analysis of the social end or need to be served cannot be accepted as an adequate account of the activities that serve it." *Capitalism, Socialism, and Democracy* (London: George Allen & Unwin, 1954), p. 282.

unrelated. The amateur subscribes, by and large, to the some-times unspoken assumption that desirable social policy can only or best result from action undertaken out of a desire to see that policy realized. But there is no reason why this should always be the case. In fact, when one considers economic activities, most people will quickly agree that the desirable consequences of that activity (the distribution of goods and services in some manner) are usually the result of activity undertaken for self-serving reasons (the attempt to maximize individual utilities). To be sure, a socialist will argue that the best distribution of goods and services is only achieved when production and distribution are undertaken out of community-regarding rather than private-regarding motives; thus the slo-gans, "production for use, not profit," and distribution "to each according to his needs (or abilities)." But most amateur Dem-ocrats, though liberals, are not socialists; indeed, many of them are conspicuously successful in their economic occupa-tions and will defend the consequences of action undertaken to maximize their wages or profits. But although they may not be economic socialists, they act as if they desired to "socialize" politics. Obviously, they are convinced that politics must be based on principle even though economics is based on interest.

This anomaly is seen most clearly, of course, when the ama-teur politician is a conservative Republican rather than a lib-eral Democrat. The amateur conservative typically is out-spoken in favor of an economic system which depends on the pursuit of private interests to provide a common good through the intervention of the "invisible hand" of which Adam Smith wrote; at the same time, the conservative urges politicians to act on principle.

## *Evaluating the Amateur Democrat*

Since people who read books about politics are likely to be instinctively sympathetic to the aims, if not the achievements, of amateur politicians, the contrast (necessarily oversimpli-fied) between the amateur and the professional sketched in this chapter may make the choice appear an easy one. Politicians, one immediately feels, *ought* to be high-minded and committed to policies; they *ought* to "talk sense" to voters rather than rely on empty slogans, selfish appeals, and political payoffs; elective officials *ought* to vote and act on the basis of conscience rather than at the dictate of party "bosses." But the choice is not a simple one. An amateur politics of principle may make certain highly valued ends difficult or impossible to attain, whereas a politics of interest may, under certain circumstances, realize these ends much more easily. Institutions should be judged by the ends they serve, not by the motives of their members, and on this basis it is an open question whether the professional politician is not the person best equipped to operate a democratic government in a way that will produce desirable policies. A preoccupation with the propriety of methods, while a legitimate concern, can be carried too far. No one used the power of patronage more ruthlessly than Abraham Lincoln; no one appealed more cleverly or more successfully to "irrational" sentiments of nationalism and race pride than Fiorello H. La Guardia; no one relied more heavily on big-city machines than Franklin D. Roosevelt.

Adlai Stevenson, the man who, more than anyone, has served as the patron saint of the amateur politicians, voiced similar concerns when he raised but did not answer these questions:

> It does not belittle the movement to ask some questions, as a perceptive California friend of mine has done, about at least the West-Coast type of club development. What are the effects of an almost exclusively "ideological" political motivation? Is some degree of instability the likely price of a lack of the restraint of economic interest and of part-time interest in politics? What are the implications of all-out election campaigning by highly vocal groups who assume little responsibility for legislative follow-up of either their nominees or their programs? What is necessary to prevent hit-and-run politics—even by one's highest minded political friends? These seem to be worthwhile questions.[15]

[15] Adlai Stevenson, "So You Want To Be in Politics?" Review of *Elm Street Politics*, by Stephen A. Mitchell, in *New York Times Book Review*, April 12, 1959, p. 1.

These questions can be placed in perspective by suggesting some historical parallels. America has had many experiences with political reform, and although the goals and strategies of the reformers have changed from decade to decade, the essential features of the reform mentality have not. The Yankee Protestant political ethic can be detected in the writings of the municipal reformers, the advocates of the direct primary, and the supporters of party reform.

Each successive political reform has proved many times to be either unattainable or defective, and hence the aims of the reformers have steadily shifted. The commission form of government advocated by reformers did not prevent Frank Hague from becoming the boss of Jersey City.[16] The initiative and the referendum are devices often used, not for "direct democracy," but for overloading state constitutions with amendments protecting special-interest groups.[17] The direct primary has, at least in some states, weakened party organization to the point that responsibility for government action is diffuse and hard to assign.[18] The 1936 reforms in New York City resulted in a charter which was workable for Fiorello La Guardia but apparently for no other mayor, since the changes praised by the reformers in 1936 were damned by them fifteen years later.[19] Cross-filing, once hailed in California as a device for returning government to the people, became, to a later generation of reformers, an obstacle to good government which they labored mightily to eliminate. Non-partisanship

[16] Cf. Francis P. Canavan, "The Revolution That Failed," *America,* July 1, 1961, pp. 483–87, and Dayton McKean, *The Boss: The Hague Machine in Action* (Boston: Houghton Mifflin Co., 1940), pp. 37–38.

[17] V. O. Key, Jr., and Winston Crouch, *The Initiative and Referendum in California* (Berkeley: University of California Press, 1939); Winston W. Crouch, "The Initiative and Referendum in Cities," *American Political Science Review,* XXXVII (June, 1943), 491–504; Joseph G. Lapalombara and Charles B. Hagan, "Direct Legislation: An Appraisal and a Suggestion," *American Political Science Review,* XLV (June, 1951), 400–421.

[18] V. O. Key, Jr., *American State Politics* (New York: Alfred A. Knopf, 1956), pp. 145–64.

[19] Rexford G. Tugwell, *The Art of Politics* (Garden City, N.Y.: Doubleday & Co., 1958), pp. 30–31.

proved to be ineffective in Chicago because the machine continued to control "nonpartisan" aldermanic elections; in Detroit and Los Angeles, on the other hand, it proved to be so effective that liberal amateurs now regard it as a principal institutional block to the success of the Democratic party at the local level.

At the same time, there have been certain reforms which have attained some of the goals of their proponents. Civil service legislation, where it has been enacted and defended, has unquestionably reduced, if not eliminated, patronage. The city manager form of government has taken hold in 38 per cent of all American cities (although in only 6 per cent of those over 500,000 population).

The mentality of the amateur and the reformer shows a remarkable continuity with the past, even though previous efforts at reform have been as often a cause for disappointment as for rejoicing. Some sense of this mentality can be obtained from a cursory examination of the groups supporting the introduction of the direct primary around the turn of this century. The direct primary was an effort to deal with the fixation of party loyalties occasioned by the Civil War. So many states, north and south, were in effect one-party states that the professional politician's habitual disinterest in issues was not checked by forcing him to compete with a rival party which had some chance at success. The primary permitted a contest *within* the dominant party to replace the meaningless contest between the two parties.

Such a reform was instituted as a result of a movement which drew together a heterogeneous group of political leaders with little in common at that time other than the desire to reform some aspect of the American political system. This group included in its ranks journalistic muckrakers who exposed the "interests," Mugwump Republicans dissatisfied with their party's conservative policies, and agrarian radicals confronted with an economic crisis. The direct primary had the advantage of appearing to satisfy all of these aspirations. Mugwumps would have a means of challenging conservatives for control of the party; Populists would have a means of weakening party organization and giving more power to the people.

For some of its spokesmen, the movement had certain substantive goals (including regulation of industry and railroads, antitrust action, minimum wage and hour laws, and so forth), but a central preoccupation which all of its members shared was a concern for procedural or formal changes in political institutions. The movement was only partly based on the economic interests of the members. A crisis in farm prices had brought agrarian radicals into the movement, but the urban middle class which supported Theodore Roosevelt, Woodrow Wilson, and various municipal and party reforms was not economically disadvantaged at all. Professor Hofstadter suggests that they were the victims of a "status revolution" rather than of economic privations—i.e., they were afflicted by a redistribution of power and deference, rather than of income, as a result of the growth of big business and city machines.[20] The traditional social elites were disturbed by the emergence of the new men of power and the new men of wealth and campaigned for devices that would enable them to check the power, both economic and political, of these new groups. The direct primary was one such method.

These progressives were typically young, middle-class, urban members of a well-educated, professional group with secure family positions.[21] They became active in politics during a period of general prosperity and rising prices, when the threats to the established order occasioned by the Populist movement and the Bryan candidacy in the 1890's had passed and before a world war diverted their attention to other matters.[22] They came to politics from a conservative background, often one produced by inherited wealth and business connections.

[20] Hofstadter, *The Age of Reform*, p. 135.

[21] Alfred D. Chandler, Jr., "The Origins of Progressive Leadership," in Elting Morison, ed., *The Letters of Theodore Roosevelt* (Cambridge: Harvard University Press, 1954), VIII, 1462–65, and George Mowry, *The California Progressives* (Berkeley: University of California Press, 1951), pp. 87–104.

[22] Hofstadter, *op. cit.*, pp. 168–69.

Among their spokesmen were clergymen who appealed to the "social gospel" and university professors who advanced a new social science.

The reformers, although agreed on many subsidiary goals, were not always in agreement on more general ends. The movement can be divided into at least two broad streams which may be called the Populist and the Progressive.[23] The Populists, who in the main were agrarian radicals with rural or small-town leaders, shared a conviction that the cure for the problems of democracy was more democracy. The people were fundamentally good and their intuitions could be trusted if they were freed from institutional constraints and the blandishments of self-seeking leaders. Political organization generally, and political parties specifically, were at best necessary evils which should be shackled. Populism represented a distrust of organization and a commitment to direct democracy. The problem to be solved was not simply bad organization but over-organization. The direct primary was one means of making direct democracy possible, and the initiative, referendum, and recall were others. Grass roots control of both parties and government would produce better policies and better leaders, thereby reducing the influence of moneyed interests.

The Progressive view differed from this in conceiving the central problem of democracy as one of improving the quality of leadership. If better leaders were the goal, then society would be better served by less "procedural" democracy (i.e., fewer opportunities for popular choice and less accountability of leaders to the led) in the interests of more "substantive" democracy (i.e., better decisions and policies). The Progressives, largely members of an established social elite, called for displacing bad leaders with good ones (which might require strengthening the executive at the expense of the voters and the legislature). Executives must have more power, not less. This would weaken or destroy the political bosses by render-

[23] The distinction is taken from Hofstadter, *op. cit.*, pp. 262–71. See also Eric Goldman, *Rendezvous with Destiny* (New York: Vintage Books, 1959), pp. 40–42, 60–64.

ing them unnecessary for operating government and by making it unprofitable for businessmen to bribe the bosses to do their bidding. Only after the success of the direct primary movement was the tension between the Populist and Progressive goals exposed.[24]

From the beginning of this century, there has been a chronic dissatisfaction of one segment of the urban middle class from conventional business mores and political practices. This disaffection was endemic among certain members of the educated professions; these persons regarded big business and machine politics as two manifestations of gross incivility based on materialistic self-seeking.[25] When prosperity ended the agricultural crisis, the farmers abandoned populism. Later they joined organizations, such as the American Farm Bureau Federation, which eventually sought only to participate in the economic and political life of the country for the purpose of enlarging the farmer's share of the national income by the use of the conventional strategies of pressure politics and business organization. They participated in the system under the traditional rules rather than by attempting to alter the system or define new rules.[26]

The disaffection of the progressive elements of the urban middle class persisted, however, for it was based not on economic but on social grievances. Throughout this century, there has always been a "reform mentality" in American politics and in this broad sense the amateur Democrats have their forebearers in the Progressive and municipal reform efforts of

[24] The direct primary was adopted in 17 states between 1903 and 1910. See Key, *op. cit.*, p. 91.

[25] Talcott Parsons observes that what distinguishes the professions from business is a belief that they are "disinterested," while business is "self-seeking." Talcott Parsons, *Essays in Sociological Theory* (Glencoe: Free Press, 1949), p. 186. An attempt to account for the anti-business, liberal cast of intellectual thought is found in F. A. Hayek, "The Intellectuals and Socialism," *University of Chicago Law Review* (Spring, 1949), p. 417, reprinted in George B. de Huszar, *The Intellectuals: A Controversial Portrait* (Glencoe, Ill.: Free Press, 1960), pp. 371–84.

[26] Cf. Grant McConnell, *The Decline of Agrarian Democracy* (Berkeley: University of California Press, 1953).

fifty years ago. The non-business urban middle class has sought to implement the Yankee political ethic. That many, if not most, contemporary amateurs are Jews, while the earlier group was Anglo-Saxon Protestant, has not affected the premises of the reform mentality, for the Jewish tradition is similar in most important respects.

Today, the major thrust of the liberals active in local party politics has been, not to institute the direct primary, but to take advantage of it. The hopes of the early reformers had been dashed; the procedural reforms in strong-party states such as Illinois had not led to the emergence of "good" leaders, and in weak-party states such as California the procedural reforms had led to a situation in which virtually no leaders at all, good or bad, could emerge. And there were still some states, such as New York, where no procedural reforms had been adopted (in great part because they had always been two-party states). It was obvious that reforms were not enough; those concerned with improving the quality of public life would have to enter it on a long-term basis in order to *become* the leaders which they had originally hoped the new mechanisms would generate spontaneously. In the postwar world, the prosaic and intensely partisan administration of Harry Truman and the business-oriented administration of Dwight D. Eisenhower offered ready targets for those who distrusted professional politicians and big businessmen and the "interests" that motivated them.

## The Plan of This Book

This analysis of the amateur Democrat will be principally concerned with the nature of the organizations amateur politicians have created in order to advance their cause and the constraints which the maintenance of those organizations place on amateur political efforts. Thus, a great deal of attention will be paid to the means by which amateurs are induced to contribute time, effort, and money to politics and this, in turn, will lead to a concern for the consequences of the use of these incentives for the structure, operation, leadership, and ends of the party organization. This concern, it should be noted, is part of a larger interest in the nature of organizations generally. Organizations, I feel, can best be understood by assuming that the central problem facing any organization is how to concert the wills of the members; that, for this purpose, a system of incentives is employed by the executives of the organization; and that the use of any incentive system makes certain demands on the goals, tactics, and leadership of the organization.[27]

For example, the concern for principles and ends is as important to the maintenance of the amateur political club as patronage is to the maintenance of a party machine or income to the maintenance of a firm. A concern for principles, ranging from unsophisticated slogans to elaborate policy statements, is a crucial incentive for club politics. Earlier reform movements never endured in great part because they could not develop a set of inducements which would continue to elicit contributions of time, money, and effort from members beyond the initial assault on the "system." Club politicians, realizing that simple reform never lasts, endeavor to provide a positive program which will attract members on a permanent basis. The clubs are resolved to generate issues, not simply respond to issues which are readily available.

If a political organization seeks to attract volunteers by demonstrating a concern for, familiarity with, or commitment to a set of general ideas and principles, this commitment offers advantages to the club (it can thereby distinguish itself from other kinds of political clubs which may rely on material rewards to attract workers), but it also creates constraints. The club espouses a set of principles which are attractive to

[27] The approach is broadly derived from Chester I. Barnard, *The Functions of the Executive* (Cambridge: Harvard University Press, 1938). Barnard's basic argument is extended and elaborated in a paper which provides the conceptual foundation for the present study of party organization: Peter B. Clark and James Q. Wilson, "Incentive Systems: A Theory of Organizations," *Administrative Science Quarterly*, VI (September, 1961), 129–66.

volunteers but which at the same time renders the club susceptible to sectarianism. Those principles provide a rationale for attacking the existing political order, but they may also raise obstacles to the creation of a viable alternative to that order.

Not all amateur clubs are identical, and the club movement is not monolithic. A major task is to account for the differences among clubs and leaders. These differences can be explained, in most cases, by describing the tension between the general and uniform demands of principles and rhetoric on the one hand and the specific and varying requirements of organizational maintenance on the other. These maintenance requirements are shaped by the political system of the community and by the character of the neighborhood, constituency, and cadres, and make unanimity in club politics inherently unobtainable. Various efforts at greater unity are continually made, however. Since the clubs are often engaged in a contest with a more or less common enemy, and inasmuch as that enemy has frequently become less conciliatory, the struggle itself provides a measure of unity. But even in the heat of battle, only an imperfect unity results.

Amateur politicians in three communities (New York, Los Angeles, and Chicago) were studied for certain obvious but important reasons. First, these are the three largest cities in the United States, and presumably the stakes of local political activity are here the highest. Second, each city represents a distinct political and social system and the three communities taken together cover much (but not all) of the variety to be found in big-city and big-state politics. In Manhattan, the traditional political machine is faltering: it is strong enough to resist but weak enough to be defeated. In Los Angeles, where there has never been a political machine, club politics has filled a vacuum rather than defeated an enemy. In Chicago, the Democratic organization is powerful and well-entrenched. Chicago and Manhattan have local institutions which are partisan; in Los Angeles, these institutions are nonpartisan. Manhattan and Chicago are older, densely populated cities, with many immigrant and racial groups. Los Angeles is a newer, less dense city, with a more homogeneous white population but a sizable number of Negroes and Mexican-Americans.

The study begins with three chapters which contain a brief factual account of the club movement, together with essential background information on the political system of each city. The remaining chapters are analytical in nature, discussing and explaining the principal features of club or amateur politics. First, there is an exposition of the beliefs and goals of the movement. An attempt is made to infer from the statements of the leaders what conception they hold of the proper conduct of political life. Second, the rewards of the club movement and the extent to which these incentives are assets or liabilities will be considered. In these chapters, we shall try to characterize the internal life of the clubs and the constraints placed by this internal life on those who must lead the clubs in their relations with the outside world. Third, the relationship between the clubs on the one hand and the constituency and leaders of the party as a whole on the other will be analyzed. The tensions between professional and volunteer politicians and the class basis of the club movement will be considered. Fourth, a tentative assessment of the power of the clubs will be offered. Finally, the principal themes will be brought together for summary treatment, followed by a brief appraisal in which an attempt will be made to evaluate the movement's importance for the Democratic party, party competition, and governing institutions generally.

# 2 New York
# The Struggle for Power

Late in the 1950's, Tammany Hall was challenged by a vigorous group of insurgents who styled themselves "reformers." It was an attack stronger and more sustained than any the regular Democratic party in Manhattan had withstood since the days of the Seabury investigation and the subsequent regime of Mayor Fiorello H. La Guardia. The leader of the Democratic party in New York County, Carmine G. De Sapio, was the principal object of the attack, and the issue was soon described as a choice between the "boss" and the "people." Unlike reformers in the past, however, these men and women were not attacking the regular party organization from the outside in general elections, nor were they relying on legislative investigations, newspaper crusades, or grand jury indictments. Instead, these reformers were challenging the regular organization from within, contesting primary elections in which control of the district and county leadership was at stake. The reformers were bent, not on changing the system from the outside, but on capturing the system itself.

By mid-1960, this new strategy of reform was no more than ten years old. Already, substantial gains had been registered. Since 1953, when the first "reform" club gained power (in the Ninth Assembly District), eight Tammany district leaders had been defeated and replaced by reform leaders, together with their female co-leaders. The Executive Committee of the Democratic County Committee of New York County has 66 members (33 male and 33 female district leaders) who have a total of 16 votes distributed among them (one vote for each assembly district, often split into halves or thirds to reflect the divi-

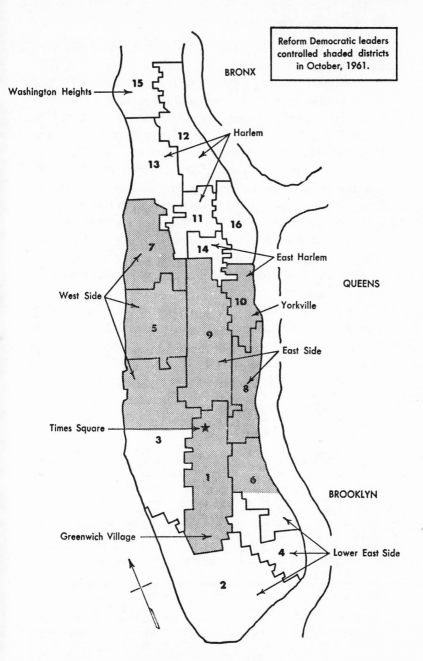

Reform Democratic leaders controlled shaded districts in October, 1961.

MANHATTAN ASSEMBLY DISTRICTS
(1961)

sion of districts among leaders). In 1960, the reformers numbered 16 of the 66 members and cast 4 1/16 votes.[1] In 1961,
the reformers, running together with Mayor Robert Wagner
in the Democratic primary, increased the number of seats they
held on the county executive committee from 16 to 30 and the
number of votes from 4 1/16 to 6 5/6—only a fraction more
than one vote shy of absolute control of the committee, and
theoretically enough for them to be a powerful force in naming
the new county leader. The man they had sworn to defeat,
Carmine De Sapio, had lost in his own fight to remain district
leader in Greenwich Village and was thus no longer even a
member of the executive committee. In the general election,
Wagner easily defeated his Republican and independent opposition and was returned to office closely identified with the
reform movement.

The political clubs which sustained these reform leaders
were scattered throughout Manhattan and had, in the summer
of 1961, a total of about eight thousand members. In addition
to these, other "insurgent" reform clubs in Manhattan had
about five hundred more members.[2] These people were an

[1] Cf. Wallace S. Sayre and Herbert Kaufman, *Governing New York
City* (New York: Russell Sage Foundation, 1960), pp. 122–41, for a
description of the formal party machinery.

[2] Some working definitions are in order. I shall speak of three kinds
of Democratic clubs. "Regular reform" clubs are those whose district
leaders are members of the "Reform Democratic Leadership Caucus"
which was formed in August, 1960 (see *New York Times,* August 5,
1960). Most, but not all, of those leaders had previously been identified as reform politicians because of their association with the New
York Committee for Democratic Voters and because they had abstained
in the September, 1959, vote for county leader and had signed the
"reform manifesto" of February, 1959. The definition of reform clubs
is made purposely broad so as to include all who have any claim to the
title. Necessary distinctions will be introduced in later chapters. "Insurgent reform" refers to those reform-oriented clubs which have not captured the leadership of their districts but which have challenged the
existing Tammany leaders. Both regular reform and insurgent reform
clubs are part of the reform movement; the former hold power in their
districts, the latter are out of power. "Tammany" clubs are those which
have not been associated with the reform movement and whose leaders
voted for De Sapio in the September, 1959, election. Excluded from
this definition of reform clubs are those in Harlem under the leadership
of Representative Adam Clayton Powell, Jr. Although these Negro lead-

extraordinary new force in Manhattan politics, and, to a remarkable degree, they had a more or less common set of characteristics, beliefs, and goals. It should be understood, however, that despite their many similarities, the reformers had
important differences as well. Indeed, many reform leaders
refused to consider their colleagues "true" reformers. As we
will suggest at a later point, there were profound disagreements among them and a great variation in political styles,
constituencies, attitudes, and goals. At the time, however, these
differences were overshadowed by the victories they had won.[3]

---

ers also abstained in the September county leader election, neither they
nor the reformers consider them to be "reform." The conflict between
Tammany and Harlem has been intense and significant, but unrelated
to the reform issue. For a classic description of the nature of New York
political clubs, see Roy V. Peel, *The Political Clubs of New York City*
(New York: G. P. Putnam's Sons, 1935). The reform clubs are consciously endeavoring to break with the pattern Professor Peel described.

Given below, as of October, 1961, are the names of the male reform
district leaders, the names of their clubs, and the date on which the
club first won the district leadership. In some cases the original district
leader has been replaced; this is indicated by an asterisk, with the
earlier leader's name below.

| Assembly District | Male Leader | Name of Club | Date |
|---|---|---|---|
| 1st South | James S. Lanigan | Village Independent Democrats | 1961 |
| 1st Middle | Alan Finberg* | Samuel J. Tilden Democratic Club | 1953 |
| 1st North | Charles Kingsolving† | Murray Hill Citizens | 1959 |
| 3d North | Jerome Kretschmer | Ansonia Independent Democrats | 1961 |
| 5th South | Robert Wechsler | Reform Independent Democrats | 1961 |
| 5th Middle | Leonard Cohen | West Side Democratic Club | 1951 |
| 5th North | Irving Wolfson | FDR-Woodrow Wilson Democrats | 1959 |
| 6th North | Shanley Egeth | East Midtown Reform Dem. Club | 1961 |
| 7th | Franz Leichter‡ | Riverside Democrats | 1957 |
| 8th South | Edward Costikyan | New Democratic Club | 1955 |
| 8th North | Mal Barasch | Lenox Hill Club | 1961 |
| 9th | Richard Lane§ | Lexington Democratic Club | 1953 |
| 10th South | John Harrington | Yorkville Democratic Club | 1959 |
| 10th Middle | Henry Sedgwick | East Side Democrats | 1961 |
| 10th North | Carlos M. Rios | East Harlem Reform Dem. Club | 1961 |

\* Replaced Millard Midonick in 1961.
† Replaced S. Arthur Glixon in 1961.
‡ Replaced William Fitts Ryan in 1960, when Ryan was elected to Congress.
§ Replaced Jean P. J. Baltzell in 1961.

[3] The Manhattan insurgent reform clubs affiliated with the New York
Committee for Democratic Voters in October, 1961, were:

| Assembly District | Name of Club |
|---|---|
| 3d South | New Chelsea Club for Democrats |
| 15th South | Heights Reform Club |

In addition, there were 19 clubs, none of which had won power in district leadership fights, in the other boroughs: 8 in Queens, 5 in the
Bronx and 6 in Brooklyn. This study is based almost entirely on the

The momentum of reform carried them along despite their differences. As that momentum built up over the years, the reform movement became increasingly outspoken, militant, and uncompromising. The later additions to the ranks of the reformers were, in many cases, far more doctrinaire than earlier entrants. At a later point the differences between factions of the reform movement will be described and some explanations offered to account for these differences.

## Insurgency and Reform

The history of New York City politics has been the history of insurgency. It is the normal, not the exceptional state of affairs in the Democratic party, at least during this century. At times insurgent leaders have been part of or allied with a "reform" movement dedicated to changes in the forms and personnel of government; usually, however, insurgents have been fighting intraparty contests for power with no thought of fundamentally altering the rules governing city politics. In 1930–32, Professor Peel found 683 Democratic political clubs of various kinds in New York City and of these 120 were "revolt" clubs contesting with the regular neighborhood, district, and county organizations for power.[4] Since the middle of the nineteenth century, there have been a few strong Tammany leaders in Manhattan, such as William Tweed, Richard Croker, and Charles F. Murphy, who have enjoyed long periods of relatively undisputed authority, but at no time has the Tammany leader been completely free of intraparty opposition and usually that opposition has been intense. Between the eras of the strong bosses there has usually been a sequence of weaker leaders who retained power for only three, four, or five years.

Manhattan clubs; resources were insufficient to examine the other boroughs. In any case, the reform movement is Manhattan-led and Manhattan-financed and, for the most part, Manhattan-staffed. Over three-fourths of the 124 members of the General Committee of the New York Committee for Democratic Voters were, in the summer of 1961, from Manhattan.

[4] Peel, *op. cit.*, pp. 273, 334.

The constant ecological change in which one ethnic or national-ity group has replaced another in the neighborhood, com-bined with the keen ambitions of rival leaders who were lured by the high stakes of politics, has made the post of Democratic county leader of Manhattan a tempting but insecure prize.

Complicating city politics has been the struggle among the leaders of the five county organizations for pre-eminence. Tammany, confined to Manhattan, has always had as rivals the Democratic party organizations in Brooklyn and the Bronx. An old battle-cry of the Brooklyn organization has been, "don't let Tammany cross the bridge"—that is, keep Tammany's in-fluence limited to Manhattan and maintain the independence of the organizations in the other boroughs. When Tweed, Croker, and Murphy were leaders of Tammany, it tended to dominate the Democratic party in the city as a whole; when lesser men were in office, Tammany had to contend with strong, and sometimes superior, rivals in the other counties. As Professors Sayre and Kaufman point out, it is largely a myth that Tammany has "run New York City" or even that it has controlled the Democratic mayors of the city. Tammany has controlled the mayor for only about fourteen of the more than sixty years since 1897. This period has been exceeded both by those mayors who owed their election to the Brooklyn organi-zation and by those "Fusion" or good-government mayors who were elected by reform movements. Brooklyn had dominant access to the mayor for almost seventeen years, Fusion mayors were in power for eighteen years, and anti-Tammany insur-gents from Manhattan have been in office for almost thirteen years.[5]

From time to time the normal pattern of intraparty com-petition within Tammany and between Tammany and the other county organizations has been caught up in a reform movement. Reformers, who generally have entered politics from a non-political background in civic associations, have capitalized on an accumulation of public grievances against party government and on cleavages within the party itself to

[5] Sayre and Kaufman, op. cit., pp. 688–89.

win office for a reform mayor, usually by creating a "Fusion" party which would campaign in alliance with Republicans and dissident Democrats. Reform or Fusion mayors have won office in New York three times in the last sixty years.[6]

Seth Low was elected mayor in 1901 after a special investigating committee of the Republican-controlled state legislature had made public certain scandals in city affairs and after Rev. Charles Parkhurst had dramatized the evils of "boss rule" under Richard Croker. John Purroy Mitchell, the second reform mayor, was elected in 1913 at the peak of the Progressive movement in the city. Tammany leader Murphy and his mayor were relatively clean and able, but the nation-wide reform sentiment was too strong to be resisted, particularly when Mitchell had the backing of President Woodrow Wilson. Progressivism had already won several procedural victories in New York City, including the introduction of the direct primary and the extension of the merit system in the civil service. The third and most colorful reform mayor was, of course, Fiorello La Guardia, who served from 1933 until 1945. He came into office on the wave of public indignation created by the Seabury investigations of the regime of Tammany Mayor James Walker and with the support of President Franklin D. Roosevelt.

All of these early reform movements in New York City had certain features in common. First, they were triggered by a series of public scandals and exposures, often revealed by investigating committees sent down from the Republican legislature to embarrass the Democratic opposition in the city. Second, the Republicans were never able to take advantage of these opportunities by themselves; in each case they needed the support of independent and dissident Democrats who could be brought together in a Fusion-Republican coalition. Third, the City Fusion party, which was always a principal force in the reform movement, never endured. Low and

[6] The following material on reform mayors is taken from Theodore J. Lowi, *At the Pleasure of the Mayor* (New York: Columbia University Press, forthcoming), chap. viii, by the kind permission of Professor Lowi, who made a manuscript copy available to me.

Mitchell only lasted for one term each. La Guardia was able to survive despite the collapse of the Fusion party because he became the nominee of the American Labor party, which had been created in 1936 to provide a means whereby anti-Tammany Democrats could support Roosevelt in Washington and La Guardia in New York without giving aid and comfort to other Tammany candidates locally. Fourth, the local reform movement usually had powerful outside assistance from national Democratic politicians whom Tammany had alienated. In 1912 Tammany had, as usual, backed a loser, Champ Clark, instead of the winner, Woodrow Wilson, and Wilson threw his support to Mitchell, the anti-Tammany candidate for mayor. In 1932, Tammany opposed the nomination of Roosevelt in the Democratic National Convention, and thus Roosevelt, who had the backing of Edward Flynn's Democratic organization in the Bronx, threw his presidential support to La Guardia the following year. Finally, the Republicans have always been disappointed by their support of the Fusion candidate, for his victory never produced that access to power and flow of patronage which the professional Republican politicians felt was their due. As a result, they refused to renominate Mitchell in 1917, and they tried to dump La Guardia in 1937.

The men and women who were attracted to the City Fusion party and the reform movement entered politics to defeat an enemy, to "clean up" government, and to replace bad men with good. Few of them had a positive program to offer beyond the procedural reform of the political structure. Further, they disliked the practice of politics and rarely remained active beyond the initial victories. For these and other reasons, reform never endured. As Lowi suggests, there has been a "reform cycle" in New York City: "Each time its onset was widespread, energetic, irresistible. But once there was a partial redress of the Democratic imbalance of power, the components dispersed. There has been no club core; no central bureaucracy; thus, reform has not been institutionalized."[7]

[7] Lowi, *op. cit.*, pp. 214–15. A similar point is made in Roy V. Peel, "New Machines for Old," *Nation*, September 5, 1953, pp. 188–90.

The reform movement of the 1950's and 1960's began with a reasonably clear realization of these problems. The leaders resolved at the outset that the Democratic party could not be "reformed" from the outside because, as a party, it could outlast any external enemy. Instead, the party must be captured from within. Reform must acquire control of the district clubs, staff the party hierarchy, and capture the party bureaucracy. The only way to insure that bad men would be replaced with good in government posts was to make certain that bad men were replaced with good in party posts.

La Guardia in New York and Roosevelt in Washington absorbed during the 1930's the energies of the young liberals, reformers, and intellectuals who were interested in a politics of principle. The Second World War diverted attention from local politics. After the war, veterans returning to New York and even younger leaders just then coming of age politically looked about for a means of reasserting the reform principle in city politics. La Guardia and Roosevelt had left office in 1945; the party, nationally and locally, had returned to the hands of the conventional party leaders.

But the party these men now led was far weaker than the party of the 1920's. Reform, although not permanent, had left its mark. The merit system had drastically curtailed patronage. The hostility of Wilson and Roosevelt had deprived Tammany of federal patronage when the Democrats were in power nationally. When the Democrats were in power in Albany under Governor Herbert Lehman, Tammany managed to alienate itself from the full political resources of that office; Thomas E. Dewey, the Republican governor, went out of his way to attack the Democrats generally and Tammany in particular. Only under Democratic Governor Averell Harriman, who appointed Tammany leader Carmine De Sapio as his Secretary of State, did the Tiger enjoy the full blessings of state patronage. Otherwise, Tammany was compelled to sustain itself during the Depression and war years largely through its control of the courts.[8] So low was its estate in 1943 that it was compelled for

[8] Cf. Sayre and Kaufman, *op. cit.*, p. 541 n.

financial reasons to sell its headquarters building to a labor union and retrench to more modest rented quarters on Madison Avenue.

Further, ecological changes in Manhattan had proceeded to the point that it was doubtful whether any political machine, even one endowed with ample resources, could continue to govern without a radical redistribution of power internally. The influx of Negroes and Puerto Ricans and the exodus of Irish and Italians made a party organization led by Irish and Italians vulnerable to attack by new groups seeking recognition. Normal population movements out to less congested boroughs such as Queens and to the outlying suburban counties had been accelerated by land clearance programs which replaced older, blighted structures with either vacant land, new medium- and high-rental apartments, or hospitals and other institutions.[9]

Land clearance has driven thousands of older residents out of the lower end of the West Side and the middle East Side, while the attractions of home ownership and a suburban style of life have drawn more thousands of Irish and Italians out of Greenwich Village and the lower East Side. The spaces vacated have often been filled by young married couples and

[9] Manhattan Congressional Districts all suffered a population loss between 1950 and 1960:

| Congressional District | 1960 | 1950 | Per Cent Decline |
|---|---|---|---|
| 16............. | 301,574 | 336,441 | −10.4 |
| 17............. | 260,235 | 316,434 | −17.8 |
| 18 ............ | 269,368 | 317,594 | −15.2 |
| 19............. | 301,499 | 336,122 | −10.3 |
| 20............. | 279,475 | 336,203 | −16.9 |

The Twentieth District is on the West Side, where reform clubs are particularly active in the Third, Fifth, and Seventh Assembly districts. Part of the decline can be explained by land clearance. Sixty-two slum clearance projects were undertaken in New York City between 1950 and 1960, displacing an estimated 124,266 persons. The bulk of these were in Manhattan. (Census data from U.S. Department of Commerce, Bureau of Census, "Population of Congressional Districts: April 1, 1960." *Supplementary Report* PC[S]-2, April 11, 1961. Land clearance data from *New York Times*, September 6, 1960.) A redistricting plan proposed by Republican leaders and passed by the state legislature reduced Manhattan's congressional districts from five to three as a result of these population losses. *New York Times*, November 11, 1961.

single people for whom the attractions of life in Manhattan are worth the congestion and cost of living. This has been particularly true on the West Side. Reform politics has, in great measure, become possible because the class structure of Manhattan has undergone a fundamental change. It is coming to consist of three groups: the wealthy, often older, residents of the East Side, where new luxury apartments are rising at an incredible rate; the lower-income Negroes and Puerto Ricans of Harlem and East Harlem; and the highly educated young professionals, often married but frequently with few or no children, for whom Manhattan has an irresistible fascination. Gone or leaving is the conventional middle class, composed of people of moderate or skimpy means, average education, a high proportion of children, and no particular commitment to the presumed cultural and social advantages of life in Manhattan. These people have moved to Queens, the upper Bronx, New Jersey, and even farther.

Almost all politicians, reform and Tammany alike, agreed that this change lies at the root of reform politics. A reform leader on the West Side spoke of the Fifth and Seventh Assembly districts as about "the only area left in Manhattan in which young, professional people can find decent homes in rent-controlled apartments—people with education and little money, predominantly Jewish." Greenwich Village, which thirty years ago was perhaps one-half Italian,[10] today is about one-third Italian. The new group is composed in part of bearded bohemians and social nomads, but more and more it consists of young middle-class families who regard the atmosphere of Village life as culturally and intellectually stimulating. The characteristics of the new group are graphically summarized by one observer:

> A growing number of the real residents hold down regular jobs [most often in what is now called "Communications" . . . ], have husbands, wives, babies, and grocery carts. The main distinction in material possessions between them and

[10] Cf. Caroline F. Ware, *Greenwich Village, 1920–1930* (Boston: Houghton Mifflin Co., 1935).

the older Italian residents is that they have hi-fi instead of television sets. In the afternoon, they buy the *Post* instead of the *Journal-American,* and are likely to wear toreador pants or slacks instead of skirts and dresses when they wheel their babies into Washington Square Park. Many of them spent the protest years of their youth here, and when they closed that chapter with marriage, they decided to stay on.[11]

The areas of Manhattan vary considerably in the kinds of people attracted to them. Even though the older ethnic neighborhoods were being broken down, the young people who were moving into the city tended to sort themselves out on the basis of income, occupation, and family status. This meant that the constituencies of reform clubs were not identical. Members of the VID in Greenwich Village, for example, were younger than reform members in the Riverside or Lexington areas; fewer of them had children; and a greater proportion were in communications or the arts. The West Side, on the other hand, had more teachers and doctors, more married persons and fewer divorced individuals.

All of these factors contributed to the instability of the Manhattan Democratic party which was manifest throughout the postwar period. After La Guardia, each of the three mayors elected came, sooner or later, to a break with the Tammany leadership, but none except Wagner was able to serve as the rallying point for a new reform effort. William O'Dwyer became mayor in 1945 after serving as a gang-busting district attorney in Brooklyn. Soon he found himself in difficulties, in part arising from his own inability to master the role of mayor, in part because Tammany refused to accept his nominees for offices, and in part because of certain scandals which were uncovered. After less than five years in office, he resigned to become Ambassador to Mexico. Vincent Impelliteri, his successor, broke with Tammany and, in the special election of 1950, formed his own "Experience party" and defeated his Tammany opponent for the mayoralty. Tammany returned to

[11] Dan Wakefield, "Greenwich Village Challenges Tammany," *Commentary,* October, 1959, p. 308.

power by backing Robert Wagner, son of the famous former Democratic senator, in the mayoralty contest of 1953. Wagner was re-elected in 1957 by an overwhelming majority. However, Tammany's brief period of grace in the City Hall was cut short when Wagner, under heavy pressure from reform forces in the city, publicly broke with Tammany leader De Sapio in early 1961.

De Sapio had been chosen county leader in Tammany Hall in 1949. Democratic party leadership in Manhattan had been in a perpetual state of flux since Charles F. Murphy had left that post in 1924, and it was De Sapio's hope that he could rebuild the party's strength and consolidate his own position in part by making overtures to liberal and reform sentiment in the city rather than by following the policy of antagonizing them with deliberate rebukes. But the changing character of the electorate in Manhattan, the shortage of political resources, and the disfavor and disunity into which Tammany had fallen made this task exceptionally difficult. For a brief period, De Sapio scored some limited successes. During his early years in power, he was hailed in feature articles in national magazines as a "new-style boss," an "enlightened political leader" with an interest in civic reforms and improving the reputation of the party.[12]

Throughout this period, when De Sapio was establishing himself in Tammany and Tammany in turn was struggling with O'Dwyer and Impelliteri, young insurgents were active in various parts of the county on a limited scale. The returning veterans and the new reformers entered such organizations as the New York Young Democrats, the Americans for Democratic Action, the Fair Deal Democrats, and the Liberal party. Each of these groups became a focus for insurgent, anti-Tammany activity. Before 1956, however, these reformers were not a major force in the borough; that had to wait on the emergence of a set of prestigious state and national leaders who could extend the appeal of the reform cause.

[12] Cf. Robert Heilbroner, "Carmine De Sapio: The Smile on the Face of the Tiger," *Harper's*, July, 1954, pp. 23–33.

The first two postwar reform efforts by the young liberals were the formation in 1949 of the Lexington Democratic Club on Manhattan's fashionable East Side to contest for the Democratic district leadership in the two halves of the Ninth Assembly District and the creation in the same year of the Fair Deal Democrats on the West Side to support Franklin D. Roosevelt, Jr., in his contest for a congressional seat. These two organizations not only were formed on opposite sides of the city, but they represented opposite philosophies of how best to attack the established organization. The Lexington Club leaders refused to join the Fair Deal Democrats. The former group took the position that it was first necessary to capture the assembly district leadership and become an integral part of the party before contesting for elective offices and that in so doing, one should not become closely identified with any public officials who were not firmly committed to reform. The Fair Deal Democrats, on the other hand, were prepared to wage a general election contest for various elective posts before capturing the local leadership and in the process were willing to form an alliance with such officials as Mayor O'Dwyer. This, of course, was the classic issue of reform: whether to fight the party or fight its candidates. Within a very few years the former approach became the dominant one in the reform clubs, and the Fair Deal Democrats, after some reversals at the polls, disintegrated.[13]

During this period De Sapio was able to stabilize his position as county leader. Although he had been defeated when Impelliteri won over Tammany's mayoral candidate and young

[13] The Fair Deal Democrats were active in the victorious campaign of F. D. Roosevelt, Jr., in the special election of May, 1949, for the congressional seat on the West Side vacated by the death of Rep. Sol Bloom. The FDD also supported O'Dwyer for Mayor in 1949, after he had broken with the dominant De Sapio faction in Tammany Hall, and backed Robert Wagner for Manhattan Borough president in 1950. But it lost in local races for assemblyman and city councilman in 1949 and 1950. Roosevelt also had powerful support from the ADA, the Young Democrats, the CIO, a rebel Tammany leader, and the Liberal party. See Arthur D. Morse, "ADA's *New* New Deal," *Survey,* July, 1949, pp. 351–55, and *New York Times,* February 16, March 29, March 30, April 25, April 29, May 3, and May 18, 1949.

Roosevelt won over its congressional candidate, De Sapio now entered a period of successes. After the May, 1949, congressional election, the rebel Tammany district leader who backed Roosevelt was removed.[14] In the 1951 elections for district leaders, nineteen of the forty regular leaders faced challengers, but the regulars under De Sapio scored decisive victories in most of the contests.[15] De Sapio followed this victory with a move which, by reducing the total number of Democratic district leaders in Manhattan from forty-one to thirty-five, eliminated three district leaders who had been close to De Sapio's enemy, Mayor Impelliteri.[16] In January, 1952, he announced that Tammany would adopt certain reforms in procedure, including the direct election of district leaders and permanent personal registration. At the same time, the forces of Mayor Impelliteri abandoned their efforts to oust De Sapio. The following year, the Tammany candidate for mayor, Robert Wagner, won, and in 1954 Averell Harriman became governor of New York with Tammany support. De Sapio joined the governor's cabinet as chief patronage dispenser. Although by this time the reform candidates of the Lexington Club had won the district leadership in the Ninth Assembly District, reform had generally made little progress and De Sapio seemed firmly in control in the city and in Albany. In 1954 he completed his rise to dominance in the party by becoming the Democratic National Committeeman from New York.

Although De Sapio continued to encounter opposition to Tammany (in August, 1953, twelve of the thirty-five district leaders backed Impelliteri for mayor[17]), by and large he was successful in dealing both with conventional party insurgents and with reform-minded club leaders. After Impelliteri's defeat by Wagner in 1953, nine Impelliteri leaders were dropped from Tammany.[18] In the 1955 elections for district leader in

14 *New York Times,* May 31, 1949.

15 *Ibid.,* August 22, 1951.

16 *Ibid.,* September 5, 1951.

17 *Ibid.,* August 1, 1953.

18 *Ibid.,* October 1, 1953.

Manhattan there were nine contests, but only one of these was a battle between a "reformer" and a "regular"; the rest were normal contests between ins and outs, and, of these, men backed by De Sapio won in almost every case.[19]

But beginning in 1956, the tide turned. De Sapio came under concerted attack by reformers in several parts of the borough and by 1959, substantial reform victories had been won. The crucial events which seemed to have triggered this change were the candidacy of Adlai Stevenson for President in 1956 and the controversial state Democratic party convention at Buffalo in 1958. The former provided a national figure with whom local club leaders could identify; the latter created an issue and brought into the reform camp well-known Democratic leaders, principally former Senator Herbert H. Lehman.

By 1959, De Sapio's gains had been all but wiped out, his credit as an "enlightened" leader had been seriously impaired, and his brief run of electoral victories had been cut short. After controlling the primaries in 1951, 1953, and 1955 and electing Wagner in 1953 and Harriman in 1954, De Sapio began to suffer reversals. He failed in an attempt to "purge" Negro Representative Adam Clayton Powell, Jr., in the 1958 congressional primary.[20] Harriman was defeated by Nelson Rockefeller for governor in 1958 and De Sapio's senatorial candidate, Frank Hogan, lost badly to the Republican Kenneth B. Keating in what was elsewhere a strong Democratic year. The Buffalo convention which had selected Hogan left bitter feelings in the party and antagonized some of its "elder statesmen," notably Lehman and Mrs. Eleanor Roosevelt. In the 1957 primary, De Sapio himself was challenged in his own district by an insurgent reform candidate who made a strong showing and a Tammany leader was defeated by another re-

[19] The "reform" contest was in the Eighth District South, where Edward Costikyan defeated a regular, Connolly, who had been thrown off the ballot and was conducting a write-in campaign. *New York Times*, September 15, 1955.

[20] On the Powell incident, see David Hapgood, *The Purge That Failed: Tammany v. Powell* ("Case Studies in Practical Politics" [New York: Henry Holt & Co., 1959]).

former on the West Side.[21] In the 1959 primaries, there were about twenty contests for district leader, seven of which were won by reformers and three by Negro (but not reform) insurgents led by Representative Powell. Only half the contests were won by regular Tammany leaders. De Sapio himself only barely defeated a reformer in his Greenwich Village district.

In 1960, De Sapio reluctantly supported John F. Kennedy for the Democratic presidential nomination, probably as the only alternative to losing control over the delegation altogether. As it was, De Sapio's ally, State Chairman Michael Prendergast, was forced to give up his seat on the delegation to the anti-De Sapio leader, Herbert Lehman. Kennedy owed little to De Sapio for the support he received from New York. At the same time, the reformers sought to put Stevenson supporters on the delegation. New York Democrats, regular and reform, were in a poor position to rely on presidential support in settling their intraparty contest.

The 1960 campaign was conducted under a temporary and imperfect truce, and scarcely had Kennedy won when De Sapio and the reformers exchanged heated attacks, accusing each other of bad faith.[22] De Sapio promised a "purge" of all reform district leaders. Mayor Wagner, after much urging by reform leaders, publicly broke with De Sapio and urged his removal as county leader.[23] The immediate cause of the rupture was the conflict between Wagner and De Sapio over who should be appointed by the City Council to replace Manhattan Borough President Hulan E. Jack. Jack had been convicted and sentenced for improperly accepting funds while in office. The Mayor's candidate, a Negro who was an independent Democrat (Edward Dudley, a justice in the Domestic Relations Court), was appointed over another Negro who had De Sapio's support.[24] The break with the Mayor cut De Sapio

21 *New York Times,* September 16, 1959.

22 *Ibid.,* January 24, 1961.

23 *Ibid.,* February 4, 1961.

24 Dudley defeated Assemblyman Lloyd E. Dickens by a vote of four to two. The vacancy was filled by the six city councilmen from Manhat-

off from the patronage resources under the Mayor's control and the selection of a new borough president who was obligated to the Mayor rather than the Tammany leader threatened De Sapio's access to patronage in that office.[25] Throughout this period, the new Democratic administration in Washington acted as if it were seeking a change in party leadership in the state and city by refusing to channel the federal patronage through either State Chairman Michael Prendergast or National Committeeman De Sapio.[26]

Thus, by 1961 many of the classic elements of a reform movement were present in Manhattan politics. There had been a series of individually minor but cumulatively significant scandals in the city administration involving policemen, city inspectors from various departments, and the Manhattan Borough president. A Republican state legislature had sent an investigating committee to New York City and its findings, although not shocking, were sufficient to lead many prominent figures to call for a new city charter. Tammany had partially isolated itself from its allies. The Mayor had broken with it,[27] it had lost control of the borough president's office, and a Democratic president in Washington seemed to be withholding important federal patronage as a means of forcing a change

---

tan (five Democrats and one Republican). *New York Times*, February 1, 1961.

[25] Three Tammany district leaders had jobs in the borough president's office and there were "several hundred" low-paying posts as street workers in addition. *New York Times*, February 1, 1961.

[26] *New York Times*, December 3, 8, 9, 11, 12, and 21, 1960, January 8, 9, and 26, February 12, 16, and 17, and March 13 and 23, 1961.

[27] The Mayor's break with De Sapio had one immediate effect. A bill in the 1961 state legislature, which had joint Democratic and Republican backing, would have created thirty-seven new judgeships in New York City if it had passed. These posts would have added greatly to De Sapio's patronage resources and thus strengthened his hand in dealing with intraparty strife. The bill failed of passage because Mayor Wagner refused to write a letter to the Governor certifying that the city needed the posts. Had the letter been written, the bill almost certainly would have passed. It was widely believed that Wagner refused as a means of preventing De Sapio from getting control of these patronage resources. *New York Times*, March 27, 1961.

in local party leadership (despite the fact that Tammany in 1960 had, untypically, backed a winner rather than a loser at the Democratic National Convention). Weakened in its own borough, powerful rivals in other boroughs with strong organizations moved to extend their influence. Tammany district leaders, most of whom thought De Sapio able, were disturbed that his leadership had led to electoral defeat at the state level and that his name had become a symbol of bossism at the local level.

The opportunities for reformers could not have been better, but they proved difficult to seize. The 1961 mayoralty election was viewed as the decisive event for the reformers. Sworn to defeat De Sapio, they now had to choose whether to field a candidate of their own in the primary, endorse Wagner if he were willing to run, or do nothing. To do nothing, it was felt, would be fatal; the movement would disintegrate without a candidate. To accept a De Sapio candidate was impossible. But Wagner, until February 1961, had *been* a De Sapio candidate who had personally endorsed not only De Sapio but every other regular organization county leader in the city. Several reform clubs passed resolutions declaring they would not support Wagner if he chose to run.[28] Efforts to settle on a reform candidate for mayor, however, were unsuccessful. Finally, at the very last minute, on June 22, Wagner announced he would run with a hand-picked slate of candidates for controller and president of the city council. Wagner knew De Sapio would not accept him; there is some doubt about whether he hoped for regular organization endorsement from the other four county leaders.[29]

But De Sapio had no trouble convincing the others that to

[28] Such sentiments were expressed by the Village Independent Democrats, the Riverside Democrats, the New Chelsea Club for Democrats, and others.

[29] As late as June 19, three days before his announcement, Wagner was reported as conferring with Bronx Democratic leader Charles Buckley over endorsements. The day before, when his decision was still but a rumor, the belief was attributed to Wagner by newspapers that his ticket could be acceptable to both the reformers and the non-De Sapio regulars. *New York Times,* June 18 and 19, 1961.

support Wagner was to support reformers who had committed themselves to eliminating "bossism"—and not just in Manhattan.[30] In any case, the regular leaders announced their support for a rival slate headed by State Controller Arthur Levitt, the reformers endorsed Wagner, and the fight was on. After a bitter contest, in which he made full use of the epithet, "boss," Wagner won resoundingly, defeating Levitt three to two and sweeping into party office as district leaders all the reformers who had run on his "line"—i.e., those who, by endorsing him and in turn being endorsed by him, appeared on the same line on the voting machine, enabling the voter, by pulling a straight-ticket lever, to vote for reformers as well as Wagner. The reformers elected fourteen new district leaders and re-elected sixteen and won the Democratic primary for four city council candidates in Manhattan and Brooklyn. Since only Manhattan district leadership seats are contested in the odd-numbered years, the regular organization in the other four boroughs remained intact. The victory in Manhattan, however, was substantial, but fraught with one ominous portent: the enemy, De Sapio, who for years had served as a rallying cry and hence as a source of reform unity, was gone. He had lost his own district leadership to a reformer.

It must be understood that the reform movement *preceded* the uncovering of the scandals, the Buffalo convention, the inauguration of a Democratic president, the Mayor's break with De Sapio, and the state investigations. The Manhattan reformers acquired, by these events, a set of issues with which to wage the fight, but their disaffection from Tammany and De Sapio was prior to and independent of these issues. For some, that disaffection sprang from nothing more than the personal ambition which drives young politicians to seek ways of rising in politics more quickly than the party ordinarily permits. But for others this disaffection was a revolt against the very nature of politics and political organization. In Manhat-

---

[30] It is rumored De Sapio played a tape recording of a television program to the other leaders on which a reform leader had said that Buckley and others were "next" on the reform list.

tan, an assault on Tammany became feasible because of the ecological changes, intraparty strife, organizational weakness, and tactical errors which afflicted the regular party. The antipathy to Tammany had always existed, and it was brought to a focus, not by De Sapio's actions, but by the entry of large numbers of new party activists anxious to support Adlai Stevenson for President.

## The Stevenson Impact

The significance of the Presidential elections of 1952 and 1956 can scarcely be exaggerated. Adlai E. Stevenson was and is a figure of great emotional significance to the young reformers. To these people, many of whom were raised with the belief that politics is a dismal and mercenary process of choice between unpalatable politicians backed by corrupt bosses and party hacks, Stevenson seemed to embody sensitivity and intellect, liberalism and self-doubt in a way that was powerfully compelling. Said one reformer of his colleagues, "Stevenson is associated with a great event in their lives—their discovery of politics." It was the lure of a *national* campaign on behalf of a *national* figure that first brought most of the reformers into politics as part of the Volunteers for Stevenson in 1952 and 1956. The Lexington Democratic Club and the Stevensonian Democrats (an insurgent club on the lower East Side) received their real impetus from the campaign of 1952; the members of the Riverside, FDR-Woodrow Wilson, VID, Lenox Hill, and other clubs were drawn into politics as a consequence of the 1956 campaign. One of the founders of the Lexington Democratic Club, and later executive director of the reform New York Committee for Democratic Voters, was state director of the Volunteers for Stevenson in 1952 and publicity director for a comparable organization in 1956. One West Side reform leader stated, "We would never have grown up without Adlai Stevenson. He, so far as I am concerned, is the spiritual and intellectual father of the reform movement."

The public and private remarks of reform leaders and followers are filled with reverential references to Stevenson. Indeed, in one club, a lengthy debate was held among members of the executive committee over whether Stevenson had become a "father figure" for the movement and whether this "canonization" of Stevenson was a good or bad thing.

Stevenson's attraction as a candidate created a mass base for reform in Manhattan by attracting hundreds of amateurs into local politics, initially for the purpose of electing their leader and then for the purpose of punishing those party officials who had failed to demonstrate comparable enthusiasm. In the Stevenson period, unlike in the Roosevelt era, the liberals and intellectuals were prepared (or forced) to enter politics at the bottom rather than at the top; to generate issues rather than resolve them; and to grasp power for themselves rather than utilize power assembled for them by others. They had discovered that American politics is fundamentally local politics, that political parties are national in name but local in fact.

Stevenson's appeal was a powerful catalyst for political change, and it is important that we understand it. Like all important subjects, however, it is an elusive one. Stevenson seemed to be a liberal, but then Harry S. Truman and John F. Kennedy were conspicuously more "liberal," and neither of them generated the enthusiasm or dedication produced by Stevenson.[31] He was urbane and witty, he often uttered speculative rather than declamatory remarks, he keenly felt the ambiguity of the political situation and the complexity of public issues. He generalized and dealt in abstractions, and his generalities and abstractions were fresher, more polished, less obvious or chauvinistic, than those of his predecessors. But again, there have been other excellent phrase-makers among Democratic candidates; many of Kennedy's set speeches re-

[31] In fact, Stevenson, as Hofstadter has noted, was a "sober and circumspect gentleman" whose ability to arouse such immense enthusiasm from young people was evidence of the "conservatism" of this group. They were anxious to conserve liberal gains which had already been won (and which, as events proved, were never really in any danger) while expressing their concern and perplexity at the "dreadful impasse of our polarized world." Richard Hofstadter, *The Age of Reform* (New York: Vintage Books, 1960), p. 14.

flected a rather high order of rhetoric, imagery, and literary allusion. To the intellectual reformer, the crucial factor was the conviction that in Stevenson's case, the classical urbanity was genuine and ingrained, while in Kennedy's case it was spurious and hastily learned, "Kennedy is just a Democratic Nixon," said one university professor in the reform movement.

The theme that Stevenson was "genuine" occurred repeatedly in the remarks of these men and women. The basic factor in his appeal was not simply his intelligence, wit, or sophistication, although all were essential. Beyond these elements was the belief he engendered that he was a true intellectual, and more than that, a true American aristocrat. Stevenson and Roosevelt represented to their admirers examples of whatever authentic American aristocracy might exist. Both represented moderate, not excessive, old-family wealth which had been used to produce men of a certain breeding and style of life, with the accents and poise (if not the substance) of the best American education.

Compared to Stevenson, Kennedy was viewed, at least before his election, as a *nouveau riche* Irishman who had acquired a Harvard education, whose wealth still belonged to the man who had created it, and who had risen too far too fast. This could only be possible, in their eyes, because he was rich and "calculating." And a suspicious or hostile attitude toward Catholicism has always been one of the many unresolved paradoxes in the American liberal creed. A majority of the leading reformers were Jewish; given their religious and ethnic background, they were keenly aware that they were excluded, in all but a few cases, from the peaks of American society. Only wealth and accomplishment could raise their status; wealth alone is suspect, for it sometimes leads to unfavorable references to the presumed vulgarity of "rich Jews." Accomplishment, notably in the educated professions, is the principal cachet of the only accessible elite. Neither blunt midwestern politicians nor recently arrived Boston Irishmen can display the background necessary to generate enthusiasm among these people. The young Jewish intellectual is too antiprovincial to approve of the former, and too ethnically competitive to accept the latter.

Indeed, so great was the feeling for Stevenson and so marked was the coolness toward Kennedy in 1959 and 1960 that Manhattan reform leaders more than once had to deny explicitly that they were "anti-Kennedy." Herbert Lehman attacked the rumor that his group was anti-Kennedy, expressing concern lest this rumor hurt the reformers in their contest for the district leadership in areas with a large Irish-Catholic vote.[32]

It is essential to remember that Stevenson fascinated as a man rather than as a candidate, and this explains many of the patent absurdities in the remarks of some of his more ardent followers. Kennedy, for example, was criticized for being the nominee of a "boss-controlled" convention; if anything, the "bosses" had more power in 1952 and 1956 than they did in 1960. Indeed, the very lesson of the Kennedy victory was that he made it impossible for the bosses to reject him. Other Democratic candidates were attacked for not repudiating the support of Tammany Hall, but Stevenson would never have repudiated it, either before or after the nomination.

After Kennedy began his campaign, and particularly after his television debates with Vice-President Richard Nixon, reform sentiment began to shift in his favor. And by the time of his inauguration, he had captured the imagination of many club leaders, who were impressed with his skills, strength, and rhetoric. They were not so captured, however, that they could refrain from urging Kennedy to appoint Stevenson as his secretary of state in terms which suggested that no alternative could reasonably be considered.

The process whereby this commitment to a national figure and this participation in a national campaign were transformed into a commitment to a set of *local* goals and participation in a *local* political effort is of central importance in understanding the nature of the Manhattan reform movement. It was in this

[32] *New York Times*, June 18, 1959. Another reform leader, Thomas Finletter, issued a similar denial on a radio program. See *New York Times*, June 1, 1959.

process of transformation that the goals and beliefs of the reformers were articulated and their appeal to the politically uncommitted was defined. In the course of the transformation, the reform movement came to attack Carmine De Sapio personally and as a symbol of a certain political order.

Carmine De Sapio and Tammany Hall, together with the Democratic political allies of De Sapio (such as State Chairman Michael Prendergast, Bronx leader Charles Buckley, and Brooklyn leader Joseph T. Sharkey), were attacked by the reformers because they were "reactionary," "undemocratic," "unrepresentative," and lacked a "concern" for the community. Stevenson supporters in Manhattan were angry at what they regarded as the treachery of De Sapio in not giving full support to Stevenson. This was particularly true in 1956, when De Sapio had backed Governor Averell Harriman for the presidential nomination against Stevenson and, after Stevenson was nominated, had appeared to "sit on his hands" in the fall campaign. Although regular organization leaders deny it, almost all reformers were thoroughly convinced that the Tammany workers failed to work for Stevenson and concentrated instead on the lesser offices of greater immediate importance to the machine (in terms of the patronage rewards). The mass base of reform opposition to Tammany was formed in part out of the conviction that Tammany had betrayed Stevenson.

There were reform groups before the Stevenson campaign, such as the Fair Deal Democrats and the Lexington Club. But the Stevenson movement was the principal means by which reformers were mobilized, with older leaders providing the cadres. Said one:

> In 1952 when we were setting up the Volunteers for Stevenson clubs throughout the state, we planned that the clubs would be the nucleus for insurgent Democratic clubs in New York City. . . . Of course, you lose most of the volunteers you get into the Stevenson campaigns. In 1952, I'd say we had maybe 10,000 Stevenson volunteers in the state and that 500 stayed in afterwards for the local campaigns. But these 500 that stayed in tended to be the natural leaders.

Another reform leader explained how this transformation from national to local organizations occurred: "I thought that it was a pity that we could only get organized as a volunteer group once every four years at the Presidential election. After the [1956] election about three of us got together and had a meeting at my house. We decided to try to stay together."

An active reformer on the West Side has described how the Stevenson volunteers in his district became aware that a national candidate and a national party are, in the last analysis, tied to the local party organization.

> [Our] experience made one point clear: the connection between local machine politics and liberal national candidates usually hurts the latter. An easy inference was the need for better local organizations interested in more than the personal advantage of their own members. Therefore, Bill Ryan called a meeting attended by ten persons, to talk about the possibility of starting a new club.[33]

When the issue was joined, of course, the attack on De Sapio and Tammany Hall moved far beyond resentment at the alleged anti-Stevenson posture of the regular organization. A whole catalogue of Tammany evils was promulgated. The use of patronage, for example, became a prime target. "The regulars think only of pay-offs," said one reformer. "They believe that only a pay-off, patronage or something, will keep people active in politics." Patronage is wrong, the reformers think, if it is used by the leader to enforce his will on party workers and club members. Although the reformers differed among themselves over the extent to which political appointments should be eliminated, they agreed that sinecures were bad. Not only are the holders of such jobs parasites on the public payroll, but what is worse, they are parasites who must take orders. Control of their jobs gives the leader a "string" by which he can compel discipline and force workers to sacrifice their independent judgment.

Although conceding that in some cases De Sapio had nomi-

[33] Robert Lekachman, "How We Beat the Machine," *Commentary*, April, 1958, pp. 290–91.

nated reasonably attractive and qualified candidates for offices at the top of the ticket (such as Harriman and Wagner), reformers felt that party hacks had been picked for the lesser, "low visibility" jobs. Particularly in the judiciary, the regular organization candidates appeared to the reformers as weak and incompetent men who were rewarded for party service and little else.

## Buffalo and the CDV

A dramatic ground for attacking "bossism" was provided in 1958, when the state convention of the Democratic party held in Buffalo nominated Frank Hogan, district attorney of New York County, for the United States Senate over the candidacies of Thomas K. Finletter and Thomas E. Murray. Finletter had the active backing of many reformers, particularly from the Lexington Club (of which he was a member), but little support elsewhere in the party or the state. The events of the Buffalo convention are confused, and the reformers and their allies (including, so the reformers felt at the time, Governor Harriman and Mayor Wagner) were not blameless. Nevertheless, the result was that De Sapio was branded as a "boss" and the convention became the symbol of a "boss-ridden party."[34] To one reformer, "it appeared as if [De Sapio] were ramming through the bosses' choice against the popular choice. De Sapio got a bad public image [the proceedings were televised] and ... Herbert Lehman, Eleanor Roosevelt, and Finletter used the Buffalo convention as a reason for creating the New York Committee for Democratic Voters." An interview with another prominent reform leader from the West Side reveals how the convention appeared to him:

[34] Cf. Robert Bendiner, "De Sapio's Big Moment, or, The Rout of the Innocents," *Reporter,* October 16, 1958, for a balanced view of the Buffalo convention and a sympathetic grasp of De Sapio's role in it. The vote in the convention was: Hogan, 772; Murray, 304; Finletter, 66. At the time, reporters stressed that the Murray and Finletter backers could not agree to join forces and that party leaders were anxious to cut the liberals down to size. *New York Times,* August 27, 1958. See also the perceptive account by an "insider": Daniel P. Moynihan, " 'Bosses' and 'Reformers,' " *Commentary,* June, 1961, pp. 465–67.

The entire convention sat assembled, sitting around on their hands for eight hours, waiting for the boss to tell them what to do. This was a terrible public spectacle. It gave rise to the charge of bossism that De Sapio will never live down. Of course, Harriman and Wagner were weak and vacillating.

Q. But what if De Sapio had ordered the convention to vote for one of your candidates like Murray or Finletter? Would that have been bossism?

A. Well, now, of course, if they'd told them to vote for Finletter, to be frank with you, I don't suppose that would have been looked upon so much as bossism. The thing is, Finletter didn't have any grass-roots support but he was very popular with many reform leaders. . . . But anyway, De Sapio didn't do this and he created this great symbol of bossism.[35]

The reformers charged that De Sapio had let the convention "sit around" while he made "deals" in the "back room." In fact, the people he was trying to deal with were Mayor Wagner and Governor Harriman, who were also in the back room. Nobody but a handful of reformers wanted Finletter to be the nominee, least of all Wagner and Harriman, who preferred Murray. Hogan got regular support for the Senate nomination for the simple reason that he was a good man (no one ever disputed his probity) who had the overwhelming advantage of being an Irish Catholic. Since no such person had been nominated in the last election, it was essential to do so now. To the amateurs, such an explanation was unacceptable, and Buffalo became the shibboleth of reform.

The immediate and vital result of Buffalo was the formation of the New York Committee for Democratic Voters (CDV) by Herbert Lehman, Mrs. Eleanor Roosevelt, Thomas Finletter, and a few others. Although only a committee, and with no formal ties to the already-existing reform clubs, it provided an indispensable source of funds and, even more important, of prestige for the movement. After a reorganization a year later,

[35] Neither Governor Harriman nor Mayor Wagner, whose prestige was most directly involved in the Buffalo fiasco, attacked De Sapio then or in 1959. They backed him throughout 1959, and Harriman never repudiated him. *New York Times*, April 17 and 26, 1959.

it acquired a paid executive secretary, allied itself somewhat more closely with the reform clubs, and shortly became known to the press and the regulars (if not to the reformers) as the "leadership" of the movement. How much it in fact "led" was a matter of dispute; what is beyond dispute is that it gave to reform the use of the politically potent names, Lehman and Roosevelt.[36]

The attack on the regulars was intensified after 1958. Reformers charged that the Tammany organizations discouraged the participation of "outsiders," that they refused to admit women on an equal basis, that they were subservient to the "bosses" in choosing candidates, that they were overly concerned with "ticket balancing" among major ethnic and religious groups, that they were not representative of districts in which they hold power, and that they took no interest in their communities. Given their undemocratic nature, it was contended, community-minded, liberal people could not enter them and reform them from within. Thus, it became necessary to overthrow the old clubs and replace them with democratic clubs. The reformers, by and large, failed to see any advantages that might accrue from the older political system. At most, they would reluctantly concede that De Sapio was probably the best (or at any rate the least bad) county leader in the city and that the other county leaders, none of whom had been seriously threatened by a reform movement, were even more reprehensible than he. But basically they felt that the system had no benefits; it was simply a liability.

The charge that the older clubs were undemocratic cannot be fully understood without grasping the extent to which the reformers found these organizations alien, hostile, and repelling. Underlying the charge of bossism was a profound sense of difference in style of life—what we may call, albeit imprecisely, a feeling of class distinction. This attitude was reflected in statements by reform leaders:

[36] Neither Wagner nor Harriman endorsed the CDV. See *New York Times,* January 23, 1959.

I remember when I walked into the club on the West Side, how foreign it all seemed to me, seeing those political hacks sitting around, doing nothing. I asked for posters for the Stevenson campaign and, of course, they took me aside and told me that our man was Dan Fink, who was running for judge of the Municipal Court. . . . It was the first time I even knew [the club] was there, and certainly the first time I'd been in it. There were a lot of seedy types hanging around. This sort of hit me hard.

Another reform leader, also from the West Side, described his first contact with organized politics:

Joining that club in Brooklyn was a shattering experience. It was an old-line club and the district leader was boss. Everybody was in it for something. They all wanted jobs or favors. There was no sense of policy or program, or finding the best man for the job, or finding somebody with ideas who would give the club creative leadership.

Many reformers felt strongly these class distinctions that separated them from the old-line political leaders and their followers. The reformers were articulate, intelligent, well-educated, and well-mannered. The natural hostility of "outs" for "ins" was reinforced in this case by the conviction that the existing order of politicians was a different breed of men, from a different background, with a wholly different outlook on politics and life. And, of course, to a great extent they were right. A typical expression of this felt difference was found in the remarks of one reform leader:

Our success is basically due, I think, to an aroused middle-class interest in politics. [We] realize for the first time, or at least for the first time in recent years, that politics affects [our] daily lives. Politics was formerly in the province of the upper classes who paid the bills and the lower classes who did the work. Now the middle classes, or at least the educated segment of them, are getting in on that. . . . There's a standing joke around that we're the first white Anglo-Saxon Protestants in Tammany in many, many years. There've been Negroes and Catholics and Jews for a long time, but a white Protestant showing up is a real revolution.

The term "middle class" in such remarks as this must be interpreted with care. The distinguishing criterion of class, for the reformer specifically and the amateur generally, was less income than education and style of life. Many Tammany politicians were wealthy men and few were impoverished. The reformers were neither the corporate rich nor, except in a few cases, the old-family elite. They were members of the newly educated, the sons and daughters (in some cases grandsons and granddaughters) of families that lacked educational and professional opportunities. An education, often made possible only by veterans' benefits and postwar prosperity, enabled the young people to break away from an older, to them constricting, mode of life. They rose in status, not because of money, but in spite of it. The Tammany political leader was seen by these people, therefore, as the man who sought status with money and power but not education or intellect; he was the vulgarian, the materialistic son of the immigrants, the man who never broke with the past or rebelled against the old order.

Not all reform clubs, however, were exclusively composed of Protestant and Jewish middle-class young professionals. Some clubs endeavored, amidst charges that they were "unrepresentative," to attract lower-income Catholic, Negro, and Puerto Rican members. Other clubs, like the Riverside Democrats, inherited older political workers from pre-existing organizations. Perhaps twenty-five workers, many of them poorer Irish who lived in West Side tenements, entered the Riverside club. There was a fundamental dissimilarity between the young reformers and the older group. Because of the polyglot character of the district, each group needed the other, but the views of politics held by the two elements were far from identical. The young reformer looked upon his older co-worker with doubts and uneasiness mixed with a certain attraction for the "colorful" and curious manners of the latter.

The exclusion of women by the regular clubs or their confinement to an auxiliary organization had an important impact on the reformers, who included not only the young lawyer but also the young housewife and the single woman just out of college who wanted to "do something" in the Stevenson campaigns. Said one reform club member, "The regular club excluded women. Stevenson's appeal was felt very keenly by women and many of them were anxious to work for him. Being excluded from the regular clubs was a real shock."

Being confronted by attractive young girls with a yen for political work must have been a surprise for the regular organization as well. One observer noted:

> The De Sapio forces just don't understand the type of modern-woman-in-politics view that is part of the newcomer's code. One young lady who worked as a poll watcher in the 1957 contest was asked with honest curiosity by one of the Tamawa [the regular club in Greenwich Village run by De Sapio] watchers [male, of course] at the polling place, "What's a nice girl like you doing in a place like this?"[37]

Women played an active part in reform politics. In addition to the female district leaders, three club presidents and one candidate for assemblyman were women.[38]

The reformers, members of what one social worker referred to as "the disenfranchised white middle class," often exaggerated the unresponsiveness of older clubs to neighborhood problems. In fact, many regular clubs performed services for their constituents on a scale comparable to that of the reform clubs. The crucial point was that the services were largely of a different kind (personal services rather than neighborhood "projects") and distributed in a different manner (through direct personal benefactions instead of community organizations and committees). The social differences this implied are suggested by Wakefield:

> During the . . . campaign I asked this particular girl [why she was working against De Sapio]. She [named various charges against De Sapio] and then said the club wasn't

[37] Wakefield, *op. cit.*, p. 310.

[38] For a review of women in reform politics, see "Politics and Pulchritude," *The Democratic Voter* (official publication of the New York Committee for Democratic Voters), April, 1960.

really serving the local people with such things as legal and rent clinics. I pointed out that they did, indeed, have such services, and after a moment the girl said, "Yes, but I really wouldn't feel I could take my own problems to them."

No—any more than an aged Italian widow would feel easy about taking her problems to the bright young [reformers]. It is the same reason that the Puerto Ricans in East Harlem don't often take their problems to the local city councilman, John Merli. He and his club are Italians. We belong to different tribes, and trust our own.[39]

For the reformers, Carmine De Sapio had become the living symbol of all that they disliked in the regular organizations. He embodied the traits—ideological, social, and political—that alienated them from the regulars. Indeed, some moderate reform leaders felt that reformers were blindly and excessively anti-De Sapio. But if De Sapio had not existed, it would have been necessary to invent him.

One newspaperman, endeavoring to summarize the nature of the rift between the reformers and the regular organization and explain, in part, the successes of the former, brought together several of the themes to which others have alluded when he wrote:

> What beat him [De Sapio] in the end was the middle class where he sought so long to make his place. A man was saying yesterday that New York, without knowing it, has become a middle-class city. Slum clearance was the final blow to Tammany. Slum clearance in New York is middle-class housing. The poor are displaced and leave cursing the Democrats, and the middle class comes in hating the machine.
>
> Carmine De Sapio is facing for the first time . . . the influx into his neighborhoods of young couples inherently distrustful of him because he is a symbol of everything the middle class has been taught to dislike and distrust. And the self-improver in De Sapio—a natural substitute for conscience—is without power to resist because he believes they are right.[40]

[39] Wakefield, *op. cit.*, p. 310.

[40] Murray Kempton, *New York Post*, June 9, 1960, p. 30.

# 3 Chicago
# The Surrender to Power

Club politics in Chicago is principally shaped by the existence
of a powerful Democratic machine which the amateurs can
neither defeat nor endure. The very factor which makes change
seem so necessary has made change impossible. The story of
club politics in Chicago is the story of the efforts made by
various amateur political organizations to adapt themselves to
the existence of the strongest big-city Democratic machine in
the United States.

The Chicago experience suggests that a strong political machine, if it is led by a shrewd boss, can cut the ground out
from under amateur Democrats by making certain kinds of
concessions and refusing others. The alternatives for the amateurs then become either to reach an accommodation with the
professionals or to cease being a Democratic club and become
instead an "independent" organization for whom the existence
of a powerful Democratic machine is a unifying rather than a
divisive force. There have been two important club movements
in Chicago in recent years; one of these has taken the former
course, and the other the latter. The events in Chicago also
provide an opportunity to draw certain revealing comparisons
between that city and New York. Both leaders of the regular
organization, De Sapio in New York and Daley in Chicago,
were in many ways similar men with similar ambitions. Both
felt that a shrewd, "modern" party leader would adopt the
slogan, "good government is good politics"; both sought to
strengthen their hand by making concessions to reform and
liberal demands; and both became the personal symbol of the
organizations they headed. But the results were far different.

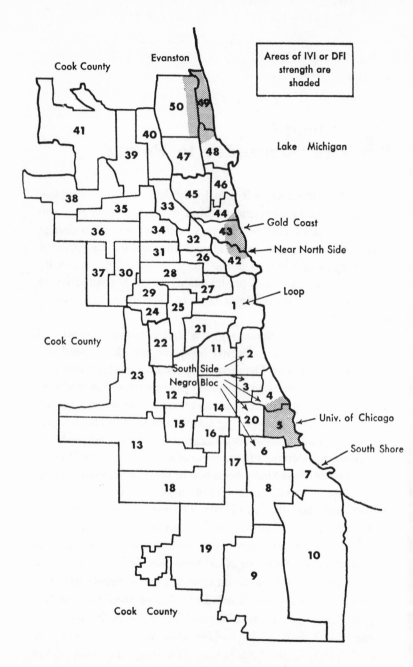

Cook County

Evanston

Lake Michigan

Cook County

Gold Coast

Near North Side

Loop

South Side
Negro Bloc

Univ. of Chicago

South Shore

Cook County

CHICAGO WARDS
(1961)

Daley not only survived but prospered; De Sapio was defeated. This chapter will recount the history of the amateurs in Chicago to indicate some of the reasons why reform was unsuccessful. In part, these explanations involve factors over which the New York and Chicago leaders had no control; in part the explanations involve mistakes made by one leader and not the other.

The Chicago regular Democratic organization is the closest modern approximation to the fast-disappearing machines which were so conspicuous a feature of American city politics forty years ago. Although it is not unbeatable in general elections (in 1956 Eisenhower carried Chicago and the Republicans elected the state's attorney of Cook County), it has been virtually unbeatable in the primary elections. The regular organization candidates almost invariably win the primary, not only in Chicago, but in Illinois as a whole. In thirty years, only one Democrat, former Governor Henry Horner, has won nomination to an important office without regular organization backing.

The conditions in Chicago which encourage the continuance of the machine have been frequently described.[1] Formal governmental power in the city and the county is widely dispersed among scores of independently elected officials. The mayor has few legal powers and can be checked at almost every turn by the fifty-man City Council. Each member (alderman) of the Council is elected from a small ward which tends to be racially, religiously, and ethnically homogeneous. Besides the mayor, the other principal executive officers—the city clerk, the treasurer, the clerks of the various courts, the sheriff, the county assessor, the state's attorney—are all elected by the voters and hence are legally in a position to exercise independent power within their own domains. The only way to overcome this formal decentralization of political power is to re-centralize it in-

[1] Harold Gosnell, *Machine Politics, Chicago Model* (Chicago: University of Chicago Press, 1939); Martin Meyerson and Edward C. Banfield, *Politics, Planning and the Public Interest* (Glencoe: Free Press, 1955); and Edward C. Banfield, *Political Influence* (New York: Free Press of Glencoe, 1961).

formally. The Democratic machine is the means by which this is done and the boss of that machine, whatever his nominal title, is in fact the boss of Chicago. Since 1955, the boss and the mayor have been the same man—Richard J. Daley.

The machine is based on its thorough organization of the fifty wards of Chicago and the townships of Cook County. It is strongest in those wards and townships in which relatively low-income, culturally unassimilated voters live. Ethnically, Chicago is extremely diverse, with large blocs of Poles, Bohemians, Scandinavians, Germans, Italians, Irish, Negroes, rural Southern whites, and Puerto Ricans. Although its Jewish community is sizable (around half a million), it is not nearly so large as the vast Jewish population of New York City (over two million). The ethnic character of neighborhoods changes slowly in Chicago and the lines separating them are often sharply drawn and bitterly defended. Although land clearance has made certain changes—principally in the Negro areas, where it has resulted mainly in large, virtually all-Negro public housing projects—it has not remade the center of the city in the way that land clearance has remade Manhattan. With the exception of two or three small urban renewal projects, there has been no significant revitalization of the residential areas lying near the center of the city, and the people who in New York would live on Manhattan's East Side in Chicago have moved to the suburbs. Their places have been taken by newcomers, for the most part low-income Negroes, who now constitute one-fourth of the city's population. Only two or three small islands of middle-class intellectuals and professional people are found in the center city—one in Hyde Park around the University of Chicago, another along the "Gold Coast" on the Near North Side, and a third in Lake Meadows and Prairie Shores, two high-rise urban redevelopment projects in the midst of a Negro slum.

The Democratic organization maintains its support in the working-class neighborhoods with many of the traditional resources of machine politics—personal loyalty to familiar precinct captains, the exchange of favors, assistance in finding jobs, and help in dealing with social workers, welfare agencies,

policemen, building inspectors, and courts. The precinct workers who provide these services are themselves sustained by a
reduced but still considerable stock of patronage jobs in the
city, county, and state governments. Although no reliable
count is available, a conservative estimate places the number
of such full-time jobs from city and county sources at perhaps
fifteen thousand and from state sources at another thirteen to
fourteen thousand.[2] In addition to jobs, there are many opportunities for lawyers, insurance salesmen, real estate brokers,
labor union leaders and contractors who seek to do business
with the government.

In 1960, the forces which elsewhere appeared to be eliminating the big-city machine as an important political organization
had seemingly passed Chicago by. Although the nationaliza-
tion of welfare services under the New Deal, the steady accul-
turation of immigrants, the heightened newspaper scrutiny of
public affairs, and the growing middle class based on continued American prosperity had all presumably affected Chicago equally with New York, Detroit, St. Louis, Philadelphia,
and other cities where machines were in decay or had been
routed, the Chicago organization seemed to be as vigorous as
ever. It controlled forty-seven of the fifty aldermen, a comfortable majority on the board of county commissioners, and
the mayor's office; it had beaten the local Republicans into a
state ranging from quiescence to connivance; and it had never
been seriously challenged by a reform movement. The period
which saw La Guardia raised to power in New York witnessed
in Chicago only the consolidation of the machine's position
under the regime of Mayor Edward Kelly. Chicago had no
Seabury investigation and no Fusion movement; instead of
alienating the Democratic governor and Democratic president
during the New Deal, the machine worked with them, and
Franklin Roosevelt depended on Kelly at the very time he was
supporting a rival to Tammany influence in New York.[3]

The strength of the Chicago organization in 1960 was not,

[2] See *Chicago Sun-Times,* November 20, 1960.

[3] Harold Ickes described this commitment by FDR to Kelly in his
diary: "Frank [Murphy, attorney-general] then said he wanted very

however, of long standing. Indeed, from 1947 to 1955, the machine had passed through a serious crisis. Scandals during the Kelly regime had discredited the organization in the eyes of many; in an effort to recoup its losses, the machine, led by Colonel Jacob Arvey, persuaded Kelly to step down and slated a "blue ribbon" candidate for mayor, Martin Kennelly. Paul Douglas, who unsuccessfully fought the machine for United States Senate nomination in 1942, found it handed to him in 1948. Adlai Stevenson, a political unknown from outside Chicago, was endorsed for governor. Although these moves partially stilled newspaper attacks on the organization and raised its public standing, they created severe internal problems. Kennelly was a weak and ineffectual mayor, who could not command the organization. As a result, it split into several fiefdoms, each headed by a powerful ward committeeman, and some of these factions became locked in internecine warfare. Stevenson, although elected governor against a scandal-ridden Republican administration, disappointed party regulars in his handling of patronage and crucial party business. The party had no boss; in the mayor's office and the governor's chair were blue-ribbon candidates whose distaste for party affairs was matched by the resolution of party leaders that these officials would be excluded from the conduct of these affairs. In the absence of a single strong leader, the party was governed by a committee of the "Big Boys."

By 1955 the party was ready to dump Kennelly and replace him with a "regular." Amidst outraged protests from the newspapers, Kennelly was not slated; instead, the city clerk, Richard J. Daley, Democratic committeeman of the Eleventh

---

much to clean up Chicago because he thought it was the worst mess in the country and that he hoped 'they' would let him go ahead. I found out that it was surmised that the President would not permit Murphy to go ahead with this investigation on account of Ed Kelly. . . . Murphy told me that the Department of Justice had all the goods that it needed on the Chicago crooks and apparently he is only waiting for the green light which probably will not flash." *The Secret Diary of Harold L. Ickes,* III (*The Lowering Clouds*) (New York: Simon & Schuster, 1954), 94.

Ward, was picked. When Daley won the primary fight against Kennelly, he faced a strong candidate backed by Republicans and independents, Robert Merriam. The Chicago version of a Fusion movement, though hastily assembled, put on a creditable showing and Daley, although the victor in the general election, entered office under a cloud of newspaper suspicion, business hostility, and egghead distrust. Ominous predictions were made that Chicago would once again become a "wide-open city" and the treasury would be raided by party hacks.

The following year, Daley, who had also become party leader (chairman of the Cook County Democratic Committee) faced his first major electoral test and failed. Despite newspaper exposure of gross thievery in the Republican state administration, the Democratic party was unable to win the gubernatorial election, failed to carry the city for its presidential candidate, and lost control of the politically important office of state's attorney to an ex-Democrat-turned-Republican with reform backing.

Three years after this low point, however, Mayor Daley was re-elected by a huge majority after a campaign in which he had the backing of almost every newspaper and civic group in the city, and the endorsement (and contributions) of an impressive list of normally Republican big businessmen. In the state elections of 1958 and 1960, the Democrats won control of almost every important office in the city, county, and state, from state's attorney to governor. Republicans and reformers had either joined the enemy, quit politics in despair, or were marking time in hope of some fortuitous improvement in the low state of their political prospects.

The success of the Chicago machine and Mayor Daley in rebuilding its strength so dramatically was due largely to a series of shrewd concessions to the substantive goals of important segments of the population. The city was not opened up (although keeping it entirely closed seemed beyond the power or will of the Chicago police). Prestigious citizens and blue-ribbon bureaucrats were appointed at least to the more visible offices in the city government and to the Board of Education.

An intensive street light and street cleaning program was begun; the University of Chicago received powerful backing for its thirty-million-dollar urban renewal program; the police and fire departments were enlarged; presentable candidates were found and endorsed for offices at the top of the ticket; a site was cleared for a new University of Illinois campus in the city; a new international airport was financed; port development was pressed; budgeting and personnel practices were improved; and a new convention hall was built on the shore of Lake Michigan. Although many persons contributed to these improvements, Mayor Daley personally identified himself with each one and usually managed to take credit for them. Indeed, the credit was often well-deserved, for with Chicago's badly fragmented formal government, a boss like Daley was required to clear away the political obstacles to these changes.

The efforts of the amateur political clubs in Chicago and Illinois can only be understood against this background of a powerful machine rebuilding and consolidating its power by serving the ends of the outer-city and suburban middle class without at the same time relinquishing its base of power in the "river wards" of Chicago's inner city. It made substantive but no procedural concessions; it turned its energies to "good government" measures but not to party reform.

To be sure, the Chicago organization gave away some of its power through reducing the number (or at least the size) of the favors aldermen could do for their constituents. Posts given to blue-ribbon candidates were perforce denied to organization candidates, and thus some lieutenants became restless. But the structure and personnel of the party remained intact and unchanged. The Democratic committeeman remained the party boss in his ward; his precinct captains were appointed and removed by him without constraints; ward organizations were devoted strictly to the business of politics. They were neither clubs for pinochle games among old cronies nor miniature town meetings for the exercise of Robert's Rules of Order or the passage of resolutions about Red China. Organization discipline could not be as strict as in an earlier era when those aspiring to be a precinct captain were hungrier than they are today, but neither was it so loose that a committeeman ever felt it necessary to submit his decision to a vote of organization members.

Amateur Democrats in Chicago were thus faced with the problem of devising a means to challenge an organization that was willing to grant certain substantive concessions (if the ends sought were not too controversial) but impatient with any suggestion of party or procedural reform. The machine would support liberal ends and liberal candidates, but it would not liberalize the party. And there were, of course, limits to the liberal ends it would support. It would do little (and perhaps could do little) about segregated schools, racial discrimination in housing, or slum neighborhoods. Only a major scandal in 1960 compelled the party to move in the direction of much-needed police reforms; when it did, however, the Mayor —whatever his personal misgivings about the direction reform was taking—stood firmly behind his new police superintendent in the face of heated public attacks from patrolmen and strong private remonstrations from politicians.

Most important of all, however, the machine made little or no use of the young, middle-class professionals and eggheads who felt they could help the liberal cause on the local and national scene. Machine politics in Chicago had suddenly become almost respectable, but the party was still composed of the same old faces—mostly Irish faces, and few which were willing to smile on the earnest ambitions of the Jewish intellectuals and Protestant reformers. Many of these amateurs saw the organization as a means of furthering both desirable social policies and their own political aspirations. But the machine was strong enough to choose which young intellectuals it wanted, and it did not want many. Beyond this, of course, was the fact that relatively few persons responsive to the appeals of amateur politics live within Chicago's city limits, far fewer at any rate than live in Manhattan, in the very center of New York.[4]

[4] Some rough measure of this fact can be inferred from census data. In 1950, 10.2 per cent of the population, twenty-five years old and

The two major amateur reform movements in Chicago were both organized as a result of the defeat of a popular Democrat. In 1944, the Independent Voters of Illinois (IVI) was formed after two years of discussion following the defeat, in 1942, of Paul Douglas in his bid for the Senate nomination. In 1957, the Democratic Federation of Illinois (DFI) was created following the defeat of Adlai Stevenson and Democratic candidates for governor and senator the preceding November. In each case, the circumstances were similar. A popular liberal figure (Douglas in 1942, Stevenson and Senate candidate Richard Stengel in 1956) had lost. Charges were made that the regular organization had "dumped" these men or "sat on its hands." Douglas lost the 1942 primary to a weak regular candidate who in turn was defeated by his Republican opponent. Leaders of the IVI (at that time called the Independent Voters League) felt that a "deal" had been made whereby in return for a weak Democratic senatorial candidate, the Republicans had agreed to give Mayor Kelly only token opposition the following year. Stevenson and Stengel lost to the Republicans because, in the opinion of the amateurs, the Chicago organization nominated a weak gubernatorial candidate (whom they later had to replace in mid-campaign when he withdrew under newspaper charges of financial irregularities in his office of Cook County treasurer) and because the organization was so interested in retaining control of the state's attorney's office that it did little about the presidential and senatorial contests. These charges would sound familiar to a Manhattan reformer; the choice of candidates is "dictated" by party "bosses," the machine only works for the "political" offices at the bottom of the ticket, and "deals" are made with the Republican opposition.

There was an important structural difference between the DFI and the IVI, however. The former sought to be a state-wide organization; the latter was confined to Chicago. The

---

over, in Manhattan had a four-year college education or better; only 5.7 per cent of Chicago's population had a similar level of schooling. The disparity in 1960 is likely to be greater. In Cook County *outside* Chicago, on the other hand, 10.9 per cent had a college degree.

reason for this difference is to be found in the differing constituencies of the two organizations. Whereas the IVI was composed almost entirely of urban liberals, the DFI was a mixture of urban liberals and downstate Democrats who had a variety of motives, many having little to do with liberalism, for opposing the Chicago organization.

To appreciate in full the situation of amateur Democrats in Chicago, therefore, we must introduce the politics of downstate Illinois. Downstate (and by that is meant all counties outside Cook County and the four suburban counties of Will, Kane, DuPage and Lake) is the stronghold of rural and small-town Republicanism. South of Chicago, there are only two counties of over 175,000 population with significant Democratic strength—St. Clair and Madison, the former an important industrial area. The Cook County Democratic organization, however, completely dominates the statewide party. Voting in the state central committee is heavily weighted in favor of Chicago. Each state central committeeman (one chosen from each congressional district) can cast as many votes in the committee as were cast by the voters in his district in the preceding Democratic primary election. Any Democrat hoping to win statewide office must, therefore, have Cook County backing. But downstate Democrats seeking offices which are *not* statewide are, of course, free of Chicago control. In most northern states, where downstate (or, as in the case of New York, upstate) is heavily Republican, this is unimportant, since no Democrat can win local office. But Illinois electoral law has an unusual feature which permits Democrats to win where Republican voters are in a clear majority: the cumulative voting system. Under this arrangement, each state representative district elects, not one, but three representatives. Each voter may cast three votes, divided as he sees fit among any number of candidates, up to three. Thus, an ardent Democrat can cast all three of his votes for one Democratic candidate in hopes that, if enough other Democrats do the same thing and if the Republicans split their votes among two or three candidates, the Democrats can win office with a minority of the votes cast.

In theory, any candidate for state representative can win with only 25.1 per cent of the total vote in his district.

Cumulative voting has meant, in practice, that one Republican usually gets elected from even heavily Democratic districts in Chicago, and sometimes one Democrat gets elected from heavily Republican districts downstate. Indeed, the parties often facilitate this by arranging their nominations so that there is, in effect, no contest for state representative. Thus, by tacit (and sometimes explicit) agreement, the majority party will put up only two candidates for the three state representative posts and the minority party will put up one; all three will automatically be elected.[5]

This situation has created in downstate Illinois pockets of rural Democratic "strength" which have been sufficient to keep in the state legislature certain politicians, some of whom have become quite powerful. One of these is Paul Powell, Speaker of the Illinois House of Representatives, where he has served for twenty-three years. Powell is the shrewd leader of a group of downstate, anti-Chicago Democrats, some of whom display the style and hold the views of rural Southern Democrats. Powell and his associates are not interested in reform, liberalism, or club politics; indeed their position in the legislature, where they often hold the balance of power between Chicago Democrats and downstate Republicans, demands a tactical flexibility and a pragmatic orientation to politics which any permanent commitment to dissidence would hamper. These Powell politicians always maintain an anti-Chicago posture, for in downstate Illinois Chicago is viewed with chronic suspicion as the scandal-ridden center of hostile urbanites who are all foreign Catholics, slick Jews, or criminal Negroes. But beyond reflect-

[5] Between 1920 and 1954, the two parties split the nominations 2–1 or 1–2 in 56.5 per cent of the state representative elections throughout Illinois. The bias of the parties is very conservative in this respect. In the 45 cases in which the Democrats won 75 per cent of the total vote, and in which they could therefore have elected all three representatives, they nominated three in only 9 per cent of the cases. See Jack Sawyer and Duncan MacRae, Jr., "Game Theory and Cumulative Voting in Illinois," *Proceedings* of the Social Statistics Section, American Statistical Association, 1959, pp. 71–78.

ing this attitude, the Powell forces are usually only willing to fight Chicago seriously if it results in patronage or power; lesser stakes do not interest them.

In addition to the Powell forces, however, there was a group of Democrats from the downstate industrial areas where labor is strong and anti-Chicago feeling high. These leaders, who (unlike Powell) owed little to the Republicans and who (unlike the Chicago amateurs) did not need to fear the consequences of antagonizing the Chicago machine, were a ready source of strength for any organized effort to challenge the party leadership. These Democrats from St. Clair and Madison counties included intellectual liberals such as Paul Simon, a young newspaper publisher and state representative, and certain labor leaders such as Mike Haas.

Such is the background for amateur Democratic clubs in Illinois. The crucial question which any club movement had to answer concerned the attitude the clubs would take toward the Chicago machine. Potential dissidents and reformers in both Chicago and downstate were divided on the issue. The Chicago liberals were split between those who believed one had to fight the machine, even if one lost, in order to establish some base of power, and those who felt the machine was too strong to make a fight worthwhile. The downstaters were divided between those who wanted to fight Chicago in order to reform the party on behalf of liberalism and those who wanted to fight Chicago in order to extract from the party patronage and office.

## The IVI

The IVI was formed because certain prominent Chicago liberals were dismayed by the Chicago machine's performance in a national election. From the beginning, these liberals all considered themselves Democrats, and in 1947 the IVI affiliated with the newly formed Americans for Democratic Action. The IVI members sought initially to extend the appeal of the Democratic party by attracting liberal and intellectual support in Chicago to national Democratic candidates. It almost never supported Republicans and only rarely offered a challenge to the regular organization in the primaries.

The IVI at the outset had little in the way of a precinct organization, relying as much on its money and the prestige of its members as on doorbell ringing to attract voters. Further, its internal structure was centralized and not notably democratic. There were two classes of members; only the "governing" members could elect the Board of Directors, and only the board could choose new governing members. Its leadership was self-perpetuating. The lack of membership control over leaders was justified on the grounds that democratic procedures would permit the IVI to be infiltrated and captured at the grass roots; liberal political action needs strong central direction in order to survive.

This early arrangement proved unworkable, however. Soon certain members began pressing for greater rank-and-file participation in decision-making as a condition of their continued support. Many of these rebels were members of the extreme left wing; some were known to be Communist sympathizers. But their demands were successful, and in 1947 the IVI adopted a new constitution which abolished the two classes of members and permitted the ward clubs to elect 60 to 80 per cent of the Board of Directors.[6] After 1948, Communists were driven out of the IVI by the anti-Communist policy of the ADA and attracted by the formation of the Progressive party supporting Henry Wallace. The internally democratic structure persisted, however.

The IVI has never been a large organization. No reliable membership figures are available, but they have probably never been more than two or three thousand, and often much less. After the 1952 Stevenson campaign, the membership stood

[6] On these events and the early history of the IVI generally, see Florence Medow, "Policy Formation in the Independent Voters of Illinois" (M.A. thesis, Department of Political Science, University of Chicago, 1947), and Irving Horwitz, "Political Campaigning of a Non-Party Group" (M.A. thesis, Department of Political Science, University of Chicago, 1954).

at about 2,500. In 1955 and 1956, when the IVI was locked in an internal conflict over goals, membership fell sharply, to less than one thousand.

The IVI from the first drew its strength principally from Chicago's Fifth Ward, then a heavily Jewish, middle-class area which is the site of the University of Chicago. Within a mile of the campus live almost all the students and 80 to 90 per cent of the faculty in the social sciences (administrators and medical and business school faculty seem to show greater preference for the suburbs). In addition, the organization enlisted members from the Gold Coast and the Jewish wards on the North Side.

Attracting liberal support for national Democratic candidates proved to be an insufficient inducement for many IVI members. During the 1950's, a split developed in the organization between older members who favored the existing policy and newer members who were eager for a primary fight and ready to take on the regular organization. This younger group felt that the IVI was simply the liberal tail to the organization dog. Only by creating its own precinct organization and challenging the machine in primary fights over local candidates would the IVI make itself felt in the party. Machine leaders, it was argued, only respect power and power must be demonstrated to be believed. Furthermore, the IVI ought to stress the development of issues and programs.

The first major effort to realize this new perspective was made in 1950 when the IVI supported a Negro labor leader, Willoughby Abner, against the regular organization candidate for state senator. The IVI joined with the United Auto Workers Political Action Committee in an anti-organization primary fight, but their candidate was beaten badly, by more than two to one in both the district as a whole and in the Fifth Ward, the center of IVI strength.[7]

This experience only reinforced the conviction of the IVI

[7] This campaign is described in Fay Calkins, *The CIO and the Democratic Party* (Chicago: University of Chicago Press, 1952), and in James Q. Wilson, *Negro Politics* (New York: Free Press of Glencoe, 1960), pp. 125–26.

militants that a strong precinct organization was necessary. The older members, on the other hand, pointed to the Abner campaign as proof of the folly of primary contests. In their eyes, if the IVI were to follow a "reform" course, it might weaken the ability of the Chicago Democratic party as a whole to aid national Democratic candidates, and thus weaken the national party and its liberal leaders.

The militants carried the day. In 1954 the IVI supported two non-machine candidates in primaries and when one of the most prestigious of the IVI's founders, Leo Lerner, protested, he was reprimanded by the young leadership. Lerner advised the IVI to "be careful about fighting ward committeemen and local candidates who support the national liberal candidates."[8]

The watershed for the IVI was reached in 1955. Over the strong protests of some older members, it endorsed a Republican candidate for mayor against Richard J. Daley. Robert Merriam had been Fifth Ward alderman since 1947, when he was elected with the joint support of the IVI (who proposed him as the candidate) and the regular organization ward committeeman (who accepted him in hopes of defeating the incumbent). By 1955 Merriam, who had been an independent alderman, favored public housing, was felt to be pro-Negro, and had identified himself with the anti-organization "Economy Bloc," had switched party allegiance and announced that he was henceforth a Republican and available for the nomination for mayor. The struggle in the IVI was intense; endorsement was not finally announced until a few weeks before the election. Although the vote of the board was 28 to 6 in favor of the Merriam endorsement, most of those who opposed it eventually left the IVI and rejoined the regular organization.[9] Merriam carried twenty-two wards but lost to Daley in a fairly close race. Shortly thereafter he departed from Chicago to accept a position with the Eisenhower administration in Washington.

The following year the IVI again endorsed a Republican for a top elective office. Benjamin Adamowski, a Polish politician

[8] Quoted in Horwitz, *op. cit.*, p. 74.

[9] One IVI founder, in fact, was later elected alderman by the regular organization in a North Side ward.

and a former Democrat, received IVI backing for the post of state's attorney of Cook County—a powerful office because of its control of law enforcement machinery and its large number of patronage positions. Again the endorsement divided the IVI, the older group expressing fears that the split ticket the IVI had backed would hurt Stevenson's chances in the presidential race.

These events in 1955 and 1956 were the dramatic climax to changes that had been under way for over five years. Before 1950, the IVI was simply a liberal faction within the Demo-

TABLE 1

IVI ENDORSEMENTS IN CHICAGO

| Year | Total Endorsements | Democrats Endorsed | Republicans Endorsed |
|---|---|---|---|
| 1946......... | 22 | 21 | 1 |
| 1948......... | 24 | 23 | 1 |
| 1950......... | 72 | 46 | 26 |
| 1952......... | 27 | 21 | 6 |
| 1954......... | 58 | 40 | 18 |
| 1956......... | 35 | 21 | 14 |
| 1958......... | 44 | 29 | 15 |
| 1960......... | 65 | 44 | 21 |

cratic party. As such, it endorsed Democrats almost exclusively and it was principally concerned with the top of the ticket. After 1950, it endorsed large numbers of Republicans and took an interest in many local offices. These changes can be seen in Table 1. The tripling in the number of endorsements between 1948 and 1950 suggests that the IVI was now challenging the machine, not simply over national offices, but across the board. This shift not only drove out older, less militant IVI members (by 1956, almost all the IVI directors who had voted against the Merriam endorsement had resigned), it also meant that the IVI lost its connection with organized labor, which, in Chicago, feels it must remain close to the regular organization. Further, the IVI declined in resources. In one early campaign it spent over $50,000; by 1960 it spent only $10,000.

The greatest successes of the IVI have come in aldermanic and state representative races in the Fifth Ward. It not only elected Merriam alderman but elected his successor, Leon Despres, and re-elected him in a heated contest with a regular organization candidate. This success in part was due to another anomaly in the Illinois electoral law. The office of alderman is legally non-partisan.[10] No party designation appears on the ballot. Thus, independent groups such as the IVI can campaign among Republican voters for support in the aldermanic primary.[11] Further, the IVI managed to nominate in the Democratic primary and then elect a state representative, Abner Mikva, in the district which includes the Fifth Ward. This victory against the regulars was made possible by the cumulative voting system which enabled Mikva to win office with only about 40 per cent of the vote. Even so, it was regarded as a considerable achievement to beat the machine at the local level.

These events—the endorsement of Republicans, the contesting of aldermanic and state representative primaries, and entering the mayoral race—placed the IVI squarely in opposition to the regular organization. To the professional politicians the IVI was an enemy, more reprehensible than the Republicans because it could not be handled in the same way that Democrats had traditionally handled the weak Republican opposition and because it crossed party lines unpredictably. Although the IVI's relations with the machine were thus firmly settled, one crucial issue had been postponed. Would the IVI attempt to take over some part of the regular organization by contest-

[10] Except in the legal sense, this non-partisanship is largely a fiction. As a powerful alderman is fond of saying, "The City Council is composed of forty-seven non-partisan Democrats and three non-partisan Republicans."

[11] Technically it is not a "primary" at all. Under the non-partisan system in Chicago, one election is held with no party labels and open to all candidates. If the top vote winner receives an absolute majority, he is declared elected. If not, a second "run-off" election is held a few weeks later, limited to the top two candidates. In fact, since the party organizations almost always control the aldermanic races, the first election serves the function of a primary.

ing one or more ward committeeman posts? The ward committeeman is the real source of power; the elective officials (unless
they also happen to be committeemen in their own right) are
often little more than errand boys. The Lexington Club in
Manhattan had decided as early as 1949 that winning *party*
office must take precedence over winning public office; that
choice was postponed in Chicago for another ten years.

The reasons why so little serious consideration should be
given to winning the ward committeeman post are in themselves an interesting commentary on the state of amateur politics in Chicago. Although we shall return to this subject later,
it will suffice here to observe that to most amateur politicians
and reformers, the strength of the Chicago machine was such
that there seemed no real possibility of making any significant
gains in this way. At best one ward could be captured, and the
County Democratic Committee was perfectly capable of not
recognizing a victorious reform candidate for committeeman.
Further, unlike Manhattan, there is no intermediate party organization between the Cook County organization and the
individual ward organizations. The Chicago Democratic party
is a unitary, not a federal structure; there is only one boss, and
he is chosen by the fifty ward committeemen in the city and
thirty township committeemen in the county. There are no
"boroughs" and hence no borough party organizations. As a
result, unlike New York, a few ward victories by reformers
cannot be parlayed into control of a borough leadership post
with its own autonomous powers and rules.

In the IVI, the issue of whether to seek the Fifth Ward
committeeman's post came to a head in 1959. An IVI leader,
Lou Silverman, was an active candidate for the job. Silverman
had, more than anyone else, been the leader of that group of
IVI activists who had favored contesting local primaries and
creating a precinct organization that could do battle with the
regulars. To Silverman, the IVI's stature could be no greater
than the power it won for itself in direct combat with the
machine. Silverman quickly became the leading figure in the
local IVI and was widely known as a hard-working, able poli-

tician. He entered politics in 1954 as the campaign manager for an unsuccessful candidate for state representative. The following year, he put together a coalition organization that elected Despres Fifth Ward alderman against machine opposition. In 1956 he ran the campaign of Mikva for state representative. As early as 1956 Silverman became interested in running for Democratic ward committeeman in the Fifth Ward,[12] but his real chance came in 1960. The regular organization committeeman, Barnet Hodes, was not popular in the university community, was frequently out of the city, and had lost support among several of his lieutenants and precinct captains. The time seemed ripe for a challenge.

Two difficulties arose, however. First, Silverman had made some important enemies during his leadership of the IVI. Not all liberals approved of his power-oriented perspective or of some of his tactics. The IVI and the Fifth Ward are populated with articulate individualists, many of whom do not take easily to the kind of strong, central direction and tactical flexibility a combative political club requires. It was, therefore, only probable but not certain that the IVI and other liberal forces would have backed Silverman. But the second difficulty soon made the first question academic. Mayor Daley and other regular politicians were also aware of Hodes' weakness as a ward committeeman and they moved to forestall a fight. State Senator Marshall Korshak, a regular organization man (he had, indeed, beaten Abner, the IVI candidate, in the 1950 senatorial primary) who also maintained good contacts with the liberal and amateur wings of the party, announced he was a candidate for Fifth Ward committeeman. Although Hodes might have been a vulnerable target, Korshak was not. He was shrewd enough to have developed a certain appeal for university liberals, and the IVI had twice endorsed him for state senator after their early unsuccessful battle with him. State Representative Mikva, an IVI and liberal hero, quickly an-

[12] The ward committeemen in Chicago are elected every four years in the presidential primary. They are rarely opposed. There is no tradition of insurgency similar to that found in New York.

nounced that he was supporting Korshak. Despres, the alderman, decided not to take part in the campaign. Silverman's potential support began to evaporate. Finally Mayor Daley let it be known that he would prefer an orderly transfer of power from Hodes to Korshak. Most of the precinct captains fell in line. Silverman decided not to run, and Korshak was elected.[13]

In mid-1961, the IVI was rapidly becoming an organization with little to do. It opposed the machine, but except for a state representative and an alderman, the machine seemed impregnable. The ward committeeman was secure. IVI leaders found themselves in the position of being far more critical of the Daley organization than most liberal opinion. The Democrats under Daley won in 1958 and 1960, and their control of the governorship only increased their strength. A friendly administration which had received powerful support from Daley, at and after the Democratic convention, was in office in Washington. Well-known Chicago liberals backed Daley as a man who could deliver, even though they caviled at some local practices in such areas as race relations. The IVI had become a holding operation, waiting for the machine to blunder. In the meantime, it could act as a kind of pressure group on behalf of certain liberal goals in fields such as housing, urban renewal, and race relations, and gird for a battle to defend its alderman in 1963.

## The DFI

Although the DFI was formed out of an alliance of more diverse groups than those represented in the IVI, it had from

---

[13] In one sense, Korshak was the Chicago equivalent of Ludwig Teller in Manhattan. Teller had been put in, with De Sapio backing, as district leader in a West Side area thickly settled with intellectuals and liberals. He was a law professor and had Liberal party backing; his mission was to rehabilitate the appeal of the regular party for the amateurs and thus forestall a fight. He failed. Korshak, under similar circumstances, succeeded. The reason seems to be that De Sapio and Teller were reforming from a position of weakness, while Daley and Korshak were acting from a position of strength. Concessions by the former only encouraged reformers; concessions by the latter deterred them.

the outset to face the same critical issue: how far to go in attacking the Chicago organization. The DFI's solution to this problem was different from the IVI's; it went out of its way to accommodate, rather than to fight, the organization. Thus Chicago offers the interesting case of two approaches to the problem of maintaining an amateur political club: the combat clubs (the IVI) and the accommodation clubs (the DFI). This characterization is, of course, something of an exaggeration, for the IVI on occasion was accommodating and the DFI on occasion was combative. But the general distinction is correct, and illuminates the problems which the DFI faced.

The DFI was created as an alliance between two or three major groups.[14] The first of these was a number of young Chicago Democrats, many of whom had once been active in the administration of former Governor Stevenson or in the campaigns on behalf of Paul Douglas and Richard Stengel. Unlike the members of the IVI, they preferred to work within the Democratic party on behalf of Democratic candidates but wanted a voice in the selection of candidates and the formulation of issues. Some had political ambitions of their own, and activity in the IVI would have been viewed with great intolerance by the regular organization. Most of these people, however, sought nothing for themselves; they were interested in good government.

After Stevenson left office in Springfield and was defeated in the 1952 presidential election, the Stevensonites who had worked for him in the party or with him in his administration sought ways to continue their role in politics. A group of young Chicagoans formed the Committee on Illinois Government (CIG). One of its leaders was Daniel Walker, a lawyer who had been an administrative assistant to Stevenson. Walker described to an interviewer his hopes for the CIG:

[14] The entire treatment of the DFI in this chapter draws heavily on a manuscript by Professor Bruce Mason, formerly of the University of Illinois and now at Arizona State University, entitled "The Democratic Federation of Illinois." I am grateful to Professor Mason for making this available to me, although he is not responsible for the way his material has been used or for the conclusions I draw.

After 1952 a group at my instigation formed the Committee on Illinois Government. The purpose of the Committee on Illinois Government was to focus attention on the short-comings of the state government under [Republican Governor] Stratton and develop ideas for legislation and improved state administration. In the initial period I hoped that it would turn into an action group. I felt that there was a need in the state for people who wanted to work for and with the Democratic party but not as a part of the regular organization. A lot of people don't like to go to ward meetings and become assistant precinct captains, but are Democrats because of the issues. I felt that there was a need to make these people feel wanted. I had hoped for an ideal of an action group that would have an impact on the regulars, not in the sense of contests, or power, but influence. It would help get candidates like Stevenson and Douglas slated, and campaign on issues rather than personalities. If you just had the Committee on Illinois Government as an idea organization it wouldn't have as much influence.

Although the CIG did research and provided help in the campaign of certain Democrats, it never developed an action group. After the Democratic defeat in 1956 in which the machine, in the eyes of most of the amateurs, had let Stevenson down badly, some CIG leaders joined with other young Democrats to seek ways to form an "action group."

It is interesting to note that the Stevenson campaigns of 1952 and 1956 brought many volunteers into the IVI who were or quickly became "independent" amateurs, willing to fight the regular party. The Stevenson men who joined the DFI after 1956, however, were not of this type; they were "party" men who sought to "liberalize" it without defying it. One explanation for the difference between the orientation of the two groups of amateurs may be the fact that the early DFI leaders were already *in* politics before they joined the DFI. Their service in Springfield had placed them on the "inside" and had given them a taste of power before they thought of creating an amateur club movement.

The Chicago group had, as significant allies, a number of

important downstate politicians. One group came from liberal, intellectual backgrounds, and looked to Representative Paul Simon of Troy as their spokesman. Another group was connected with organized labor in St. Clair County (which contains the city of East St. Louis) and was led by Mike Haas, an older man who already held a patronage job in his community. Indeed, those attending the initial meeting to explore the possibility of creating the DFI were almost evenly divided between Cook County and downstate. The Chicago group was composed almost entirely of urban, middle-class liberals; the downstate group was much more diverse. Some were professional politicians who were feuding either with the Chicago machine or with their own county leadership. Others were professors from provincial colleges. Some were elective officials who had already defeated the regular organization in their districts.

But the cleavage which from the first divided the embryonic DFI was not an urban-rural, Chicago-versus-downstate fissure. Paradoxically, it was not the downstate professional politicians who sought to guide the DFI into a moderate, accommodating role while the urban intellectuals tried to breathe militancy and combativeness into it. On the contrary, for the most part the roles were exactly reversed. The downstaters, including both the professionals and the amateurs, were eager to fight Chicago because they had nothing to lose and a great deal to gain by striking a pose as giant-killers. The Chicagoans, on the other hand, felt the power of the Daley machine all too keenly and knew that discretion had to be the better part of valor. If the DFI embarked on a reckless course of fighting Daley and failed (as was almost a certainty), the Chicago members could expect little help from the machine in their future political careers. But even this description of Chicago and downstate factions is too simple, for in both areas there were moderates and militants.

The first exploratory meeting was held in July, 1957, not in Chicago, but downstate, in Bloomington. Many of those in attendance were generally familiar with the California club movement and the CDC, and later some of them went to considerable effort to learn more about it. There was some hope of creating an Illinois equivalent of the CDC, but one issue had to be resolved immediately: Since the DFI could not fill a vacuum, as in California, how could it win a place for itself in the political sun?

In New York, confronted with a vulnerable machine, the clubs had raised the slogan of reform. In California, with no machine at all, club members were preoccupied with substantive goals, and their rallying cry was liberalism. In Illinois, the cry of reform would only antagonize the regulars, who were too strong to be threatened. As one DFI member put it, "I never did regard the DFI as a 'Democratic party reform movement.' The New York people have been trying to depose De Sapio. Our concept was to supplement the Democratic party, to open it up, but not to take it over."

Members of the DFI were liberals, but, as the IVI had discovered before them, there were structural difficulties in the way of liberal goals in Illinois. They wanted to remain in the Democratic party but also to "open it up." The DFI was thus faced with the problem of developing an approach that could appeal both to its amateur constituency and to the regulars. Kelly's idea was "that we should avoid a challenge to the regular party, and therefore should de-emphasize the power aspects. The key word in our efforts should be 'participation.'" To some extent "participation" caught on as a slogan; the idea that produced it was certainly the dominant view of the Chicago DFI leaders. By "participation" or "open up" they meant, in a general sense, to increase the participation of liberal, middle-class elements and thereby to enhance the "image" and broaden the appeal of the party. There was much personal recrimination against the Daley organization at the Bloomington meeting, especially from downstate, but a proposal immediately to establish clubs was rejected on the grounds that they might come into conflict with the regular Democratic organization. Instead, a committee was formed to sound out local opinion. The goals adopted by the Bloomington meeting indicate the character of the DFI: (1) to build a broader base for the Democratic party; (2) to co-operate with the regular Democratic organization; (3) to provide a vehicle for the co-ordination of statewide Democratic efforts; (4) to encourage the candidacies of young men of the caliber of Henry Horner, Adlai Stevenson, and Paul Douglas. Representative Paul Simon and CIG leader Dan Walker were named co-chairmen.

After the Bloomington meeting, two Chicago DFI leaders, Frank McNaughton and Angelo Geocaris, went around the state making contact with local Democrats who might be receptive to the club idea. They found many. A list was made, invitations were drafted, and a letter went out signed by Simon and Walker inviting "all voting Democrats" to an organizing conference in Springfield on September 28, 1957. Four hundred came.

It is interesting to compare the manner in which the DFI and the IVI were created. The IVI was formed by a small group of leaders who established the organization and its internal structure (initially undemocratic) before making any attempt to enlist a mass membership. The struggle over the proper role of the IVI thus came some years *after* its formation and hence was a struggle over *goals* but not over the *existence* of the organization. The DFI began with a mass meeting and thus the question of goals was from the very first inseparable from the problem of creating the organization. As it turned out, the question proved insoluble.

The notion of "participation" begged the real issue of whether one did or did not participate in primary contests against the regular organization. It soon became clear that for most DFI leaders, there were to be no such contests. The DFI was to take the road tried by the early IVI—attract liberal amateurs into the Democratic party on behalf of liberal candidates and issues.

Indeed, the DFI went out of its way to get into contact with the regulars. The Democratic State Chairman, James Ronan, was advised of DFI plans and is reported even to have suggested the DFI's name. Conversations were held with Mayor Daley, who maintained a friendly but aloof attitude toward the new group. He frequently addressed meetings of the DFI, usually with a calm plea for party unity. A resolution which denounced Mayor Daley by name, brought by a downstater to the first DFI convention in Springfield, was not introduced at the request of some Chicago delegates. The DFI constitution "recognized the County and State Central Committees as the legally constituted instruments of political administration." An effort by one delegate to make this stronger by adding an amendment which stipulated that DFI clubs could not be formed without the approval of the Democratic party county chairman (in Chicago, that would have been Mayor Daley) was defeated.[15]

After the first convention, DFI volunteers set about organizing neighborhood clubs. The greatest successes were had in the suburban countries around Chicago and in the areas where the IVI had found adherents. By May, 1958, an estimated fifty-five or sixty clubs had affiliated with the state DFI, and the organization could claim three thousand members. The question of dues was left to each club, and in many cases no dues were remitted to the state organization. Hence, an accurate membership figure could not be obtained. In areas where clubs were numerous, as in DuPage and St. Clair counties and in Chicago's Fifth Ward, local co-ordinating councils were formed.

At the 1958 convention, the question of primary fights again arose. Several delegates opposed pre-primary endorsements, but it quickly became clear that if the clubs could not participate in primaries, many would have no reason for existence. Hence, the convention went on record as permitting pre-primary endorsements without, however, committing itself to campaigning on behalf of its endorsees if they were opposed by the regular organization.

Another question plagued the DFI. One group of leaders, headed by President Walker, wanted a centralized organiza-

[15] A similar provision, of course, is part of the constitution of the CDC in California, but there the county chairmen are rarely figures of great political power.

tion with a full-time, paid executive secretary. Another group opposed spending the money and delegating the authority this would involve. Walker's views prevailed, and Victor De Grazia was hired at $9,000 a year as the executive. The DFI had little money and few prospects; it quickly went into debt from which it never fully recovered. But aside from objecting to the money being spent, Walker's opponents were fearful that centralized authority would enable him to restrain the more militant members who sought active combat with the regulars.

Many DFI members were interested in issues, and at the 1958 convention prominent liberal speakers appeared, including Adlai Stevenson, Mrs. Eleanor Roosevelt, and Senator Albert Gore. A platform treating substantive policy issues was adopted.

In the meantime, the DFI had to deal with two statewide elections. In 1958, the only state offices vacant were treasurer and superintendent of public instruction, and for these posts the regular Democratic party nominated men to whom the DFI could not object. Joseph Lohman, a former University of Chicago lecturer, a party "maverick," and recently Cook County sheriff, was selected for treasurer, and George Wilkins, a downstate school administrator, was picked for the other post. Having no cause for a primary fight, the DFI could only "help get out the vote."

By 1960, the DFI had virtually ceased to function. The local clubs, most of which were no longer active in the statewide organization, had with a few exceptions begun to fall apart. The final blow, however, came as a result of the 1960 gubernatorial contest. Republican weakness and disunity that year suggested that a Democrat could win control of the state. Interest in the dying DFI picked up somewhat at the prospect of endorsing a candidate for this office.

One candidate was already in the field. Stephen A. Mitchell, a Chicago lawyer, prominent Catholic layman, and Democratic National Chairman in the Stevenson campaign of 1952, had been unofficially campaigning for the Democratic nomination since the spring of 1959; in October he formally announced his candidacy. He had unsuccessfully sought the nomination in 1956. Since then he had remained active in politics and had published a book, *Elm Street Politics,* in which he described the formation of a Democratic club in his neighborhood, recounted the history of similar clubs in New York, California, and elsewhere, and advocated the extension of the club movement as a new force in politics. Because of these views, many people thought of Mitchell as the godfather of the DFI and hoped he would base his campaign on it. In fact, Mitchell took no part in its organization and contributed no money to it; the DFI leadership was in good part hostile to his candidacy.[16] However, he did hope to obtain its endorsement at its convention, and a few pro-Mitchell DFI clubs sought to make this possible.

Since he had already been refused in 1956 by the Chicago machine, Mitchell had little hope of getting its support in 1960. He was therefore determined to wage a primary fight. The DFI clubs which were prepared to help him were, as a result, those suburban and downstate clubs which opposed the DFI's posture of accommodation toward the Daley organization. The Daley machine delayed its choice of a candidate to the last minute, and there were rumors that Daley himself might decide to run for governor. But the choice facing the amateurs suddenly was seriously complicated by the announcement that a second "good government" candidate was available—Joseph Lohman. Lohman had strong support in that large part of the DFI from Chicago's Fifth Ward. He entered the race with a bold attack on "bossism" even though the Chicago "bosses" had made him Cook County sheriff in 1954 and state treasurer in 1958. One candidate with amateur appeal was enough; two threatened to split the organization. But Mayor Daley com-

16 Mitchell, in a letter to the author, said his relations to the DFI were confined to advising some of its leaders on its constitution, helping them get some speakers for their conventions, and encouraging local clubs to form. Beyond this "I did not at any time, directly or indirectly, take active part in the state or regional DFI activities but made a special effort to stay apart from those activities." (Letter dated November 7, 1961.)

pounded the confusion by shrewdly picking as the regular organization candidate a blue-ribbon county judge, Otto Kerner, a thoroughly presentable man of unimpeachable reputation. It was hard to think of good reasons for opposing Kerner.

Although it was likely that Mitchell had the most support among the delegates, it was even more likely that an outright endorsement would have badly divided the movement. In the end, the convention lamely voted not to endorse anyone but to express a "preference" for Mitchell without prejudice to the other two contenders.

The strength of the DFI had already been slipping for nearly a year. The conflict over relations with the Chicago machine had led many clubs to withdraw and stop paying dues. In the 1959 Chicago mayoralty contest, twenty-two Chicago DFI clubs voted unanimously to endorse Mayor Daley for re-election. President Dan Walker announced late in 1959 that he was resigning in order to be free to seek the *regular* organization nomination for state attorney-general. (He tried very hard to obtain it but was passed over in favor of a close Daley ally.) Soon thereafter the executive secretary, De Grazia, quit. The results of the three-way 1960 gubernatorial primary were the final blow. Kerner won easily, collecting almost twice as many votes as his two opponents together. But Lohman was second and Mitchell, whom the DFI had preferred, was a poor third.[17] And when Kerner won the general election and became the new governor, he promptly brought many leading DFI members into his administration. Others went to Washington as part of the Kennedy administration. The DFI as a statewide movement was, for all practical purposes, finished.

Remnants of the DFI persisted in certain localities, however. Clubs in the suburbs, particularly DuPage County, formed the Northern Illinois Council of Clubs. In these heavily Republican counties, the regular Democratic party was weak, and the amateur clubs had less to fear from an independent course. The leaders of the council resolved to keep it that way by stay-

[17] The vote was: Kerner, 649,253; Lohman, 232,345; Mitchell, 184,651.

ing out of Chicago. Another large group of clubs led by Haas in downstate St. Clair County continued, concerned with local affairs and the traditional perquisites of politics, including patronage. A few scattered clubs also managed to persist, including groups in Evanston (where the amateurs managed to take over a weak regular organization), Rockford, and southern Lake County. But there was little talk of any statewide merger; the memories of that were still too painful. Within Chicago, a handful of small and typically weak clubs could be found in the traditional areas of political dissidence—the Fifth Ward and the Near North Side.

In Chicago the DFI repeated the IVI's experience. The IVI evolved from a pseudo-Democratic organization which supported national liberals to a group oriented to fighting the power of the local Democratic machine. The DFI attempted to avoid this choice by trying to "open up" and change the Democratic party from within. It ended in schism. One group went back into the regular organization and attempted to influence it from administrative or advisory positions at the top. The other, still attempting to build a grass roots organization, was determined to stay out of Chicago. The IVI's course has antagonized many liberal Democrats, but the evolution of the DFI raised the question whether a liberal organization could maintain an independent existence in Chicago if it attempted to work within the Democratic party. Whether cut off from power, or swallowed up by it, reform in Illinois had to await a challenge to the machine from forces stronger than the reformers were able to command.

# 4 Los Angeles The Search for Power

California politics has been less a struggle and more a search for power. The reforms instituted by an earlier group of amateurs and progressives in part stimulated and in part frustrated the present generation of volunteers. By effectively destroying local party organization, these "reforms" provided the opportunity for the present club movement; by removing elective officials from dependence on the party, they prevented the club movement from winning a complete victory.

Partisan activity continues to be deeply molded by the anti-party legacy of Hiram Johnson and the statutory restrictions on political parties enacted over forty years ago. Johnson and his followers in the progressive wing of the dominant Republican party sought to break the hold of the Southern Pacific Railroad over the government of the state by curbing, through legislation, the party machinery which translated economic into political power. In the desire to eliminate a bad party, party itself was all but destroyed. A direct primary law had, in 1909, already supplanted the party convention as a means of selecting nominees. After Johnson's Lincoln-Roosevelt League captured control of the Republican party by taking advantage of the direct primary system, it moved in the legislature to insure that never again would a political party be strong in the state. Between 1911 and 1913, a presidential primary election and the direct election of United States senators were authorized, straight-ticket party voting was made laborious by eliminating the party circle from the ballot, the legal party organization was fragmented and reduced to impotence, all city and county elective posts were made non-partisan, and cross-filing

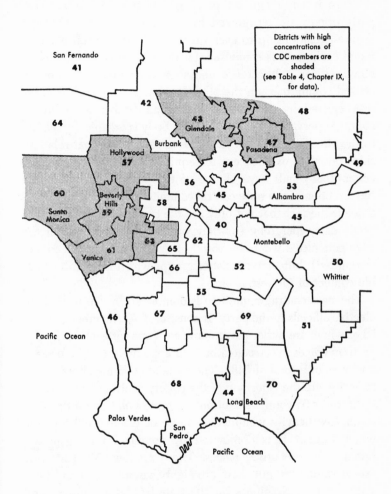

San Fernando
**41**

**42**

**64**

**43**
Glendale

**48**

Burbank

Hollywood
**57**

**47**
Pasadena

**49**

**54**

**56**

**53**
Alhambra

**60**

Beverly
Hills
**59**

**58**

**45**

Santa
Monica

**45**

**40**

**61**

**62**
**65**

Montebello

Venice

**66**

**52**

**50**
Whittier

**55**

**46**

**67**

**69**

**51**

Pacific  Ocean

**68**

**44**
Long Beach

**70**

Palos Verdes

San
Pedro

Pacific  Ocean

LOS ANGELES COUNTY ASSEMBLY DISTRICTS
(1961)

was introduced.[1] The result was the creation of a political vacuum which has never been filled.

There is no integrated party structure in the state. Two party organs are recognized by law, but they bear only the slightest relationship to each other. The state central committee of each party is composed, for the most part, of the party's nominees for public office and their appointees; the county central committees, on the other hand, are composed of members elected by the voters from small (either assembly or county supervisor) districts. Neither body is organically related to the other, and the law has little to say about what relationships ought to exist except to require that the county central committees "shall have charge of the party campaign under the direction of the state central committee."[2] Of crucial importance is the fact that not only are the two bodies not part of a single party hierarchy (as they would be, for example, if the state committee were composed of delegates from the county committee), but they consist of groups which have an inevitable conflict of interest.

The state central committee is dominated by the incumbent elective officials in the party. It consists of 706 members, all but 58 of whom are either party nominees (one for each of the 162 partisan offices in the state) or their appointees (three for each nominee, or a total of 648). The remaining 58 members, a tiny minority, are the chairmen of the county central committees of California's 58 counties. Not only is representation on the state committee heavily weighted in favor of elective officials and nominees, but it is dominated by nominees for legislative, rather than executive, offices. There are only six statewide executive officers, but there are eighty assemblymen and forty state senators. Nominees for the state legislature thus control 480 seats on the committee, while nominees for executive posts control only 24. Further, nominees who win office and who

[1] On the Johnson era, see Dean R. Cresap, *Party Politics in the Golden State* (Los Angeles: Haynes Foundation, 1954), chap. i; Chester H. Rowell, *The California Progressives* (Berkeley: University of California Press, 1951).

[2] *Elections Code,* secs. 2831, 2832.

stand for re-election year after year are able to retain seats for themselves and their appointees on the committee for long periods of time, whereas unsuccessful nominees serve only two years and then are replaced by a new set of nominees (except for those few times when defeated candidates stand again for election). This means that incumbent officeholders tend to acquire seniority and a fund of experience in and knowledge about committee affairs that usually enables them to exercise leadership in this group. In 1961, a law was passed which strengthened even further the power of the incumbents by increasing the number of committee members each could name from three to five.

The county central committees, on the other hand, are dominated by elected members. The Los Angeles County Democratic Central Committee, the largest in the state, consists of 249 members, 217 of whom are elected in primaries for two-year terms, seven from each assembly district. The remaining 32 are the party's nominees for assemblymen and state senator from the county. These nominees, who usually control the state central committee, are a small minority on the county committee. Whereas the chairman of the state committee is almost always either an officeholder or the appointee of one, the chairmen of the county committees rarely are. The elected county committeemen are the only party officials chosen directly by the voters. This election is, of course, hardly a deliberative process of any consequence. Owing to the lengthy and complicated California ballot and the absence of party control over the electorate in primaries, the choice of county committeemen is, in the words of many party leaders, a "hopeless lottery" in which the sound of one's name and the nature of one's occupation, together with one's position on the ballot in the list of candidates for that post, are the most important factors in determining election to the committee. Nevertheless, despite the fact that the average county committeeman is almost entirely unknown to the voters and owes his post as much to chance as to ability, he is placed—by virtue of his election—in a position which inescapably gives him a point of view different from that of the state legislators and congressmen who control the state committee.

Not only are the two official party organs predestined to conflict, but in addition the legal party lacks any base in city or county politics. Affairs at the local level are by and large nonpartisan.[3] Legally, the city does not exist for the party organization, and there is little patronage in city government with which to strengthen party organization even if the parties could successfully intervene in local affairs.

Most important, however, the official party organs have relatively little power. To decentralization and internal conflict is added impotence. The state committee by law cannot take part in primary contests, and only recently have the county committees, by a lower court test, won a cloudy right to make pre-primary endorsements. But even local endorsements by a county committee are often unimportant, for there is no official party organization in the precincts that could make effective the decisions of the leadership. The Elections Code prescribes in careful detail what the state central committee may do. It meets every two years, principally to elect officers.[4] Although contests for these offices are often heated, in a committee with so many members and in a state with so few means for assembling political power, it becomes extremely difficult to control the election process. Further, the law requires that the chairmanship of the committee be alternated between the northern and southern parts of the state. This means not only that no state committee chairman can succeed himself, but also that for this and other reasons, the party organization is split in half. North and south function virtually as separate political entities. The state committee has two vice-chairmen, one from each region. In effect, when the chairman is from the north, party affairs in the south are conducted, not by the chairman, but the vice-chairman for Southern California, and

[3] See Eugene C. Lee, *The Politics of Nonpartisanship: A Study of California City Elections* (Berkeley and Los Angeles: University of California Press, 1960), chap. vii.

[4] In 1961, a law was enacted changing the Democratic party state convention from biennial to annual.

vice versa. There can never be a single statewide party chairman with influence commensurate with his title, nor can there be, except under the most fortuitous circumstances based on informal personal understandings, any real continuity of party leadership.

The Los Angeles County Committee is probably the most active in the California Democratic party. In comparison to many other county committees, some of which scarcely ever meet and a few of which lack a full complement of members, it is exceptionally effective. In comparison with a county party organization in a large eastern city, however, it is feeble and inconsequential. An active member of it, addressing a meeting of its executive committee, urged it to be more active in certain party affairs. "Twelve to fifteen years ago," he observed, "the County Committee was a laughing stock. We have grown in stature some, and we want to grow even more. Not many years ago, hardly any politician would even talk to us. Now, many will. We have to up-grade ourselves."

In cities where parties are strong, that strength results from the existence of an effective precinct organization, the ability to determine who shall be the party's nominees, and control of the patronage resources of the government. In California, all three of these sources of strength are lacking. There is no precinct organization within the regular party, no way to deliver nominations to endorsed candidates at the local level, no way even to make endorsements at the state level, and parties are excluded from city and county affairs. Only from the state and national governments may the parties receive patronage. In California, the merit system is effective at the state as well as the local level, and only a few desirable jobs, most of them judicial appointments, are available to state officers. Edmund G. "Pat" Brown, a Democrat who later became governor, told an interviewer that there were no more than six hundred political appointments available to the top state official.[5] Most

---

[5] Quoted in Robert E. G. Harris, "California's Democratic Party: A Health Report," *Frontier*, February, 1956, p. 9. By comparison, the state administration in Illinois can probably make 13,000 to 14,000 political

of the discretionary appointments are to honorific posts which carry no pay. Judgeships and department heads, under the control of the governor, and inheritance tax appraiserships, under the purview of the controller, are almost the only important state patronage.

But even these meager resources are not used to build party strength. Because of the factional character of Democratic politics, patronage must be distributed to competing leaders and rival groups. There is enough patronage to make these forces struggle for it, but not enough to compel them to follow a single leader. Further, the elective officials who control these jobs are concerned with re-election. Knowing that the prospects for building a strong organization are almost nil under present laws, jobs are awarded in order to reward personal supporters and overcome objections to re-election rather than to consolidate political strength in a single organization. Indeed, elective officers, both Democratic and Republican, are keenly aware that a strong party would weaken their own authority and place burdensome constraints upon them. This gives them additional reasons for spending patronage in a way one powerful California party leader termed "unwise." The state controller told an interviewer that criticisms of his practice in awarding inheritance tax appraiserships, many of which are very lucrative, were known to him. But he defended giving such jobs to persons who in some cases were weak Democrats or even known Republicans. "To make appointments only to strong party workers in the Democratic organization would make it appear as if I were attempting too consciously to build a political machine. We don't want it to look machine-like, so I am spreading the appointments around so that as a result, some Republicans and weak Democrats get them."

After the Democrats won five of the six statewide offices in

---

appointments. In Pennsylvania in 1957, there were 46,671 state jobs not under Civil Service. See James Reichley, *The Art of Government: Reform and Organization Politics in Philadelphia* (New York: Fund for the Republic, 1959), pp. 24 n., 102 n.

1958, no central patronage-dispensing office was created, much to the disgust of party functionaries. A powerful member of the State Central Committee observed glumly:

> What he [the Governor] needs to do is to pick a State Chairman and back him—decide who is going to get the patronage and centralize the control of it in somebody . . . with continuity. . . . For a while there we were trying to run all this through one man, but [the Governor] keeps pulling the rug out from under him. For a while I was handling all the patronage, and then the Governor would make a couple of appointments himself to people he had to satisfy, and there I'd be, standing on a bare floor with no clothes on. . . . He won't designate one person to handle this.

These debilitating factors have been aggravated by others. Until 1954, it was possible for one candidate to file for nomination in the primaries of both parties without indicating his party affiliation on the ballot. Cross-filing, in the view of every writer on the subject, undoubtedly reduced party organization to very nearly an empty charade. Effective in 1954, the law was changed to require that party memberhip be shown on the ballot after the name of each candidate. The results were dramatic. In 1952, 72 per cent of all elective offices had been won in the primary by cross-filed candidates who captured the nomination of both parties. In 1954, after the introduction of the party label, only 26 per cent were decided in the primary.[6] Having won the nomination, many Democrats were then able to go on to the general election and, drawing on the Democrats' four-to-three lead in registration, turn Republicans out. (In 1954, the number of Democrats in the state senate increased from eleven to sixteen, and in the state assembly from twenty-six to thirty-two.) In 1959, the legislature abolished cross-filing altogether.

[6] Robert J. Pitchell, "The Electoral System and Voting Behavior: The Case of California's Cross-Filing," *Western Political Quarterly*, XII (1959), 459–84. See also James C. Findley, "Cross-Filing and the Progressive Movement in California Politics," *Western Political Quarterly*, XII (1959), 699–711.

*Consequences of Party Weakness*

Given the rapid growth and high mobility of California's population, it is questionable whether an effective precinct organization could have been constructed even if the formal party machinery had been legally strong and patronage plentiful. It has been estimated that about one-fourth of the persons in the state did not live at their present address one year ago.[7] Organizing the grass roots when the population turnover is so high would be exceptionally difficult under the best of circumstances.

The principal consequence of this political vacuum in California is that any number of persons, groups, and community organizations seek to fill the void and that in the effort to establish themselves, these forces endeavor not so much to wrest power from those who hold it as to create power where none has existed before. The search for power in this fluid situation, in which the formal party apparatus is both incomplete and fragmented, is an extraordinarily difficult and taxing enterprise. But it offers great rewards to skilful men who have the ability to manipulate large groups of people and the energy to struggle for intangible ends in a highly uncertain situation. The absence of a hierachical party, with authority clearly distributed in some regularized pattern, means that men with ability but little seniority can rise rapidly. Paul Ziffren, the former Democratic national committeeman from California, rose to that office almost out of nowhere, his talents more than compensating for his lack of preliminary work in the lower ranks of the party and his recent arrival in the state from Illinois. Joseph L. Wyatt, Jr., became the second president of the California Democratic Council after having lived in the state only eight years. Jesse M. Unruh, one of the two or three

[7] The 1950 census, based on a 20 per cent sample of households, found that 495,970 of the 1,929,025 persons one year of age and over in the Los Angeles urbanized area did not live at their 1950 address in 1949. See *Census of the Population*, Vol. II, Part 5, Table 34, p. 5-100.

most powerful politicians in the state, Speaker of the Assembly and head of the Kennedy presidential campaign in Southern California in 1960, was just thirty-eight years old and a member of the assembly only since 1954.

This is true throughout the party. An able young leader who had risen quickly observed:

> Power accrues to him who works hard and becomes known as a leader. If you're willing to be vigorous and active, if you're willing to do the work, sooner or later you're going to become known as a leader. It's inevitable. Leadership tends to go to the person most active, and thus power goes by default to the person most interested in obtaining it.

There is no table of organization to fill, and hence no energy-sapping career ladder which requires new arrivals to wait at the lower levels until party leaders die or resign. "The party is young and in flux," said a rising young leader. But this same flux which has as its advantage the creation of opportunities has as its price the creation of uncertainty. Those most anxious to attain power are least confident that they have it or know where it can be found. No matter how high they rise, claims are always made on their authority by others and decisions must always be shared with many. Since decision-making is highly decentralized and based in great measure on persuasion and consensus, those mose influential in making decisions are those most adept at persuading and creating the correct mood or set of expectations. A majority of the 249 members of the Los Angeles County Committee must be persuaded (threats are almost useless) in order to endorse a primary candidate for the least important offices. To choose a state chairman, the votes or proxies of a majority of 706 state central committeemen must be obtained.

The absence of a clear party organization, with easily visible and generally recognized leadership, means that roles are vague and tend to overlap. Conflict is intensified simply by the multiplication of the number of people who can advance some claim to having their views considered. Deprived of formal responsibilities, leaders of county committees often fall to wondering just what they are supposed to do. Said one in Los Angeles:

> What are we supposed to do? What is power? We are supposed to have it, but we don't seem to. The Election Code gives us the right to conduct the affairs of the party in Los Angeles County under the general direction of the State Committee. But the State Committee tends to be meaningless as a source of direction. We really don't know what we are supposed to do down here.

"Capturing control" of the county committee is almost an empty phrase. There is not enough at stake in control of that committee, or indeed in the control of any party organ, to justify the effort or to make the results significant. A young, ambitious leader may well be able, after a heated fight, to become chairman of the Los Angeles County Committee. But he would not find that he could then speak as the "leader" of the Democratic party in Los Angeles County, and should he attempt to do so, others would laugh at him. A California political scientist recently commented:

> The [county] committee commands little respect, manifests a high degree of disagreement, and, because of a rigid California code, is generally hamstrung in its operations. As a result, county central committeemen, frustrated by their inability to act, are reduced to the status of party caretaker, content to discuss issues, mold empty plans, and contemplate the disadvantages of ineffective organization.[8]

Committee members are fully aware of their weak position. As a result, there is a high absentee rate at meetings even though the law stipulates that anyone who is absent more than three times without an excuse forfeits his seat. At every meeting of the committee, new members are selected to fill such vacancies. Over 38 per cent of the members of the 1960 Los Angeles County Committee had not been members of the previous committee. Nearly two out of every five members had either resigned, not sought re-election, or been defeated. In

[8] William Henry Vatcher, Jr., "California's Chaotic Political Structure," *Frontier*, January, 1961, p. 5.

1950, one student discovered that there was no contest for county committee seats in about 36 of California's 58 counties.[9] In another study made in 1956, over one-third of a random sample of all county committeemen (of both parties) had held their seat for one year or less.[10] The same can be said for the state committee. Only 32.3 per cent of the members of the 1954 Democratic State Central Committee had served on the 1952 committee.[11] Few county committeemen receive the kind of reward which could be expected by their counterparts in many eastern states. In 1956, only 2.2 per cent of a sample of county committeemen (of both parties) gave their occupation as government employee or officeholder.[12] An active member of the Los Angeles County Committee, chairman of one of its subcommittees, noted that some influential members opposed the county chairman, but little had been done.

> The turnover is so high and the lack of interest is so great that nobody thinks it's worth much to organize an effective campaign against him. There has never been any well-programmed opposition to the present leadership of the County Committee. The reasons for that are, first of all, the Committee is so big and the county is so large that it's almost impossible to organize it to do anything. And secondly, it's simply not worth the effort it would take to control it. If you control the committee, what do you have? Just a large, unwieldy body in which most people don't even take any interest at all.

The incomplete and disjointed nature of the party organization makes the crucial question of party finance a perplexing one. With no clear center of political gravity and no recognized leadership, many party agencies and individuals raise money

[9] Cresap, *op. cit.*, p. 21. The situation would be different today.

[10] John H. Duke, "The County Committeeman and His Role in California Politics" (Ph.D. thesis, Department of Political Science, University of Southern California, 1956), p. 104.

[11] Cf. Charles G. Bell, "A Study of Four Selected Factors Which Have Contributed to the Inability of the Democratic Party To Successfully Mobilize Its Latent Majority in California" (M.A. thesis, Department of Political Science, University of Southern California), p. 61.

[12] Duke, *op. cit.*, p. 71.

in independent and often conflicting ways. With the lack of a patronage-sustained precinct organization, abundant campaign funds are vital. Yet precisely because the legal party apparatus is ineffective, donors are often reluctant to give any sizable contribution to a committee which carries little weight. Unions, businesses, and individuals with interests they are anxious to advance are far more likely to give money directly to candidates, particularly incumbent candidates. A person who both spent funds on behalf of a local special-interest group and served on the county committee told an interviewer that it would be absurd to consider giving much to the party organs. "You might as well throw your money away. . . . If you have any money to give, you give it to the individual candidate directly." Lacking adequate funds, the party committees find it even harder to control party nominations. Each prospective nominee first decides whether he can find a personal finance chairman who can raise the money he needs; if he can, he need rarely worry about having the approval of the county committee, for a failure to win its support would not be very costly in terms of withheld funds.[13]

The decentralization of party finance has in the past, at least, given inordinate influence to certain generously endowed interests which found that money could provide more influence than party control.[14] In recent years this has changed somewhat, with the public exposure of some of the more notorious donors, a tendency toward greater organization and routinization of party finance, and the growth of the extra-legal party groups which have been sources of volunteer labor that reduced somewhat the need for large sums in campaigns.

All of these factors—the high turnover of county and state committee members, the diffuseness of political power, the

[13] The importance of finance and its personal basis in California are alluded to in Alexander Heard, *The Costs of Democracy* (Chapel Hill: University of North Carolina Press, 1960), pp. 271 n., 275 n., 330. See also Francis Carney, *The Rise of the Democratic Clubs in California* (New York: Henry Holt & Co., 1958), p. 14, on the lack of finance causing one prospective nominee to withdraw.

[14] Cresap, *op. cit.*, pp. 80–81, gives some instances.

weakness of the legal party machinery, and the tendency of political funds to go directly to incumbent candidates—have served to enhance the position of the elective officials. In the past, these men have often been the only visible sign of party life at all, and even today, despite the partisan revitalization, they have as large or larger a claim to influence within the party as anyone. Such influence has often been used to keep the party weak and divided, for this condition removes one restraint on their freedom of action and permits the broad appeal to voters which has been so successful in the past. One of the themes of this study will be the fundamental conflict between elective officials and the amateur politicians who make up the California Democratic Council, but it should be remembered that this tension between incumbent and party workers existed long before the creation of the CDC. Earl Warren found that the Republican state organization was of little help to his candidacy and its intervention reduced the effectiveness of his bipartisan appeal. He rejected its pre-primary support and refused to become identified with it in the election campaign.[15] Democrats have been somewhat more partisan, in an effort to capitalize on the Democratic lead in registration, but even they have looked upon the party as a group which should work hard and remain silent. In 1951, and again in 1961, the legislature passed a bill which, if the Governor had signed it, would have allowed each nominee for state office to appoint some members to his county central committee.[16] In effect, this would have converted the county committees into smaller replicas of the state central committee.

## The Democratic Resurgence

The partisan vacuum created in California by the absence of formally organized political power was, of course, filled by a variety of competing forces. In the effort to supply an alternative to party organization, the Republicans for decades enjoyed

[15] *Igid.*, pp. 84, 90.
[16] *Ibid.*, p. 19. The bill was S.B. 759 (1951).

an unmistakable advantage. California state politics, although legally partisan, were in fact non-partisan, and Republican candidates were better able to take advantage of this situation for the same reasons that they are more successful in cities which are governed by non-partisan institutions.

Republicans could provide more campaign money; they had the support of almost all the newspapers, including the three most influential (the *Los Angeles Times,* the *San Francisco Chronicle,* and the *Oakland Tribune*); they had been the incumbents in a system which favored them by placing their name first on the ballot and labeling them as incumbents; and they had in greater measure those attributes, such as free time, business success, civic reputation, and social respectability, which are vitally important in an elective process that is based on personal qualities rather than party affiliation.[17]

The result was that, in 1952, Republicans held all the state-wide offices, both U.S. Senate seats, half the membership of the State Board of Equalization, nineteen of the thirty congressional seats, and eighty-three of the one hundred and twenty seats in the state senate and assembly. Six years later, the proportions were almost exactly reversed. The sweep of 1958 carried the Democrats into control of both houses of the legislature, the congressional delegation, the Board of Equalization, and five of the six state constitutional offices, including the governorship.

A continuous argument rages, with no end in sight, over what factor should be assigned the credit for this dramatic improvement in the fortunes of the Democratic party. Almost simultaneously, two important changes had occurred in the state. One change was organizational, the other legal. In 1953, the California Democratic Council was formed to unify and expand the club movement which was rapidly building on the enthusiasm and political interest created by the presidential campaign of Adlai E. Stevenson. The CDC had as its immediate objective the making of local and statewide pre-primary

[17] Carney, *op. cit.,* p. 2, makes the same point, as do almost all other writers on California politics.

endorsements (which the state central committee could not do) as a means of enabling bona fide Democrats to win primary nominations against Republicans who cross-filed against them. At the same time, the CDC hoped to provide an army of volunteer workers to carry the Democratic campaign in the general elections at the precinct level. The CDC and the club movement are given major credit, by their supporters, for returning the Democrats to power in the state.

The legal change was the requirement, introduced in 1954, that on primary election ballots the party registration of each candidate must be indicated. Although candidates might still cross-file, they must now reveal their party affiliation by adding the letters "Dem." or "Rep." after their names.

There is no way by which credit can be decisively apportioned among these factors. Volunteers prefer the organizational explanation; elective officials prefer the legal one. The legal change was probably more important in rehabilitating the primary as a means of choosing party candidates. The number of Democrats who voted for registered Republicans in the Democratic primary fell precipitously, but at the same time, the number of Republicans who voted for Democrats in Republican primaries fell by a nearly equal amount.[18] The role of the CDC might explain the former change, but it cannot explain the latter. The number of assembly races decided in the primary fell from 75 per cent in 1952 to 28 per cent in 1954. In 1950, half the congressional seats, fifteen of the twenty state senate seats, and fifty-nine of the eighty assembly seats were virtually uncontested. In 1956, the number of uncontested races fell to three in Congress, ten in the state senate, and ten in the assembly.[19]

[18] The percentage of Democrats voting for Republicans in Democratic primaries fell from 44 per cent in 1952 to 24 per cent in 1956; the percentage of Republicans voting for Democrats in Republican primaries fell from 28 per cent in 1952 to 19 per cent in 1956. Pitchell, *op. cit.*, pp. 778–79.

[19] The number of contested elections rose from 28.2 per cent of the total in 1952 to 75.6 per cent of the total in 1956. Pitchell, *op. cit.*, p. 465. See also Mary Ellen Leary, "The Two-Party System Comes to California," *Reporter*, February 7, 1957, p. 36.

The CDC was undoubtedly important in the resurgence of the Democratic party. Some measure of its effectiveness will be attempted in a later chapter. But whatever its significance in affecting the outcome of elections, there can be little doubt that it has deeply affected the style of politics in California. The political vacuum in the state offered an opportunity for the entry of amateur politicians who would be attracted by the intangible rewards of politics and who would not have to unseat an entrenched political machine. The absence of an established party leadership was both an advantage and, as we shall see later, a liability. But for a variety of reasons, the volunteer movement did not exist to any real extent before 1952. The distrust of politics and parties, which the early California Progressives had enacted into law, has always been widespread and has probably equally affected intellectually oriented persons and the average voter.

The Democratic party has always been split along a broadly liberal-conservative axis. Every two years since at least 1948, there has been a contest between a coterie of party regulars and some liberal challengers in California, or among the regulars themselves. In 1948, Harry S. Truman was opposed by an enthusiastic Independent Progressive party (IPP) led by Henry Wallace. In 1950, James Roosevelt, former state chairman and national committeeman, ran for governor over the opposition of many wealthy party contributors, such as Edwin W. Pauley and E. George Luckey. In 1952, many anti-organization liberals supported Senator Estes Kefauver's successful bid in California's presidential primary against the "stop Kefauver" slate headed by Edmund G. Brown. None of these intraparty battles fundamentally altered the composition of the party or created any organizational home for the intellectual liberals. But the 1952 victory of the Kefauver forces paved the way for the creation of just such a structure, for it led to the replacement of the established party leaders by a new group who were concerned about consolidating their position.

Following their victory in the presidential primary, the Kefauver backers and other liberals took over the major statewide party offices. State Senator George Miller, Jr., became state chairman, John Anson Ford replaced Roosevelt as national committeeman, and Mrs. Clara Shirpser replaced Mrs. Edward H. Heller as national committeewoman. A year later, Paul Ziffren replaced Ford and began to be identified as the state's leading Democratic organizer. This group worked energetically on behalf of Adlai Stevenson after he had won the nomination from Kefauver at the Chicago convention. When Stevenson lost to Eisenhower and failed to carry California, these new party leaders began to consider ways in which the California Democratic party could be revitalized instead of returning to the old pattern of an amorphous, faction-ridden collection of party regulars, financial contributors, and inactive county committees. In December, 1952, Miller, supported by Ziffren and others, sent out a call for a conference to be held at Asilomar to consider how to rebuild party strength and defeat the Republicans who controlled the state.

At the same time, the impact of the Stevenson candidacy was being felt at the grass roots. Democratic clubs had existed in California, mostly in Los Angeles County, at least since 1942, and perhaps earlier.[20] But they were of little significance, largely created to support a particular candidate on a personal basis or to provide a forum for liberals. As in New York City, so in California, the nomination of Stevenson galvanized many hundreds of young people with a desire to "do something" in politics on behalf of their candidate. "Six months after Stevenson made his acceptance address at Chicago," Professor Carney writes, "the number of clubs had risen from 75 to 175."[21]

The enthusiasm for Stevenson transcended his defeat. Having discovered politics and an intellectually gratifying leader, the new club members were anxious to continue after 1952 in hopes of electing him in 1956. An early organizer of clubs in Los Angeles, Mrs. Helen Myers (then the organization chairman of the Los Angeles County Democratic Central Committee) described this period to an interviewer:

[20] This account of the early history of the club movement and the CDC follows Carney, *op. cit.*

[21] *Ibid.*, p. 6.

> As soon as I got back from Chicago from the convention, there was a stack of phone calls on my desk—people calling in wanting to know if they could work for Adlai Stevenson. New people, people we hadn't heard of before. This was our big advantage. The Stevenson people came into politics just at the time when we were trying to create a new structure in the county. . . . I collected all the names, found out what assembly district they lived in, and sent them out to the campaign manager in that district. The fascinating thing is that the defeat of Stevenson didn't dim their enthusiasm in the slightest. In a *post mortem* meeting right after the election, 150 to 200 people turned out wanting to know what they could do to help Stevenson and the party. There was a great deal of sentiment expressed that we hadn't done enough. I suppose you could call it a guilt feeling. People felt that if they'd only done more, Stevenson would have won.

In the absence of any pre-existing precinct or district structure, there were few guide-lines for the organization of clubs. They sprang up without any real geographical jurisdiction, based on cadres of mutual acquaintances and neighborhood groupings. There was no place from which politics could be "learned" in California. In Manhattan, the club system of political organization had existed for generations, and the clubs were recognized party entities based on assembly district lines. The nature of club organization could be learned by Manhattan reformers even if they rejected the manner in which the Tammany clubs functioned. In California, there was no model and the club had to be invented with only the sketchiest previous experience upon which to draw.

## Organization of the CDC

The early club members were not at all certain what they were supposed to do, what the laws and customs of politics were, or how they would occupy themselves until Stevenson ran again four years hence. At this same time, however, the liberal party leadership in the state was calling the Asilomar conference in the vague hope that the embryonic club movement could be the basis for party reorganization and revitalization. If the clubs were workable local units, then they could be given the task of working outside the legal restriction on the formal party to re-establish Democratic control over the Democratic primaries. The conference endorsed the idea of a statewide extra-legal party organization, similar in purpose to the California Republican Assembly. A convention held in Stockton in May, 1953, carried the idea further by ratifying a proposal made by Alan Cranston, a political associate of State Chairman George Miller, for developing the means of making pre-primary endorsements in northern California. The basis of such a machinery would be the councils of Democratic clubs, formed in each assembly and congressional district to work for the nomination of a single, endorsed Democratic candidate in the primaries. Later, after trips to southern California, where they discovered the club movement mushrooming, another convention was called for November, 1953, in Fresno.

Over five hundred delegates at Fresno approved a constitution for the new California Democratic Council which would be based on the local clubs and headed by a statewide group of officers elected at a convention. Cranston was elected the first president. Three months later, in February, 1954, the CDC held its first state convention for the purpose of endorsing Democratic candidates for a United States Senate seat and for other offices. For most offices, there was a fight, but the most heated contest developed for the Senate seat between Congressman Sam Yorty and Professor Peter Odegard, a political scientist at the University of California at Berkeley. Yorty was a well-known House member from Los Angeles, but one who was not attractive to those many club members who sought someone about whose liberalism they were more confident and who could "evoke those strong, ideological sentiments that had originally propelled the delegates into political activity."[22] Odegard, a last-minute entry, was more to the liking of the CDC. He was a "club type" of candidate—"a liberal, an intellectual, an amateur in politics, and a witty and effective speak-

22 *Ibid.*, p. 13.

er in the bargain."[23] But the CDC leadership was divided. Some, such as Paul Ziffren and State Senator Richard Richards of Los Angeles, along with most of the party regulars, supported Yorty. Others, including State Chairman Miller, opposed him. CDC Secretary Joseph L. Wyatt, Jr. (later CDC president) and Mrs. Helen Myers of the Los Angeles County Central Committee backed Yorty because he had a better chance of winning in the primary against the Republican incumbent, who was cross-filing.

In the end, the convention backed Yorty after Odegard announced he would not be a candidate. He had been unable to assure himself of adequate financial backing. The endorsed slate, including Yorty, easily won the Democratic primary in June, but all were defeated in the general election except Pat Brown, who was elected attorney-general. In 1956 the CDC again held an endorsing convention, and this time rejected Yorty's bid for a second try at the Senate in favor of State Senator Richard Richards. Yorty, knowing he could not win the endorsement, attacked the CDC in a bitter speech at the convention and aroused the delegates to a blazing fury. He entered the primary against Richards, but was beaten easily. Again, however, the Democratic ticket was defeated in the November election. In 1958, CDC endorsed a slate of state officers, headed by Pat Brown, who was the unchallenged candidate for governor. Three endorsements were contested. Representative Clair Engle was endorsed for the Senate against Los Angeles County Supervisor Kenneth Hahn and Professor Odegard, and a Mexican-American newcomer to politics, Henry Lopez, was given the endorsement for secretary of state in preference to a well-known Democrat, John Anson Ford. Stanley Mosk was unopposed in the convention for attorney-general but had to meet a Democratic challenger in the primary, State Senator Robert McCarthy, who did not seek the CDC endorsement. The CDC slate won in the primary and went on to win every statewide office with the exception

[23] *Ibid.* The entire section by Carney on the 1954 convention is a detailed and revealing account of the character of the CDC.

of secretary of state, where Lopez was defeated by a Republican incumbent. In 1962 the CDC re-endorsed all statewide Democratic incumbents and gave Richards a second chance at the Senate seat. The opportunity to campaign against Republican gubernatorial candidate Richard M. Nixon was a great source of unity and spirit for the amateurs.

The CDC is more than simply an organization of Democratic clubs. It claims to include every element of the party. Membership is open not only to all chartered Democratic clubs but to representatives of every other official party organ and to party officers and nominees. Although many, if not all, of these groups send delegates to the annual CDC convention, the organization is in reality clearly oriented to the local Democratic clubs.

In order for a club to affiliate with the CDC, it must have a minimum of twenty paid members, support only Democrats for public office, hold regular meetings, levy dues, and be chartered by the appropriate county central committee (or, in the case of Young Democrat clubs, by the California Federation of Young Democrats). The chartering requirement was written into the CDC constitution at the 1953 organizing convention at the insistence of Mrs. Helen Myers and others who were anxious that the clubs be firmly linked to the official party structure.[24] Chartering had been employed as early as 1948 as a way of weeding out clubs which sought to use the name "Democratic" but which were in fact supporting the Progressive party of Henry Wallace. The Los Angeles County Central Committee, which has been the most active in chartering clubs, has a set of minimum standards in addition to those laid down by CDC. These include requirements that the club's request for a charter be made only after two club meetings within a specified time and that it be reviewed and accepted by the county committeemen from the appropriate assembly district. All members must be registered Democrats (or at least 18 years of age and a declared Democrat), pay dues, and be

[24] A similar proposal was rejected by the DFI because in Illinois the county committee is more likely to be a body of considerable power.

on a membership list sent to county committee headquarters. Further, the county committee and the chairman of the county committee delegation from the appropriate assembly district must be notified by mail in advance of all meetings and other business. The club must meet at least four times a year and elect officers annually.[25]

The requirement that clubs affiliating with CDC first be chartered by their county committee is an obvious source of potential conflict. In effect, it means that although all CDC clubs must be recognized by the county committees, the county committees need not require that clubs they charter affiliate with CDC. There are thus CDC and non-CDC clubs throughout the state. In Los Angeles, where there are more clubs and more members than in any other county, nearly one-third (31 per cent) of the chartered clubs were not affiliated with CDC in February, 1961. Of the 219 clubs the County Committee had chartered, 68 were not accredited to CDC for the purpose of sending delegates to the annual convention.[26] This study is primarily concerned with CDC clubs.

In February, 1960, there were 400 clubs in California affiliated with CDC (not counting Young Democrat clubs), with a total membership of 26,706, an average of about 67 members per club.[27] The clubs ranged in size from those which had the minimum of twenty members to the Beverly Hills Democratic Club, which in early 1961 had over 720. The twenty largest clubs at the 1960 convention had between 195 and 455 members each. Of the twenty largest, ten were in Los Angeles

[25] These requirements, as well as other material on club organization, are from the *President's Manual for Democratic Clubs*, published by the Los Angeles County Democratic Central Committee (July 25, 1959).

[26] Figures obtained by comparing County Committee and CDC lists of Los Angeles County clubs. The total number of clubs attending the CDC convention would be higher than the 151 affiliated clubs, for CDC also admits Young Democrat clubs.

[27] Figures from the February, 1960, list prepared for the 1960 CDC convention. A preliminary count in February, 1961, showed 151 CDC clubs in Los Angeles County, excluding the Young Democrats. Total CDC membership in 1962 is significantly higher than these figures as the result of an intensive membership drive.

County. In all, Los Angeles had 172 of the 400 clubs in the state, with 11,304 members. Although Los Angeles is clearly the largest county in terms of club activity, this is closely proportional to its population. In June, 1960, Los Angeles County had 40 per cent of the registered Democrats in the state and 43 per cent of the CDC clubs and 42 per cent of the CDC membership.

These local clubs are often grouped together into assembly district and congressional district councils for the purpose of making endorsements in local contests and carrying on campaign and fund-raising activities. Such councils must have at least three member clubs, and also include the members of the County Central Committee, the State Central Committee, and officers of the CDC who reside in that district. Club delegates to such councils are usually in proportion to the membership of the clubs, although there is no uniform rule governing this except that (beginning in 1962) there must be at least one delegate for every twenty members. Practice has varied widely in this regard, and each local council presents some unique features in organization and functioning.

The existence of chartered clubs not affiliated with CDC raises problems in the composition of these councils. Until the bylaws were amended, effective in 1962, assembly and congressional district councils could be composed of clubs not part of CDC. Indeed, in several cases, the local council was dominated by clubs and leaders who were hostile to CDC. These councils, usually acting through a special local convention called for that purpose, may endorse candidates for local offices: assemblymen, state senators, and congressmen. The CDC itself, as a statewide organization, cannot make local endorsements; it can only ratify the endorsements made by these local councils. It could refuse ratification, but in practice this is rarely, if ever, done. The CDC constitution stipulates a set of "minimal requirements" for local endorsing procedures before the CDC will "recognize" that endorsement. These include the requirement that the local convention or council be "representative" and "deliberative," consisting only of delegates from clubs affiliated with CDC, with proportional representation of clubs.

The statewide convention of the CDC not only endorses candidates, but elects CDC officers and adopts resolutions and policy statements. These officers include a president, secretary, and treasurer, plus five vice-presidents, one for each of five regions of the state. (Los Angeles County is Region II.) The Board of Directors consists of these officers, plus a legal counsel, three trustees, and one director from each of California's thirty congressional districts. Each congressional district director ("CD director") is elected by the delegation from his district to the state convention. He, in turn, appoints directors for assembly districts and senatorial districts, and acts as the chief link in CDC between the state and local organizations.

Power within the CDC leadership is thus widely dispersed. The thirty CD directors, each owing his election to local club representatives, greatly outnumber the twelve state officers. The Board of Directors itself is so large as to make control by any clique extremely difficult and render it wide open to local pressures and the glare of publicity. The twelve state officers were, in 1960, evenly distributed between north and south, with the president, secretary, legal counsel, one vice-president, one trustee, and one executive committee member coming from Los Angeles County.

Similarly, the convention is a large and club-oriented body. Each club may send one delegate for every twenty paid members. Local district councils are also entitled to one delegate each. In addition, delegates may attend from all other party organs, including party nominees and incumbents, the officers of the CDC and the Young Democrats, delegates from all county central committees, the officers of the state central committee, and CD and assembly district directors. The CDC can boast, in theory, of being a genuinely representative convention of the entire party. In fact, the club delegates greatly outnumber those from any other body. In 1960, they were entitled to about 1,335 delegates, while the nominees and county and state central committees combined could send only about

417 at most. The volunteer club members of the party out-number the elective and appointive officials at least three to one in the CDC convention and, considering that many state, national, and county central committee members and Young Democratic delegates are sympathetic to the club movement, the margin is actually greater.

This is not to imply that there are two homogeneous groups within the CDC who oppose one another along clear and simple factional lines. Far from it. But there can be little doubt that the CDC's center of gravity is in the clubs and, as a later chapter will suggest, this is resented by many in the professional wing of the party.

## North-South Differences

The general picture of a political vacuum into which the Stevenson candidacy lured liberal amateurs is generally correct, but, as with so much of California's politics, there are important regional differences that must be explained. The club movement has, in the opinion of almost all CDC leaders and political observers, flourished more in Southern than in Northern California. Although Los Angeles County has only a few more clubs than its population would warrant, the clubs tend to be larger and more vigorous than those in, say, the Bay Area of San Francisco and Oakland. The CDC vice-president for the Bay Area, when asked, said that "it is true to say that CDC is better organized . . . and stronger in the south." The first president of CDC, himself a northerner, observed that the club movement "is weak in San Francisco County."

There appear to be a variety of reasons for this difference. Examining them is one way of pointing up some of the important inner dynamics of party politics and club organization in the state. For one thing, Los Angeles can take advantage of certain economies of scale. With over six million people living in a single county, even a territorially large county, club organization is somewhat simplified by the greater ease and lower cost of communication and transportation. To reach as many people in the north, one would have to travel throughout the northern half of the state, an area of several thousand sparsely populated square miles. A northern CDC leader stated this succinctly when he remarked to an interviewer that "since organization depends on communication, and since communication is costly in time and money, things are less well organized in the north than they are in the south, where these costs are less."

A second reason is that the regular party in the north is weaker at the county level. In the north, the county central committees have been largely ineffectual when compared to the Los Angeles County Central Committee. In San Francisco, the county committee usually meets only to engage in factional quarrels over the election of officers, and does little or nothing to encourage the formation of new clubs even though it is the body which must charter them. In Los Angeles, the committee, even before Mrs. Myers became its organization chairman, has been very active in stimulating club growth. The committee soon hired a full-time executive secretary who was charged primarily with the task of organizing clubs. He, together with three field representatives and an office staff, spent most of their time organizing and chartering clubs and providing them with manuals, speakers, and literature. This is not done entirely for disinterested reasons. Each club must recharter with the committee every year, and to do so must pay a fifteen-dollar fee. With over two hundred clubs in the county, this produces more than three thousand dollars a year, a substantial part of the committee's annual income.

At the state level, the situation is almost completely reversed. The northern wing of the state central committee has been under relatively steady leadership for over a decade. It has had the services of an able full-time executive director and has been largely free of the bitter battles for supremacy which have characterized the southern part of the state committee. In the south, leadership has alternated between those who were sympathetic and those who were hostile to CDC and the club movement. From 1954 to 1956, Mrs. Elizabeth Snyder, a state committee appointee of Congressman Chet Holifield, was the chairman in the south. She was outspokenly hostile to the club movement from its inception and worked to organize an alternative volunteer group called "Dime a Day for Democracy," open to all who could contribute $36.50 per year to the party. From its inception, CDC in the south had a powerful enemy to face. Early CDC leaders rejected Dime a Day as limited to the fairly affluent and under the control of the regular party; Mrs. Snyder and her allies rejected CDC as amateurish and open to any kind of dilettante or irresponsible adventurer who could pay two or three dollars annual dues.

Control of the southern half of the State Committee shifted, however, when William Rosenthal, a close associate of National Committeeman Paul Ziffren, succeeded Mrs. Snyder for the period 1956 through 1959. Rosenthal was more friendly to the club movement and did not raise obstacles. With Mrs. Snyder off the scene, the Dime a Day movement disintegrated. But in 1959 Rosenthal was replaced by William Munnell as southern Chairman, a state legislator then close to Jesse Unruh, and less than an enthusiast about CDC.

This complex situation, with the north having a strong state and weak county committees, and Los Angeles having a divided state but a fairly effective county committee, is of great importance to the club movement. In the north it has meant that while the county committees did little to encourage club growth, neither they nor the state committee opposed it. Indeed, the state leadership adopted a welcoming attitude toward such clubs as wanted to form. In the north, CDC has had no enemy to fight, and as a northern vice-president stated, "CDC people thrive on adversity." The northern state chairman received the new clubs kindly. "Roger Kent," said one CDC officer, "has been so receptive to the club movement that the club movement, I think, has been hurt. It hasn't had a bogeyman. Kent says, 'Come on in to headquarters. Glad to have you.' But when they're so receptive, it sort of takes the steam out of your operation." Alan Cranston, the first president of CDC and a northerner close to the state leadership, agreed with this estimate. "In the north, the State Central Committee and the CDC are virtually the same. They share the same offices. Roger Kent and I worked very closely together. . . . There have been no serious differences of opinion in the north between the two organizations."

Paradoxically, the stability and unity of the northern leadership of the state party may have been a detriment to the growth of the club movement. It was not simply because this meant that there was less of a vacuum to fill. On the contrary, at the precinct and assembly district level, there was no more of a party in existence in the north than in the south. Leadership continuity did not mean thorough organization. Rather, it meant the existence, in formal party offices, of men who were reasonably secure in those posts and who did not feel threatened by club activity. There were no county committees active enough to represent a serious challenge to the state committee in themselves, or vigorous enough to encourage the formation of clubs tied to county committee leadership. Further, the instigators of the CDC had been the liberal northern leaders around George Miller and Alan Cranston who, in 1953, took the initiative in creating the statewide organization of the volunteer movement. There has always been a certain pride of parenthood in the state committee offices at 212 Sutter Street in San Francisco. In the south, on the other hand, formal party leadership was in a state of flux. The state and county committees were both strong enough to be rivals but neither was strong enough to become pre-eminent. A handful of people on the county committee in Los Angeles saw the club movement as a means of creating a link between the county committee and the precincts and strengthening the liberal elements in the party. The state committee, on the other hand, was cool to the idea and sought to weaken the movement. Its leadership became the first enemy of CDC, and CDC drew strength and purpose from having an enemy to fight. A northern CDC officer summed up this situation to an interviewer:

> In the south, the CDC always had an enemy to fight—Liz Snyder, Chet Holifield, organized labor, people around the

State Central Committee generally. This has motivated people. . . . There were greater opportunities for adversity in the south and hence more opportunities for thriving on that adversity. In the north the regular leaders were not bad enough to motivate the clubs by attacking them or serving as an enemy. Nor were they good enough to lead the CDC and stimulate it by organizing it and promoting its membership.

Although the club movement brought young liberal ama- teurs into grass-roots Democratic politics throughout the state, we are concerned here with their experiences in Los Angeles. But unlike New York, it is impossible to examine the city apart from the state, for in California, partisan politics has had no relationship to urban government, and the California Democratic Council is organized on a statewide basis rather than, as with the New York Committee for Democratic Voters, on a citywide basis. As a consequence, local California politi- cians, professional and amateur, are preoccupied with state and national affairs, and look to Sacramento and Washington, rather than to Los Angeles or San Francisco, for cues, guid- ance, and gossip. The political scoreboard is tallied on a state, rather than a city, basis.

# 5 The Goals of the Amateur

The stated goals of the amateur politician vary with the political system in which he is competing. In New York, the amateurs have been preoccupied with defeating the regular organization and displacing the old-line club leaders. Thus, although almost all members of the New York reform movement are liberals, the fundamental goal of the movement has been not liberalism but "reformism." In California, on the other hand, where there was no entrenched machine to overthrow, the primary task was from the outset defeating Republicans and defeating them with outspokenly liberal candidates. There was no intraparty enemy to correspond with the New York reformer's conception of Carmine De Sapio, and hence little immediate concern with party reform. Liberalism became the overriding issue. In Illinois, where the Chicago Democratic machine was too strong to be defeated, the amateurs vacillated between outright attacks and a circumspect attitude in which they simply called for "secret primaries," "better candidates," and "participation." Thus, while the CDV in New York wrote into its "Plan of Structure" a definition of reform and intraparty democracy, the CDC in California drafted a "Policy Statement" on the major national and international issues of the day and the DFI in Illinois adopted a platform on issues and then searched its soul for something appropriate to say about party organization.

Given the need to find inducements to maintain the efforts of the amateur, the club leader is constrained to adapt his statements of purpose to existing conditions. It would be foolish in Manhattan to base the appeal simply on liberal ends, for there are far too many rival organizations which have already pre-empted liberalism. In California, relatively little enthusiasm can be generated by demands that the party be reformed; the party must first be created before it can be either corrupted or reformed. However rational the stated goals of the amateurs may be from the standpoint of sustaining the movement, however, there is little assurance that these goals are likely to be rational in terms of improving the quality of civic life. In fact, the use of certain ends as incentives for political action can easily lead to a situation in which these ends are effective as incentives in inverse proportion to the likelihood that they will be realized. The theme of this chapter and the three following is that the use of reformism and liberalism as the motive power for political action by amateurs places important limits on the ability of the leaders either to reform the party or to attain liberal ends. These limits in general arise out of the need of amateur leaders continually to commit themselves on issues and to follow the logic of their position beyond the point where it can any longer be the basis for the formulation of public policy.

## Reformism

To an outsider, the distinction between reformism and liberalism may seem academic; to those involved, it is of great significance, in principle and in practice. The distinction is made repeatedly by moderate reformers who accuse the militants of tactical inflexibility, by regular leaders who accuse insurgent leaders of self-seeking, and by some candidates for public office who feel that reformers are more anxious to win primaries than to win general elections.

Liberalism refers broadly to a related set of substantive goals which include civil rights, government intervention in the economy for welfare purposes, concern for minority groups, and "internationalism." Reformism, on the other hand, is concerned with reorganizing the procedures, recruitment, and tactics of the New York Democratic party and with replacing its present leadership with leaders acceptable to (i.e., drawn from the ranks of) the reformers.

Many reform clubs have promulgated a set of principles or purposes in order to define reformism. One of the earliest of these was the statement adopted by the Lexington Democratic Club.[1] Essentially, the eleven points of that statement can be summarized as three major demands: the democratization of the party machinery, an improvement in the caliber of party leaders and candidates, and an emphasis on program and principle in attracting both party workers and voters. Of these, the first was clearly of greatest importance, both as a goal of the reformers and as a key to understanding their tactics and problems. The reformers were convinced, by and large, that if the first goal (democratizing the party apparatus) were attained, the other two would follow almost as a matter of course. Then, politics would be in the hands of an educated, professional middle class that would fill all posts with qualified applicants. "Blue-ribbon" candidates would be selected, not only for the important, highly visible posts at the top of the ticket, but also for the less visible posts at the bottom. The use of patronage would be restricted (if you were a moderate reformer) or abolished altogether (if you were a militant). Voters would be offered candidates who run on an elaborate, meaningful platform to which (in the eyes of some reformers) they would be explicitly committed. With such an appeal, there no longer would be a need for such "outmoded" practices as tickets which are "balanced" from a religious, racial, or geographic standpoint. Once elected to office, officials would be held responsible for vigorously supporting comprehensive programs of substantive legislation and procedural reform.

Reformism is, of course, related to liberalism in one crucial respect, for it is another way of stating the amateur conviction that the ends of government ought to provide the motivation for underaking political action. After all, any kind of political organization, even the most corrupt and boss-ridden, can sup-

[1] James S. Ottenberg, *The Lexington Democratic Club Story* (2d ed.; New York: Lexington Democratic Club, 1960), pp. 44–46.

port and has supported liberal and even radical ends. Indeed, many non-reform liberals in New York prefer to work with the regular organization, so long as it supports liberal goals, or with the Liberal party, which has affected the choice of many elective officials because of the sizable vote it can command. Amateurs rarely enter the regular organization or the Liberal party, however, because they are internally undemocratic. Reformism is a way of committing a party to certain liberal goals *whether or not* they are politically expedient. One VID leader in Manhattan was at pains to explain this:

> This confuses a lot of people. They confuse liberalism with reform. The old-line leaders, for example, wouldn't be for liberalism. They might say publicly they were in favor of civil rights, but they'd never do anything about it. It's just a politically expedient position for them. Some people in our group feel it's enough if we are just more liberal than Tammany. It's not. All reform people are liberal, but not all liberal people are reform. . . . Reform refers to the party structure, and creating a democratic procedure within that party structure.

In other words, the party must be "genuinely" liberal—i.e., it must profess liberalism out of conviction rather than expediency. The only way to insure this is to capture and reform the party machinery so that liberal activists can compel the leadership to reflect their beliefs. This view is not limited to the Democrats. Certain elements in the Manhattan Republican party are equally concerned about party reform, and these people—who, like the Democrats, are intellectually oriented persons with professional careers—are eager to change the party from a broker of interests, which supports substantive goals when it is in its interest to do so, to a committed agent of social change which will support these goals even when it is not in its interest. In the United States, where political parties have traditionally been brokers, this would be a change of fundamental importance.

Democratizing the party machinery means making party leaders responsible to party members. To realize this goal, many specific reforms are envisaged. These are spelled out in the "Statement of Principles" of the CDV and in its Plan of Structure under the rubric of the "Democratic Standards" which local clubs must comply with in order to become affiliated with the CDV. The general theme is maximum citizen participation in the party: "it is of the utmost importance that as many Democrats as possible participate in party decisions through their local clubs." In order for these clubs to be considered "reformed," they must have a written constitution; membership open to all without regard to race, color, sex, creed, or national origin; regular elections of officers and executive committee; endorsement of candidates for public and party office by secret ballot of the members; annual reports of income and disbursements; membership lists available to members; membership dues not in excess of ten dollars per year; and membership meetings at least four times a year after five days written notice of time and place.

The democratization of political machinery would not, of course, be confined to the district club. The entire party organization, from the state committee down, would be made internally democratic. No definitive statement of such higher level changes has been set forth by the reformers, but some specific changes have been suggested. The most important of these have included the direct election of the county leader (now chosen by the district leaders), regular financial statements by all party levels, and the elimination of "patronage abuses." In the so-called "reform manifesto" presented to Tammany Hall in February, 1959, by certain reform district leaders, demands were made that the use of the party name be denied all clubs not operated in accordance with democratic standards, that committees in Tammany be established to pass on qualifications of candidates for office and appointments, that policy statements be prepared, and that local clubs be required to issue financial reports.[2] Whatever else their differences, the reformers agree almost to a man on the importance

[2] *New York Times,* February 13, 1959. The reform leaders were Baltzell, Costikyan, Midonick, and Ryan and their female co-leaders.

of intraparty democracy. Indeed, reference to the goal often takes the form of a slogan, "small-d democracy." When one reform leader was asked what the goal of the movement was, he replied:

> We plug the democatic process. This is the key part of the whole thing. Our goal is to be democratic. . . . By democratic we mean the clubs should have an open membership and encourage people to join, should not discriminate against people on racial grounds or religious grounds, should have regular membership meetings, should have written constitutions, and the election of officers.

In the majority of the reform clubs, intraparty democracy is not only advocated but practiced. One need attend only a few meetings of the more militant clubs to sense the flavor of the movement. The number of people present is in direct proportion to the interest of the agenda. Meetings begin late and end very late, often in the early hours of the morning. Everyone may speak, and virtually everyone does. Robert's Rules of Order is very much in evidence; indeed, it is perhaps the only source of authority one can detect. Certainly relatively little deference is paid to elected officials or club leaders. They must compete for expression with the lowliest rank-and-file member. Debates are lengthy and conducted with passion and considerable parliamentary skill. Motions are made, amended, and the amendments are amended in complex patterns. Points of order, of information, and of personal privilege are frequently raised. The club president plays a relatively passive role at meetings, recognizing speakers impartially and without restriction, rarely attempting to impose a point of view or even guide the discussion into predetermined channels. The rulings of the chair are frequently challenged from the floor, although they are usually upheld in the vote. The reports of committees are thoroughly debated and, although they are generally adopted in substance, modifications are not unusual and outright rejections not unheard of. Nominations for club office are typically initiated by a nominating committee, but nominations from the floor or by petition are often accepted. Elections are frequently close, and few, if any, "king-makers" can be detected behind the scenes. While the district leader dominates the proceedings in Tammany clubs, he is important but not preeminent in reform meetings and, of course, non-existent in insurgent clubs. Women play an active and vocal role (at least three club presidents are young ladies) and meetings of both the general membership and the executive committee are open to the public. If the officers or executive committee often win their way in the reform clubs, it is only because they have anticipated objections, argued down opponents, and conformed to the expectations of the members. In some "moderate" reform clubs, to be sure, the district leader or the executive committee have greater discretion than the foregoing would indicate. These differences are important and will be treated at a later point. For now, it is sufficient to note that the practice of reform clubs generally follows their principles—indeed, it may even exceed them. Given such a high level of intraparty democracy, one would assume that confusion, indecision, and ineffectiveness would be the inevitable result. Certainly such problems exist, but what is remarkable is that despite the confusion (or perhaps *because* of it), the reform clubs have organized and led strong campaigns against entrenched organizations and have defeated them. What is surprising is not that intraparty democracy is "inefficient," but that it is not a greater problem than it is.

One of the major premises of reformism is the conviction that democratic processes will generally produce correct or wise decisions; another is that persons interested in reform can work in harmony with those interested in liberalism and social welfare. On the first page of its booklet, the Lexington Club observes:

> Basically we believe in the desirability of widespread participation in the Democratic Party. We assume that people are fundamentally good and consequently both government and politics will improve as more and more people understand and participate. . . . Actually the Club combines two American traditions: that of the good government reform

liberals, interested in honesty and efficiency in government, and that of the social reform liberals concerned primarily with working toward the abolition of poverty and inequality of opportunity.[3]

This statement, of course, touches on a favorite topic of speculation among students of political philosophy, the conflict between "procedural" and "substantive" democracy—that is, between the view that democracy should be defined and justified in terms of the procedures it requires for the election of officials and the enacting of laws, and the view that the substance of democracy (the elimination of poverty and inequality and the protection of individual freedom) may be better served by institutions which are to some extent "undemocratic." But speculation such as this is rare in the reform movement, although the issue is raised indirectly in a number of ways.

It arises most frequently in the criticisms of those who argue that reform has no program other than to put reformers in power. The absence of any substantive program gives some plausibility to charges that "reform" is simply a slogan devised to justify the transfer of political power from one class to another—from the Irish and Italian politician with his local orientation and professional attitude to the Yankee and Jewish cosmopolitan amateurs in their Wall Street law offices. Even liberals sympathetic to the general approach of the reformers sometimes think there is more to be said for supporting a professional politician whose policy on crucial matters can be inferred from his record in office than an amateur who has no record and whose official pronouncements are silent on most important matters.[4]

This may explain a phenomenon which disquiets many reformers. Few, if any, of the liberal journals seem to have much enthusiasm for reform, even though reformers consider them-

[3] Ottenberg, *op. cit.*, p. 7.

[4] Murray Kempton, a principal columnist for the liberal *New York Post*, observed that "the Reform Democrats talk about many things, but they have never offered a serious program to meet the conditions that make New York as conspicuous for the sweatshop as it is for the slum." *Post*, August 4, 1961.

selves a principal part of the audience of such magazines as the *Reporter, Commentary,* the *New Republic,* the *Nation,* and *Dissent. Commentary* has repeatedly disheartened certain reform clubs with stories which stressed the middle-class basis of the reform movement and seemed to display more sympathy for the Italian housewife who supported Carmine De Sapio or John Merli than the Jewish co-ed who supports the VID.[5] The *Reporter* printed a noncommittal story which gave points to both sides.[6] *Dissent,* the journal of American intellectual socialism, published a hostile article attacking reform for lacking a program. "No clear-cut decision has been made as to the purpose of a political club. . . . There is . . . an absence in the reform movement of a mature civic idealism." Liberal "fat cats," it was charged, are using reform for their own selfish purposes and therefore talk of party reform is "mere political hogwash."[7] Reform in Manhattan has not resulted in any general mobilization of the intellectual Left.

Of the seventeen proposals contained in the "Statement of Principles" published by the CDV in 1961, only two referred to matters of substantive public policy. One of these was a demand for "equal job, housing, and educational opportunities"; the other was the vague assertion that "the complexities of metropolitan life make necessary the use of the most advanced techniques in research and study of the problems of housing, education, juvenile delinquency, traffic, etc." To be sure, the CDV did appoint a committee to prepare a "City Affairs Platform," and the committee, in the spring of 1961, did submit to the General Committee a proposed platform containing 152 numbered proposals dealing with the promotion of trade and industry, transportation and traffic, labor relations,

[5] Dan Wakefield, "Greenwich Village Challenges Tammany," *Commentary,* October, 1959, p. 308.

[6] Meg Greenfield, "Tammany in Search of a Boss," *Reporter,* April 13, 1961, pp. 28–31, and "The Decline and Fall of Tammany Hall," *Reporter,* February 15, 1962, pp. 33–37. The latter is a sympathetic account of De Sapio's un-boss-like qualities.

[7] Mary Peret Nichols, "The Politics of Virtue, Or, The New Tammany," *Dissent,* Summer, 1961, pp. 366–70.

education, civil rights and integration, health and welfare services, fiscal management, public personnel, police and fire protection, cultural and community programs, youth services, and housing. The platform was never adopted; indeed, it was never even seriously discussed by the General Committee. In part this was because other matters, including endorsements for the mayoralty primary, intervened; many reform leaders, however, believed that no such detailed platform could be adopted, regardless of how much time was available for deliberation, because of the conflicting points of view within the CDV. Most reformers, being liberals, would probably assent to planks dealing with the classic issues of liberalism: civil rights, integration, increased welfare services, collective bargaining, and the need for "comprehensive planning." Getting agreement on questions affecting mass transit, urban renewal, tax assessments and valuations, zoning, traffic and parking, where no simple "liberal" position is easy to discover, would be far harder.

Other than party reform, the only area in which the CDV has taken a comprehensive position has been charter revision. A Charter Revision Commission, appointed by Mayor Wagner, issued a report in July, 1961, in which it found "the basic structure" of the present charter to be "sound" but recommended a "reallocation of powers" in the direction of strengthening the mayor's executive authority and increasing the legislative powers of the City Council. These proposals were a slightly watered-down version of changes suggested earlier in the year by the state Commission on Governmental Operations appointed by Republican Governor Rockefeller.[8] The CDV, along with several other good government groups in the city, testified at hearings before the Charter Revision Commission and urged that it go much further in creating a strong mayor. It advocated eliminating the Board of Estimate and the office of borough president and reducing the comptroller from

[8] Text of the recommendations of the state body, known as the Moore Commission, were printed in the *New York Times*, January 16, 1961, p. 16.

a powerful elective official to a council-appointed auditor of the city's books. Initially the regular Democratic organization set out to oppose charter revision, but when it became evident that the proposed changes were relatively minor, it altered its position.[9] Even so, the proposed transfer of certain functions from the borough presidents to the central administration would significantly reduce the employees in the borough presidents' offices (and thus the patronage available to local leaders).[10]

The CDV, of course, wished to go much further than this as a way of weakening the regular organization by reducing the amount of patronage available to it and restricting or eliminating its access to the formal government which the weakness of the mayor's office and the power of the party-oriented Board of Estimate had made possible.

Both of these approaches—party reform and charter revision —had as their central focus the weakening of the position of the district leader. In many reform clubs, but particularly in the more militant ones, the power of the district leader has been severely restricted; indeed, most of his functions, except that of serving as the messenger of the club to the party's county executive committee, have been transferred to the club officers and executive committee. The insistence on democracy within the club, even at the expense of endless haggling and speech-making, was felt to be necessary in order to keep the district leader from gaining power over the club because of his formal position in the party.

The emphasis on reformism and the absence of any con-

[9] The party fought the appointment of the Charter Revision Commission in the City Council and the Board of Estimate and challenged its legality with a taxpayer's suit. By July, however, Arthur Levitt, regular organization candidate for mayor, endorsed charter revision, saying "I . . . believe in a strong Mayor." *New York Times,* April 14 and 16, May 2, 6, 12, 13, 16, and 19, and July 14 and 21, 1961. The Charter revisions were approved by the voters in November, 1961.

[10] The borough president of Queens, John T. Clancy, estimated his office would be reduced from 1,800 to 200 employees. *New York Times,* July 14, 1961.

structive program in the movement can be exaggerated. Particularly at the club level, reformers do take positions on substantive matters, and in any case, their position can often be inferred or predicted from the general liberalism of the membership. But reformism has been the major citywide preoccupation of the New York amateurs, and although this program has certain disadvantages—it exposes reformers to the criticisms of liberals who feel the movement is excessively negative—it has certain advantages as well.

Reformism, more than liberalism, enables the club to sustain interest among the members. Liberal goals are only slowly realized, if at all; reform goals are as close as the next primary. Liberalism tends to divert attention to the national scene; reformism focuses attention on the local scene. Further, reformism permits the clubs to differentiate themselves sharply from other liberal organizations. The reform clubs offer something unique—the chance to fight city hall—and thus they are not competitive (except among themselves) with other liberal and intellectual groups.

The strength of the reform movement lies precisely in the fact that its "ideology" does not specify in any detail the concrete goals of the clubs. If liberalism were the operative ideology, it would be difficult (but not impossible) to avoid indicating the substantive ends the movement sought. But so long as reformism is a general program which calls for "democratizing" the party, making it more "representative," and turning the rascals out, it need offend no potential club member. It can be specific where a broad consensus prevails (as, for example, in deploring the poor quality of lower-court judges); it must be abstract where no such consensus exists.

Differences on goals frequently come to the surface in club affairs. The committee on public schools of one West Side club was "split down the middle between two factions." The committee's work had been paralyzed by an inability to agree on what they wanted or how to get it. A heated debate occurred in an East Side club over what position to take on the proposed redistricting of a public school in the area, the effect of which would be to integrate the school in a manner that would give it a student body that was perhaps one-fourth white and three-fourths Negro and Puerto Rican. That was a "real donny-brook," according to a club leader. "I doubt that in the short run it is going to help us—in fact, it [the position the club took] will probably cost us some votes of some parents who object to having the school so heavily integrated. But in the long run, I think it will help us." Here, a club was led by the members' concern for the question of school integration, not only to conduct an acrimonious discussion within the organization, but to take a position in the community which a more prudent club would have avoided. Clearly, ends were not merely (as some Tammany leaders often allege) a "cover" for a simple bid for power, but a vital aspect of the club's relations to its members, an aspect which might be expensive in votes.

On many local issues, it is unlikely that the club membership will be divided because they have stakes in the outcome. Given the character of the persons recruited into reform politics, few will object to slum inspection programs, anti-crime campaigns, or neighborhood conservation projects. Most of these efforts will not only gratify the members' sense of justice, they will improve conditions for them in their own areas. But there are just as many issues which will divide the members, either because of conflicting views of the public interest or because of conflicting stakes in the outcome. Among such issues are racial integration in housing and schools, land clearance projects, parking regulations and facilities, zoning ordinances, and so on.[11]

As long as democratizing the party and defeating Carmine De Sapio could be invested with sufficient moral fervor, there was little real need for agreement on more substantive ends. This was particularly true so long as the reformers had not won the county leadership, the borough presidency, or the mayoralty. Until then, reformers were not called upon to make

[11] Professor Bert Swanson of Hunter College contends that there is evidence of a growing "liberal position" on urban affairs and that his research suggests its major dimensions. (Letter to the author.)

significant choices among competing alternatives, to decide issues of public policy, or to bear responsibility for their actions.

Reformism offers a rationale which can justify challenging regular Tammany leaders and candidates without inquiring into their qualifications. In California, the CDC clubs do not contest even half of the Democratic primaries; most incumbents are endorsed. If the candidate meets the clubs' definition of liberalism, there is no reason to oppose him (unless, of course, he is a liberal who has attacked the clubs head-on). In New York, on the other hand, reformism can justify challenging *all* non-reform candidates and leaders, regardless of their liberalism, on the grounds that no matter how able the individual, he is supported in office by an evil machine and that machine must be broken. Thus, reform primary contests are found wherever there is a reform club in existence, regardless of the merits of the case. Insurgent clubs tend to collapse if they have no struggle to motivate the members; reformism justifies incessant struggle.

Reformism is particularly valuable as a means of forging alliances with non-liberal groups and with dissident Democrats whose motives for attacking the organization are not identical with those of the reformers. The issue of bossism has undoubtedly helped reform clubs spread into Brooklyn, Queens, and the Bronx in districts where the upper-middle-class amateur might ordinarily have no appeal for the voters.[12]

Further, *party* reform (as contrasted to government reform) has provided greater opportunities for ambitious young politicians. Earlier reform movements had difficulty in sustaining themselves in part because they could offer no continuing in-

[12] The 1961 mayoralty primary, when Wagner was the anti-organization candidate, brought all kinds of insurgents and dissident Democrats into the mayor's camp as "allies" of the reformers, who soon became leery of their good faith. "Reform" provided a useful slogan for several factions in the party which were not interested in reform so much as in winning power in their own districts. Thus, certain regular clubs in the Bronx and Queens took advantage of the primary to break with their county leaders. There were no wholesale desertions, however. See *New York Post*, August 1, 1961.

centives for the ambitious. Party reform gives them a more lasting base of power from which they can negotiate on behalf of their political careers without losing everything when the reform mood leaves the electorate and the party recaptures control of the chief governmental offices. In the past, rising in the party bureaucracy was painfully slow for the young lawyer; reformism can make that rise very rapid indeed. The power of the reform slogans has deprived the regular party of its single greatest resource: the ability to absorb new entrants into politics in an orderly manner and thus maintain the system by rewarding the most ambitious and aggressive and punishing the others. Reformism, arising out of the need to sustain organizations created almost overnight by the sudden influx of hundreds of amateurs motivated by some measure of idealism, has meant that the regular party could not absorb these new leaders by the traditional means, for the alternative opportunities open to these young men—the opportunity, not simply to enter, but to capture the party—were more attractive than the party could offer—the opportunity to work one's way slowly up the ladder of political recognition.

Interestingly, in upstate New York counties, where the traditional party was weaker and less identified with bossism, the Stevenson supporters who entered politics after 1952 were, by and large, absorbed by existing party mechanisms without a dramatic struggle between "bosses" and "reformers." Instead, the regular leaders simply became more liberal and "Stevensonian" as a result of a rather orderly transfer of power.[13]

## Liberalism

Where no single issue such as reform provides a unifying theme for amateur Democratic clubs, the goals of the club movement become at once more substantive and more diffuse. The Los Angeles clubs are both smaller and more numerous than their New York counterparts, and there are several clubs

[13] See Robert Bendiner, "The Provincial Politics of the Empire State," *Reporter*, May 12, 1960, p. 22.

which, by CDC standards, are conservative and even reactionary. However, if the sixty or seventy clubs not affiliated with CDC are set aside, and if one is concerned primarily with the larger, more active clubs which provide the vocal leadership of the CDC, much of the diversity is submerged in the general liberalism of the movement. This becomes particularly clear in reading the policy statements of the CDC and examining the kinds of candidates that are endorsed. Ultimately, as we shall discover, the differences between professional and amateur politicians in the California Democratic party became so important that the club movement more and more became concerned with intraparty strife and problems of party "reform." Similarly, the Democratic Federation of Illinois twice adopted platforms which set forth liberal positions on labor legislation, increased welfare expenditures, civil rights, planning, and state support for education. A prime attraction for DFI club members attending the state conventions was the opportunity to discuss such matters and to hear prestigious liberal spokesmen, such as Eleanor Roosevelt, Senator Albert Gore, and Adlai Stevenson. But from the first, the crucial question was always: What shall be the relations between the DFI and the Chicago machine headed by Mayor Daley? On this they could say little.

Regardless of the extent to which people participate in club politics for the fun of the game, for the game to be attractive to the liberal amateur it must espouse unmistakably liberal goals. Liberalism provides in California the programmatic focus which reformism provides in Manhattan—or, to state it more correctly, reformism preoccupies those volunteers in Manhattan who otherwise would, like their Los Angeles brethren, be engaged in the definition and pursuit of liberal goals. In California, this process has been institutionalized in the vitally important CDC Issues Conference.

The Issues Conference, begun in 1959, is an annual meeting at which club delegates come together to provide the CDC (and hopefully, the party as a whole) with a platform. But unlike conventional party platforms, this is not a series of bland statements worked out behind closed doors by a small commit-tee of party leaders anxious to placate special-interest groups and devise plausible appeals for blocs of voters. Rather, it is an elaborate, highly organized process of discussions in which almost every delegate participates while professors and other "resource persons" offer background material and discussion papers. The end product is a lengthy "policy statement" which is assembled overnight by collating the conclusions of dozens of individual discussion groups into a single document that is then debated and voted on by the conference in plenary ses-sion. In the words of a reporter for the *Christian Science Mon-itor,* quoted with pride in CDC literature, "It was the most unusual political meeting ever held in this state. It seemed more like a huge university seminar than a political conven-tion."[14]

Until 1959, the CDC had been largely concerned at its con-vention with making pre-primary endorsements. At each con-vention, in addition, a number of resolutions were presented on substantive matters, placing the organization on record on a wide range of issues. The creation of the first Issues Con-ference in 1959 was explicitly designed to maintain the or-ganization in the absence of any opportunity to make state-wide endorsements. A CDC officer explained to an interviewer:

> We have to have annual conventions. And we have to make them interesting. We've got to get people to come and we've got to create enthusiasm among them. It's easy when we're endorsing candidates for public office. Every-one wants to get in on that. But . . . in 1959, 1960, and 1961 there were no statewide offices up for election. This really put us on the spot. What do we do—how do we hold the organization together for three years? We had the idea, therefore, of having an issues conference in 1959.

A CDC staff member agreed: "We started it, frankly, because we weren't making any statewide endorsements in those years. It was a gimmick—something to do at our annual conventions to get us over the lean years." The first chairman of the Issues

[14] Quoted in California Democratic Council, *Policy Statements,* adopt-ed at Second Annual Issues Conference, Fresno, February, 1960, p. 1.

Conference described it as an effort to "provide an organized forum for the discussion of issues in order to maintain spirit and enthusiasm and a sense of purpose for the CDC membership." The conference proved to be immensely popular with the delegates. Although meetings on problems of CDC organization were held simultaneously with the Issues Conference, it proved difficult to get many people to attend those sessions as compared to the issues panels.

Until 1959, stands on issues had been taken in the form of resolutions passed at endorsing conventions, as well as by local councils, conventions, and clubs. Many of these resolutions were contradictory, none was subject to any centralized scrutiny, and all could be construed as representing the "official" position of CDC. Some were a source of embarrassment to CDC leaders. These officers, more sensitive than the rank and file to the virtues of circumspection and timing, realized that a concern for issues and a liberal ideology was vital to the club movement. The question became, how could the expression of that concern be placed under some control without, at the same time, weakening intraparty democracy and mass participation in decision-making? The Issues Conference, with all delegates discussing policy matters in panels but with no formal expression of view by the organization as a whole, was tried in 1959. Nothing was put in writing except a "Summary Report" of the various views expressed. The convention itself did not act on this report, it was not adopted or ratified as CDC policy, and no attempt was made to resolve differing points of view and produce a consistent document.

This, however, proved to be inadequate for the delegates. Outspoken militancy had been sacrificed to discretion. "Many delegates were dissatisfied with this," said a conference leader. "They wanted to take positions. They wanted to have something concrete. They wanted the organizaiton to act on these issues and produce something in writing which could be taken back to the clubs." As a result, several changes were made before the 1960 Issues Conference. First, a standing Issues Committee was created within the CDC to meet regularly and prepare study kits, assign discussion leaders, and hold regional conferences. Second, leadership conferences were held to train discussion leaders. Third, regional issues conferences were held in order to prepare the delegates on the issues to be discussed in Fresno. Fourth, it was decided to draw up a "Policy Statement" at the conference at the conclusion of the panel discussions on which the convention could then vote. This policy statement was to be a coherent document, not a series of resolutions, and it would not represent all points of view. At the conference in February, 1960, the various parts of the Policy Statement were written Saturday night by drafting committees working into the early hours, assembling recommendations from the leaders of the various discussion groups. It was mimeographed and presented to the delegates Sunday morning, debated, adopted, and printed. At the same time, however, separate resolutions were introduced in the convention via a Resolutions Committee, and these were acted on before and without reference to the Policy Statement. As a result, inconsistencies appeared and many positions were taken which later proved vulnerable to conservative attack. Besides, the resolutions were time-consuming. Thus, for the 1961 Issues Conference, the CDC leadership decided to eliminate all resolutions and allow the convention to speak only through the Policy Statement.

The 1960 statement was a revealing document. The conference considered six areas: United States foreign and atomic policy, human rights, agriculture, water and power, United States policy toward underdeveloped nations, and economic and governmental problems. Of the sixty-two specific proposals presented in boldface type, forty-four referred to national and international affairs and only eighteen to state and local matters. In all, about 125 recommendations were contained in the statement, 75 of them requiring federal rather than state action. The CDC and its members, in the Issues Conference and in more routine matters, evidence an absorption in the large issues of the day. Although a state, rather than a national party, the CDC is oriented to the national scene and gives serious attention to only certain kinds of local matters. Of the forty state and local issues mentioned, the largest group (fifteen) referred to civil liberties and civil rights. There was little or no mention of such mundane matters as state fiscal policies, taxation, state control over natural resource development, urban renewal, highway programs, and air and water pollution. The only areas, outside of libertarian issues, of concern to the CDC at the state level were the state water program (which was to be on the ballot as a referendum measure), agriculture (particularly farm labor), and education.

Although not all clubs within the CDC occupy an identical position on the political spectrum, the recommendations of the Policy Statement left little doubt of the outspokenly liberal character of the movement. Among the more controversial positions taken in the statement were proposals calling for opposition to any increase in American military appropriations, initiation of "detailed total universal disarmament proposals," expansion of disarmament negotiations to include France and Communist China, abolition of the House Committee on Un-American Activities, abolition of all state and federal "non-disloyalty oaths," abolition of capital punishment, opposition to further governmental controls relating to pornography and obscenity, strengthening the state housing anti-discrimination law, creation of a universal state or federal health insurance plan, passage of the Forand bill for medical care for the aged, formation and encouragement of more farm and consumer cooperatives, increasing capital gains taxes, and elimination of the oil depletion allowance.[15]

Elaborate preparations were made in 1961 to insure that participants in the conference would be well-informed on the issues to be discussed and considerable pains were taken to

[15] See *Policy Statements,* Second Annual Issues Conference, 1960, *passim.* The club concern for substantive liberal issues has affected the Los Angeles County Central Committee as well. As early as 1955 it passed a resolution expressing support for the Fund for the Republic and the United Nations, which were then under attack by certain conservatives, and in 1960 it adopted a resolution calling for the abolition of capital punishment. (See *Los Angeles Times,* October 12, 1955, and March 3, 1960.)

provide an opportunity for a full discussion of all points of view. These precautions enabled the conference to function fairly smoothly in those topic areas in which there was general agreement and widely shared knowledge. But in such areas as foreign policy, where there was a fundamental cleavage of opinion with detailed knowledge possessed by only a few, the conference procedure was clumsy and the result open to criticism. Although a sixty-page background paper containing a scholarly debate was distributed well in advance to all members, the discussion groups (there were twenty) could hardly cope with the complexities of the subject in the time available. Observations of several discussion groups indicated that most began late, were chaired by discussion leaders who had little preparation for the task, and lasted only two or three hours. The panels typically involved a protracted debate over procedure, followed by either a colloquy among a few well-versed members while the majority sat silent, or an effort by the well-versed to explain the rudiments of the issue to the uninformed. In one of the larger panels, only four of the thirty people in attendance indicated that they had even read the background paper. Under such circumstances, and in the brief time available, only the sanguine could hope that a well-reasoned, spontaneous expression of policy would emerge.

The drafting committee began its work, not *de novo*, but by bringing forth a draft statement that had been prepared in advance but not shown to the discussion groups. Representatives from these panels were then asked if anything said in their discussion contradicted or modified any point in the pre-arranged draft statement; if not, the statement would be considered approved. This statement was then taken to a plenary meeting of all members of the foreign policy section (several hundred delegates) where an attempt was made to debate it. It was immediately evident that a sizable and vocal minority opposed it. Since the proceedings were under Robert's Rules of Order, an attempt to discuss the substance of the issues quickly collapsed into a parliamentary wrangle over procedure, with the majority accusing the minority of dilatory tactics. Finally, after nearly three hours of such maneuvering, a "gag rule" was adopted under which each item in the draft statement was to be voted on with no debate and no amendments. By two o'clock in the morning, the statement was approved with practically no changes.

Later that morning, the entire conference considered the draft statement, but under a severe time limitation on debate. The most controversial portion, a paragraph calling for diplomatic recognition of Communist China by the United States, was deleted by an amendment offered by popular State Senator Richard Richards and seconded by State Controller Alan Cranston and Lieutenant-Governor Glenn Anderson. These public officials called for greater "responsibility" and adherence to the national platform and policies of the Democratic party and President Kennedy. Emotional references were made to Adlai Stevenson, who by then was ambassador to the United Nations and on record as opposing the recognition of Red China. Opponents of these speakers argued that the issue was "honesty, not expediency" and that the CDC could only be vital when it did not "fear to embarrass party leaders" and did not hesitate to put "country above party." But the standing and appeal of the elective officials carried the day, and the Chinese recognition paragraph was eliminated by an overwhelming voice vote. Further efforts by other leaders to water down the statement were rejected. It remained an extremely liberal policy statement, calling for admission of Red China to the United Nations and suggesting negotiations for the general disengagement of military forces and the reciprocal withdrawal from foreign bases.

In 1962, the CDC convention was able to devote its attention to candidate endorsements. The more controversial issues were side-stepped. The resolutions committee reported out only 24 of the 145 proposals submitted to it, and none of those reported dealt with Red China, capital punishment, or unilateral disarmament.

If this involvement in liberal issues is an attraction for club members, it may also be a liability for the party as a whole.

Many elective officials express dismay and even hostility to the actions of CDC, the unofficial wing of the party, in adopting policy statements which then become known, incorrectly, as the platform of the party as a whole.[16] Candidates, many running in districts where pronounced liberalism is not considered an asset, become identified with the CDC platform, particularly if they seek, as most do, CDC endorsement. This raises the question of whether the concern for liberal ends works against the ability of the CDC to elect officials who will serve those ends.

No conclusive answer can be given to this question. The CDC leadership is itself divided on the effect policy statements have. A chairman of one Issues Conference felt that the conference gave "the Republicans their platform on a silver platter. There's no doubt about that in my mind." A past president of the CDC felt that "the issues and resolutions have created problems for us." A leading party official, closely identified with the CDC, felt that the earlier Issues Conferences "did go off half-cocked in some areas, concerning matters outside California [like] Red China." A CDC vice-president felt that "some of those resolutions have put some candidates on the spot." How serious this liability was cannot be determined. But there is no doubt that several Democratic candidates were attacked by their Republican opponents and by the conservative press for being identified with the "ultra-liberalism" of the CDC. The political editor of the *Los Angeles Times* charged that the CDC was an organization with "all the potentials of a political machine" that posed "a threat to a free and independent Democratic party." He went on to list, in critical tones, the more extreme of the policies CDC was alleged to stand for, including the release of Caryl Chessman (under sentence of death for nine years) and Morton Sobel (imprisoned

---

[16] The actual California Democratic party platform is written by the state convention of the party, composed of all the party's nominees for partisan offices, which meets for one day every two years to draw up a platform and for nothing else. *Elections Code,* secs. 2807-9. The document attracts little attention in most cases. Beginning in 1962 the convention will be held annually.

on espionage charges).[17] In fact, no reference was made in the Policy Statement to either Chessman or Sobel, and a CDC protest was followed, three weeks later, by a printed apology.[18] But to most conservatives, many of the other issues with which the *Times* and the Republican party linked CDC candidates were both extreme and represented the actual position taken at the second Issues Conference.[19] The CDC never described its Policy Statements as binding on candidates, and they were not the party platform, but such distinctions are often lost on the average voter. In Contra Costa County, a Republican candidate for state senator distributed a pink handbill headed "Democrats and Republicans Alike Shocked by CDC Meeting at Fresno" and containing a list (with some inaccuracies) of CDC policy positions.[20]

Several other candidates for state and national office were subjected to similar attacks.[21] Some of these attacks misstated

[17] Kyle Palmer in *Los Angeles Times,* February 28, 1960.

[18] *Los Angeles Times,* March 20, 1960. A resolution had been passed in an early-morning session of the 1960 CDC convention concerning the Sobel case, but it was not part of the official Policy Statement. It was one of the factors that led CDC leaders to decide against permitting resolutions in the 1961 conference.

[19] Republican campaign chairman Pat Hillings demanded that CDC "clarify" its "obscure attitude toward Red China." (*Los Angeles Times,* March 25, 1960.)

[20] Quoted in *The Liberal Democrat,* December, 1960, p. 2.

[21] In Monterey County, an advertisement in a local paper by a Republican candidate cited CDC stands on six controversial issues and linked them to his Democratic opponent, State Senator Fred S. Farr, who had been the head of the county's delegation to the conference (*Monterey Peninsula Herald,* October 13, 1960). Five days later, Senator Farr published in the paper a repudiation of the CDC positions, stating that "I was not present when the resolutions were adopted and had no part in them. I went there primarily to hear the candidates. As a matter of fact, the resolutions were adopted by a small group after most of the delegates had left the hall." He expressed disagreement with CDC in its stand on abolishing the House Un-American Activities Committee and on disarmament. He stated that "the CDC stand on these and many other issues does not represent the view of the majority —if any— of the Democratic members of the Legislature or of the Democratic Central Committee, or of the Democratic Platform, or of the rank and file of the Democrats of California, or even of the majority of the

or exaggerated the actual CDC position, but there is little doubt that many Republicans regarded even a scrupulously accurate account of CDC views as politically valuable material. Not all Democrats so attacked repudiated CDC positions, at least openly.

It is difficult to assess the extent to which CDC policy statements harmed the campaigns of CDC-endorsed candidates. Senator Fred Farr was re-elected, winning 57 per cent of the vote despite the attack on him. Assemblyman Gordon Winton, similarly attacked in Madera and Merced counties, won even though he, unlike Farr, defended CDC.[22] James C. Corman won a congressional seat in the San Fernando Valley although he was attacked for his CDC affiliation.[23] The Democratic congressional candidates in Los Angeles County polled nearly 20,000 votes more than President Kennedy, with only one incumbent losing. Democrats retained control of both houses of the state legislature. CDC President Joseph L. Wyatt, Jr., in a report to the CDC board, expressed his view that the "sleazy and dirty" anti-CDC attacks had not been effective. Candidates were elected "in spite of this attack, or perhaps because of it."[24]

There can be little doubt, however, that there were many elective officials, both liberal and sympathetic to CDC, who were deeply concerned about the impact of the issues program. Although only Senator Farr, himself a liberal, publicly repudiated the resolutions, several were willing to do so privately.

---

CDC members. They are certainly not my views." (*Ibid.*, October 18, 1960.)

The CDC legal counsel charged that the original Republican advertisement was "libelous and false," but the paper replied that the advertisement was generally a fair statement of CDC positions, and followed that with an editorial the next day stating that, although it was not accusing the CDC of being Communist, "there are parts of this program which are identical with the program of the American communist party." (*Ibid.*, October 20 and 21, 1960.)

[22] See *The Liberal Democrat*, December, 1960, p. 12.

[23] See *ibid.*, January, 1961, p. 21.

[24] *Ibid.*

One state legislator, a former CDC officer, said after his re-election that "something has to be done about CDC. I had to run against those damned resolutions my last time up." A liberal Democratic candidate for Congress wished that "the clubs would shut up and just work." A CDC-endorsed candidate for Congress, referring to the primary election, felt that the Issues Conference had not hurt his campaign only because "word had not gotten around yet:"

> The ultra-left nature of some of the CDC actions in Fresno didn't become generally known around here until after the primary, which was in June. It would have killed me if it had become known, though. . . . As it was, CDC clubs in this area helped me greatly. But it would have been a different story if people had known what kind of organization it seemed to be. This is pretty much a middle-of-the-road district.

Rightly or wrongly, liberal Democrats who welcome CDC endorsements are concerned about the ideology with which that endorsement is encumbered. At the same time, however, it is precisely these ideological encumbrances which, in the eyes of CDC leaders, make it possible to stimulate volunteer work on behalf of the endorsees. Even CDC leaders who see difficulties in the Issues Conference agree that the Conference is crucial. A club president stated the issue clearly:

> You must realize the importance of these Issues Conferences to us. They may hurt us in some races, although I don't think they do. But we have to have these issue to get us to work. We're volunteers. We have to have the feeling we are working for a cause in which we believe in order to work at all. . . . If we didn't have this cause to believe in . . . we wouldn't work at all.

As it is, some club leaders are restless with even the limited extent to which the Issues Conference is controlled by CDC leaders. Eliminating resolutions dissatisfied those who looked upon their passage as a form of concrete "action" more meaningful than "policy statements." Other club members dislike the extent to which dissenting and minority views have been eliminated from the policy statements and would like to enhance the power of individual discussion groups to shape the contents of these statements, free of even the most general guidance from drafting committees and CDC leaders. But as one club president who was also an Issues Conference leader remarked to an interviewer:

> The CDC Issues Conference moved more and more in the direction of more formal statements—policy statements —in order to prevent [Republican misconstruing]. But . . . this militates against the open, democratic, free nature of issues discussions. If you're going to produce carefully phrased policy statements which will represent your views precisely with a minimal opportunity for distortion, it means you have to organize the structure of the Issues Conference to a greater degree. The purpose of having these people together is to get them to talk freely. The two goals seem to be in conflict.

Those CDC leaders who recognize the dangers of even a careful statement of the organization's extremely liberal views are, however, emphatic in agreeing that the Issues Conference is vital, though risky. A CDC vice-president remarked:

> What can we do when people use these tactics [of attacking CDC for its policy positions]? One of two things— either drop the Issues Conference and let the whole thing go by default and thereby shrink our own consciences, or second, say to hell with them. I think we should do the latter—to hell with the opponents. I think we'll still win, resolutions or not.

Former National Committeeman Paul Ziffren agreed. "The party has to stand for something in order to get volunteers. You have to take a firm stand on issues or you can't attract the kind of person you want into politics. It can't be a Tweedledum and Tweedledee situation."

The problems attending the CDC issues program indicate the benefits the New York clubs have reaped by basing their appeal on procedural reforms rather than substantive issues. Reformism, at least at present, provides little leverage for the conservative opposition, and thus the reform cause can attract conservative and "good government" support from newspapers, civic associations, and some businessmen. However, reformism, if it makes enough gains, may succeed in so altering the distribution of power in the community that groups with tangible stakes in the existing distribution (e.g., businesses and labor unions which have worked out an advantageous *modus vivendi* with the party that enables them to use the party to advance their interests within the weak and decentralized formal government) will begin to oppose reform. And, if reform's victory is complete and it can no longer maintain itself with reform slogans, it will in all likelihood begin to develop appeals based on liberalism which will expose it to the same kinds of counterattacks that the CDC experiences. This possibiity must be qualified, however, by the fact that there is on the whole more deference to liberal causes in New York politics than in California (owing, perhaps, to the differing ethnic composition of the two areas);[25] New York will probably be more tolerant of an outspokenly liberal political organization.

## Limited War

In Chicago, where machine strength was a prime consideration for the amateurs, neither the IVI nor the DFI has been able to develop a "reform" program. The former realized that it was hopeless, the latter that it was dangerous. But since stated ends were vital incentives for the members, both organizations had to find a set of substitute goals. The IVI chose to become, in effect, a pressure group on behalf of certain liberal causes (without, of course, relinquishing its desire to contest primaries) while the DFI sought to avoid the problem of power by in many (but not all) cases devoting itself to "getting out the vote" and "finding" good candidates. Total war on behalf of reform ends was impossible; both organizations had to settle for a kind of limited war.

In 1961, no IVI leaders described the immediate goal of their

[25] The political differences between New York and other cities as revealed by their receptivity to liberal causes is discussed briefly in James Q. Wilson, *Negro Politics* (New York: Free Press of Glencoe, 1961), chaps. ii, v.

organization as being the defeat of the Daley machine. The IVI could only seek to command respect from the regulars by fighting them for attainable local offices (such as alderman) and trying to switch votes to certain Republican candidates. "You can't compete with the machine," said one IVI leader. "You have to wait for them to make a mistake." He continued by speculating on what the mistakes might be. "Daley's approaching that on the Negro issue. Or the machine may become too expensive or inefficient for State Street [Chicago's financial and business section]. But they will stand a lot of corruption. Or there [may be] a fight between the city and the federal machine." Others mentioned the possibility of serious scandals rocking the organization. In the meantime, little could be done. "Reformers moderate conditions that never change," said another IVI leader. "Occasionally . . . a reform group will win . . . but usually the machine will . . . be dominant. La Guardia won in New York because of FDR. We won't change the basic structure, but we will air the stink over public health. We will get open residency. We may get better schools."

Unlike the Manhattan reformers, the IVI was concerned mostly about specific issues, but unlike the California clubs, these issues were mostly local, rather than national, in character. The machine's perceived strength was sufficient both to shift the focus to substantive goals and to tie those goals to local—i.e., "machine-caused"—conditions. The independent alderman elected by the IVI saw his role as that of a gadfly: "The more independent you are, the more they give you things so you won't make so much noise." Being a gadfly and circulating petitions demanding an "open occupancy" ordinance in the city were, of course, not necessarily in conflict with the Silverman approach of building a "power base" through effective precinct organization, but there remained a latent tension in the IVI over how resources should be allocated between these two strategies. Usually, the IVI did a little of both.

The DFI, on the other hand, had a harder time finding substitute goals. Reform could not be considered, and "good government" seemed, in the Chicago context, both naïve and an implicit attack on that organization which completely dominated the city's government. DFI leaders almost never used such words as "reform" or "bossism" to an interviewer, even though Daley's power made De Sapio's in Manhattan seem innocuous by comparison. Even when "reform" was used, it meant something far different from that word in Manhattan. It meant getting the "right kind" of people into the party, not revolutionizing the party structure or procedures. It was frustrating in the extreme to discover that the regulars seemed to have no need for the amateurs; "participation" was not *simply* an empty slogan (although it was surely at least that), but in addition a way of expressing anger at exclusion. One person who had run for office with DFI backing observed:

> The tightness of the Democratic party means that those who want to be active but aren't a part of the Democratic party can't join. It is almost like the Communist party [in Chicago]. You almost have to be born into it. If you are a product of Harvard Law School, you just don't join the organization in [this] ward.

Although "participation" skirted the central issue of whether the DFI would be willing to force its way into the regular party if the latter refused to let it participate in any other way, the goal still had some meaning. Where the regular organization was weak, it could mean getting upper-middle-class Democrats to do something about trying to build up the party's vote in their Republican neighborhoods. In certain areas even in Chicago, the DFI could prove useful by canvassing in the expensive, high-rise apartment buildings on the Gold Coast which were often closed to regulars. Not all DFI leaders were by any means satisfied with this arrangement; there were many who, had they lived in Chicago, would probably have been members of the IVI. They were eager for a primary fight. Since such leaders were generally found *outside* the city, in the suburbs or downstate, it was here that the conventional anti-boss slogans of the reformers were heard most frequently. In Evanston, where the amateurs managed to take over the regular party organization, the goal of "party reform" was often stated, but hardly anywhere else. It would appear that success or the prospects of success encourage the formulation of reform goals by amateurs; defeat or a conviction that defeat is inevitable lead the amateurs to try to devise alternative goals. This is not easy.

## Ideology and the Amateurs

It is tempting to refer to the amateur club movement as representing the "ideological" wing of the Democratic party. This is true only if by ideology is meant simply a set of general ideas concerning political life, particularly those ideas, however vague, which are characteristic of a certain class or stratum. If ideology is used in its narrower sense as referring to a comprehensive world view which explains and offers a moral judgment on social phenomena (as does, for example, Marxism), then there is very little ideology in contemporary amateur politics.

The use of issues or slogans as a main incentive for political action usually means that the amateurs will represent the extreme wing of the party's membership. This is not to say that all amateurs are extremists on policy matters, but only that the use of slogans and appeals to principle by club leaders will generally be governed by the needs of the extremist members who demand a steady reaffirmation of these principles as a condition of their support. Many rank-and-file members state, as one of their complaints about club life, that there is too much talking and arguing about remote or abstract issues.[26] Similarly, active officers often profess themselves more concerned with organizational, tactical, and political problems and regret the time which they feel must be given to talking about issues, either reform or liberal. Interviewing members and officers privately, one soon begins to wonder why, when

[26] Mail questionnaires returned by members who were not officers of the clubs in both Los Angeles and New York almost invariably cited "talking" and "bickering" as their principal grievances.

neither group enjoys the endless talking, so much talking takes place.

In fact, both officers and members probably get more enjoyment out of it than they are willing to admit. They are extremely sensitive to the charge that amateur politics is "nothing but a debating society." But even if one feels the time given to some abstract matter could be better used for other purposes, there is an almost irresistible urge among the intellectual amateurs to get into the discussion in order to attack a weak argument, display a fact, dissect an inconsistency, or make a point. It is difficult for them to take a purely instrumental view of debates—that is, to indulge without rebuttal some members' need for eloquence because it is necessary in order to keep them involved in the club. An active club leader finds it hard to let foolishness or contradiction pass unchallenged.

The tendency to take extreme stands on policy matters is sometimes checked by the existence of a more conservative membership or constituency (reform clubs on Manhattan's East Side, the area of high-income Jews, are generally more moderate than those on the West Side, the area of middle-income Jews), by the existence of some powerful constraint (one Manhattan club came into politics early enough to get several patronage jobs which it was later reluctant to jeopardize by militant reformism) or by the fact that the important battles have already been won (regular reform clubs which control district leaderships are often less interested in fights than insurgent reform clubs which are still trying to win the leadership).

Most amateurs are not "ideological" in the same sense that a Socialist is ideological. Indeed, many seem actively to shun ideology and go out of their way to display what they feel is a properly "tough-minded" and pragmatic attitude toward politics. Perhaps this is an expression of their fear that otherwise they might be thought "naïve," the way "reformers" and "do-gooders" are traditionally supposed to be naïve. Perhaps it is because the issues strike them as too complex for simple views.

Whatever the reason, the character of the contemporary amateur Democrats is thrown into sharp relief when, as is sometimes the case, an amateur club will contain both young volunteers and older men and women who come to club politics out of a background in the Socialist or American Labor parties or Upton Sinclair's EPIC (End Poverty in California) movement. The absence of any viable alternative to the two-party system today means that such persons with a strong and comprehensive ideology may be forced to participate in club politics within a major party if they are to participate in politics at all. The alternatives which formerly existed are gone with the collapse of the Socialist, American Labor, Progressive, and other ideological third parties.

But most of the club members are not urban radicals in the tradition of the American Socialist left. By the very fact that they have joined the two-party system in order to refashion it from within, they express a belief that whatever ideological cleavages are important in the country can be compassed by the traditional parties, if given new leadership. The contemporary liberals are, for the most part, neither "proud independents" who believe it the part of civic virtue to remain outside and above partisan conflict nor urban radicals who see a new party of the left as the only hope for a new era.

The politically involved amateur today believes that "proud independence" was largely an empty and ineffectual pose and that history proves the futility of third-party movements. He espouses a liberalism that has lost most of its doctrinaire ideology and, lacking an ideological foundation, can be adapted to existing institutions. Where a Marxian ideology provides a single world view which relates political questions to the nature of society as a whole, and calls for new organizations outside the existing institutional framework to make possible fundamental changes, the more *ad hoc* liberalism of the club intellectual lacks such a world view, pronounces no judgment on society as a whole, and demands incremental rather than fundamental changes. With such a perspective, an accommodation to the two-party system is possible if one is persuaded that those parties can be given new directions.[27]

The club movement lacks a manifesto, and there is rarely heard any appeal to the traditional heroes and slogans of American radicalism. These club leaders came of age politically when American socialism was already dying and few, if any, attempts have been made in their many speeches and scattered writing to identify themselves with any sort of radical or reforming past; indeed, the opposite has been more nearly the case. The contemporary reformers carefully distinguish themselves from the "naive" reformers of the past by pointing to their more "realistic" understanding of local politics and the inadequacy of externally imposed reforms and structural changes. In the Issues Conferences of the CDC, where the most intense and articulate concern for liberal goals has been displayed, little in the way of coherent ideology can be detected. The emphasis on fact-finding, *expertise,* research, background papers, and "resource persons" has not been simply politically useful cover; rather, it has reflected an awareness of the complexity of issues, the difficulty of stating general solutions for specific problems, and the need to establish the plausibility of proposed solutions by some means other than deductions from an a priori ideology. If such an ideology

[27] Some young Jewish intellectuals lament this. One wrote, "I mourn—uselessly—the absence of that generation of Jewish socialists who considered it an obligation and joy to radically question the organization of society. . . . Most of today's 'engaged' young 'political' Jews are careful warriors in 'reform' politics. . . ." Nat Hentoff, in his contribution to "A Symposium—Jewishness and the Younger Intellectuals," *Commentary,* April, 1961, p. 328.

Two common themes of social criticism today involve a dispute over whether there has been an "end of ideology" in America and the extent to which American intellectuals are "alienated" from their society and from social action within it. Without entering into these subjects directly, it suffices to say here that the amateur club movement has goals without an explicated ideology, and the involvement of these young leaders in local political action suggests that, although intellectual producers may be "alienated," these intellectual consumers are not. Cf. Daniel Bell, *End of Ideology* (Glencoe: Free Press, 1960), and Edward A. Shils, "Ideology and Civility: On the Politics of the Intellectual," *Sewanee Review,* LXVI (Summer, 1958), 450–80.

existed and was widely shared, it could provide its own justification for specific programs. The CDC is hardly, in Phillip Selznick's phrase, an "organizational weapon" acting forcefully in pursuit of ideological goals central to the lives of its members; it is a loose, ambivalent congress of organizations which does not play a central part in the lives of any but the most active members.[28]

The need to maintain *organizations* composed of amateur politicians may constrain leaders to engage in more quasi-ideological appeals than they privately prefer, however. Whereas professional politicians attempt to avoid issues because the loyalty of their workers is commanded by other means, amateurs generate issues because there seems to be no other way to command these loyalties. There is thus a thrust toward extremism which may be imparted more by considerations of organization than by the intent of members.

In Wisconsin, the extremism that is the result of the club movement can be seen in both parties. There, both the Democrats and the Republicans rely on extra-legal, club-based party organizations. The former party reflects a strong New Deal–Fair Deal point of view, while the latter was enthusiastic in its support of Senator Joseph McCarthy in the early 1950's. The Republicans not only endorsed McCarthy, but actively sought in 1956 to replace the internationalist Senator Alexander Wiley (then the ranking Republican member of the Senate Foreign Relations Committee) with an isolationist, pro-McCarthy candidate.[29]

In Great Britain where the local party organizations rely almost entirely on a cadre of middle-class volunteer workers organized into constituency associations, a similar phenomenon

[28] This may be the crucial point distinguishing club politics from earlier radical organizations. A Socialist in the 1930's adopted the party, in most cases, as a way of life; the CDC and the Manhattan clubs are rarely a "way of life" for their members. Indeed, many club activists spread their organizational loyalties around, and belong as well to the ADA, the American Civil Liberties Union, the League of Women Voters, and other "bourgeois" associations.

[29] Leon D. Epstein, *Politics in Wisconsin* (Madison: University of Wisconsin Press, 1958), pp. 85–86, 94–95.

can be found. In those cases in which the constituency associations of the British political parties have acted to discipline members of Parliament, they have revealed that association activists are more extremist than the M.P.s and often more extremist than the party leadership. A survey of constituency refusals to readopt M.P.s after the Suez crisis of 1956 shows that all ten of the Conservative M.P.s who opposed intervention in Suez were criticized, induced to resign, or dropped as candidates, while not one of the twenty Conservatives who favored *greater* intervention lost his seat and many were warmly defended, even though at the time opinion in the country on the crisis was sharply divided.[30] "Pressure from constituency associations . . . tends to be that of relatively extreme partisans," and as a result, "Conservative activists showed a tolerance for the pro-Suez deviants that was denied the anti-Suez M.P.s."[31]

However, the concern for goals displayed by amateur political clubs not only tends to thrust them in the direction of extreme statements of these goals, it also imparts a quest for goals of general or national significance. This can be checked where reform is an issue, and hence local CDV clubs in Manhattan and IVI organizations in Chicago have (with certain exceptions) made local affairs their major preoccupation. Where reform is not an issue, as in California, there is little to restrain a desire to emphasize issues of the most general significance. This was clearly evident in the history of the CDC

---

[30] Leon D. Epstein, "British M.P.s and Their Local Parties: The Suez Case," *American Political Science Review,* LIV (June, 1960), 374–90. At the time of the Parliamentary crisis, a British Institute of Public Opinion poll showed that 72 per cent of Labour voters opposed the Suez intervention while 76 per cent of Conservative voters supported it. *Ibid.,* p. 376.

[31] *Ibid.,* p. 385. That volunteer activists tend to be militants is, of course, a familiar point in various analyses of European political parties, particularly Socialist parties. See Philip Williams, *Politics in Post-War France* (2d ed.; London: Longmans, Green & Co., 1958), pp. 60–61, 67–68, 72–76, 366–73, and Maurice Duverger, *Political Parties,* trans. Barbara and Robert North (2d ed.; London: Methuen & Co., 1959), pp. 109–16.

Issues Conferences, and it is underscored by the electoral activity of the clubs.

The California clubs are not involved, to any great extent, in local politics, in great part due to the non-partisan character of city and county elections. There is little doubt that many voters would resent the open intrusion of political parties, even unofficial ones, into city elections. And non-partisan offices are rarely attractive to ambitious, well-known Democratic politicians. The office of mayor or city councilman is usually a dead end; only rarely do incumbents rise to state or national office, or even enter partisan politics at all.[32] Given voter expectations, the prestige of the party is not implicated in city elections. Winning such elections is not necessary to the maintenance of the party, either in terms of patronage (which is almost non-existent at the local level) or a reputation for power.

But these are probably incomplete explanations, for not only is there little club activity in local races, there is very little interest expressed in them by club leaders. The absence of *interest* can probably be explained by the fact that nothing of importance to club members appears to be at stake in city politics. There is no machine to reform and there are no issues of ideological significance with which to arouse enthusiasm. A former CDC president said to an interviewer:

> There's very little interest in my organization in city elections. I received only *one* letter urging us to put up a candidate for this mayoralty election—only one letter, and we have thousands of members in southern California, all of whom are notorious letter-writers. . . . The big reason, I suspect, is that there are no issues at stake in city politics. The issues are pretty small potatoes.

[32] This seems to be a general characteristic of non-partisanship. See Charles R. Adrian, "Some General Characteristics of Nonpartisan Elections," *American Political Science Review*, XLVI (September, 1952), 766–76. Some facts on California's experience with non-partisan officials running for partisan offices are given in Eugene C. Lee, *The Politics of Nonpartisanship* (Berkeley and Los Angeles: University of California Press, 1960), pp. 108–10. Of 162 partisan officials in 1960 thirteen had once been mayors and seven councilmen.

The best evidence that it is ideology more than political structure that deters participation by the clubs in city politics is the fact that they have engaged, often with vigor, in races for seats on the Los Angeles Board of Education. These offices are also non-partisan and political dead ends to which no outstanding partisan figures are attracted. But the Board of Education has been, in recent years, seized with ideological questions of precisely the character that arouses club interest. A conservative majority on the board opposed the classroom discussion of certain matters, such as UNESCO, close to liberal and intellectual hearts. After a bitter fight, three liberals won seats and when two of them stood for re-election in 1961, not only most clubs but the club-oriented Los Angeles County Democratic Central Committee endorsed them, voted funds for their campaigns, and did some precinct work. As one club president remarked, "The Board of Education . . . attracts people because it affects women who feel strongly about schools and because we've had an old reactionary group in power. There's a lot of ideology involved in the Board races now."

# 6 The Rewards of the Amateur

The rewards which club politics offers to the amateur are as varied as the members themselves; to generalize about them at all is to oversimplify drastically. At the same time, however, the incentives which club leaders must (or think they must) distribute to the members in order to maintain their interest in the organization are perhaps the single most important constraint on the freedom of action of those leaders. The need to act and speak in certain ways in order to conform to the expectations of the members is a crucial limitation on leadership discretion. Thus, although this account of the rewards of the amateur Democrats may be more plausible than accurate, it is vital to an explanation of their behavior.

Generally speaking, clubs of amateur politicians are examples of "purposive" organizations.[1] Most people belong because of the goals they feel the clubs serve rather than from any hope of material gain or because they enjoy the sociability the clubs provide. This does not mean that the goals need be specific—indeed, in many cases they are scarcely given more than the most general statement. Nor does it imply that the members never derive fun, companionship, prestige, power, or even material gain from politics. What it does mean is that the amateur, unlike the professional, must feel that any rewards other than the satisfaction of serving a good cause and idealized principles are and must be secondary or derivative; mainly, one participates in politics because one ought to.

[1] Peter B. Clark and James Q. Wilson, "Incentive Systems: A Theory of Organizations," *Administrative Science Quarterly*, VI (September, 1961), 129–166. The present analysis relies heavily on this conceptual framework and is, in many respects, a case study exemplifying the theory presented there.

Although many clubs in various cities offer their members reduced air fares to Europe on charter flights, a full schedule of social events, forums featuring prestigious speakers, and the opportunity to play the political game, and although some members join simply to find a mate quickly or get to Paris inexpensively, if the clubs should cease to define themselves as organizations devoted to liberalism or reformism or similar worthy causes, they could not for long sustain the interest of any but the handful who simply enjoy the company of others or like being district leader.

Many members joined initially in response to the lure of a powerful national personality, such as Adlai E. Stevenson or John F. Kennedy, others in reaction against the unspecified evils of bossism and machine rule. Questionnaires returned by club members in New York and Los Angeles indicate the range of these initial motives. In New York, the most frequent answer to the question, "why did you join your club?" was a statement which related to the creed of reform. Such statements as "better politics," "good government," "increased democracy," "reform," "clean and honest government," "anti-Tammany," "rid New York of bosses," and "get rid of Tammany domination" occurred repeatedly. Far fewer mentioned any substantive goal, such as cheaper housing, improved race relations, better schools, or urban renewal. In Los Angeles, there were, in contrast, practically no references to reform in the questionnaires, but many references to the duty to participate in politics, the need for better candidates, the desire to make the party "stand for something," and the hope of forwarding the liberal cause.

The number of personal motives of the amateurs is, of course, infinite. Many volunteers are rootless, transient newcomers searching the city for a means of associating with like-minded people. Others are individuals with a deep sense of moral indignation at the corrupt and self-serving basis of city politics. They are liberals who would like to see the local Democratic party converted into their image of the national party, thereby ending the painful contrast between the national

Democrats (whom they see as liberal, upright, community-regarding statesmen) and the local Democrats (whom they consider materialistic, devious, self-regarding hacks). In between can be found every variety of personal motive.[2] But the clubs are more than a mixture of overeducated neurotics and party reformers, for all these personal motives are refracted through the lens of political involvement. It is with this political involvement that this study is concerned; the ultimate, deeply rooted personal motives will be left to those with a taste for mass psychiatry.

While it is true that several clubs devote a great deal of effort to holding social functions, attracting important speakers, and organizing group excursions to places of scenic or political interest, such clubs are in a minority in all three cities. In any case, only the larger clubs, like the Lexington in New York and the Beverly Hills in Los Angeles, have the resources for such programs. But *no* club fails to devote much of its time to the discussion of candidates and issues, passing resolutions on substantive matters as well as procedural reforms, and debates over policy. Equally important, no club fails to attempt, often to an astonishing extent, to involve the mass of the members in the work of the club; broad participation is always the desideratum and usually the reality of amateur club politics.[3]

Even for those who seem to derive satisfaction only from the social aspects of club life, it is important to remember that they choose to obtain such satisfactions from a *political* organization rather than from a Masonic order, a wine-tasting society, a country club, a Parent-Teachers' Association, or a bowling

[2] Many politicians, both amateur and professional, delight in speculating on the motives of the amateur. Many explanations, some ingenious, are propounded, all lacking in evidence. One Tammany supporter with an unusually abstract turn of mind suggested to me that the New York reform clubs are composed of frustrated, aggressive women who act out their hostility to males by attacking Carmine De Sapio, whom they unconsciously see as a handsome, sinister symbol of masculine virility. I shall try to avoid such unsupportable generalizations, tantalizing as they may be.

[3] "Broad" participation is a relative term, of course. Most clubs are fortunate if they can involve on a continuing basis even 15 per cent of their members. But at club elections, the turnout is much higher.

league. Some of these organizations are, of course, rejected because of class differences between Ivy League lawyers and the typical members of bowling clubs or Masonic orders, but even this choice has political implications. In effect, the person who joins an amateur political club in order to make friends and have fun is giving expression to that part of the Anglo-Saxon–Jewish ethic which says that organizations ought to have serious purposes; one ought to have fun on behalf of a worthwhile cause. A person wants friends who resemble what he would like to be: interesting and amusing, to be sure, but also idealistic and right-thinking.

Those who do join such clubs as the Beverly Hills or the Lexington for social reasons rarely become active members or do much club work. Rather, they are exploited by the active members in order to obtain resources for the club's political activities. The Beverly Hills club holds a regular Sunday afternoon cocktail dance every month at a lavish nightclub on the Sunset Strip, an inaugural ball and a pre-election extravaganza at luxurious hotels, and lawn parties for candidates. Twice a year trips to Palm Springs are organized, and additional trips have been provided to Catalina Island, Las Vegas, and Mexico City. There are frequent theater parties. Large sums of money are raised by these events,[4] but relatively few politically active members or club officers attend. The affairs are designed for the socially-minded inactive members who in this way, and no other, can be induced to provide the sizable budget for the club's political work.

The politically active members heatedly deny and deeply resent the accusation that the primary reward of club politics is social.[5] "The club movement is not basically a social move-

[4] These affairs are almost always a financial success. Package tours are arranged out of which the club takes a fixed percentage rebate from the commercial entrepreneur, usually amounting to $7.50 to $10.00 per person. The hotel parties can produce as much as $1,300 to $1,800, a good trip to Mexico City $1,000, and a Las Vegas excursion $700.

[5] The leading example of this interpretation is Seyom Brown, "Fun Can Be Politics," *Reporter,* November 12, 1959, pp. 27–28. It was challenged in letters to the editor written by Los Angeles club leaders.

ment, except perhaps in Beverly Hills," said a CDC officer. "My social friends are not in the clubs. I don't go to the homes of the people I know in the clubs and they don't come to mine." Leaders of such large and affluent clubs as the Beverly Hills (which has over 720 members) concede that social opportunities and parties are the primary inducement for a great many, perhaps most, members. But club leaders can be quite deliberate about this. An officer of the Schiller Banks club in Chicago, located on the Gold Coast, observed: "Knowing the snobbery of the building . . . we tried to have meetings in penthouses. We got the kind of speakers with prestige. . . . [But] it is very difficult to get people to do precinct work. We had two hundred people to [a penthouse] party. We couldn't get ten to work."

The Beverly Hills club is not typical of all or even many clubs, and even here the activists are a separate group within the club which remains apart from the fun-minded rank and file and which derives its satisfaction from aspects of club life that are unrelated to pure sociability. An officer of the Beverly Hills club described his club as "basically a social vehicle" for the average member, who is young, female, and single. But almost all the officers and activists were married. "Frankly, I prefer married people," he said. "Married people are more interested in politics and less interested in social things."

Indeed, anyone attending the meeting of a typical club would find very little of a social character that seemed attractive. Meetings are long and often dull in the extreme, with a seemingly endless agenda and interminable speakers. There is much discussion from the floor, business is transacted in minute detail, and the routine of parliamentary procedure is constantly rehearsed. Although a handful of clubs can afford prestigious speakers and elaborate social affairs, most simply lack the resources for this sort of thing. It is hard to believe that many people find an average club meeting "fun."

In understanding the rewards of politics for amateurs, the role of the club itself is crucial. If the lure of Stevenson's personality or the force of powerful ideals were alone sufficient to motivate political effort, then the club would not be essential. Individuals, attracted by a candidate or cause in which they believed, could serve as precinct workers directly under the county central committee or under district or block captains appointed by that body. Indeed, such tactics have been tried from time to time by the Los Angeles County Committee, but all have met with failure. A committee official was at pains to reassure an interviewer that they had not overlooked the possibility of what he termed the "Eastern system" of precinct work:

> A lot of Easterners come out here and tell us we've got the system all wrong. What we ought to do is appoint a precinct captain in each precinct and give him the responsibility for getting out the vote, and organize the county in that way. But we've tried it. We're not closed to such ideas. We're interested in all alternatives to what we're doing now. But . . . they don't work. You can't get people to take responsibility for a precinct and . . . work in it.

The club is the vital intervening link between the formal party and the volunteer workers. Without it, precinct work is ineffective and whatever organization is created does not endure. With it, enthusiasm can be aroused and effort sustained. The same county committee official observed that

> the basic organization of the County Committee depends on the club movement. . . . We have to have group support or consensus [for the members]. . . . You've got to realize, it's not just ideals that gets people into politics. If it were only ideals, then the precinct system would work. If it were ideals simply, then you could persuade people to work alone in their precinct . . . in order to realize their ideals. But you can't persuade them to do this. You can only persuade them to work through a club. The club atmosphere, the "groupness," is vitally important.

So convinced was he of this that he had become fascinated by the theory of group dynamics in an effort better to understand the clubs' role. The reason for the importance of the club is probably related to the character of the incentives it can distribute to members. If the County Committee had a large stock of patronage jobs, the clubs would be unnecessary except for the convenience of decentralizing precinct operations and giving district or ward leaders a means of exercising control over their subordinates. Workers would perform their tasks for tangible incentives, such as jobs, because such rewards would be received regardless of the outcome of the election so long as the worker himself performed creditably—e.g., by turning out a given number of Democratic voters. But if the rewards are intangible (the lure of personality or ideals), they are not substantially lessened if all workers do not perform ably (i.e., if the election is lost and the candidate defeated). And if the candidate wins, even the worker who does little derives considerable satisfaction.

In brief, the crucial distinction between tangible and intangible rewards in this connection is that the former are divisible in a way the latter are not. The distinction corresponds closely to Chester Barnard's distinction between "specific" and "general" inducements.[6] The former can be offered to one person and withheld from all others; the latter cannot. Since specific or divisible incentives can be given to or withheld from individuals, a measure of control attaches to their use, such that *individual* performance can be rewarded or punished regardless of what others may do. A general or indivisible incentive lacks this element of control—its existence may depend on the efforts of many, but not on the efforts of any single individual. Everyone gets it or no one. Therefore, no person has any compelling reason to work hard for it. If he knows his candidate may win or lose regardless of what he does, he need not work at all.

Thus, the clubs intervene between the ultimate rewards (ideals, candidate personality, the national party) and individual effort by supplying a kind of inducement which these ultimate rewards, in themselves, cannot provide. The club creates a set of proximate inducements to supplement and reinforce the ultimate ones. Both are essential; neither will suffice alone. These proximate rewards derive from the act of associating to-

[6] Chester I. Barnard, *The Functions of the Executive* (Cambridge: Harvard University Press, 1938), pp. 142 ff.

gether, and include the opportunities for office, power, and prestige in the club; the sense of approval from one's fellow members; and the opportunities for sociability which are in part dependent on club work and contributions of money or effort. None of these is as divisible (and hence as subject to control) as a tangible payoff, but all are more divisible than purely ideal benefactions.

The *initial* reason for joining the club is probably replaced, in most cases, by a *secondary* or supplementary motivation that produces a sustained contribution of effort. An early club organizer noted that "after the first blush of enthusiasm for Stevenson had worn off, it became evident that these people were going to stay in politics for somewhat different reasons." A leading CDC officer echoed these feelings: "The volunteer gets into this organization because he's interested in its ideals or because he's ambitious. But once this has passed—and these things always do pass—then he tends to become involved for other reasons."

These secondary motivations seem to derive from the attractions of playing the political game and shaping the course of party affairs on behalf of a liberal cause. Liberalism or reformism is the ultimate incentive (if the game were not liberal and intellectual, it would not be fun) and the game is the proximate or operative inducement. "The volunteer type soon acquires the habits of the professional without acquiring his means of livelihood," observed a former CDC president. "He tends to become involved in the campaign for the sake of winning . . . and playing the game." Playing the game includes winning club and CDC office and acquiring the prestige of political standing as well as participating in the making of club and party decisions. The fun, of course, is proportional to the intrinsic value of the game. When John F. Kennedy became the Democratic presidential nominee in 1960 despite intense pro-Stevenson feeling on the part of most club leaders in Los Angeles and New York, enthusiasm for campaign work quickly dimmed and there were muttered threats of "sitting on our hands." By and large, this did not materialize, for Kennedy, particularly in his television debates with Richard Nixon, soon began to impress many club members and, in any case, the prospect of sitting by while Nixon won was unsupportable. But many leaders, particularly at higher party levels, were eager to participate on the "inside" of the campaign regardless of who the nominee was. For a variety of reasons, including the appeal of Kennedy, the dislike of Nixon, and the irresistible lure of the game, the predicted revolt against Kennedy by the Stevenson-oriented clubs never really developed beyond scattered instances.

The importance of the lure of political activity is underscored by the failure of the DFI in Chicago. An amateur club must have something to do; it cannot be simply a debating society. Almost without exception, ex-DFI leaders blamed the organization's failure on "too much talk, not enough action." Said one leader, "We went down there [to the DFI convention] in 1958 and spent three days passing a constitution. This was fine. The next year we spent three days debating amendments." That was not enough in the absence of electoral successes. "I have been around a lot of ADA [Americans for Democratic Action] chapters but the thing that impresses me about the IVI is that we don't sit around and talk about Indonesia but we do real precinct work." These were the remarks of leaders. How the rank and file felt cannot be accurately assessed, but there was probably a good deal more enthusiasm for "talk." At a DFI convention, the hall was packed to hear Mrs. Roosevelt and Senator Gore; when they finished, so many delegates left that there was no longer a quorum for the transaction of vital organization business concerning the budget, staff, and rules.

The distinction between leader and member, and hence between initial and secondary motives, means that a good deal of what transpires publicly at club meetings or conventions is ritual. The talk on the floor of the meeting is heavily charged with slogans, references to goals and ideals, and allusions to club heroes. In the corridors and hotel rooms, however, the private conversation is almost indistinguishable (except in syntax) from that of professional politicians. The subjects are candidates, nominations, power-plays, and party gossip. But if the floor speeches are ritual, they are not meaningless ritual. The amateur politicians require a rhetoric when they are together in large numbers in public that they do not require when they are alone or in small groups.

A leader in the Riverside Democrats in New York felt that "the principal motivation for many of these people [i.e., active members and leaders] is the sheer fascination of politics. It's certainly not civic dedication. That wears thin in short order."[7] An officer of the VID shared this view:

> I think a big attraction for most people in the club is the fun of politics. I think the people who are attracted because of their interest in some goal or purpose are in the minority. The social functions are a very big part of our club, and of course, a big source of money. Many people are attracted to the club just because they're lonely and want human contact.

This fun may be nothing more than the opportunity to let off steam. "All day long," said one member of the FDR-Woodrow Wilson Club, "I can't shout back at the boss, I can't shout back at the wife, I can't shout back at the kids. But I come here in the evenings and I shout at these people, and I go away feeling like a new man."

Almost all amateur clubs endeavor to diversify their incentives such that there will be some reward in political activity for almost anybody who chooses to join. The range of club work is staggering. The Lexington Democratic Club, for example, had in 1960 thirty standing committees with a total of sixty-one chairmen and vice-chairmen. The purposes of these committees ranged from finance and campaigning to art, charter flights abroad, community affairs, and newspaper publication. (In fact, two members admitted that they had joined the club solely in order to take advantage of the cheap air travel

---

[7] The fun of the game attracts people into other kinds of organizations as well. Frank H. Knight asserts that it is important in the understanding of businesses. *Ethics and Competition* (New York: Harper & Bros., 1935), pp. 60–61.

rates provided by the charter flights committee.) Other clubs, although not so large as the Lexington, had proportionally sizable committee structures.

In addition, the club also provides for the discussion of issues and topics in current affairs. The reform clubs vary considerably in the resources they devote to such forums, and this is an important distinction among them. The Lexington Club on the East Side, the oldest, largest, and wealthiest of the reform clubs, devotes by far the most to forums; clubs on the West Side and in lower Manhattan devote significantly less energy to such matters.

When Lexington Club members were asked what club activity they liked most, more answers referred to forums and the discussion of large issues than to any other activity. The club contributes amply to such interests. Scarcely a month passes in which a prominent speaker is not heard at the club. In two years (January, 1958, through January, 1960) there were twenty-eight such events, featuring such persons as Professor Arthur M. Schlesinger, Jr., Mrs. Eleanor Roosevelt, William Zeckendorf, Jr., Senator Albert Gore, Senator Harrison Williams, Thomas K. Finletter, Dr. Edward Teller, and others. The topics were almost evenly divided between local and national or international matters, and between the concern for reformism and the concern for liberalism.

Most professional politicians freely admit that their clubs sponsor no "forums" and are genuinely puzzled about why the reformers should consider this a failing. Who needs forums? One Tammany club, however, prodded by an egghead who had defected from reform and joined the regulars, did hold, in 1960 and 1961, three forum series. Put off by titles such as "The Constitutional and Legislative Authority for the Prerogatives of Elective Office," "Psychological Factors in Election Campaigns—Prejudices, Neuroses, etc.," and "American Politics as Portrayed in Modern American Literature," the regular party workers were at first suspicious and reluctant to attend but were relieved to discover that, by and large, the "forum" participants quickly turned to the familiar gossip about politics which is the staple fare of clubhouse evenings.[8]

*Community Service*

The opportunity for community service is another important club activity which can generate incentives for members, although such activities are largely confined to the New York clubs. The Lexington Club has been in existence longer, and thus has a greater list of such activities, but in any given year other reform clubs could duplicate the number of projects undertaken. Allowing for a certain degree of exaggeration in describing the extent to which reformers were the key agents in these activities, the list is nonetheless impressive: stimulating building inspections north of Ninety-seventh Street; publishing a booklet for tenants explaining rent control and eviction laws; initiating the organization of a group which secured a neighborhood conservation project for Ninety-seventh and Ninety-eighth streets; advising tenants on relocation; sponsoring an adult organization to provide services for problem children in Public School 612; lobbying to continue the free performance of Shakespeare in Central Park; administering over 1,000 polio shots in 1958; conducting public forums on local and national issues; arranging for a bookmobile to provide library services; pressing for re-opening of the Ninety-seventh Street public library; passing resolutions supporting laws to end racial discrimination; and backing a 500-million-dollar school construction bond issue.[9] Another reform club, the Riverside Democrats, engaged in similar activities, including organizing a picket line to demonstrate sympathy for southern

[8] The club was the James J. Farley Association (James J. Farley, district leader). The forums, organized by a writer, Mary Bancroft, were a reply to the Lexington Club. Neither reformers nor regulars could believe that such a thing was taking place in a Tammany club. A Tammany club on the lower East Side once held, to the astonishment of its members, a forum discussion of the Dead Sea Scrolls.

[9] From Lexington Democratic Club, "Community Affairs Fact Sheet," March, 1960 (mimeograph).

Negro student "sit-ins," conducting a housing inspection, and organizing a neighborhood conservation project on West 103d Street.

Most reform club leaders tend to exaggerate the difference between reformers and regulars in this respect. Although the scuttle of coal and the free Christmas turkey are no longer very valuable resources for a Tammany organization, some of them have adapted quite well to the changing needs of their constituents. Tammany clubs provided free polio shots sooner than many reformers. On the lower East Side, Tammany clubs have been operating free "housing clinics" for years, advising tenants on rent-control laws, eviction notices, and the availability of public housing as well as defending them in court against landlord suits. Regular clubs have "law committees" which provide legal aid to constituents (indeed, this may now be the main service which political clubs perform). In the spring, assistance is frequently provided voters in filling out tax returns. Although regular clubs have not been as conspicuous in the field of checking on housing and building code violations as have some reformers (after all, landlords and building inspectors often have close ties to regular clubs), they have done more than the lop-sided publicity of the reformers would imply. One regular leader was quoted as complaining that he has handled hundreds of housing complaints over the years, but "every time Bill Ryan [a CDV-backed congressman] finds a hole in the wall somewhere they take a flash bulb of it and send it to the papers."[10] The *New York Post* has always crusaded against slum conditions, and the reformers have from the first enjoyed better access to its pages than the regulars.

But there remain important differences between at least the style, if not the substance, of community service as practiced

[10] Meg Greenfield, "Tammany in Search of a Boss," *Reporter*, April 13, 1961, p. 30. Tammany leaders themselves distinguish between "oldline" clubs where an aging leadership has failed to adapt to new conditions and those clubs with younger, more aggressive leadership which have entered into "community service" activities. Tammany seems to have been, in 1961, about equally divided between the two kinds, with the Jewish and Italian leaders among the more aggressive and the older Irish leaders among the less adaptive.

by a reform amateur and a Tammany professional. First, many of the amateur club functions are likely to be run by persons who have little time to give to what they regard as minor problems. A reform lawyer, who is rapidly rising in a lucrative Wall Street practice, has not the endless hours which constituent service would require. His temptation is to send such people to the Legal Aid Society attached to the local law school. A Tammany lawyer, dependent on political contacts for much of his business and hoping for a judgeship in time, can often be induced to give more time to "clubhouse law."

Second, the amateur clubs like to provide community services for the middle-class intelligentsia as well as for the lower-class voter. Thus, the West Side Democratic Club sponsored an annual month-long art exhibit in its clubhouse, the Tilden Club sponsored a tour (at three dollars a person) of the apartments of three important New York art collectors, and the New Democratic Club gave an amateur performance of Handel's "Messiah" with the district leader conducting.[11] By contrast, although at least one professional politician who is a New York club leader is an amateur violinist of note and a graduate of the Juilliard School of Music with a brother who was an important official of the New York City Center (devoted to music, drama, and ballet), the leader never let this intrude in clubhouse affairs on the grounds that "politics and culture don't mix."[12] Culture doesn't mix, in part because—to the professional—it is irrelevant to politics and in part because most voters would not feel comfortable in an organization which catered to such tastes.

Third, community services, while necessary in both reform and regular clubs, are even more important to the former than to the latter. The reformers cannot offer the voters patronage nor can they intercede in their behalf at city hall. In fact, with the advent of civil service and the reforms already instituted in city government, not even Tammany captains can offer much in the way of patronage, fixed traffic tickets, soft police

[11] *New York Times*, October 16, 1959, and January 31, 1960.
[12] *Ibid.*, October 16, 1959.

administration, or other city hall favors to their voters. District leaders who supported De Sapio were the first to admit that the days when they could perform political services for their constituents were almost over, much to their regret. They, too, had to turn in some measure to other kinds of voter appeals. But although the need for such services has been felt by political clubs of all kinds, for the reform clubs the need has been compelling. Many Tammany clubs and Chicago ward organizations can draw on a resource denied to the reformers —a reservoir of personal loyalties which have been developed between voters and election district captains. Many Tammany and Chicago captains have been active in politics for twenty to fifty years[13] and can (at least in those neighborhoods which have not undergone rapid sociological change) call upon old friendships as a means of mobilizing votes. The young reformers find it more difficult to develop such personal loyalties. Being young, they are sometimes not taken seriously by older residents; at the very least, they cannot appeal to any long-standing friendships. Given the high turnover of captains, relatively few election districts are staffed by the same person for more than two or three years—too short a time in which to develop any personal loyalties.[14] In such a situation, the community activities of the club serve an important function. The reformers deliberately seek to build a pattern of voter loyalties to the *club,* rather than to the captain or the district leader. The club is institutionalized in the district through the services it performs and the ideals it seeks to embody. Said one reform leader:

> We have a big turnover of election district captains. That's our biggest problem. . . . The average person only lasts one or two years in the job. We really rely on the club to build the contacts with the voters as a whole, rather than the individual election district captains. . . . The big thing you have to understand is that the club is the center of political life, not the individual captain. We try to bring

[13] Five captains in just one Tammany club had lived in and worked the same election districts for over forty years.

[14] For data on turnover among captains, see below, chapter viii.

the whole community into or around the club. We know we can't build up that pattern of personal loyalties between the voter and the captain which in the poorer districts Tammany has been able to do in the past.

Fourth, the community-service system provides an outlet for the energies of the active club members and a means to engage the interest of the inactive members. The excitement of the political campaign is brief and exhausting; it occurs only at intervals of six months or a year; and it does not always satisfy the desires of members to give expression to their ideals or frustrations. Committee work related to some immediate goal, such as housing inspections, can provide an outlet for energies throughout the year. The positions created by multiplying committee chairmanships (a Manhattan reform club, depending on its size, will have anywhere from thirty to nearly one hundred offices) are an effective means of distributing status to a large number of members. When few, if any, members receive material rewards from reform politics, the distribution of prestige and the opportunity to work toward goals is of crucial importance in maintaining the club.

In these respects and others, the Los Angeles clubs are at a disadvantage. California clubs are more difficult to maintain than their New York counterparts. Being smaller and more numerous, they lack the resources with which to provide forums, social affairs, and publicity campaigns.[15] Being extra-legal and unofficial, there is less at stake politically in their control and fewer incentives for being leader or president. There are no "district leaders" in California politics. There is no cause, such as reform, which can provide a single obvious and dramatic appeal for the members. Further, the ecology of Los Angeles makes any community service program difficult or impossible.

Whereas Manhattan is a heterogeneous cross-section of all income, ethnic, and religious groups living in close proximity, Los Angeles, with its lower population densities, consists of a vast collection of relatively homogeneous local communities.

[15] In 1961, the average size of a Los Angeles CDC club was 77 members; the average size of a Manhattan reform club, regular and insurgent, was over 530.

Since the most active clubs are found in middle- and upper-middle-class areas, and inasmuch as these areas are often located as far as ten or twenty miles from the nearest low-income Negro or Mexican slum, the possibilities of involving club members in community work on behalf of less fortunate people are rather slim. A very active club leader and organizer spoke wistfully of this situation to an interviewer:

> We have no real community service activity in these Democratic clubs at all. We've talked about it a lot, but what is there to do? I suppose if there were tenements to be inspected or people to help get on relief, or something like that, we could turn our clubs into community service agencies. But we've never been able to think of anything, although it's often discussed.

The Beverly Hills Democratic Club, situated in one of the wealthiest communities in the United States (although a majority of the club's members are not wealthy and do not live in Beverly Hills), has a committee on community problems, but it is difficult to find problems in a community as amply endowed as Beverly Hills. Although the Beverly Hills club is quite similar, in size, membership characteristics, and vigor to the Lexington Democratic Club in Manhattan, it has no Irish or Puerto Rican tenement areas in which it can arrange a neighborhood conservation project, conduct building inspections, or advise tenants on relocation. At most it can suggest the need for a new library. The incentive system of the Los Angeles clubs is victimized by the affluence and dispersion of the city.

*Intraparty Democracy*

The rewards of amateur Democratic politics are brought to a focus in the demand for mass participation and its procedural corollary, intraparty democracy. The amateur Democrat believes that people ought to participate in politics, that clubs ought to have a broad base, and that the making of proper decisions and the endorsement of qualified candidates will be best assured by making party leaders responsible to the party members. If one considered only New York, where these views are part of the demand for reform, it would be easy to dismiss the belief in intraparty democracy as merely a convenient slogan to justify taking power away from the old-line Tammany leaders and giving it to "reform" leaders who would then revert to the old methods of centralizing power. Indeed, this is just what the Tammany regulars believe the reformers are trying to do. But when one considers the experience of the CDC clubs in California, it quickly becomes evident that intraparty democracy is not merely a tactically expedient slogan, it is an inherent feature of amateur politics and represents a fundamental break with the professional style.

Mass participation and intraparty democracy are crucial to the nature of amateur politics for both theoretical and practical reasons. Theoretically, the amateur argues that the only way to guarantee that the ends of government will provide the motivation for political action is to hold party leaders responsible to the disinterested party membership, thereby making certain that they act on behalf of certain ends because they share them and not merely because the exigencies of the two-party contest make it expedient. Further, since public policy ideally ought to be set deliberately and rationally, by intent rather than as the unintended consequence of partisan or interest-group competition, and on the basis of the merits of the issues rather than as a result of "deals" arranged among economic, ethnic, or regional interests, then the citizenry ought to be consulted directly. Since "direct democracy" would be unwieldy—all citizens cannot be consulted—then the best-informed, most articulate, least selfish, and most highly motivated ought to be consulted: in short, the amateurs ought to be consulted. A man's right to press his views in a political organization, therefore, ought not to depend on his power or position in that organization, but on his ability and knowledge. Hierarchy and ex officio authority, the foundation stones of the professional political organization, must be destroyed or severely limited.[16]

Practically, intraparty democracy is a crucial incentive for stimulating amateur—i.e., volunteer—efforts. Almost all active club members speak of the importance to them of sharing in party decisions, particularly the selection of candidates and the shaping of issues. "The opportunity to make pre-primary endorsements is the big source of enthusiasm for the club movement," said a CDC officer. "Once you feel you've had a hand in naming the candidate, you can work for the party with a good deal of enthusiasm." A club organizer was convinced that no club could be successful that was not brought fully into the decision-making process in the party. "The big thing that keeps them active is the feeling of participation they get, shaping the Democratic party and in selecting the candidates of the party. . . . It is my firm conviction that you can't get people to work on a volunteer basis unless they feel they've had a part in making the decisions which lead to that work.[17]

The difficulty experienced in persuading the 1954 CDC convention to accept with any enthusiasm Sam Yorty as its senatorial candidate in preference to Professor Odegard, the "club type," illustrates this condition. The CDC rejected Yorty with exuberance in 1956, delighted to be able to refuse a party professional, and exhilarated by their endorsement of Richard Richards, who, although he was also the choice of many party

[16] This, of course, is close to what I earlier (chapter i) referred to as Populism. Not all amateurs go this far, and hence not all are Populists. Many retain the elitist notions of the Progressives. Indeed, the unresolved tension between the two theories of government is a steady source of concern to the more reflective amateurs; this may be one reason why none has evolved any systematic philosophy of government. Accommodating the needs of power to the desire for democracy is not simple.

[17] This estimate of the nature of membership motivation is probably accurate, but it is also useful to the leaders of the CDC. The focal point of their continual struggle to maintain and enhance their own positions in the party as a whole has been the right to determine party nominees. If it can be shown that mass participation, by volunteers, in that process is essential to retaining the services of those volunteers (who are the party's only grass-roots workers), then CDC leaders can claim a greater share in the selection of candidates and enlarge the stature and powers of their organization.

regulars, was "the overwhelming popular choice, a hero of the movement cast in the mold of the 'club type.' "[18] In 1958, however, the leading senatorial candidate was not a club type, but a party regular, Congressman Clair Engle. No real alternative to him appeared, but there was grumbling reported among the convention delegates in having to accept him. The opposition was not personal so much as it was "an attempt of club members to let the party leaders know they would like to have more of a voice in the selection of the party's candidates."[19] The convention disliked what some delegates called "rubber stampism."

The requirements of providing organizational inducements thus lead to the same concern for intraparty democracy and broad participation in decisions in Los Angeles as indicated in Manhattan. In the latter case the rationale is reformism; in Los Angeles, where reformism is not a burning issue, the justification is phrased in terms of the utility of intraparty democracy and the requirements of the theory of group dynamics. The results are similar: the proliferation of offices, the decentralization of decisions, the devolution of power, the elimination of secrecy, and the multiplication of the number and size of delegations to higher party levels.

Not all amateur clubs insist as rigorously as CDC and CDV clubs on internal democracy and the right to participate in the selection of candidates. Although studies of the volunteer membership of the Wisconsin Democratic party show that it is in many ways comparable to New York and California clubs, there is as well an important difference.[20] There the Demo-

[18] Francis Carney, *The Rise of the Democratic Clubs in California* (New York: Henry Holt & Co., 1958), p. 15.

[19] *Los Angeles Times,* January 12, 1958. At the same time, many CDC leaders were proud of the "responsibility" and "practicality" the convention showed in endorsing Engle, an experienced politician of moderately liberal views, over Professor Odegard, an amateur who was popular with many rank-and-file members.

[20] See Leon D. Epstein, *Politics in Wisconsin* (Madison: University of Wisconsin Press, 1958), and "Party Activism in Wisconsin," *Midwest Journal of Political Science,* I (November, 1957), 291–312; Frank J. Sorauf, "Extra-Legal Political Parties in Wisconsin," *American Political*

cratic clubs not only do not endorse candidates in primaries, but the constitution of the Democratic organization specifically prohibits such endorsing, and this provision is strongly supported by club activists who have resisted attempts to rescind the rule.[21] Thus, the claim of New York and California club leaders that participation in candidate selection is a vital inducement for club members is not invariably true. Where, as in Wisconsin, there is a long tradition of "open primaries" and a vivid memory of an older machine era, anything that resembles party control over nominations is attacked as undemocratic.

Furthermore, some amateur political organizations are willing to place a much lower value on intraclub democracy than are typical club leaders in New York and California. In Chicago, the IVI is continually criticized by the DFI on the grounds that it is "undemocratic." Although this is not entirely true, many IVI leaders are quite prepared to admit that their organization is more centralized than the typical amateur club. They defend this centralization on the grounds that it increases the efficiency of the organization and permits part-time volunteers to work directly on electoral campaigns with a minimum of organizational waste motion. An IVI leader scoffed at what he termed the DFI's "collegiate mentality" which involved it in endless caucuses and constitution-making. If there is some truth in this distinction between the IVI and other amateur clubs, how can it be explained? Why should the IVI alone require less intraclub democracy?

Several answers are possible. First, the IVI is, unlike all other club movements, an *independent* organization, not part of the Democratic party. Thus, since it does not seek to play a part in the party in the same way as the CDV or CDC clubs, it does not feel required to provide a "model" of democratic club procedure.

*Science Review,* XLVIII (September, 1954), 692–704, and "The Voluntary Committee System in Wisconsin" (Ph.D. thesis, Department of Political Science, University of Wisconsin, 1953).

[21] Epstein, *Politics in Wisconsin,* pp. 92–96.

Second, being an independent organization, its attraction for its members derives from the role it endeavors to play *between* the two parties as a local "balance of power." The IVI is in some ways the Chicago equivalent of the Liberal party in New York, and the Liberal party has never been internally democratic. Both the IVI and the Liberals seek to influence the choice of Democratic candidates by threatening not to support poor ones in the general election. In contrast, the typical amateur clubs—such as the DFI, the CDC, and the CDV—being *Democratic* (not independent) clubs, cannot threaten to support Republicans in the general election. Their influence must be wielded within the party; this requires an insistence on democratic procedures. The IVI can induce members to participate because they can influence the election of officials without having to play a role in their nomination; other amateur clubs can *only* wield that influence by participating in the nomination process.

The difference between the attractions of most amateur clubs and the attractions of the IVI can, perhaps, be inferred from a comparison of reasons given by members for joining most amateur clubs (noted earlier in this chapter) with this statement of a leading IVI activist:

> I don't suppose it occurred to me in a million years that I would vote for a Republican. But there was a bad slum fire, and in the course of the investigation it became clear that it had occurred because a building inspector had been bribed. I remember brooding over this and thinking, how many people have to die because I can't bear to pull the Republican lever, or so Stevenson can get some votes?

For such a person, the opportunity the IVI presented for striking out at the machine directly by supporting the Republican opposition made it unnecessary for it to offer an inducement based on the chance to participate in the selection of Democratic candidates.

This matter of intraparty democracy raises an important intellectual question. Liberal amateurs seem to be more demanding about the forms of politics (such as internal democracy) than are the conservative amateurs, but it is not immediately obvious why this should be so. Both the Conservative and Labour parties in Great Britain have constituency associations in which the active leadership is largely in the hands of the militants. But whereas the Labour associations are well known for their insistence on intraparty democracy, the Conservative ones allow their parliamentary leaders to run the party unhindered. Labourites must be given the appearance (although rarely the substance) of intraparty democracy, while the Conservatives seem content with appeals to an elitist tradition.[22] Similarly in California, the CDC leadership argues that internal democracy and an avoidance of conventional party practices is essential; the California Republican Assembly, on the other hand, has never stressed such matters.[23] A similar difference is found between the Democratic and Republican extra-legal parties in Wisconsin.[24] Thus, it is not only voluntarism but liberalism as well that shapes the character of the club movement.

Several explanations are possible. One concerns the goals of the movement. For the liberal amateur, equality is of crucial importance. Indeed, equality—both in the treatment one receives before the law and in one's right to certain minimal welfare services—is close to the center of the liberal creed. Equality in general implies equality in power and in the opportunity to make one's wishes felt. Procedural equality (i.e., democracy) is thus felt to be good because equality generally is good, but also because it is thought to be a necessary condition for achieving equality as a substantive outcome of political decisions. For example, if everyone votes (procedural equality), income is more likely to be redistributed (substantive equality). The extreme conservative amateur, on the other hand, is likely to feel that procedural equality is a defect in our system of government. The measures he opposes—

[22] Leon D. Epstein, "British Mass Parties in Comparison with American Parties," *Political Science Quarterly*, LXXI (March, 1956), 97–125.

[23] On the California Republican Assembly, see Hugh A. Bone "New Party Associations in the West," *American Political Science Review*, XLV (December, 1951), 1115–25.

[24] Sorauf, "The Voluntary Committee System in Wisconsin."

redistribution of income, the regulation of business, and vast welfare expenditures—are seen to be the direct result of dema-goguery. Universal suffrage, he believes, has meant that poli-ticians responsive to the will of the masses have been kept in office as a reward for taking from the rich and giving to the poor. Thus, the extreme conservative asserts that the United States is a "republic," not a "democracy." It would be surpris-ing if these contrasting attitudes toward democratic political institutions did not affect the internal organization of amateur political clubs.

But this explanation, while perhaps useful in accounting for the behavior of extreme conservatives, does not explain the behavior of other conservatives. The California Republican Assembly, for example, is completely unlike the John Birch Society in attitudes and organization, but it has no mass base similar to the CDC's nor does it show any real concern for the democratic character of its internal procedure; it is a leader-ship-oriented organization.

Conservative amateurs are perhaps not caught by the ten-sion between Populism and Progressivism that afflicts so many amateur Democrats. They are more ready to accept an elitist view of government, deriving, perhaps from their experience in business, as contrasted to the liberal's experience in the pro-fessions. The professions are characterized by a kind of com-mercial egalitarianism in which *expertise* is regarded as the determinant of success and reputation. A businessman, on the other hand, is part of a hierarchical organization in which suc-cess depends on attaining unambiguous substantive goals (maximizing profits in the simple case) and in which the rep-utation of the executive is hard to separate from the success of the enterprise. Thus, a lawyer may conduct a defense that, in the eyes of other lawyers and judges, is brilliant, only to see his client go to jail for twenty years; a surgeon may operate with extraordinary skill, only to see his patient die. A business-man who loses money is in a different position. His record is easier to judge, and his judges are harsh.

The conservative political club differs from the liberal in the same way and for perhaps the same reason that a business-men's civic association differs from a local branch of the NAACP. A business-oriented civic organization rarely has "members"; instead, it has "contributors."[25] It exists to raise money to employ staff and other experts and to pay for essential services such as public relations agencies. Supporters of the organization have little *personal* involvement. Contests for offices are rare. The chief resource the conservative brings to civic—or to political—action is economic: money, corporate power, and the personal contacts flowing from business position. The liberal, lacking money, brings numbers and personal contributions of time and effort. The conservative organization, to the extent that it is successful in mobilizing money and prestige, incapacitates itself for direct political action insofar as the people it recruits are successful in business or their careers; personal success leaves them little time for or interest in personal participation. The contributors are at a point where political action can offer little in status or recognition—indeed, such action is more likely to be considered harmful.[26] This lack of personal involvement may produce an indifference to organizational forms and procedures and an emphasis on organizational goals. To say the same thing another way, whatever incentives a conservative club can offer will derive from its stated goals; direct participation itself is not an important reward to the member, and internal democracy is therefore not of crucial significance to him.

*Conflicts among Amateurs*

Amateur clubs everywhere reflect differences in constituencies, size, affluence, and relations with professional politicians. In all three areas, there are clubs which are filled with intel-

[25] See the discussion of this point in Clark and Wilson, *op. cit.*, and in Peter B. Clark, "The Chicago Big Businessman as a Civic Leader" (Ph.D. thesis, Department of Political Science, University of Chicago, 1959).

[26] The "business in politics" movement typically involves the junior executives and white collar workers in political campaigning.

lectual, middle-class Jewish lawyers with a seemingly insatiable appetite for controversy, internal politicking, and extreme positions. There are also clubs with older, wealthier members with vague but strongly held convictions, who are more willing to compromise and more disposed to defer to a handful of active leaders. There are even clubs with Negro or Puerto Rican members whose major interests are often at considerable variance with the main thrust of reform or liberalism.

The variety of club life can be more easily seen in Los Angeles than in Manhattan, because in the former city there are both more members and more clubs. The large number of small clubs without any prescribed geographical jurisdiction means that each club tends to acquire a certain character, perhaps imparted by a circle of like-minded friends who were its founders, and that character serves to attract further members who are responsive to it and who, in turn, strengthen and institutionalize it. The Mary Bethune, Walter White, and Thurgood Marshall clubs are almost entirely Negro; the Baldwin Hills and Cheviot Hills clubs are largely Jewish; the Beverly Hills club is widely known for its social character; the Harry S. Truman and San Pedro clubs are working class and close to labor unions; the Hancock Park and FDR-Pasadena clubs are upper-middle class; the Pacific Palisades and the Claremont clubs are filled with practicing intellectuals; the Long Beach Women's Study Club is filled with middle-aged and elderly ladies who enjoy teas and corsages; and the Mid-City club is a mixture of many kinds of people, Negro and white.

In New York, in addition to differences in constituency and membership, there is the vital difference created by the legal structure of the party. Manhattan clubs are partly "regular reform" and partly "insurgent reform." Electing a district leader converts a club from an organization seeking power to one attempting to conserve power, and this change in status profoundly affects the needs and tactics of the club.

First, an insurgent club must seek out contests; a regular reform club is often more interested in avoiding contests. The elected leaders become more concerned with using power than with attaining it, with getting re-elected rather than elected. Getting elected always means defeating a Tammany incumbent; getting re-elected could mean—at least until 1961, when the skirmishing between De Sapio and the reformers became total war—negotiating a settlement with Tammany so that a primary fight is avoided and one need defeat (if running for public rather than party office) only the Republican. To regular reform clubs, war is more costly than peace, for a primary contest wastes resources and jeopardizes offices already won. For an insurgent club, however, peace is more costly than war; lacking any office, the club can maintain membership interest only by continuing the battle. Although defeat may lead to frustration, inaction leads to disinterest. Contests justify the existence of the organization, hold out the promise of power, and provide a means of resolving or deferring potentially divisive internal problems.

When one West Side club was being formed, a leader gave a candid account of its sudden decision to challenge the Tammany club for the district leadership: "An organization gets formed and then casts about for a purpose. We decided to have a leadership fight in order to hold the organization together, to give it a sense of purpose and some momentum." Another West Side leader agreed: "The only thing you can give the workers in reform politics is an object for their enthusiasm."

A CDV officer, responsible for running an organization whose ruling General Committee consisted in 1961 of forty representatives from regular clubs but forty-six from insurgent groups, felt this difference in status very keenly. By and large, insurgent clubs favored a primary fight against Mayor Wagner in 1961; regular clubs, with certain important exceptions, were more willing to endorse the Mayor and avoid a fight. The CDV official said:

> The regular clubs fight less. The insurgent clubs, on the other hand, are eager to fight. The more primaries they can contest, the better they like it. In fact, insurgent clubs

seek out primary fights in order to build the reform movement. The regular clubs, on the other hand, have won their
primaries. They're now the established leadership. A primary for them is costly. . . . The regular clubs tend to
avoid primaries if they can. These differences are what
you might call built-in instincts. They're fundamental differences. There's no way of getting around it.

Second, once the primary contest is over, a regular reform
club, as the official agency of the Democratic party in the district, has an obligation to support the Democratic ticket, even
if its primary candidates did not get on it. But the enthusiasm
of club members for political work is directly proportional to
the perceived virtues of the candidates, and therefore the reform clubs are often required to find a compromise solution to
the problem of satisfying membership demands that only good
candidates be supported and party demands that all candidates be supported[27] Sometimes such compromises are not
possible. Although the reformers were backing Wagner in the
1961 mayoralty election, many clubs simply could not induce
their members to work for him. A VID leader complained that
he "couldn't get anybody to work for the Mayor because they
thought he'd sold us out." A Lexington club leader lamented
that since their control of the district leadership was not challenged in 1961 by Tammany, it proved very difficult to motivate club workers. "They'll campaign for our own candidates,
but they usually aren't very interested in the mayor."

A related problem arises out of the fact that *insurgent* reform clubs have no obligation at all to support Democratic

[27] The Lexington Club, for example, stipulates in its constitution that
all nominated Democratic candidates are deemed to have the club's
endorsement unless two-thirds of the club members present at a meeting
vote otherwise. Similar rules are found in other reform constitutions. In
most cases, the clubs back the regular ticket in the general election, at
least formally. Remaining consistent in reform politics is often very difficult indeed. In 1961, the Lexington Club argued that it had to step
outside the regular Democratic party to support Wagner for mayor
because the character of the candidate was more important than loyalty
to the party label. In the same year, however, it supported a Democrat
in opposition to the Republican city councilman, Stanley Isaacs, even
though Isaacs was acknowledged on all sides to be the very embodiment
of liberalism.

candidates of whom they disapprove. Thus, whereas a regular reform club was often willing to work in a common front with Tammany clubs in the general election against the common Republican foe, many insurgent reform clubs have seen such an alliance as a threat to their autonomy and an instance of capitulating to the intraparty enemy. This was the case in 1960 when great efforts were made to form an all-faction organization to work for the election of John F. Kennedy as president, and, at a lower level, for Democratic candidates for the state senate, state assembly, and Congress.[28]

General-election organizations require at least the semblance of unity. Regardless of one's true feelings, it is usually considered only proper that one say nothing derogatory about one's colleagues, at least while the campaign is on. For regular reform clubs, this rule of the political game is usually not hard to observe. Democratic candidates from both Tammany and reform clubs will receive, at least formally, equal support. But for an insurgent reform club, this rule is difficult to observe. Saying uncomplimentary things about Tammany and Tammany candidates is precisely the way in which the club keeps alive anti-Tammany feelings for the next primary fight in which, hopefully, the Tammany leader will be replaced by the

[28] See *New York Times,* July 7, 22, 25, 27, 28, 29, 30 and August 2 and 22, 1960. One of the problems facing the insurgent clubs was getting access to the polls. For this, poll-watchers' slips were required. These can only be issued by a regular party organization or a candidate. Tammany and regular reform clubs obtain them as a matter of course. Insurgent clubs, however, are not "regular" and do not constitute a separate party; they are therefore not entitled to such credentials. In those districts in which the insurgents operate, the Tammany clubs which control the district leadership receive the slips. The importance of this factor extends beyond simply watching the polls on election day to check against irregularities. The real reason for concern over this is that, by being present in the polls, party workers can discover who votes. With this knowledge, they are better prepared to conduct voter registration drives and solicit favorable votes in the election districts. This, in turn, enables them to build their strength for the crucial primaries the following year in which the insurgent club will dispute the leadership with its Tammany opponent. Getting poll-watchers' slips is therefore a form of recognition for the clubs, a means of providing club workers with the status accruing from official credentials, and a source of strength in registration and primary campaigns.

insurgent leader. Thus, insurgent clubs will often go to considerable lengths to dissociate themselves from the Tammany portion of the Democratic ticket in order that none of their workers or supporters will think that the insurgents have "sold out" or gone over to the enemy. Further, the insurgent clubs will make strong demands that the Democratic candidates for office explicitly renounce Tammany support in the general election. This was the case with reform Democratic candidates for congressman and state senator in 1960.[29] The state senatorial candidate, much to the disgust of some middle-of-the-road reform clubs, did state that he was not soliciting the help of De Sapio and his cohorts. Indeed, he worked with insurgent clubs in Tammany districts and, as a result, may have been "cut" by those Tammany leaders in the general election. The congressional candidate, on the other hand, was less venturesome, apparently feeling that—against a strong Republican opponent in a traditionally Republican area (Manhattan's East Side)—he needed all the help he could get. As a result, he was criticized, publicly and privately, for accepting the aid of Tammany when he "ought" to have relied solely on the reform movement and its ideals.[30]

A third problem which arises out of the reform-insurgent schizophrenia of the movement concerns the relations between reformers and regular Tammany leaders. After the successes of the reformers in the June, 1960, primaries, some Tammany district leaders felt that the tide was running so strongly in favor of their opponents that an alliance was worth considering. These leaders came to regard De Sapio as a liability, and were

[29] William Vanden Heuvel, candidate for Congress in the Seventeenth Congressional District, and John Westergaard, candidate for the state senate from the Twentieth Senatorial District. Both candidates were defeated in the November general election. In 1961, Vanden Heuvel supported Levitt, the regular organization candidate for Mayor, whereas Westergaard supported Wagner.

[30] The New Chelsea Club, an insurgent group in the Third Assembly District South, arranged a "truce" with the regular organization for the duration of the fall, 1960, campaign. The VID and the Stevensonian Democratic Club, however, refused such truces. Cf. *New York Times*, August 22, 1960.

fearful that should they remain too closely identified with him, an insurgent club in their own district would be able to unseat them by branding them "De Sapio's Choice." In return for some assurances about their own position, such leaders might have been willing to support reform efforts to oust De Sapio and revise the party rules. This possibility created a real dilemma for reform clubs, however. To enter into such an alliance, or to even give the appearance of negotiating with such men, would have been regarded by the insurgent clubs in the districts concerned as betrayal. They would, in effect, have felt they had been "sold out" by their reform allies. The insurgent clubs, in their own interest, had to insist on an unremitting struggle against all Tammany leaders regardless of the opportunities for alliances which were thereby foregone. To do otherwise would have been to vote themselves out of existence. Some reform leaders were interested, by temperament and opportunity, in exploring the possibility of alliances with defecting Tammany leaders. But they were keenly aware of the constraints membership in the reform movement places on them:

> This is a tough one. We're afraid to cut the ground out from under the insurgent clubs in those areas, but at the same time we'd like to be able to deal with the regular leaders. . . . People feel very strongly about this. I invited [two Tammany leaders from the West Side] to meet me in my office, but I found out I couldn't keep the appointment. . . . The other reform leaders put up a scream. They get very emotional about the idea of my meeting these guys in my office, so I have to meet them in a cocktail bar. Nobody trusts the other guy to deal with the enemy.

The most militant reform clubs opposed such deals; their sympathies were entirely with the insurgents:

> If we took these men [the Tammany leaders] who have insurgent clubs in their own districts, we would cut the morale of the reform movement very badly. People would throw up their hands and say, what's the use of trying to be a reformer, if your fellow reformers are going to sell you out?

A leader in the then-insurgent Village Independent Democrats in Manhattan explained why that club had rejected all offers of a joint slate with the "moderate" clubs and De Sapio:

> The VID wanted to get De Sapio, and it wanted to do it with candidates purely of our own choosing. Reform was a strong issue. We felt we could not allow any fuzzing of that issue. The attraction of reform would be diluted for many people in our area, we felt, if there were any compromises with the enemy. . . . I feel we cannot allow this kind of confusion to affect our voters. We've got to make the issue crystal clear. It is black or white, reform or De Sapio. . . . I see reform politics as a life-or-death war with the regular organization. Any half-way measures are no good. . . . There can be no compromise and we cannot be unprincipled.

But to some regular reformers, supporting such an insurgent club was equally vexatious. In one West Side district, the insurgent organization was considered weak and unpromising, while the Tammany leader was felt to be ripe for an alliance. Although they might well have preferred the experienced Tammany leader to the incompetent insurgent leader, there was little the reformers could do to achieve this end. There were virtually no means for exercising control over insurgent clubs, even though the CDV provided them with large sums of money. To have denied these funds to one insurgent club would have been opposed by all other insurgent clubs, since they were anxious to prevent the CDV from establishing any precedent which implied that it could or should decide what constitutes a "good" insurgent club. "We can't save the old-line leaders from the attacks of the insurgent clubs even if we wanted to," concluded one moderate reform leader.

With the defeat, in 1961, of De Sapio and almost all the other vulnerable Tammany leaders, all but two insurgent reform clubs gained regular status. For the Manhattan reformers, therefore, 1961 ended their painful dilemma of how to bargain with the enemy without alienating one's colleagues. But the problem remains in the other four boroughs of New York City, where reform is still entirely in an insurgent status.

Indeed, the problem will in all probability become more acute, for now with reformers the dominant force in Tammany Hall, relations between Tammany (i.e., Manhattan) Democratic leaders and the leaders of the party in the rest of the city will be profoundly complicated by the pressure on the Manhattan reformers to give some encouragement to insurgent reformers in, say, the Bronx who are busily engaged in trying to unseat the same Bronx leader with whom the Manhattan leaders must deal. This halfway house of partial victory may, in the long run, prove to be the greatest problem an amateur club movement must face. Amateur politicians have shown great resilience in rebounding from total defeat; they would relish total victory. But partial victory presents deep problems arising out of the need to deal simultaneously with both professional politicians and their amateur opponents; the conflict this will generate could split almost any reform movement asunder. Stated more formally, the incentives necessary to gratify reformers who have won regular status are so different from those necessary to sustain reformers who are still in an insurgent status that it is questionable whether one organization can provide sufficient amounts of both.

There are other sources of cleavage which, although they do not arise out of the political status of the clubs, are also important. In Manhattan, one such conspicuous difference is the general contrast between the "East Side" and "West Side" reform clubs. The Lexington, Yorkville, Murray Hill Citizens and New Democratic clubs, all on the East Side, are generally regarded by West Side clubs, such as the Riverside and the FDR-Woodrow Wilson, as less militantly "reform," more willing to bargain, and less opposed to the use of patronage. No simple explanation can be given for this widely recognized difference in attitude, but one may perhaps be found in the differences in constituency and membership. Most East Side clubs, like the Lexington, Murray Hill, and New Democratic, are found in high-income areas which are normally strongly Republican; West Side clubs, on the other hand, are found in middle-income, heavily Democratic areas. The West Side has a high concentration of Jewish voters and is a stronghold of the Liberal party. The differences in character of the members and voters of the two parts of Manhattan may account for some of the differences between clubs, but this study can offer no evidence on that score. One *political* difference, however, is probably of considerable significance. Because of the voting patterns, the stakes of politics are higher on the West than the East Side. The significantly higher level of internecine warfare on the West Side may be due simply to the fact that the winner of a Democratic primary there is almost assured of victory in the general election. Thus, primaries for public office attract more candidates on the East than the West Side.[31] Since the stakes are higher, the struggle is more intense and the clubs become highly combative. Further, with real prospects for realizing personal ambitions, reform candidates on the West Side are more exposed to charges by their fellow reformers of being self-seeking or materialistic; thus, it is the West Side clubs which, by and large, have placed the strongest restrictions on the acceptance of patronage. Club leaders are required to renounce such rewards when they accept office. Paradoxically, therefore, it is precisely in the areas where the rewards of political participation may be the highest that the greatest constraints are enforced by reform clubs against the acceptance of such rewards; where the tangible rewards are the lowest, as on the East Side, there are the fewest such constraints. Because victory is easier, West Side leaders need constantly to reassure their followers that they have not lost their "amateur standing"; this stance carries over, inevitably, into their relations with other reform clubs and leads to some of the charges that East Side clubs are not sufficiently militant.

Further, since the primary election is hotly contested on the

[31] For the City Council races in 1961, there were ten reform candidates seeking pre-primary endorsement on the West Side but only one on the East Side. For the congressional and State Senate races in 1960, there were three or four candidates for each post on the West Side but only one on the East Side. The reform candidates on the West Side who won the primary all went on to win the general election; none of the East Side candidates were challenged in the primary, but all lost in the general election to the Republicans.

West Side, there was a greater tendency for each reform club and candidate to attempt to outbid the other in the extent of his opposition to professional politicians generally and Carmine De Sapio in particular. The "image of bossism" which De Sapio provided in 1960 and 1961 was of great value to West Side reform clubs in defeating regular Tammany organizations (see chapter xi); after the regular clubs had been vanquished, however, the slogan persisted in the contests among reformers for the Democratic nomination. Each candidate sought to prove himself more anti-De Sapio than the next. On the East

TABLE 2

CLUB MILITANCY AS RELATED TO REFORM AND DEMOCRATIC
VOTING STRENGTH IN MANHATTAN'S
FIRST ASSEMBLY DISTRICT

| Parts of District | Wagner Vote in Club Endorsement* (Per Cent) | Democratic 1960 Presidential Vote (Per Cent) | Reform 1959 District Leader Vote (Per Cent) |
|---|---|---|---|
| South (Village Independent Democrats)............. | 65.6 | 59.3 | 46.7 |
| Middle (Tilden Democratic Club)................. | 95.1 | 58.1 | 54.5 |
| North (Murray Hill Citizens) | 100.0 | 42.6 | 63.9 |

* Endorsement vote as reported in *Village Voice*, July 27, 1961.

Side, where the problem for the regular reform clubs was not to win the nomination but to defeat the Republicans, the value of an anti-De Sapio slogan was considerably less; indeed, by calling attention to the deficiencies of the Democratic party in a strongly Republican area, it might actually increase the Republican vote.

Some fragmentary evidence for this interpretation of reform club militancy can be inferred from Table 2. The July, 1961, endorsement vote in each of the three reform clubs in the First Assembly District was taken as a crude measure of "militancy": the greater the opposition to the endorsement of Mayor Wagner as the reform candidate in the Democratic primary, the greater the militancy of the club. The table suggests that militancy decreases as the district becomes more Republican and as the position of the reform district leader becomes more secure. The more Republican the area (as determined by the 1960 presidential vote), the greater the vote for the reform district leader candidate in the 1959 Democratic primary and the greater the support for Mayor Wagner in the club endorsements.

Thus, the incentives which an amateur political club can use to maintain the enthusiasm of its members are not constant. They vary with the electoral prospects of the club and particularly with the extent to which a club is competitive with others in the same area. Competition contributes to militancy as clubs endeavor to distinguish themselves from other, similar clubs and as they seek to maintain enthusiasm while out of power in their district.

# 7 Patronage

The amateur politician's attitude toward patronage is ambiguous—not so much because he openly rejects while secretly coveting the chief reward of the professional, but because the very meaning of patronage is itself ambiguous. Every amateur politician—by definition—rejects outright low-paid governmental jobs which require that little or no time be spent on the ostensible duties of the office but much time on partisan work. These jobs—the "no-show" jobs—are what all the New York reformers would like to see abolished and what the California liberals are happy to find largely absent in their state. On the other hand, almost any amateur would be flattered to be offered the post of Ambassador to France, Secretary of State, or Director of the Budget. In between the low-paying, no-show job with the Department of Public Works and a prestigious cabinet office, there are a large number of posts which are hard to define as being either "patronage" or "non-patronage."

The reason for this is, of course, that patronage is a word which has come to have pejorative connotations. Broadly speaking, patronage refers to any benefit with some material value which a government official can award at his discretion: a job, a contract, a charter, or a franchise, or even "inside information" which the recipient can use to his advantage in private dealings. The amateur believes that the merit system and open competition should be extended to insure, insofar as is feasible, that general principles rather than private advantage govern the awarding of such benefits.

But there remain a number of appointive jobs where considerations of merit do not limit the number of satisfactory candidates to some small number or where the offices are involved in policy-making and the abstract question of "merit" becomes implicated in the controversial ends which an administration seeks to attain. It is in this area where the ambiguity about patronage prevails. To the amateur, patronage generally is bad—but which jobs are "patronage" in the bad sense of the word?

This question is most relevant in New York, where jobs are available to reformers if they want them.[1] In Illinois and California, the matter is least relevant. In the former case, patronage is abundant, but the clubs have little hope of influencing its distribution; in Los Angeles, it is practically non-existent.

When the Democratic party in Illinois controls all three levels of government (as it did in 1961), the material rewards of politics are substantial indeed. DFI and IVI leaders almost universally ascribe their defeats to the existence of the "patronage army" at the command of the regulars. Indeed, some of them exaggerate considerably the size of this army (one estimate of fifty thousand job-holders in the county was absurdly high) and the value of its remuneration (most of the jobs pay very poorly by anybody's standards). In fact, the DFI and IVI make little headway in many areas of the city for reasons which have nothing to do with patronage, as we shall see when (in chapter ix) we consider the relations between amateur politicians and the lower classes. But because no amateur club has ever won control of a ward committeeman's post, and since the ward committeeman is the principal dispenser of patronage, no amateur club *in Chicago* has had to come to grips with the question of what to do about any jobs it might inherit from the regular organization.

[1] Leo Egan in *New York Times,* August 13, 1961, p. 6E, writes, "There are nearly 500 well-paying jobs exempt from Civil Service requirements subject to the Mayor's control. In addition there are several hundred highly sought places in the lower courts that are filled by appointment of the Mayor as terms expire." In addition, the other elective officials, particularly the borough presidents and judges, control several hundred more jobs.

Outside Chicago, however, where some DFI clubs have met with local successes, attitudes toward patronage are often modified by its availability. The Evanston club, which won control of the regular organization, does not need patronage for the middle-class amateurs, but is anguished over whether it is necessary for the lower-class Negroes in Evanston's Fifth Ward. The Evanston township committeeman, who is a club member, is willing to accept jobs from Mayor Daley (who is party chairman for Cook County, in which Evanston is located). The downstate labor-oriented clubs in Rockford and St. Clair County are vitally interested in political appointments. Club members in Wheaton and South Lake County have from time to time been concerned over whether a militant action would jeopardize jobs already held or in prospect.

The IVI in Chicago is generally more hostile to patronage than the DFI; the reason seems to be that the IVI's independent role not only has eliminated any possibility of its ever being offered a job by the machine, but also has recruited into the IVI persons who were prepared, and even eager, to renounce political jobs as a reward of participation. Indeed, the tenor of many statements by IVI members is distinctly more moralistic on this subject than that of DFI leaders. One IVI activist observed that he "would like to see political organizations so clean and above-board that people will volunteer their services. . . . They [should be] moved by idealism." By contrast, a DFI leader stated that he "had no hostility toward patronage" because an elective official cannot be an "effective leader unless he 'recognizes' people." Another said that, "there is nothing wrong with patronage if you are getting qualified people who will work." If suddenly there was no more patronage, "who would work the precincts? There are not enough volunteers in [Chicago's] Fifth Ward, and almost none outside." The DFI, of course, never took a formal position on this issue because this question, like so many others, was bound up with the delicate problem of its relations with the regulars. But there is no doubt that many leaders accepted appointments after 1960.[2]

California, on the other hand, is well known for the extent to which the merit system and an alert civil service organization have reduced the number of discretionary appointments to a handful. Governor Brown, before being elected to that office, estimated that there were no more than six hundred jobs to which he could make appointments.[3] Los Angeles has far fewer jobs (the mayor only appoints a dozen or so persons at his own discretion), and what few exist are controlled by a non-partisan administration with no real ties to any party organization. Patronage which provides an income to the holder may be lacking, but honorific patronage is not. In 1959, Governor Brown made at least 346 discretionary appointments to persons in Los Angeles County alone, the majority of which carried no salary (except, in some cases, per diem payment for actual services).[4] Honorific patronage, while it is of little value in sustaining an organization designed to mobilize lower-income voters, is of considerable value in attracting contributions of time and money from middle-class Democrats for whom prestige may be as valuable as additional income. Thus, "clean," honorific patronage in California predisposes politics toward middle-class activity; the value of such appointments to their respectable recipients is not suspect because they are not made by a party boss in the same manner as, and in conjunction with, appointments of precinct workers to paid posts as street sweepers.

Those state jobs of moderate pay, such as posts in the

[2] At least three DFI leaders were appointed by Democratic Governor Otto Kerner to posts in his administration, and others sought appointments. At the same time, two persons prominent in the IVI in its early, pre-independent days, are now regular-organization aldermen. A state representative elected by the IVI remains close to it, but he has also managed to make his peace with the regulars.

[3] See footnote, p. 101.

[4] Count made from list of appointments provided by Governor's office. Of the 346 appointments, 34, or about 10 per cent, were to judgeships which, of course, are paid positions.

Disaster Control Office or with legislative committees, have gone largely to supporters of professional party leaders. The CDC has received few, if any, judgeships from the governor, and only a few inheritance tax appraiserships from the state controller.[5]

In appointing appraisers, State Controller Cranston adopted a rule that a CDC (or regular party) worker accepting an appraisership must resign from any *important* CDC or party post he held. An exception was Bernard Selber, who was allowed to remain as vice-president for Los Angeles County. Recipients who resigned high CDC offices to take appraiserships nevertheless remained active in the club movement and the CDC. What is important is that CDC has not, thus far, provided many real opportunities for tangible rewards to its leaders, despite the fact that few ideological objections are raised by club members to patronage as practiced in California.

The absence of a preoccupation with reformism has made the California clubs less concerned about the presumed evils of patronage. Not having to fight a machine supported with patronage, they are less worried about the theoretical proprieties of political appointments. Not much is available (although more than most people seem to think), patronage is not obviously the basis of the strength of the CDC's opponents, and relatively few CDC leaders have benefited from it (although some club members are fearful lest the regular party

[5] The controller, former CDC President Alan Cranston, gave appraiser appointments to Bernard Selber, CDC vice-president for Region II (Los Angeles County); Roy F. Greenaway, former CDC vice-president from Fresno; Alan Parker, a CDC committee chairman and later CDC treasurer; Joe Katz, former CDC vice-president from Region I (San Bernardino); and William W. Thomson, former CDC director in the Twenty-eighth Congressional District (Orange County). Tax appraiserships went to a few other CDC personnel, but the above list includes most of the important appointments. An appraisership can be lucrative, as the holder is paid on a fee basis according to the size of the estate. There were 145 such posts in the state as of January 30, 1961. Cranston was criticized for not giving more such posts to CDC leaders and at the same time for using these jobs as a way of taking certain people out of CDC politics.

induce CDC leaders to "sell out" by "dangling attractive offers" in front of them). The CDC itself decided to remain out of the formal patronage allocation process, which means that, since CDC never has had the power to affect the distribution of many jobs, it would not make recommendations to party leaders regarding deserving candidates. Until that time (1956), CDC had on occasion placed job requests with party leaders. The prevailing attitude seems to be one expressed by a club president: "We don't have much discussion about patronage in the club. . . . It's not a live issue. After all, California is the cleanest state in the union."[6]

## Patronage and Reform

In New York, there is enough patronage to covet but too little to live on. For example, the James J. Farley Democratic Association, until 1961 the regular club in the Eighth Assembly District North, was responsible for fifty-three election districts with nearly twenty thousand registered Democrats. Although there were fifty-three district captains, only four had political jobs.[7] It is rare for any regular Tammany club to have as many as twenty jobs, no matter how big it may be. Further, most of the unpaid captains have no prospects for jobs and know it. On the other hand, the regular district leader almost always has a job, and the "clubhouse lawyers" who serve as captains and give time on club nights to providing free legal advice to voters often have hopes of either court patronage

---

[6] Almost everyone, no matter how liberal or intellectual, accepts the belief that California is genuinely "clean" politically. The "inside dopesters" gossip mainly in terms of personalities and alliance rather than in terms of "deals" and graft. Eastern visitors often find this hard to believe. A leading Pennsylvania politician flatly refused to believe Governor Brown when the latter told him, in a private conversation at a party fund-raising dinner, that no blocs of tickets had been sold to highway contractors, but the Governor was right.

[7] There were two secretaries to Supreme Court justices, one clerk to a judge, and one part-time secretary to a congressman. The jobs paid very poorly (two to four thousand dollars a year).

(getting special guardianships, for example) or getting an appointment to the bench.[8]

Since several reform clubs have won the party leadership in their district, they have been faced with a concrete decision on the question of patronage. Most of the jobs which New York politics can provide are poorly-paid, low-status positions which would not interest a reformer in any case. And as the battle between Tammany and the reformers grew more intense, De Sapio refused to allot jobs to those clubs which were challenging him. Nonetheless, there were a small number of men and women who acquired appointive offices.[9] Accepting these jobs exposed them to considerable criticism from the more militant reformers, although in each case, the jobs were accepted with the approval of the reform club concerned. Certain reform clubs, notably those on the East Side, permit pa-

[8] The district leader, Farley, was deputy commissioner of public works in the Manhattan Borough president's office. The Farley club had twenty-three lawyers on its "law committee." In twelve years, two lawyers nominally identified with the club had obtained judicial appointments. In 1952, 77 per cent of the Democratic district leaders in New York City (80 per cent in Manhattan) had government positions at the federal, state, county, or city level. Of the 28 Manhattan Democratic leaders with jobs, 16 were employed in the court system (as law clerks, etc.). Wallace Sayre and Herbert Kaufman, *Governing New York City* (New York: Russell Sage Foundation, 1960), pp. 463, 534, 541, from New York State Crime (Proskauer) Commission, *Hearings*, Vol. VI, No. 4 (1952), pp. 53–54.

[9] In 1960, some of the most important jobs held by reformers were:

| Club | Post | Held By |
|---|---|---|
| Lexington Democratic Club..... | Law Clerk, Court of General Sessions | Club officer |
| | Law Clerk, Supreme Court (Appellate Division) | Executive Committee member |
| | Executive Assistant to Commissioner of Marine and Aviation | Executive Committee member |
| Yorkville Democratic Club..... | Confidential Aide to Board of Justices, Supreme Court | District Leader |
| Tilden Democratic Club........ | Public Relations Assistant to Commissioner of Commerce and Public Events | District Leader (female) |
| West Side Democratic Club..... | Law Clerk, Supreme Court* | District Leader* |
| | Mediator, City Department of Labor | District Leader (female) |

* Leonard N. Cohen, District Leader in the Fifth Assembly District Middle, held a post controlled by County Leader De Sapio until he broke with De Sapio after the June, 1960, primary. He then resigned.

tronage to be accepted under proper conditions and with the understanding that the jobholder will do a day's work for a day's pay. Indeed, at least one club has a Committee on Appointments to pass on applicants for such jobs.

The West Side Democratic Club, which captured the district leadership in 1951 but did not join the reform movement until 1960 (after it had supported an incumbent congressman who lost in the primary to a reform candidate), had received a substantial amount of patronage while it was still in good standing with Tammany. In fact, it had delayed breaking with De Sapio in part because this patronage was at stake. A leader of the club explained:

> I believe this was an important issue. We had more to lose in terms of patronage than the whole reform movement put together. We didn't want to be cut off. We had . . . patronage jobs worth about $75,000 a year in salaries. Of the 24 election district captains we have, perhaps 10 or 11 had jobs. . . . But although [certain other reform leaders have] had jobs . . . [they have] never had anything substantial. We did have something substantial.

For a variety of reasons, many of these jobs did not imply a political obligation to Tammany Hall. Some, such as those in city departments, were under the purview of the mayor, and the break in 1961 between Mayor Wagner and County Leader De Sapio meant that ranking city jobholders were not in jeopardy as a result of their reform activity. In the case of two law clerks, the justices involved were both liberals (they were, in fact, members of the Lexington Club) who were secure in their posts and independent in their attitude toward the party leader. The aide to the Board of Justices was responsible to the entire panel, rather than to one justice, and thus could not easily be dismissed by the action of a single man.

The few well-paying posts held by reformers have often been won in spite of, rather than because of, the desires of the county leader. Two reformers were hired as law clerks after all the De Sapio applicants for the posts had been rejected by the justices involved. Practically no jobs for the rank and file have been made available to reform clubs. Indeed, many jobholders are active in various districts in opposition to the reform club, even though it has won the leadership and would normally be entitled to all patronage assigned to the district. These jobholders were retained by Tammany as the nucleus of the anti-reform forces in the districts.

Some regular political workers joined the new reform clubs when the Tammany organization in the district had been defeated. In at least one case, the reform club came into existence when the election district captains in the regular club decided to bolt and follow a new leader. Many of those captains held jobs which they obtained through the old organization. The reaction of the county leadership to this situation has varied. Older workers who joined the reform club in, for example, the Seventh Assembly District (the Riverside Democrats) did not necessarily lose their jobs. In addition, some of the more moderate reform leaders were able to obtain a few jobs for their followers.

The reformers did not, however, have to face squarely the issue of patronage until after the 1960 election had carried a Democratic President into the White House and the 1961 election had returned a reform-oriented mayor to New York's city hall. This not only made jobs available to reformers, but made them available from what they regarded as "clean hands." This new turn of events tested the resolve of the reform purists that patronage was an intrinsic evil and ought to be rejected by all reform leaders. Less came of the federal than of the city victory. Washington jobs did not, except in a few cases, become immediately available. Some reformers went to Washington, but these were almost all appointments made on a personal basis, without any organized political clearance.[10] A leader in a militant West Side club known for

[10] Thomas K. Finletter became ambassador to NATO; Anthony Akers, ambassador to New Zealand; Harold Linden, president of the Export-Import Bank; Angier Biddle Duke, chief of protocol in the State Department; and Marietta Tree, member of the U.S. delegation to the United Nations Human Rights Commission. All these appointees were from

its criticism of patronage sought to obtain an important appointment in Washington ("That's not patronage; that's an opportunity to serve your country and to help put across the President's program.") but failed when it became evident that the Kennedy administration was, in effect, "freezing" most of the New York federal patronage until the unstable situation in the city had been resolved.

The Wagner victory, on the other hand, offered substantial opportunities to the reformers. Most of the Mayor's appointees before 1961 had been men "cleared" by the regular organization, and usually by De Sapio personally. During the primary battle between Wagner and the regulars, patronage had proved to be a poor disciplinary measure. Theoretically, the Mayor could have fired all employees under his control who supported the regular organization. With a few exceptions he did not fire anyone, in large part because he feared that such a move would permit his critics to charge that he was acting like a "boss." Similarly, De Sapio did not strip a club such as the West Side Democrats of its jobs even though the club had broken with him and gone over to the side of Wagner and reform. Both sides had, therefore, active enemies on their own payrolls. But after his general election victory in November, Mayor Wagner demanded the resignation of four hundred top appointees so that he could weed out his opponents and, presumably, reward his friends. Wagner was seeking to establish himself as the Democratic leader of New York City; to this end, he alone—without the influence of the county leaders —would appoint to patronage jobs and thus the loyalties of the officeholders would be to him and not to the party.

Even before the Wagner victory, a debate had raged privately among the reform leaders about the propriety of pa-

the Lexington Club, but none were in any way "cleared" through the club. They were almost entirely appointments made on a personal basis. A few reformers from other clubs also received lesser posts. Most of the persons listed above would probably have been appointed even if the reform movement and the Lexington Club had never existed. All, of course, had been Kennedy supporters in the presidential campaign.

tronage; the 1961 successes only brought the issue to a head. As usual when the reform clubs disagreed, the CDV could take no position. "There's a wide variety of views on patronage," said one CDV officer. "It's all a question of individual values. There isn't any group policy."

The division of opinion on this subject tends to parallel the division on the subject of contests and compromises. At one extreme are such clubs as the VID and the FDR-Woodrow Wilson Club, which categorically reject the use of patronage as a means of sustaining a political organization. In the constitution of the VID appears a provision that no officer or member of the executive committee of the club may retain his club position if he accepts a paid patronage job.[11] There is even some sentiment in the organization for requiring ordinary members to choose between a job and membership. A leader of the VID offered several explanations for this position:

> We believe that we must eliminate the control by party officers over appointive positions. The only people who should control appointive positions should be elective officials. . . . I know we are accused of being impractical and naive, and other so-called reform leaders say we don't know what we are doing. But it is a philosophy. . . . And we must have such a philosophy. Patronage is an obvious fraud and it is illegal. It is not right for party officials to take public money to perform party duties.

Even after the VID won the leadership in its district, its officers did not moderate their anti-patronage position. One bitterly observed that the CDV had held a meeting at which "the reform clubs in New York City were fighting over patronage just like old-line clubs."

Patronage at the disposal of party leaders places those who hold the jobs under an obligation to the leaders. Such an obligation prevents a free expression of opinion and thus renders intraparty democracy impossible. This view is coupled with

[11] A provision denying officers and district leaders the right to hold political jobs was adopted by the Riverside Club in July, 1961. Executive Committee members who were not officers were exempt from the restriction.

the assertion that patronage is not really necessary as an inducement for political workers. A leader of the FDR-Woodrow Wilson Club argued that

> people can be active in local politics without any payoffs whatsoever. There ought not to be any patronage. . . . [The Mayor] should appoint men without regard to local political organization at all. . . . I think it's a fallacy that the poorer assembly districts need jobs. In the first place, everyone couldn't be satisfied. You need more people to work in an organization than you can possibly take care of with jobs. . . . [It's wrong] to believe that you need patronage to get people into it—even poor people. Take the Puerto Ricans. The reason they don't participate in politics is not because they don't have jobs, it's because they don't have time, or interest in politics, or they can't pass a literacy test, or they have a fear of signing their names, or they have a fear of embarrassment, or they move around too much and can't fulfill the residence requirements. . . . I think we are on the right side of the patronage issue. I think the purest ideology will prevail.

Other reform leaders, including many of those from the "poorer assembly districts" referred to in the last statement, disagreed heartily. In such clubs as the Yorkville Democrats and the East Harlem club, one of the functions of the organization was precisely to make jobs available for workers.

> You can work on a political campaign without patronage, but you can't run a political machine without patronage. If you eliminate patronage, in my estimation, you break down the two-party system. I think you have to have it. It is a great myth that politicians don't work at their jobs. [The speaker held a post in a New York court.] I'm still out working at the club or in community activities four or five nights a week; the hours are very long and the work is hard. I think it's ridiculous to say that a person isn't entitled to remuneration for this.

Another leader, who does not hold a job himself, nonetheless rejected the idea that lower-income people could be induced to participate in politics without some material reward.

> I need it in my area here. This is a lower-income area. I can't very well ask a person to work for me five nights a

week, when he doesn't get anything for it. These people desperately need a job and if I can get them a job in the County Hospital working 40 hours a week for $3,800 a year, why, I don't think anything's wrong with that. They're not going to get rich off that kind of job, and I certainly wouldn't use it as a club over them.

It is a measure of the extent to which the reform ideology has influenced even these defenders of the patronage system that neither of them (nor, to my knowledge, any other reform leader) justified patronage in the same way regular organization leaders (such as the late Edward Flynn, boss of the Bronx) did—as a means of exercising discipline over workers.[12] Indeed, the last statement quoted above contained an explicit denial of the disciplinary function of patronage. Thus, even though there are defenders of patronage among reformers, they are forced by the rhetoric of reform to rely on weaker arguments (at least publicly). Instead of the issue being whether there *ought* to be patronage (in order to control workers, build a disciplined organization, and insure the carrying-out of party decisions), it is whether patronage is *needed* (to support indigent workers and reward the poor for party services).

If politicians ought to be professionals, rather than amateurs, and if patronage is the best means of remunerating the professional worker, then it becomes an open question whether the political worker who is a patronage recipient should do a "day's work for a day's pay." If professionalism is desirable, it would be contradictory to restrict the rewards of politics so that the jobholder must practice politics only in the evening, during his free time. If patronage is appropriate as an incentive, then its value as an incentive ought not to be vitiated. Such considerations are rarely discussed by the reformers, however.

Between the two extremes are many shades of opinion. Almost all reformers, even those who calmly accept patronage, agree that "no-show" jobs (i.e., jobs for which the employee

[12] Cf. Edward Flynn, *You're the Boss* (New York: Viking, 1947), pp. 224–25.

is not required to perform public duties) should be curtailed or eliminated and that patronage should not be allowed to interfere with the internal democracy of the individual club or to place the district leader under a disadvantageous obligation to the party leader. In any case, most reformers feel that their active club members would not be interested in "menial" jobs; on the other hand, there is no reason to prevent their being court clerks, judicial secretaries, deputy commissioners of important city departments, and the like. This middle body of opinion was epitomized by one West Side leader:

> I think by and large you don't need [patronage]. We have brought lower-income people into our club without it, but I don't think we should abolish it altogether. . . . It seems to me that you can use clean patronage for lesser posts. I don't object to helping our people try to get jobs as temporary clerks and what-not, and I think our club should be prepared to offer candidates for important executive appointments. What I do object to is any arrangement by which the person who gets the job has some string tied to him.

This leader had taken a pledge before winning office that he would not accept any appointive office so long as he was district leader. Not even this pledge had become universal practice, however; some leaders continued to hold jobs, others demanded that all jobs be abolished.[13]

But the district leadership is, for most incumbents who take it seriously, a time-consuming and expensive task. The leader must invest many hours and dollars in his political life. If reformism denies him a patronage appointment, he must provide this investment out of his own resources. Few reform leaders have incomes sufficient to defray political expenses with ease, and few have businesses which can be neglected

[13] Leaders who tolerated or actively sought patronage included Costikyan, Glixon, Midonick, Cohen, and Harrington. Wolfson and Lanigan rejected patronage outright. Ryan and others took a middle ground. By January 1, 1962, five reformers—none of them district leaders—had been appointed to posts in the new Wagner administration. *New York Times*, January 1, 1962, p. 1.

for long. One reform district leader was described by a colleague:

> The district leadership is a full-time job, and if you're going to have time to do this job, you've got to have a patronage position or a private income. But once he gets a patronage job, he gets all sorts of strings on it. This is the big problem now—how to pay district leaders. . . . Ryan [has said] that as long as he's district leader he wouldn't take a patronage position, but he's going broke doing it.

Ryan himself suggested a solution for this problem: pay the district leader.

> If the county leader and the district leader jobs are so demanding, I think we ought to pay them. We ought to pay . . . the district leader with party funds raised through party fund-raising activities—but funds which are not subject to the control of the county leader. . . . The district leader shouldn't be tied to the county leader by that payment.

To the most militant reformer, the proper incentives for political action are principles, convictions, and a concern for neighborhood conditions. This often means that not only do the militants reject patronage and other material incentives, they look with suspicion on any incentives which subordinate the concern for public policy. Thus, militants in New York will criticize the affluent Lexington Club for its social affairs while those in California attack the Beverly Hills Club for its parties and excursions. This criticism, of course, may arise from a deeper resentment owing to the singularly favorable social and economic position of Lexington and Beverly Hills Club members. Many West Side reform leaders, for example, seem eager to find grounds for accusing the Lexington Club leadership of being backsliders, "so-called" reformers, or "third-force" politicians. Unfortunately, the Lexington Club affords surprisingly few grounds for such an accusation. It is as if, to less privileged leaders, wealth and social position necessarily mean compromise and timidity in reform politics, and they are disappointed to find so little evidence of it. Although Lexington Club members have accepted a few particularly choice patronage positions, the leadership was quite willing to work with some energy for the defeat of De Sapio and the support of the reform cause. Indeed, the club and its membership have acted as financial "angels" for less opulent reform clubs all over the city and as principal supporters for the Committee for Democratic Voters. The Beverly Hills Club, likewise, has been a major financial support for the CDC in California.

As a result, critics of the Lexington Club have turned its advantages into signs of decadence and effeteness. It is criticized *because* it has money, *because* it has socially prominent members, *because* it has taken the leadership in the CDV, and *because* it uses forums and other social events as inducements. Said one West Side leader:

> In the Lexington Club, it is true, they believe in the democratic processes and they believe in getting people into office. But most of their activities are concerned with forums—getting big speakers in to talk on weighty subjects, and having Broadway actresses appear. . . . The Lexington Club is fancy and well known. And a lot of people are attracted into it by the lure of rubbing elbows with actresses and big-name speakers. In *our* club, nobody gives a s—— about these well-known people.

Another West Side leader, from another club, echoed these sentiments:

> The Lexington Club . . . is very successful, but it hasn't spread. . . . That's a silk-stocking district over there. It is a heavily Republican area. . . . They are very upper-class people. We were glad to see them successful and hoped their leadership would spread, but it didn't. They haven't won any public offices. . . . They're smothered in cream. Those rich Democrats and rich Republicans have lots of money.[14]

The ideal self-conception of the amateur includes asceticism as well as ideology. If this asceticism, as manifested in certain attitudes toward the Lexington and Beverly Hills clubs is

[14] The wealth of the Lexington Club as an organization can be exaggerated. In its early years, it had an annual budget surplus of perhaps $2,000. At one point its treasury contained $15,000. The amount is less today, perhaps by half.

essential to some activists, it may shed light on attitudes toward patronage. In addition to patronage being undesirable because of the constraints it creates, it is also evil because it destroys the ascetic spirit which ought to lie at the center of political life. Politics should be genuinely selfless in a way in which commerce is not. Perhaps alienation from the business creed and the values of the market place are reflected in the aspirations reformers bring to the practice of politics.

### Lawyers in Amateur Politics

Traditionally, lawyers have found more rewards in politics than any other single group and the backbone of most political organizations, professional as well as amateur, has been young attorneys who see in politics an opportunity relevant to their careers. But while the lawyer in a professional party organization is a common and accepted part of the system (every regular club has a staff of "clubhouse lawyers"), the lawyer in an amateur club is subject to serious constraints. On the one hand, he is regarded as an essential expert who can draft constitutions and bylaws, unravel a lengthy and complex Elections Code, and grasp the finer points of Robert's Rules of Order. At the same time, it is well known that a lawyer can benefit in many ways from politics, and the possibility of an attorney turning an amateur club into a vehicle for his own advancement is a constant concern to the purists in the movement.[15] The lawyer is the club leader most likely to be transformed by success from an amateur to a professional.

Almost all lawyers, at one time or another, probably give

[15] The genuine amateur's distrust of lawyers is expressed in statements to the effect that attorneys "want to run everything," are "out for themselves," and "love to show off their knowledge of Robert's Rules of Order." Interestingly, in Illinois there seem to be fewer lawyers in Democratic clubs which are located in heavily Republican areas and where opportunities for elective office are rare. In Du Page County, for example, the DFI leader was proud of the fact that none of the club presidents were lawyers. "We are very suspicious of lawyers. When lawyers get into politics, they only want to further their political ambitions." The presidents were teachers, scientists, staff workers of voluntary associations, and one retired businessman.

serious thought to the possibility of becoming a judge. For a judicial appointment in almost any state, some record of political participation is an asset if not a prerequisite. But there are other, less obvious rewards as well. In Manhattan, for example, a political benefit attractive to many lawyers is to be placed on the "Surrogates' List" to receive legal business from the county (as special guardians of the estates left to children) with fees which are often substantial.[16] Some moderate reform leaders have actively sought such business for their clubs, but relatively little has been forthcoming. For the young lawyer, reform politics may help his career by giving him some publicity or bringing him into contact with potential sources of law work, but there is little, if any, direct payoff. And the indirect benefits may well be offset by the controversial nature of politics and the distractions political work can create for a young man ambitious to rise in a large, conservative Wall Street firm. One reform district leader said, "I don't think it [reform politics] helps the young lawyers. Most of them work as an election district captain for a little while and then drop out. I don't think they feel this is particularly good for their careers."

The young lawyers who have been most active in amateur politics (as candidates for public office on the reform ticket) are, for the most part, in independent practice, unaffiliated with the larger law firms. An independent practice (even a small one, as in most cases) gives a lawyer greater freedom in managing his time, permits him to take the "little people's cases" which are politically useful in terms of contacts and creating a reputation for public service, does not place him under the constraints found in those big law firms anxious to avoid notoriety and political "contamination," and puts the lawyer in a better position to take advantage of any benefits which might accrue to him from political involvement. Many of these solo practitioners get their start in law by serving as an assistant district attorney (in New York) or an assistant

16 Cf. Sayre and Kaufman, *op. cit.*, pp. 467–68, 530, 541, 544, 549.

corporation counsel (in Chicago). In Chicago such appointments are almost entirely a matter of patronage, and a young lawyer who accepts one has, in effect, committed himself to the regular organization. In contrast, the district attorney's office of New York County (Manhattan) is non-political. The incumbent district attorney in recent years almost always has been nominated by all major parties and thus unopposed for re-election. Since he is free to pick his own staff without organization clearance, young lawyers who begin here are free to enter reform politics when they leave the D.A.'s office to set up their own practice.[17]

In addition to solo practitioners who stand to benefit from politics and who are likely to acquire the habits and aspirations, if not the livelihood, of a professional politician, there are active in the clubs, particularly in Manhattan, lawyers from the big firms, particularly those on Wall Street, for whom politics not only is not a source of material benefits, but perhaps is an actual detriment to their careers. The lawyer who simply serves as an election district captain or club officer and then drifts away from politics is likely to be a younger associate of a large firm. Politics, for him, is a means of attaining certain intangible benefits (arising out of ideology, the fun of the game, a dislike of Tammany, or whatever) for a short while before the necessities of his career in a demanding institution distract him.

One explanation for the militancy of Manhattan reform and for the inability of the regular organization to "buy off" the leaders of the movement may be found in the altered career prospects of the young lawyers who are likely to take an interest in politics. There appears to be under way a change in

[17] A large number of reform leaders have been assistant district attorneys, often as their first job out of law school. These include William Fitts Ryan, Seventh Assembly District leader and then congressman; Manfred Ohrenstein, elected to the state senate; Theodore Weiss, an FDR-Woodrow Wilson Club founder and later elected to the City Council; Thomas J. Sammon, defeated district leader candidate of the Lenox Hill Club in the Eighth Assembly District North; and Richard Kuh, a former president of the VID. The New York County District Attorney's office employs 85 assistant district attorneys, half of them directly out of law school. The D.A. recruits from a wider range of law schools than do the Wall Street firms. See *New York Post*, August 20, 1961.

the legal job market such that the value of the material rewards of politics has declined relative to the value of the intangible rewards. This is most clearly seen in New York.

The center of gravity of the city's legal business is found on Wall Street, in the large, conservative firms that serve the financial world and the headquarters of national and international corporations. These firms offer, in general, the most lucrative and prestigious sources of employment for the young attorney leaving law school. About 1,700 lawyers worked with Wall Street firms (as partners or associates) in 1958, in organizations ranging in size from 46 to 125 attorneys.[18] Young lawyers come to Manhattan to join these firms, and although only perhaps one in six or even one in twelve survive in the firm to become a partner, many usually remain in New York with smaller firms or corporations.

Before the Second World War, entering these firms was difficult and impoverishing. Many applied and few were accepted, and the starting salary was as low as $2100 a year. Only men at the top of their classes at Harvard, Yale, and one or two other big Eastern schools had a chance of joining. No Jews were accepted in most firms. In recent years, the boom in law business has changed this situation drastically. Now, there is a shortage of high-quality legal talent. Instead of young men coming to Manhattan to seek jobs, Wall Street firms send their most distinguished partners on recruiting trips to law schools to compete for promising candidates. In 1956–57, recruiters from 194 law firms and corporations were sent to Harvard, and a comparable number elsewhere.[19] Since 1949, the beginning salaries have risen sharply, from $3600 to about $6500 in 1958.[20] In 1961, $7200 and $7500 were not un-

[18] These data are from Erwin O. Smigel, "The Impact of Recruitment on the Organization of the Large Law Firm," *American Sociological Review*, XXV (February, 1960), 55–66, and Spencer Klaw, "The Wall Street Lawyer," *Fortune*, February, 1958, pp. 140 ff. See also Martin Mayer "The Wall Street Lawyer," *Harper's*, January and February, 1956, pp. 31–37 and 50–56.

[19] Klaw, *op. cit.*, p. 192, and Smigel, *op. cit.*, p. 62.

[20] *Ibid.* A story in the *New York Post*, August 17, 1961, gave the "going rate" as $7,200.

common starting figures, and in ten years, a good associate might expect $15,000 to $30,000. Further, the search for talent widened to include schools outside the Ivy League. The New York city schools, formerly ignored as sources of Wall Street lawyers, are now cultivated, and Midwestern and Southern schools are canvassed as well. Further, and of great importance, Jews are now hired. Once one firm began to hire Jewish attorneys, most other firms felt compelled to follow suit, and although charges are made that Jews are not given equal opportunity in promotions to partnerships, many of the old barriers have clearly collapsed.[21]

As the prospects for bright, young, ambitious lawyers changed on Wall Street, so also did the prospects for young politicians. After World War II, returning veterans who obtained law degrees with government assistance at Columbia and New York University law schools often felt that easy entry into the big, important law firms of Manhattan was closed to them. The alternatives were smaller firms of independent practice, often involving personal injury suits, negligence claims, divorce actions, workmen's compensation, and other "little people's" business. In such a situation, politics offered real rewards. It meant contacts, new business, publicity, and possibly elective or appointive office. Some chose civil service government careers, but the better jobs often depended on political connections. Patronage was not to be despised. If the old-line Tammany clubs were closed to outsiders, then the young lawyers would start their own insurgent clubs, do battle

[21] The American Jewish Congress survey of the 1951 graduating class at Chicago, Columbia, Harvard, and Yale law schools found that 35 per cent of the Jewish respondents reported that they did not apply to certain law firms because of a belief that these firms used discriminatory hiring practices. Commission on Law and Social Action, American Jewish Congress, "A Survey of the Employment Experiences of Law School Graduates of Chicago, Columbia, Harvard, and Yale Universities," mimeographed, New York, 1954. With the growing demand for topflight lawyers, this pattern could not long persist. For example, an estimated 63 per cent of the student contributors to the *Yale Law Journal* in the period 1955–57 were Jewish. See Smigel, *op. cit.*, p. 59. Today, certain Wall Street firms have already promoted some of their Jewish associates to partnerships, *ibid.*, p. 64.

in the district leadership fights and, if victorious, claim the material rewards which at the time appeared valuable. In this period, from 1947 through 1953, many lawyers became involved in what later become the "reform" movement, and many are still active.

The greater prosperity of the law market during the 1950's and into the 1960's has, in effect, changed the value placed on politics by many young attorneys. Many of the brightest, and some who are not so bright, find access to Wall Street fairly easy. A condition of overemployment exists. The value of politics is no longer so much as a source of jobs and connections but as an arena for the expression of grievances, the declaration of ideals, and relief from the tedium and materialism of law work. Indeed, since most Wall Street firms are Republican and conservative, only a few restless associates would take the time to participate in Democratic reform politics at all and practically none would continue that participation to the point that it jeopardized their careers in the firms.[22]

Thus, the new generation of lawers in reform politics includes many who derive intangible, rather than tangible, satisfactions. This probably has had important implications for the reform movement generally. It has injected into it men who have a concern for political issues and the philosophy of reform and who forego personal political objectives in order to realize these goals.

Many of them participate only a short while, and then drop out. Intangible satisfactions, as compared to tangible ones, are quickly exhausted. But while they are in, often holding important posts (some are presidents of their clubs and many are executive committee members), they are a real source of ideology. As such, they set the tone and provide the rhetoric

[22] Reform club leaders who were interviewed included members of Sullivan and Cromwell; Winthrop, Stimson, Putnam and Roberts; Donovan, Liesure, Newton and Irvine; and Mudge, Stern, Baldwin and Todd. One large firm of partners who are liberal Democrats exists: Paul, Weiss, Rifkind, Wharton and Garrison, which is located, symbolically, not on Wall Street but on Madison Avenue. Adlai E. Stevenson is a partner.

for much of the reform movement as a whole. Even the most cynical young lawyer, ambitious for political office and willing to adopt any expedient to attain it, is inevitably impressed with the need to conform to the pattern of reform politics that in many cases is set by those who do not share his ambitions. Reform clubs, as organizations, must be adaptive to the needs of both kinds of participants, and this sometimes creates strains.

To be sure, not all Wall Street lawyers are brooding, issue-oriented dilettantes, and certainly not all independent attorneys are office-seeking professionals. The inescapable ambiguity of the reform movement is that most men partake of both sets of qualities; "sincere" becomes a hopelessly meaningless adjective when motives are so thoroughly mixed and aspirations so generally obscure. But whatever blurring occurs in the average case, there is little doubt of the thrusts imparted to reform politics by each group.

One West Side leader, himself a product of the earlier era and holder of a valuable job, described these changes so perceptively that his remarks merit quoting at length:

> Practically none of the lawyers in the West Side Club are in the big firms. A very few of them are from Yale and Harvard. Most of them are from Columbia, NYU, or New York Law School and most of them are in private practice or with smaller firms. The job market for lawyers now is more attractive than it was ten years ago, and hence a job as a lawyer is often better than an exempt [i.e., a patronage] job with the city. . . .
>
> The West Side Democratic Club was composed of young people who couldn't get anywhere in the regular organization. . . . I think most of the young people in the club at that time felt that they wanted to get something out of politics. . . . The new generation . . . is very rebellious. . . . Politics is a good outlet for their general frustrations and they are fully aware of it. [They] may not really be interested in public positions the way they were ten years ago. They can get a good job on their own, but they're still interested in politics—politics for a different reason: because it is a way of expressing, what? Something, some-

> thing that is eating them. They're young and very ideal-
> istic. . . .
>
> Many of the new reformers are not interested in politics
> as a career or a profession, which it is and which it ought
> to be. To them, politics is just "interesting." It is a con-
> versation piece; it is fashionable. It's interesting to talk
> about international issues. It's a kind of play world, I think.

This may be too unkind, for it implies a lack of sophistication in the ways of politics and a naïveté about tactics and
strategy. As a later chapter will suggest, even the most idealistic reformers are often very shrewd indeed when it comes to
getting out the vote. It is interesting to note that many reformers express some degree of dissatisfaction with their careers. The steady, often routinized exertions in a large law
firm, for example, are felt to be confining, deadening, even
purposeless. One thoughtful reform leader remarked:

> I think I should say that the people in reform are . . . all
> dissatisfied with their professional lives. They can't invest
> the time they do in politics without letting their profes-
> sional life slip, and their professional lives, mine included,
> have slipped. Their professional life doesn't satisfy them
> completely. It's true in my case, as in other cases.

The year 1952 was a turning point in New York politics.
Earlier, anti-Tammany efforts had been *insurgent* movements
(i.e., outsiders seeking to break into politics), not *reform*
movements (outsiders seeking to alter the structure of politics). The West Side Democrats, and before them the Fair
Deal Democrats, were organizations through which young
lawyers sought a place in the sun. In Chicago, the Committee
on Illinois Government (CIG) had a similar purpose. In 1952
and 1956, however, the Stevenson candidacy brought hundreds
of young volunteers into politics and created thereby the raw
material for a political organization which could only be run
with reform, and not simply insurgent, slogans. At the same
time, the prosperity of the Eisenhower years was so altering
the career prospects of young lawyers that many of them
could now afford the luxury of a disinterested role in politics.
Gradually, the post-1952 group became composed of reform-

ers; by 1960, the pressure of reform was such that the West Side Democrats, which had been formed in the pre-1952 era, was compelled to break its ties with De Sapio and become part of the reform movement. In Chicago, many young lawyers saw by 1957 greater opportunities in the DFI than in the CIG; by 1960, some had made their peace with the regular party.

In Los Angeles, the rewards of politics to lawyers had never been linked with control of a party organization, for there was never a party organization to be controlled. Acquiring a judicial nomination or an inheritance tax appraisership was typically a matter of associating one's self with the personal fortunes of an individual candidate; if one chose wisely, the candidate succeeded and one benefited to some degree. The creation of the CDC did not seriously alter this pattern. Although some CDC lawyers benefited from politics,[23] they were a small minority. Many ambitious lawyers continued in the traditional paths, becoming personal campaign managers to candidates and ignoring the CDC structure.

One problem this created was the difficulty experienced in recruiting and motivating able members for the clubs. The ambitious young lawyer is hard to lure into a movement which has no prospect of taking over a pre-existing system of offices, power, and appointments, but which only fills a power vacuum and seeks to influence issues and nominations. A CDC officer said of his colleagues that "few of them have political ambitions" and as a result, to his regret, "there's not much political acumen among them." The president of one of the largest and most successful clubs agreed and lamented the difficulty he had in finding new leaders with ability for his organization. Not only are there few patronage or party posts, but California courts have generally been above influence and judges

[23] In addition to the inheritance tax appraiserships mentioned earlier, an appointment paying $6800 a year on the State Personnel Board went to former CDC President Joseph L. Wyatt, Jr., *after* he had left the CDC presidency. Such a post, although providing a small extra income, could hardly be considered a "plum" for a man who had for four years been, in effect, the head of the only statewide grass-roots party organization.

can dispense few favors to lawyers whom they come to know. And the judiciary, of course, is legally non-partisan.

> Able people don't come into the club as much as we'd like. We need at least five or six people to come into the club every year who really have something on the ball, but sometimes we don't even get that. . . . I suppose if we were fighting Tammany Hall we could get all the young lawyers in the club we wanted. But we don't have a real or obvious cause.

This shortage of opportunities for the simply ambitious is made more severe by the fact, to be discussed later, that clubs are strongest in those areas where the Democratic party's prospects are the poorest, and thus even a nomination for assemblyman or congressman, which is sometimes in the clubs' power to bestow, is often an empty reward, for it offers a chance only to be defeated by the Republican incumbent in the general election.

# 8 Organizational Problems

The amateur spirit, whether expressed in terms of reformism, liberalism, or simply "participation" and "good government," has undeniable advantages for the amateur club leader: it attracts into politics a kind of person who would never enter the politics of patronage and machines or the politics of the "cozy caucus" of big contributors and public relations experts. The moral fervor of the amateur generates considerable enthusiasm among the activists, transmutes politics into a "cause," and brings together people of similar class and educational background.

But the task of maintaining a club based on the amateur spirit is far different from maintaining a machine clubhouse or ward headquarters. The amateur must constantly find ideals, personalities, and causes sufficient to replenish the easily exhausted reservoir of enthusiasm which stimulates him. Club leaders well know that this is not an easy job. As one Manhattan reformer phrased it, "Enthusiasm . . . is a very fragile thing. It can be broken easily. You daren't lose your momentum." The very resources which are valuable in sustaining that momentum, however, create problems within the amateur clubs. These include the problems of turnover, authority, endorsements, and co-ordination. Sometimes, as with the DFI, these problems are such that the organization goes out of existence.

*Turnover*

A major problem of all amateur clubs is the turnover in personnel, particularly among the ranks of canvassers and precinct or election district captains. "We have a big turnover of election district captains," said one Manhattan reform leader. "That's our biggest problem. Our big problem is to find enough people to man all these posts. The average person lasts only one or two years on the job." Another reform leader, in a nearby district, admitted that this was difficult. "This turnover, of course, is a constant problem. During an election we manage to staff all but maybe one or two of our election districts, but it's sometimes hard in between." The magnitude of this problem varies from district to district. In some areas, such as the Ninth Assembly District (Lexington Club), there are virtually no patronage-holders among the election district captains, the members are almost all well above the median in income, and they are absorbed in promising careers or businesses. Persuading such people to work several nights a week for the two or three months of a campaign is difficult in itself, but persuading them to repeat the process in succeeding campaigns poses even greater problems. Such continuity in election personnel would, of course, strengthen the club in its district, but the people who might provide such continuity either quickly tire of the political game or are eager to assume greater responsibilities and acquire greater prestige in the movement—leaving canvassing to somebody else. In some reform districts, such as the Seventh (Riverside Democrats) and the Tenth South (Yorkville Club), there are a larger number of older political workers, some with government jobs, who are content to continue canvassing in the same areas repeatedly.

In mid-1960, half the election districts in Manhattan's Ninth Assembly District (Lexington Club) either had no captain or had a captain with one year's experience or less. One-third of the election districts in the Seventh Assembly District (Riverside Democrats) were similarly lacking in trained workers. The James J. Farley Association, a Tammany club which for twelve years (1949–61) was the regular organization in the Eighth Assembly District North, provided an interesting contrast in turnover to the two reform clubs. Of the fifty-three election district captains, more than half (twenty-eight) had served as captains in the district for ten years or more, and seven of these had served for over twenty-five years. Less than one-fourth (sixteen) had less than three years' experience (Table 3).

One aspect of the turnover problem is particularly revealing. There is a tendency, not uniform in all cases, for the greatest turnover in captains to occur in those election districts inhabited by people who are not (by class, education, profession, ethnicity, and religion) similar to members of the reform

TABLE 3

TURNOVER AMONG ELECTION DISTRICT CAPTAINS

| LENGTH OF SERVICE OF ELECTION DISTRICT CAPTAIN* | NUMBER OF ELECTION DISTRICTS | |
|---|---|---|
| | Lexington Club | Riverside Democrats |
| No captain in district..... | 6 | 9 |
| Captain with no previous experience............. | 14 | 2 |
| Captain with one year's experience............... | 20 | 9 |
| Captain with two years' or more experience........ | 38 | 37 |
| Total............... | 78 | 57 |

* Data as of August, 1960.

movement itself. On the West Side, for example, in the Seventh Assembly District, the nine election districts with no captain were concentrated in areas with old tenements inhabited by a polyglot group, including many lower- and lower-middle-class Irish. In these places (election districts 20, 25, 33, 35, 36, and 51) it was apparently difficult to find and keep effective captains who were attracted by the reform cause and who, at the same time, were in easy rapport with the voters in the neighborhood. A similar tendency, less evident because of the less heterogeneous character of the assembly district, was found on the East Side in the area led by the Lexington Club. The twenty election districts which lacked experienced captains in mid-1960 were spread throughout the area, but most were found in those parts of the community with inhabitants least like the active members of the club. A high turnover in captains could be found in the deteriorating neighborhoods along Ninety-seventh, Ninety-eighth, and Ninety-ninth streets (election districts 77 and 78), in parts of the unattractive area south of Central Park near the Avenue of the Americas (election districts 8, 17, and 19), and along Third Avenue in those blocks (such as election district 4) with walk-up tenements. To serve in these districts, reform leaders try to recruit persons with the appropriate neighborhood attachments and religious and ethnic background, but they are not always successful.

In Los Angeles, turnover is equally a difficult problem. The continuity which the club system provides, although far better than rebuilding a precinct organization before each election through the county committee's unaided efforts, is imperfect at best. The movement remains the same, and the top CDC leadership tends to remain the same (to the dislike of some members who feel that a rapid rotation in office would be more desirable), but the leadership of individual clubs passes rapidly from hand to hand. Of the 164 clubs (both CDC and non-CDC) chartered by the Los Angeles County Central Committee in 1961 which had also been in existence the year before, 107, or more than 65 per cent, had new presidents serving their first term of office. In one year nearly two-thirds of the clubs had changed leaders.[1]

In addition, there is a high turnover in the very existence of many clubs, particularly among the smaller ones. Of the 193 chartered clubs which in February, 1960, were in existence, 27, or 14 per cent, had either ceased to exist or had changed their names by February, 1961.[2] As a result, a county committee official lamented that, except for the larger, more stable clubs, he had a "totally new organization every year to deal with, even though the movement remains basically the same."

[1] Calculated from the lists of clubs and club presidents in the program book of the annual FDR dinner published every year in February by the county committee.

[2] *Ibid.*

In most of the larger clubs, there has been a fairly stable core of activists who contribute time and energy to politics over a period of three to four years and, in some cases, even longer. But because these people are fewer than the jobs which must be done, it is rare for one person to have identical responsibilities over any period of time. This situation becomes vexatious in the field of precinct work. One very large and active club in Los Angeles, which has responsibility for working 78 precincts in the county during every election, reports that only in presidential or gubernatorial elections can it staff all of its precincts on a thorough basis. And from year to year, different people work different precincts, reducing the likelihood of building up a stable pattern of relationships or personal friendships with voters. "We have no real precinct captains," said the club president. "I think there are only ten cases or so in which there are people who live in the precinct in which they do political work and who have done this more than once. For all the rest of the precincts we get people who don't live there or who haven't done it before." It must be added, however, that the high mobility of the population in many (although not all) parts of Los Angeles County would make it difficult to build any enduring precinct organization even if some way could be found to induce volunteers to participate in such work.

Membership in most clubs generally rises just before an important national election and just before a statewide CDC endorsing convention in which some contest is expected. The president of the largest club, the Beverly Hills Democratic Club, found that after the 1960 general elections, his club membership fell as much as 30 per cent.

The turnover affects even the reform district leaders in New York. In the 1961 primaries, three—Baltzell, Glixon, and Midonick—announced they were not candidates for re-election. Their reasons were revealing. One or two of the leaders hoped to become judges and, given the extent to which reform slogans place constraints on district leaders who seek government positions, these men felt their chances might be improved if they sought nomination from outside politics. More important, however, was the fact that none of the three felt any sense of vocation about politics. Being district leader was a demanding, unrewarding, exhausting, and even nerve-wracking experience; politics was a distraction from their businesses which, although it provided some brief amusement, quickly became burdensome.[3] These three leaders were, in 1960, almost half of all the reform district leaders in power.

Insurgent reform clubs are also afflicted with a turnover in candidates. For example, before 1961, the insurgent Lenox Hill Club in the Eighth Assembly District North ran five different candidates in as many years for the district leadership (elected in odd-numbered years) and the Democratic nomination for assemblyman (decided in even-numbered years).[4] Not only were the voters presented with a different face each year, but the previous candidates did not, in most cases, remain in the area. Of the four before 1961, three left the district after their unsuccessful races. This prompted the regular club to stress in its campaign literature that it provided "non-transient" leadership.

In Chicago, the DFI was similarly plagued with a turnover in workers. The IVI, however, was something of an exception. Perhaps because the organization has been in existence so long (since 1944), perhaps because it has been closely identified with several well-known elective officials (Senator Paul Douglas, State Representative Abner Mikva, and Aldermen Robert Merriam and Leon Despres), and perhaps because of its fairly close identification with the cohesive university community, the IVI in the Fifth Ward has been able to rely on a far more stable supply of precinct workers than most clubs. Interestingly, in the Fourth Ward just to the north, where the IVI has

[3] See *New York Times*, May 26, 1961: "Although different reasons were given . . . by all three, one common factor was a feeling that the time and energy required was not worth the effort."

[4] The Lenox Hill Club candidates for district leaders were Thomas Sammon (1957), Harry Le Bien (1959), and Mal Barasch (1961); for assemblyman they were Paul Bragdon (1958) and Charles Lieber (1960). In 1961, Barasch won the district leadership.

elected no officials and where few members of the university community live, turnover has been much higher.

*Authority*

The insistence on internal democracy within the amateur clubs and within those organizations, such as the CDC, the DFI, and the CDV, which co-ordinate the clubs, reduces the extent to which authority can be vested in club leaders. The absence of centralized authority in turn weakens tactical flexibility in situations calling for bargaining among clubs.

There are, of course, important differences of opinion within the club movement on how much authority a club president or a reform district leader ought to have. In New York, for example, the insurgent clubs and the West Side reform clubs place extreme restrictions on the president or leader. In these clubs, the leader is scarcely more than a messenger who casts the club vote in Tammany Hall, and the president a bearer of a narrowly construed mandate who exchanges views with other club presidents. On the East Side, by contrast, leaders and presidents often have considerably more discretion. These differences in discretion, like the differences in attitude toward patronage and De Sapio, are probably related to the differences in membership and electoral prospects discussed in the previous chapter.

By and large, however, the amateur clubs differ radically from professional organizations in the authority they vest in leaders. An officer of the CDV described what he felt was the generally accepted view of the role of the reform district leader:

> The district leader has a purely political function in the reform clubs. His job is to represent the club in Tammany and cast the club's vote in the Tammany Executive Committee. But the club president, the officer, the executive committee, the various standing committees, they do all the work.

This is a generally accurate description of the leader's role in most reform clubs. It is strikingly unlike the leader in a

Tammany club. There, the leader *is* the club: the sole source of authority and initiative, the dispenser of jobs, the judge in disputes, and the architect of all the club's activities. Officers and committee chairmen are usually election district captains who hold their posts at the pleasure of the leader. There are no meaningful club elections. In reform clubs, officers are elected for formal terms, many are not election district captains, few owe their posts to the district leader, and there is normally a great competition in innovating, planning, and executing club functions. Thus, differences among reform district leaders are marginal when compared to Tammany leaders. These differences, nonetheless, are sufficient to indicate some of the distinctive contrasts within the reform movement.

A West Side leader, after describing with scorn the "boss-like" authority of certain other reform leaders, pictured his own limited role:

> I think [another reform leader] is just like a political boss, despite the fact that he runs a democratic club. He is elevated above everybody else and his people pay him a great deal of deference. His word goes. In my *own* club, no one is conceded to have any real power. Everything is give and take. I certainly don't have any real control over them.

Another reform district leader stressed the necessity for broad leadership discretion. The reason he advanced cuts to the heart of one of the problems facing the reformers in Manhattan. Intraparty democracy and correspondingly weak personal leadership may be valuable inducements to attract and hold club members, but they may at the same time weaken the club's ability to attract and hold voters through decisive action, firm commitments, and bold community-service activities. As this East Side leader observed:

> If any kind of club, regular or reform, is going to stay in business, the only way it can do it is by providing community services. If you don't have leadership you can't provide those services. If you have too much rank-and-file participation and bickering, you're not going to have that leadership.

The consequences of the dispersion of power within an amateur political club is most evident in New York, where regular reform clubs have a dual leadership: the club officers and the male and female district leaders. In Tammany clubs, the male district leader is the boss, while the female leader and other club officers are almost always figureheads who do routine work. Many of the reform clubs attempt to reverse this pattern. In so doing, they place the district leaders in an ambiguous position. The leaders are elected by the voters of the district, not by the club, and hence their legal responsibility and basis for power are with the electorate. In fact, of course, the leader could not endure without his club's endorsement. Thus, his loyalties are of necessity divided. Reform district leaders, like other politicians, dare not outrage the electorate, but they also, unlike other politicians, dare not offend the sensibilities of their clubs. The reform leader must embody the values and ideals of his club; he cannot rely on either the indifference of members or the power of patronage to maintain his position. Reform club members are not indifferent, and few are susceptible to patronage controls.

This problem of dual loyalties vexes almost all reform district leaders. Like all politicians, amateur or professional, they are very sensitive to the fact that they were elected "by the people" and tend to become contemptuous of persons, not elected by the people, who attempt to constrain them. Some reform leaders abandoned their posts in part because they had so little status in their clubs. "You wonder sometimes why we even have the post of leader," one said. "The club blames you if you try to make a deal with Tammany, and Tammany blames you if your club fails to deliver on some commitment. You're caught in the middle."

When the club feels strongly about an issue, the leader is usually left with little discretion in defining his position. The club stands between the leader and the voter. The leaders themselves are ambivalent about this situation. On the one hand, they are restless with club efforts to bind them to specific policies and tactics. On the other hand, their belief in a

programmatic party responsive to the membership leads them
to favor greater commitment to policies on the part of party
and elective officials. One district leader reflected this duality
when he insisted strongly that club mandates should not fetter
his discretion; otherwise, his effectiveness as a bargaining
agent would be lost. At the same time, he was critical of the
Tammany leadership for not committing Manhattan congressmen to a set of specific goals:

> In my view, Carmine De Sapio should caucus the New
> York City Congressmen regularly to make them into an
> effective Congressional delegation and hammer out policy
> among them. He doesn't. There is no policy that the Con-
> gressmen from New York City consistently follows as a
> group, but there ought to be. . . . Our state committee
> ought to do more research and try to hammer out policies
> for the state party. We need to get professors to do studies
> for us and write position papers on various issues, like
> housing and education.

This same leader was unhappy with the way "rank-and-file
participation and bickering" made it difficult to exercise "real
leadership" in his club. The leader saw clearly the disadvantages of allowing his club to commit him and thereby reduce
his authority, but he, along with many other reform leaders,
did not see that equally serious questions could be raised
about committing other officials to the programs of the party.

The membership is not, of course, always united. When it is
divided, the leadership has more discretion. But this creates its
own set of problems. When there is no clear and firm expression of club sentiment, the officers and district leaders are
likely to be divided amongst themselves. The majority speaks
but does not rule. The club finds it difficult to present a united
front, and this weakens its tactical position. The male district
leader, supreme in Tammany clubs, has no way in reform
clubs to enforce his will on either his female counterpart or
the club's executive committee. On several occasions, the male
and female leaders from reform clubs have taken conflicting
positions or voted on opposite sides of the same issue in meetings of the county executive committee. The co-leaders of the

Tilden Club, the Lexington Club, the Riverside Club, the Yorkville Club, and the FDR-Woodrow Wilson Club have voted against each other in Tammany Hall and endorsed different candidates for the same office. The issues which divided them ranged from the selection of a party candidate for General Sessions Court judge to the re-election of De Sapio as county leader. The co-leaders of the FDR-Woodrow Wilson Club disagreed intensely on the endorsement for state senator, and the co-leaders of the Tilden Club disagreed on state committeemen nominations (for which one leader was a candidate). There is little or nothing one leader can do to discipline his colleague, even though they are both from the same club.[5]

One reform district leader, who had been faced with this situation himself, offered an explanation:

> The reform female leaders have always been independent. It is the usual case for them to disagree with their male counterparts in these actions. Among the regular Tammany co-leaders, on the other hand, there are very few disagreements. This is because the female leaders in the reform movement have their own base of strength within the organization. They are educated women, intelligent, and tend to be independent. They're very conscious of their own position on the policies they represent. The Tammany co-leaders, on the other hand, who rarely disagree, are usually housewives with little education who are simply picked because a woman has to be in the job and because her husband asked her to do it.

Planning any kind of joint strategy by which the reform movement will, as a group, carry the fight against Tammany is

[5] Two female co-leaders in fact deserted the reform movement altogether in 1961. Mary Barret Reis of the First Assembly District North left the Reform District Leaders' Caucus and the Murray Hill Citizens Club to found her own club (the New Frontier) and enter a slate against the regular reform leader (Charles Kinsolving, Jr.). Dorothy M. Feldman, co-leader in the Tenth Assembly District South, broke with Harrington and announced her support of De Sapio.

By contrast, De Sapio's own co-leader, Mrs. Elsie Gleason Mattura, was interviewed on television in 1959 just before the primary elections. She said that women had a voice in Mr. De Sapio's club and that they were independent. When asked whether she had ever voted against De Sapio in Tammany Hall, Mrs. Mattura looked shocked and exclaimed, "God forbid!" See Greenfield, op. cit., p. 30.

complicated by the frequent splits between male and female leaders. Further, such divisions make it difficult to form alliances with other groups of leaders. "Why," asked one Negro district leader, "should I ally myself with a group which can't even control its own votes?"

It is possible, however, to deal with a clear act of defiance against the doctrines of reform. When the vice-president of the Riverside Democrats openly refused to support the club's candidate for congressman in the 1960 primaries and endorsed and worked for his Tammany opponent instead, the club's executive committee voted to remove her from office. The officer appealed the decision to the club membership which, by the constitution, had ultimate power. After a lengthy and impassioned debate at an open membership meeting, the executive committee was upheld by an overwhelming majority and the office was declared vacated. There are few such dramatic instances of open rebellion involving going over to the side of the enemy, and thus correspondingly few cases in which leadership unity is enforced (albeit after the damage has been done).

With so many offices to be filled, and so many shades of opinion to be dealt with, it is almost inevitable that factionalism within the membership will be reflected in divergence among the leadership. When members were asked what they disliked most about their clubs, the largest percentage of respondents mentioned internecine conflict and the constant struggle for power and position. "Bickering," "factionalism," "petty quarreling," and "politicking" were most frequently cited as reasons for dissatisfaction. Given the absence of a clear source of authority in the clubs, this situation is probably inevitable. Given the goals and rewards of reformism, it is equally inevitable that disagreements which begin as the clash of incompatible personalities or the quest for office will quickly become invested with an ideological significance. But the level of this factionalism varies over time. It is probably at its highest in the period of pre-endorsement maneuvering and on those occasions (such as the issuance of policy statements or the adoption of resolutions) when it is necessary to take a position on some specific problem. During election periods, it is much less evident.

One club on Manhattan's West Side, noted for its militancy, was also a club continually in the grip of internecine quarrels. The FDR-Woodrow Wilson Club was organized in 1959 as an amalgamation of three competing insurgent groups in the district. From the beginning, it lacked a single accepted leadership. The truce among the three factions was uneasy at best. It required stipulating in great detail in the written constitution the manner in which the choice of leader would be resolved. The three groups enrolled 587 members—a very large number for a club just organizing—and the club election resulted in a victory for the man who later became the district leader. The initial struggle for power in the club was bitter, and it left its mark. The involved election procedures, the sizable initial membership, and the heat of the contest all indicated the unsteady factional alliance on which the club rested. This factionalism meant that it was necessary to compete continually in order to maintain one's position within the club. Such competition inevitably led to a sharpening of personal and ideological differences. One group walked out. An important club leader very shrewdly described the consequences of this factionalism:

> We have been in a constant state of turmoil since our very inception. . . . There was a lot of heat and dissent generated [at our inception]. . . . Ever since then there have been constant fights. There's no general agreement on leadership. Most of these fights are prompted by clashes of personality and other things, but they get invested with ideology—people attempt to prove that they are purer than the other people, ideologically speaking. The split on personality grounds has continued ever since and acquired these ideological overtones. I think the reformer basically is a very neurotic kind of person.

The inability of the New York reform leaders to commit their clubs inhibits the reform movement from making alliances with other politicians. When the CDV discussed with

Mayor Wagner the possibility of endorsing him for re-election in 1961, it ran certain risks. There was no reason why Wagner, were he sufficiently ruthless, could not have accepted reform support in the Democratic primary and then, after winning the primary, have dropped the reformers and forged a new alliance with the regular county leaders in order to obtain their support against the Republicans in the general election. The reform leaders could not extract any guarantees from Wagner in advance of voting their endorsement for the simple reason that, before the clubs actually voted to ratify the CDV endorsement, they could give no assurances to the Mayor that he would be endorsed at all. Said a CDV official:

> We got no *quid pro quo* from Wagner at all, and this kind of movement never can get them. Of course, Wagner promised us *ex post facto* that he wouldn't desert us after the primary, but that's not the same thing. . . . The reason we couldn't get guarantees in advance is because we [the CDV leaders] couldn't commit the leaders of the clubs and they in turn couldn't commit their own memberships. It's hard to stipulate conditions when you're not sure you can deliver what you are promising.

The difficulty in making commitments binding on the reform movement was illustrated in a 1961 election for two justices of the New York Supreme Court. Of the fifteen Manhattan reform clubs, six endorsed the Democratic nominees, six endorsed the Liberal party nominees, and three took no position at all. The CDV decided to remain neutral, realizing that it had no power to enforce a single slate on its member clubs.[6]

## Endorsements

The problem of authority is at no time more keenly felt than when endorsements must be made by amateur clubs. The doctrine of intraparty democracy may prescribe very well the relationships which ought to obtain between a president or a district leader and his club, or between officers and members, but it has little to say about the relationships which ought to

[6] *New York Times,* October 30, 1961.

exist among leaders from different districts. They are legally equals, and no one is willing to concede pre-eminence to any of his colleagues. The feeling that each leader is as good or better than the next man, normal enough under any circumstances, is sharpened to a razor's edge in New York by the intense competition among reform leaders for prestige and the vindication of cherished principles. If the principles of reform are an inducement which can hold a club together, they are equally a force which can drive the leaders of the clubs apart.

The problem is most clearly seen in the selection of candidates for public office. In New York and California, only one public (as contrasted to party) office is filled solely by the voters in one district—that of assemblyman. For all other offices (such as congressman, state senator, and city councilman), more than one assembly district participates in the election and hence, within the party organization, more than one district must participate in the nominating process. Several clubs or district leaders must agree on a candidate to endorse in the primary election; without unanimity, the primary vote will be split and the nomination may go to a rival candidate or a maverick. The problem is important in all cases, but it is particularly acute when (as on New York's West Side, for example) the Democratic nomination is tantamount to election. With the stakes so high, owing to the favorable prospects for the Democratic candidate, the competition for endorsements before the primary is strenuous. The principle of intraparty democracy does not offer any guidelines for making such endorsements. Furthermore, most reform leaders are roughly equal in education, age, experience, and prestige. There is no obvious basis on which one possible candidate might be preferred over another. Each leader can easily visualize himself as the nominee, and fails to detect any reason why someone else should be preferred. When William Fitts Ryan, leader of the Seventh Assembly District (the Riverside Democrats), won the Democratic nomination for congressman in 1960 after an intense struggle within the reform movement, his new prominence was not easily accepted. Said one of his leading supporters:

> My hope was that Ryan would become a natural leader of the reform movement because of his visibility and the office he will hold. . . . Of course, I have no illusions as to how many of my fellow reformers like him. Too many of them can see themselves as Congressman for them to like him personally.

Another leader, from the East Side, agreed with this assessment. Few politicians with the education and professional attainments of the reformers are modest about their eligibility for a congressional seat: "There is . . . a developing struggle for power in the reform movement. This is inevitable. People get a taste of the hereafter and they like it. They get a taste of the big jobs and they want more. We have lots of good people in this organization. . . ."

In a regular organization such as Tammany or the Chicago machine, the endorsement of candidates similarly attracts much competition. But because of the nature of the organization, this competition can be, and is, resolved in a manner unlike that found in the reform movement. In the first place, most regular organizations are willing to agree to a principle of club "recognition" in allocating choice elective posts. On the West Side of Manhattan, for example, there were six such jobs to be divided among six regular clubs in the Third and Fifth Assembly districts. In order to reduce conflict, the principle was followed of giving one job to each club. Thus, the club in the Fifth South received the congressman, the club in the Fifth Middle one assemblyman, the club in the Fifth North the judge, the club in the Third North the city councilman, the club in the Third Middle the second assemblyman, and the club in the Third South the state senator. Once this pattern was established, it persisted. It became the responsibility of each club to fill vacancies. If a redistribution was to occur, elaborate negotiations were required in which trades were effected. When, for example, a congressman retired or died and the state senator moved up to fill his shoes, the club which lost the office had to be compensated, and the club which gained the higher office had to give up its previous post to another organization.

The principle of club recognition was maintained in the face of conflicting demands for scarce jobs by negotiation and ultimately by arbitration. Negotiations among club leaders always occurred first, and settlements were often arranged involving either trades or side payments. A trade could be made immediately or over time. For example, the club leaders could either agree to switch jobs in one election, or one leader could give a job to another in exchange for the promise that, in a future election, the latter leader would support the former's candidate. If negotiation failed, the matter was referred to the county leadership for arbitration. Since the county leadership controlled both patronage and county- and citywide endorsements, its decision was final and could be enforced.

Among amateur Democrats, this procedure is unworkable. In the first place, club leaders, by and large, do not accept the principle of club recognition. Indeed, given their commitment to democracy, it would be difficult to see how they could. In a democracy, the "best man" wins. This means that, in theory at least, one club blessed with an extraordinary number of excellent candidates might be entitled to the endorsement for several offices. Other clubs, less abundantly endowed, would have to be content with nothing. In a democracy, there is no place for recognizing such artificial entities as clubs, particularly if it means taking second-best men from poorly equipped clubs, any more than there is any place for ethnic or religious recognition in "balancing" tickets. (In practice, of course, a great deal of both occur within the reform movement. Decisions are often reached regarding endorsements, based on the unstated premise that one club "deserves" to have a candidate to balance the candidate given to another club.[7] Similarly, there is often a self-conscious effort to balance tickets ethnically and religiously. A frequent combination is an Irish Catholic and a Jew.[8])

[7] This happened when Manfred Ohrenstein was endorsed for state senator in 1960 in order to "recognize" his club on the West Side.

[8] This happens when Irish district leaders are paired with Jewish female co-leaders, or vice versa (William Fitts Ryan and Shirley Kaye,

Furthermore, negotiation over endorsements is made difficult by the fact that in many cases, the district leader lacks the authority to commit himself and his club to any given settlement. Any promises made by such a leader would have to be referred back to the club membership, and the other leaders know this. Negotiation takes place, therefore, in an atmosphere of profound uncertainty. Said one West Side leader: "The reform leaders can't commit their clubs. They are dependent on club support for their positions and they cannot speak authoritatively for the clubs. The clubs' principle of internal democracy works against this."

The discretion of the leaders is further constrained by the knowledge that they cannot easily make trades or accept side payments. A "deal" is odious in reform politics, and any trade smacks of a "deal." In addition, therefore, to the fact that the leader's actions must be ratified by his club is the fact that any action involving an obvious deal will not be ratified at all. Under favorable circumstances, and with considerable haggling, one club might trade one job for another job on the same ticket. But it is very unlikely that any club would consent to being bound over time—i.e., to a commitment to support another club's candidate (perhaps unnamed as yet) at an election one or two years later.

> The club would never agree to making deals ahead of time about the nominations. They would never relinquish their prerogative to make choices on individual candidates. They insist on that. It is absolutely inconceivable that the club would permit the leaders to trade on candidates and prevent candidates for office coming up at a later time to be scrutinized by the membership.

Although clubs differ on this, the difficulty or impossibility of committing clubs, making trades, and accepting side payments are severe impediments in the endorsement process, and constitute a great challenge to amateur politicians gen-

---

Irving Wolfson and Catherine Hemenway, John T. Harrington and Dorothy Feldman, etc.).

erally.[9] Several attempts have been made to devise formal machinery to facilitate the endorsement process. But any such machinery can function smoothly only if all participants agree that maintaining the procedure is more important than the nature of the outcomes (the identity of the candidates). In effect, this is what the Tammany leaders have done all along. By placing a higher value on the mechanism (the party and its chain of command and distribution of authority and prestige) than on the offices themselves, it could meliorate interclub conflict. When greater value is placed on the identity of the candidates (and, even more, on the principles which the candidates seem to embody), then a formal apparatus will be ignored if it fails to produce the desired outcome.

Where, as on Manhattan's West Side and in Greenwich Village, victory in the primary is tantamount to victory in the general election, the most intense reform struggles over nominations have occurred. In 1960, the struggle over pre-primary endorsements had been protracted and bitter. There had been three major contests for state senator in the Twenty-fifth Senatorial District (the lower West Side), congressman in the Twentieth Congressional District (the West Side), and state committeeman in the First Assembly District (lower Manhattan). Each case was complicated by the fact that there were

[9] There is an obvious formal similarity between the endorsing problem and certain aspects of game theory. See the discussion of games of "fair division" in R. Duncan Luce and Howard Raiffa, *Games and Decisions* (New York: John Wiley & Sons, Inc., 1957), pp. 363–68, and Hugo Steinhaus, "The Problem of Fair Division," *Econometrica*, XVI (1948), 101–4. The problem essentially is how to achieve a Paretian optimum with an indivisible commodity. One method is by tossing a coin; another method is an agreement to share over time; a third method is for each player to contribute money (or some other infinitely-divisible value) to a pot, which will be split as a side payment. Tammany leaders regularly use variations of all three methods in distributing endorsements. Reform leaders are constrained by ideology (an ideology, it should be stressed, which is regarded as essential for the maintenance of the organization) from using any of the three methods. Settlements, as a consequence, are usually the result of protracted and debilitating haggling after which a highly prestigious "mediator" suggests a solution which is accepted largely because *some* solution must be agreed to (i.e., the payoff of the endorsing "game" is relevant to the potential payoff in the election "game") and the parties are too exhausted to continue the struggle.

both reform and Tammany clubs in each area and that, of the reform clubs, some were regular (i.e., controlled the leadership) and others were insurgent.

In all cases, a commitment to intraparty democracy, while important in creating or shaping the problem, contributed little to its solution. In each case, every club's preference was expressed by a vote of the membership. The result was that almost no club was united behind a single candidate; each candidate had strength in several clubs (although the greatest strength in his own).[10] Club leaders usually attempted to negotiate a settlement between the rivals but failed, and thus a second preference vote had to be taken. When one candidate, who was also a district leader, was asked whether his club would support his rival in the primary if he lost, he replied that he could not commit his club. In part, this was probably a power play intended to compel other clubs to give him the nomination. But in part it was probably an honest admission that he could not in fact commit his club to anything. In two cases, prestigious mediators from the CDV were called in to propose a compromise settlement. Once they were successful, once unsuccessful. Interestingly enough, there was a tendency for the mediators to try to reassert the principle of club recognition in suggesting a solution. On the West Side, a large reform club was recognized against three small insurgent clubs; in the First Assembly District, a large and vociferous insurgent club had its claims balanced, by means of a complex formula, against those of two smaller reform clubs. Finally, and most significant, great importance was attached to capturing

[10] For example, in the First Assembly District state committeewoman contest, the vote of the three reform clubs was divided as follows:

| Club | Candidates | Vote |
|---|---|---|
| Village Independent Democrats....... | Sarah Schoenkopf | 60 |
| | Barbara Yuncker | 2 |
| | Margot Gayle | 0 |
| Tilden Democratic Club ............. | Barbara Yuncker | 45 |
| | Margot Gayle | 32 |
| | Sarah Schoenkopf | 18 |
| Murray Hill Citizens Club........... | Barbara Yuncker | 22 |
| | Margot Gayle | 5 |
| | Sarah Schoenkopf | 5 |

the "image" of reform. The moderate amateurs tended to be forced out in all cases. Older leaders were replaced by younger ones and conservative or middle-of-the-road clubs were defeated by militant ones. Any connection with Tammany or Carmine De Sapio became a kiss of death. The state committeemen campaign centered almost entirely on charges that the one slate was "De Sapio-backed," "boss-controlled," or "compromising." The charges proved effective. The position of the so-called moderate reform clubs, the Tilden and the Murray Hill Citizens, was made untenable and after the election attempts were begun (later abandoned) to unseat the leadership in both organizations.[11] This "pressure from the left" seems to be an important aspect of much of reform politics, notably in its nascent stages.

An attempt to solve this problem of endorsements and reduce the enervating fratricide was made in 1961, when four reform clubs, regular and insurgent, in the Twenty-fifth Councilmanic District on Manhattan's West Side held a "West Side Nominating Convention" for the purpose of selecting a reform candidate for the City Council seat.[12] Four clubs were represented by a total of 180 delegates, apportioned by a complicated formula. Delegates were pledged to a total of nine candidates who had shown strength in club membership votes preceding the convention. Candidates were required to sign agreements that they would abide by the decision of the convention and not oppose its nominee. Seventeen ballots were required to obtain a majority for one candidate, and there would have been many more, except that on the later ballots, the rules required that the low man be dropped from consideration. The campaigning was intense, costly, and exhausting. All nine candidates spoke twice at each club, elaborate brochures and newsletters were mailed to all members, and countless "kaffeeklatches" were held at which candidates appeared. In the end, however, most leaders agreed that the winning

[11] See *Village Voice,* July 14, 1960.

[12] See *New York Times,* April 14, 1961, and *Village Voice,* May 24, 1961.

candidates would have been the same if the convention had
never been held and instead the club leaders had bargained
over the nomination. The nominee, Theodore Weiss, was the
candidate of the only large club in the district which at that
time had no member in elective office (the Reform Independent Democrats). In short, the principle of club recognition
was followed by the convention and would probably have
been followed if there had been no convention. The crucial
fact, of course, is that the same end could *not* have been
achieved by bargaining among club leaders because club
members would never have permitted such a procedure. The
leaders could never have obtained the authority or discretion
to enter into such negotiations.

Privately, certain higher-echelon reform leaders deplored
the use of the convention. One officer of the CDV felt that it
only created "lasting animosities" by making public the deep
conflicts on the West Side. The CDV did not participate in
the convention, and many of its leaders were unhappy with
its choice. Further, some of the CDV "angels" were fearful
that such conventions would commit the reform movement to
unacceptable candidates. To the West Side leaders, on the
other hand, these CDV reservations were just another case of
its "timidity."

Where, as in California, the structure of politics is radically
different from that found in New York, the strategy of pre-
primary endorsement is also different. The absence of a precinct organization in many areas and the episodic character
of that organization in other areas makes primaries, particularly those with no incumbent, largely unorganized events in
which the name and personality of the candidate are often of
considerable importance. It is very easy for a person to become
a candidate, another legacy of the Progressive era that has
remained in the Elections Code. To run for the state assembly, one need acquire only twenty signatures on a petition and
pay a filing fee of twenty dollars. In New York City, by contrast, candidates for similar office must collect 350 signatures

within a very short period of time.[13] Thus, it is not unusual for there to be a large number of candidates for any office in California for which the prospects of winning are at all significant. In June, 1960, the Fifteenth Congressional District primary attracted six Democratic aspirants, while the Twenty-second Congressional District contest attracted nine Republicans.

When there are so many candidates and so little organization, the problem of endowing one's name with meaning becomes crucial. Primary elections typically become a struggle for labels. These labels are usually the endorsements of important groups—labor, the press, and the official party. The CDC came into existence primarily to provide a means whereby an organization using the name "Democratic" could affix the label, "Democrat," to favored primary candidates. With the end of cross-filing, the organization persisted in large part to affix the label "endorsed" onto favored Democrats. Although the clubs have organized precincts in some parts of the state, these clubs are neither so numerous nor so disciplined that they can effectively work more than a small minority of these precincts. In campaigns, a candidate must rely on other ways of reaching the voter. One of the most important of these is through mailings. Mailings constitute the primary campaign expenses for many, if not most candidates, and the most important of these is what is known as the "slate mailer."

The slate mailer is a piece of literature, often in the form of a sample ballot, which is sent out in each assembly district and lists the official endorsements of the CDC for the entire ticket in that election. A local candidate is usually anxious to appear on this slate mailer (which is made up differently for each district, so that a single assembly and congressional candidate appears on each one along with the statewide endorsees), because in this way he can be associated with the prestigious state and national candidates of the party.

[13] For California, see *Elections Code*, sections 2605 and 2671. For New York, see Wallace Sayre and Herbert Kaufman, *Governing New York City* (New York: Russell Sage Foundation, 1960), pp. 141–42.

The difficulty is that there are few legal restrictions governing the use of the word "endorsed," and since CDC is an unofficial party organ, there is no inherent reason why other organizations, also using the name Democratic, could not spring up and make "endorsements." And since almost any group of twenty Democrats who have fifteen dollars among them can become a Democratic club chartered by the county committee, the possibilities of conflicting endorsements from competing groups are theoretically infinite.

In critical primaries (i.e., primaries in those districts in which there is no Democratic incumbent but in which the party's prospects are good), this problem is easily seen. The 1960 primary in the Fifteenth Congressional District, an area with twenty CDC clubs with over one thousand members plus seven other non-CDC clubs, was a contest over the right to use the word "endorsed." Five candidates entered the primary. In the endorsing convention held by the clubs in the district, there were two leading contenders, neither of whom received the 60 per cent of the delegates' vote necessary to win the endorsement. Since the local convention made no endorsement, the CDC itself could make none.[14] In the primary campaign, one of the five candidates precipitated considerable controversy by mailing a piece of promotional literature to Democratic voters stating that he was "the endorsed Democratic Congressional candidate." When this was angrily disputed by the president of the Fifteenth Congressional District Council, the candidate's supporters pointed out that he was endorsed by some sixteen club presidents in the district, as well as by other individuals. After several heated exchanges

[14] Whether CDC could or did make an endorsement became a heated issue in the primary. But the evidence seems clear. In a letter dated April 25, 1960, to James L. Cole, campaign manager for Norman Martell (the candidate who eventually won the primary), Edna Wiesbart, secretary of CDC, stated that the CDC executive committee had considered Martell's request for an endorsement but that "it is the judgment of this committee that it is not within the legal rights of the CDC Executive Committee to make endorsements and that our only right in this respect, according to the CDC constitution and by-laws, is to ratify endorsements made by local groups."

among factions in the district, the candidate issued another mailing which carried the names of twelve clubs in the district which had endorsed him by separate resolutions. Because of the ill-will created during the primary, in which personal attacks were made on several candidates, the winning candidate had difficulty in obtaining the support of the Fifteenth Congressional District Council even though he had captured the nomination.[15] Finally, at a special meeting held only three weeks before the election, the council voted to endorse "the entire slate" and distribute funds to the local candidates ( $150 each to the four nominees for assembly and congress).

A struggle over the right to use the word "endorsed" also occurred in the Fifty-sixth Assembly District. One candidate for assemblyman had received, along with the candidate for congress, the endorsement of the local convention. But a rival, unendorsed assembly candidate sent out a mailing in which he linked his name with that of the endorsed congressional candidate, printing the word "endorsed" on the pamphlet in such a way that it seemed to refer to both. In fact, he was not the endorsee of the local convention, but of another body, called the "United Council of Democratic Clubs," which had no official standing as a CDC affiliate.[16]

Thus, although California clubs have gone further than those in New York in establishing formal machinery for the selection of party candidates before the primaries, that machinery is subject to malfunction and its results can be disputed. When a campaign relies more on labels than on gaining the support of an established precinct organization, the endorsement machinery has few, if any, sanctions it can employ

[15] A meeting on July 5, 1960, adjourned, according to the official minutes, amidst "much confusion and commotion" and with "the meeting becoming unruly."

[16] It is interesting that rival organizations which are created to make endorsements tend to select names which include the initials "CDC." The United Council of Democratic Clubs in the Fifty-sixth Assembly District referred to itself as the "UCDC," while a club endorsing Martell in the Fifteenth Congressional District called itself the "Central District Democratic Club," or the "CDDC." Opponents charged that these were attempts to mislead the voters.

to enforce its will against a rival who is willing to create his own machinery for producing an endorsement or who is able to claim support from individual clubs which were dissatisfied with the results of the endorsing convention.

## Co-ordination

Devising mechanisms that will co-ordinate the amateur Democratic clubs while at the same time preserving the crucial features of the amateur spirit—the appearance and if possible the reality of internal democracy—has not been easy. By and large, the California Democratic Council has been the most successful—in great part because it attempts to do less than the CDV in New York. Although in California there are significant differences among the constituencies of various clubs and some conflict created by the clash of strong personalities, there is no inherent cleavage created by differences in political status. In California, unlike New York, the clubs have no geographical jurisdiction and no formal role in the party apparatus; thus, there is no conflict between those holding the leadership and those challenging others for the leadership. No California club controls the leadership of its district, because there is no leadership post to control. And because of the large number of clubs, most of which are rather small, no single club or group of clubs can dominate the CDC. Such conflict as occurs within the CDC is largely ideological rather than organizational, with the exception of a latent north-south division.[17] Perhaps most important, the CDC cannot command the resources of money and prestige that are at the disposal of the CDV in New York. The CDC cannot deploy such names as Lehman and Roosevelt nor can it call on Park Avenue donors to put up money which it can then distribute to clubs.

[17] In the 1961 election of a CDC president to replace Joseph Wyatt, who was retiring, northern and southern clubs each put up one candidate. In general, the vote followed regional lines, although the southern candidate showed considerable strength in the Central Valley and the East Bay region. Tom Carvey won handily by a two-to-one majority, drawing on the more populous southern districts.

Thus, there is less at stake in the CDC. In Illinois, the DFI had so few resources and so many liabilities (ranging from a sizable financial debt to an absence of any agreement on purpose or leadership) that it could not survive at all as a coordinating organization for the local clubs.

Because the resources of the CDC are so scanty, most California clubs conduct their day-to-day affairs with relatively little attention to the statewide organization. The president of one of the largest Los Angeles clubs observed that "most of our members have barely heard of the CDC. All they know is that once a year some of them go as delegates to its convention and watch the fun. But by and large, we are strictly a local operation and we run our own show." Further, the CDC, unlike the CDV, lacks a single strong executive director. The CDC, although it has hired some staff workers, is still for the most part a volunteer operation. The elected officials handle most of the high-level dealings between the CDC and other political forces in California. The CDV, by contrast, has an executive director who is the focus for almost all the organization's activities; although he has few formal powers, he is an important center of communications for New York amateur politics and conducts much of the CDV's business personally.

Since the CDV is an active body with strong staff leadership and considerable resources at its command, its role as a coordinating device for club politics offers the most interesting case. With so much at stake, the clubs take very seriously the distribution of power within the citywide organization. Within the first two years of its existence, the CDV was reorganized twice, once in February, 1960, when the executive director was brought in and again in the spring of 1961, when a formal "Plan of Structure" was adopted.

The CDV structure was defined as the result of a compromise between two conflicting points of view on the organization's function. In one view, the CDV ought to be a club-oriented organization that would serve as a sort of "reform county committee" in which important decisions would be made on political goals and tactics. In the other view, the

CDV should be simply a service organization and public-relations committee which would raise money and provide speakers and publicity for the reform movement.

If one accepts the first view, then the CDV becomes an important locus of power and a forum for debates. In order for this power to be acceptable to club leaders, the CDV would have to be democratically organized, with many leaders sharing authority on a roughly equal footing. Reform district leaders, although holding an official party office, would be given no more power in the CDV than any other club representative. Indeed, to insure that the leaders were not dominant, each club would have several representatives who could outvote their leader.

If, on the other hand, one accepts the "service organization" point of view, then a different set of implications follow. If the CDV is only to raise money and organize the prestigious "elder statesmen" of the reform movement, there is no need for an elaborate constitution which allocates powers precisely. Most functions could be in the hands of the staff and the senior members—in most cases, the "Advisory Committee" of elder statesmen. Since no substantive decisions on goals or tactics would be made, rigid guarantees of internal democracy would be unnecessary.

In fact, the CDV began primarily under the influence of this second point of view. The 1961 reorganization was in great part an expression of dissatisfaction by certain club leaders who wanted to make the clubs the basis of the CDV. These leaders, both reform and insurgent, saw in the "informal" or "service" CDV a threat to their autonomy—an organization using its resources free of club control and making statements which were construed by outsiders, rightly or wrongly, as the "official" position of the reform movement. Three regular reform clubs were represented on the old CDV, not by their district leaders, but by lesser officials, while one club refused to send any representatives at all.[18] At the same time, certain

[18] The Riverside, Murray Hill, and Tilden clubs were represented by lesser officials while the leaders stayed aloof. All three leaders ex-

insurgent reform clubs felt the CDV was "undemocratic" and "not responsible to anybody."

The principal change in 1961 was to shift the basis of power within the CDV further in the direction of the clubs and away from the CDV officers and advisors. Club representatives, chosen by an elaborate formula, accounted for 58 per cent of the 124 members of the new General Committee. Insurgent reform clubs were placed on a par with regular reform clubs by allowing extra representatives on the basis of large memberships, large districts, and the size of the club's last primary vote. Thus, in early 1961, a large insurgent club like the VID had more representatives than small regular clubs like the Murray Hill, Tilden, or Yorkville. Elected district leaders in the reform movement saw this as another step in the direction of downgrading district leaders and weakening their voice in the councils of the movement; insurgent clubs saw it, on the other hand, as a legitimate and tardy recognition of the rank-and-file volunteers. Several district leaders became even more dubious about allowing themselves to be committed by an organization controlled by groups which were out of power in their districts. One leader, Costikyan, refused to affiliate his club with the new CDV.

In addition, the new CDV structure placed the prestigious Board of Advisors (Herbert Lehman, Frank Adams, Lloyd Garrison, Irving Engle, and Mrs. Eleanor Roosevelt) along with the co-opted members-at-large in an even more ambiguous position. The advisors, particularly Lehman, had been *de facto* heads of the CDV for its first two years. In part this was a recognition of their status in the civic and political life of the community and in part a recognition of the fact that they gave and raised, either directly or indirectly, most of the CDV's funds. Now they were given the right only to "initiate proposals" and to be "consulted" prior to endorsing candidates, issuing policy statements, adopting platforms, amending the

---

pressed the same view: "I don't feel I should be part of any organization which attempts to speak for me." The New Democratic Club sent no representation to either the old or the reorganized CDV.

Plan of Structure, and taking "major political steps," and it was recognized that "emergency situations" might require CDV to act without such consultation. Thus, limits were imposed on the extent to which the advisors could be the major source of leadership. Herbert Lehman, a former governor and senator, eighty-three years old and with vast financial resources, was given the same vote on the General Committee as a twenty-two-year-old college student from the Bronx who had been in politics for six months.

This had several consequences. First, the logic of intraparty democracy was carried up from the club to the CDV, making difficult the problem of tactical co-ordination. Second, the recruitment of older, economically and politically successful advisors and members-at-large was rendered somewhat more difficult by requiring them to serve with one vote each on the large (over one hundred and twenty members) General Committee in a way which was often contrary to their own conceptions of their status. Stated more formally, the incentives available to the CDV for attracting contributions of time and effort from the rank-and-file amateurs were increased while the inducements available for attracting status and money were reduced. The "liberal fat cats" had to relinquish control over the organization they financed. But third, the prestige of the advisors continued to give them a leadership role despite the constitutional limitations placed on them, and this conflict between informal power and formal impotence created misunderstanding and criticisms. Because of Lehman's stature, newspapers and other politicians still looked to him as the "head" of the reform movement even though formally he was nothing of the sort. Thus, his announcement that "personally" favored the nomination of Wagner for re-election as mayor, before the CDV had acted on the endorsement placed the CDV in an awkward position. It had to choose between making an endorsement to which many reformers, although probably not most, were opposed, or repudiating an "informal" leader. Many militant clubs, such as the VID, FDR-Woodrow Wilson, and the Riverside were disturbed being "committed" in this way.[19] In sum, the tensions within the CDV arose out of the criticisms of moderate reformers and elected district leaders who felt it gave too much power to the "irresponsible" insurgents, of advisors who saw themselves contributing to an organization which they found hard to control, and of militant clubs who saw their formal power still weakened by the informal authority of the advisors.

Although California largely escaped problems of the kind that afflicted the CDV, the task of co-ordination did arise in the relation of the CDC to other party organizations. The clubs and the Los Angeles County Democratic Central Committee are, unlike their New York counterparts, allies and generally sympathetic to one another. Their staffs share the same offices and facilities. Presumably, relations between the CDC and the county committee would be close.

In fact, it is this very closeness which creates difficulties. The Los Angeles experience may presage what might happen in Manhattan if the reformers won control of Tammany Hall. Then there would be two pro-reform organizations in existence, one defending the pure amateur spirit and the other attempting to reconcile that spirit with the demands of official party office. Some of the possible difficulties can perhaps be seen in Los Angeles.

First, any two organizations with comparable goals and similar views which compete for resources from a single area in order to maintain separate identities are bound to produce a good deal of friction. What is surprising is that there is not more friction than there is. The chairman of the Los Angeles County Committee and the CDC vice-president for that region can both claim to be the leader of the party's grass-roots organization in that county. Both do make that claim, at least implicitly, and as a result there have been clashes.

Second, each organization requires slightly different incen-

[19] See *New York Times*, May 23, 1961. Earlier, the CDV General Committee had adopted a resolution opposing the possible selection of Peter Crotty, Democratic leader of Erie County (Buffalo), as Democratic State Chairman. Lehman had asked the CDV not to act in this way, but his advice was disregarded. *New York Times*, April 9, 1961.

tives to maintain itself, and the distribution of these produces a difference in emphasis in their general behavior. The CDC requires a concern for ideal benefactions and the appeals of principle and personality; the county committtee, on the other hand, is composed of persons elected to legal posts and is thus concerned more with raising funds to support its activities than with inducing people to participate. As a result, CDC is often critical of the lack of militancy on the part of the county committee, while the leaders of the latter sometimes deplore the extreme positions on issues the CDC is wont to take.

Third, the CDC is concerned with getting clubs to affiliate with it, while the county committee is more interested in getting new clubs chartered, regardless of whether they affiliate with the CDC or not. The clubs have two parents, and these parents frequently quarrel over the custody of the children (and sometimes seem to be on the verge of suing for separate maintenance). A CDC official lamented that "the CDC is the mother organization, but . . . we are a mother that doesn't give birth. If we do have offspring, it's only by adoption and even then a lot of the children we'd like to adopt remain orphans." The CDC criticizes the county committee for not insisting that new clubs affiliate with CDC; the county committee rejoins that they are lucky to get any new clubs at all, and it would be foolish to insist on something that some clubs will not consider.

This problem is particularly acute since there are few, if any, sanctions which the county committee or the CDC can use to assert control over the clubs. Although technically the county committee could revoke the charter of any club not abiding by its rules, in fact this move is almost never given serious consideration. Thus, the simple requirement that the clubs furnish the committee with a list of members is often evaded. As a county committee official explained, "We don't want to discourage growth. My God! Our problem is not in sanctioning clubs, but in getting enough of them to cover the precincts we have in the county. Our problem is to get them to do something at all—not to keep them from acting."

# 9 The Class Basis of Amateur Democrats

The amateur club movement is, with few exceptions, a middle-class phenomenon. In the long run this, more than its factionalism, will probably prove to be its single greatest weakness.

Of the thirty-three leadership districts in Manhattan, only sixteen (or fewer than one half) have clubs which are affiliated with the CDV. In addition, two other districts have reform clubs which for various reasons are not part of the movement. The gaps are revealing: there were (in 1961) no reform clubs in Harlem, none in the Irish section of Washington Heights, none in the lower-income Italian and Jewish districts of the lower East Side and lower Manhattan, and none in the Italian upper East Side.

Although there are CDC club members living in all twelve Los Angeles congressional districts, well over one-half of the members live in four districts in the north and northwest portions of the county.[1] Of the ten largest clubs in the county, eight are found in four congressional districts.

The heaviest concentration of CDC clubs and CDC members is found in a broad belt running east and west on the northern side of the county, from the Pacific Ocean along the Santa Monica Mountains inland to Pomona, and including such areas as Beverly Hills, the UCLA campus in Westwood, Hollywood, the suburban areas of the San Fernando Valley, Pasadena, and the college towns of Claremont and Pomona. This area has more CDC members at its western end than its

[1] In February, 1961, there were 6,538 of the 11,606 members in congressional districts 15, 16, 21, and 22.

eastern end. South of it are, with a few exceptions, communities with lower incomes, fewer university areas, and more minority groups. To the south, extending as far as the harbor at San Pedro and Wilmington, are areas of working-class families. In the center, in such places as Watts, Willowbrook, Compton, and West Adams, is the large Negro community, now numbering over 461,000 persons.[2] To the east of the Negro area is the equally large Mexican-American district around East Los Angeles, Montebello, and Boyle Heights. Not only are there fewer clubs south of the northern area, but there are fewer members per club and a higher percentage of clubs unaffiliated with CDC.

Some of the central facts about the amateur clubs can be seen in Tables 4 and 5. In Table 4 the assembly districts of Los Angeles County are ranked in order of the Republican percentage of the 1960 presidential vote. The most heavily Democratic districts are at the top; the most heavily Republican districts are at the bottom. For each district is given the number of CDC-affiliated club members per thousand registered Democrats as of the end of 1960. In Table 5 the same data is given for Manhattan. The assembly districts are ranked on the basis of the Republican percentage of the total 1960 presidential vote, with the most Democratic (i.e., least Republican) districts at the top and the most Republican districts at the bottom. For each district the number of members of CDV-affiliated clubs per thousand registered Democrats is also given.[3]

Several inferences can be drawn from these tables. First, Democratic club strength tends to be concentrated in Republican areas. In Los Angeles, the three most heavily Democratic

[2] U.S. Department of Commerce, Bureau of the Census, *U.S. Census of Population: 1960,* Final Report PC (1)–6B, *California,* pp. 6–196. The figure is for Los Angeles County, where Negroes are 7.6 per cent of the total population. In the *city* of Los Angeles, the Negro population is 334,916, or 13.5 per cent of the total.

[3] The Manhattan chart includes the membership of the New Democratic Club in the Eighth Assembly District South because it is generally considered a "reform" club even though it has not voted to affiliate with the CDV.

assembly districts had an average of 1.0 CDC members per thousand Democrats while the four most heavily Republican areas had an average of nearly 17.2 CDC members per thousand Democrats. Of the three most Democratic districts, two (55 and 62) are largely Negro and one (40) is heavily Mexican. Of the four most Republican districts where the highest

TABLE 4

CDC STRENGTH IN LOS ANGELES

| Assembly District | Republican Percentage of Presidential Vote, 1960 | CDC Club Members per 1,000 Registered Democrats |
|---|---|---|
| 62......... | 17.1 | 1.5 |
| 55......... | 21.6 | 0.9 |
| 40......... | 22.5 | 0.6 |
| 61......... | 31.6 | 10.0 |
| 51......... | 35.4 | 3.5 |
| 65......... | 36.8 | 2.2 |
| 45......... | 36.9 | 3.7 |
| 66......... | 37.2 | 0.0 |
| 68......... | 38.5 | 1.5 |
| 63......... | 39.8 | 11.8 |
| 67......... | 41.8 | 1.4 |
| 69......... | 45.2 | 5.0 |
| 59......... | 48.4 | 36.0 |
| 52......... | 48.5 | 5.1 |
| 42......... | 48.6 | 5.9 |
| 41......... | 48.7 | 6.8 |
| 57......... | 50.5 | 17.1 |
| 56......... | 50.8 | 8.7 |
| 64......... | 51.6 | 7.0 |
| 44......... | 52.2 | 7.0 |
| 58......... | 52.5 | 9.6 |
| 70......... | 52.7 | 1.1 |
| 50......... | 54.1 | 0.4 |
| 54......... | 55.3 | 3.2 |
| 49......... | 57.9 | 7.8 |
| 46......... | 58.1 | 7.0 |
| 53......... | 59.4 | 0.0 |
| 60......... | 60.5 | 33.6 |
| 47......... | 64.9 | 12.2 |
| 43......... | 67.1 | 10.7 |
| 48......... | 68.3 | 12.2 |

Note: (1) The Republican percentage is of *total* vote, not the major party vote.
(2) Absentee ballots not counted. In this election, the absentee ballots, which totaled about 80,000, swung the election to the Republican candidate.
(3) Not all CDC members live in the same assembly district as the club to which they belong.

concentration of CDC members is found, all are high-income areas, and two (60 and 47) are near the sites of large universities (UCLA faculty live in the Pacific Palisades area of the Sixtieth Assembly District, California Institute of Technology faculty in the Pasadena area of the Forty-seventh Assembly District).

TABLE 5

CDV STRENGTH IN MANHATTAN

| Assembly District | Republican Percentage of Presidential Vote, 1960 | CDV Club Members per 1,000 Registered Democrats |
|---|---|---|
| 14......... | 18.7 | 0.0 |
| 11......... | 21.2 | 0.0 |
| 4......... | 21.7 | 0.0 |
| 12......... | 23.4 | 0.0 |
| 13......... | 24.5 | 0.0 |
| 16......... | 24.6 | 0.0 |
| 2......... | 27.7 | 0.0 |
| 15......... | 28.9 | 1.4 |
| 7......... | 29.7 | 30.2 |
| 5......... | 32.0 | 48.7 |
| 3.... .... | 34.9 | 16.6 |
| 10......... | 39.5 | 32.3 |
| 6......... | 40.0 | 8.7 |
| 1......... | 43.1 | 42.5 |
| 8......... | 51.8 | 31.4 |
| 9......... | 57.2 | 81.4 |

Note: (1) The Republican percentage is of *total* vote, not the major party vote.
(2) Absentee and military ballots not counted.
(3) Not all CDV members live in the same assembly district as the club to which they belong.

In Manhattan, four of the five most Republican districts (1, 8, 9, and 10) are areas of intense reform club activity. Reformers control the district leaderships in all parts of all four of these districts. Interestingly enough, they came to power in the *most* Republican parts of these districts at an early date; they acquired power in the *least* Republican parts of these areas only in 1961. Thus, they were first in power in the Murray Hill and Gramercy Park sections of the First Assembly District but not in the heavily Democratic Greenwich Village section until 1961. In the Tenth Assembly District, they first came to power in the Irish and German Yorkville section but not until 1961 in the Puerto Rican and Negro areas of East Harlem to the north. In the Eighth Assembly District they first came to power in the Republican Tudor City section in the south and only much later in the Democratic tenement section to the north. And in the most Democratic assembly districts (14, 11, 4, 12, 13, 16, and 2) they are not only not in power, they have no clubs at all.

In the 1961 New York City election, the natural Republicanism of most reform districts was of great importance in affecting the demands which reformers could make on Wagner, their successful candidate for mayor. Although he beat his Republican and independent opponents handily, the four Manhattan districts he failed to carry were all entirely or partly led by reformers, while his biggest majorities came from Negro and Puerto Rican areas.[4] Although the reformers were among Wagner's most active *primary* election supporters, they were (with the exception of the Seventh and Tenth Assembly districts) almost powerless to deliver in the general election. (In areas such as Greenwich Village there was so little enthusiasm for Wagner that very little *effort* was made on his behalf.) The result of this situation, of course, was to increase greatly the difficulty of translating reform successes in capturing *party* offices (such as district leader) into success in influencing *public* officials (such as the mayor). The Harlem leaders, by contrast, were not faced with this dilemma.

Both the Los Angeles and Manhattan tables reveal certain important exceptions to this general pattern. In Los Angeles, the Sixty-first Assembly District is both heavily Democratic and has a large number of CDC members. In Manhattan, the Fifth and Seventh Assembly districts are strongly Democratic but also have a large concentration of CDV club members and

[4] He lost the First, Sixth, Eighth, and Ninth Assembly districts and only narrowly carried the Fifth. These reform districts also showed the greatest decline in the Wagner vote between 1957 and 1961. The Harlem districts scarcely declined at all. Seven reform districts gave Wagner in 1961 an average of 45 per cent of the vote; the four Harlem districts gave him an average of 78.5 per cent.

the reformers are in power in both areas. These three "deviant" districts (61 in Los Angeles and 5 and 7 in Manhattan) can be explained for the most part by the high concentration of Jewish voters residing in them.[5] The Sixty-first Assembly District, for example, includes the communities of Culver City and Venice and the Beverly-Fairfax, Wilshire-Fairfax, Cheviot Hills, and Mar Vista neighborhoods. These have the highest concentration of Jewish families of any part of the county (with the exception of Beverly Hills). In 1959, the Jewish Federation of Greater Los Angeles calculated, on the basis of a sample survey, the Jewish population of these areas, all of which lie largely within the Sixty-first Assembly District:[6]

| Community | Jewish Population as Percentage of Entire Population |
| --- | --- |
| Wilshire-Fairfax | 63.0 |
| Beverly-Fairfax | 70.0 |
| Beverlywood–Cheviot Hills–Mar Vista | 27.2 |

In that district, one out of every hundred of the more than 93,000 registered Democrats was a CDC member, the eighth highest concentration in the county and the highest for any district with more than 62 per cent registered Democrats. Other areas with large numbers of CDC members were similarly heavily Jewish. The Fifty-ninth Assembly District, about half of which consists of the city of Beverly Hills, which in 1959 was estimated to be 52.6 per cent Jewish, had the highest concentration of CDC members—36 per thousand Democrats.[7]

[5] Explanations for the effect of Jewishness in offsetting the normally conservative influence of high socio-economic status are offered in Lawrence H. Fuchs, *The Political Behavior of American Jews* (Glencoe: Free Press, 1956), and Werner Cohn, "The Politics of American Jews," in Marshall Sklare, ed., *The Jews* (Glencoe: Free Press, 1958), pp. 614–26.

[6] Fred Massarik, *A Report on the Jewish Population of Los Angeles* (Los Angeles: Jewish Federation Council of Greater Los Angeles, 1959), p. 8.

[7] Not all CDC members live in the same assembly district in which their club is found. Over half the members of the Beverly Hills Democratic Club live outside Beverly Hills. But this is the exception. In general, the clubs take on the character of the neighborhood in which they are chartered.

In Manhattan, the Fifth and Seventh Assembly districts have traditionally been the two areas of greatest Liberal party strength. Amateur Democrats and Liberals are both found in large numbers in these areas despite the large number of registered Democrats for the same reason: voting the Liberal party ticket and joining the reform clubs are both ways for persons to support Democratic candidates at the *national* level while opposing unacceptable Democrats at the *local* level. In Table 6 the Manhattan districts are ranked by the average percentage of the total vote won by the Liberals.

TABLE 6

CDV CLUB MEMBERS AND LIBERAL
PARTY STRENGTH

| Assembly District | Average Liberal Party Vote as Per Cent of Total* | CDV Club Members per 1,000 Registered Democrats |
|---|---|---|
| 7 | 13.1 | 30.2 |
| 5 | 12.8 | 48.7 |
| 4 | 11.8 | 0.0 |
| 15 | 11.4 | 1.4 |
| 1 | 11.4 | 42.5 |
| 13 | 10.7 | 0.0 |
| 6 | 10.1 | 8.7 |
| 12 | 9.9 | 0.0 |
| 11 | 9.2 | 0.0 |
| 14 | 8.9 | 0.0 |
| 3 | 8.7 | 16.6 |
| 2 | 8.6 | 0.0 |
| 9 | 7.3 | 81.4 |
| 8 | 6.9 | 31.4 |
| 10 | 6.5 | 32.3 |
| 16 | 6.4 | 0.0 |

* Since the Liberal party sometimes endorses major party candidates and sometimes runs its own candidates, the percentages in this column are an unweighted average of the Liberal percentage of the total vote in three elections: the 1956 presidential election, the 1958 Attorney-General election, and the 1960 election for Judge of the Court of General Sessions of New York County. These three were chosen because they represented the range of possible endorsement patterns. In 1956, the Liberals endorsed the same candidate as the Democrats (Adlai E. Stevenson); in 1958 they ran their own candidate (Edward Goodell) independently of both major parties; in 1960 they endorsed the Republican (Samuel Pierce). The assembly districts maintained roughly the ranking given above no matter whom the Liberals endorsed, but the *size* of the vote varied considerably. The Liberal party vote was lowest when the party endorsed the Democrat, highest when it endorsed the Republican, and fell between these extremes when it ran its own candidate.

The bulwark of the Liberal party, of course, has always been the major Jewish labor unions—the International Ladies Garment Workers Union and the United Cap, Hat, and Millinery Workers.[8] The Fifth and Seventh Assembly districts, in the heart of Manhattan's West Side, are part of an area with a large middle-class Jewish population.

Amateur Democrats are not simply found wherever there are Jews, however. The third most Liberal assembly district, the Fourth District, is an area of many Jewish families, and there are large numbers of Jews in Washington Heights, which is part of the Fifteenth Assembly District. Neither the Fourth nor the Fifteenth Assembly districts has any CDV club members to speak of. The explanation for this seems to be that Jews must be of a certain income and occupational status before they become recruits to reform, even though Jews of all income levels will support the Liberal party. In 1957 there were five Manhattan neighborhoods with a Jewish population estimated at one-fifth or more of the total. But, as Table 7 suggests, the class characteristics of these areas varied significantly.

The Jewish areas with a small percentage of people in professional and managerial occupations and with few persons with incomes of ten thousand dollars a year or more were the lower East Side and Washington Heights. These correspond, more or less, to the Fourth and Fifteenth Assembly districts, which have a high Democratic and Liberal party vote but little reform club activity. On the other hand, Park West, Times Square, and East Central Park, which correspond roughly to parts of the Fifth, First, and Eighth Assembly districts, were areas with many upper-income Jewish professionals and hence with extensive club activity.

There is evident in Los Angeles another kind of deviation from the general correlation between Republican strength and Democratic club membership. Districts 50, 53, and 70 are be-

[8] The rank and file of the two garment unions is today predominantly Negro and Puerto Rican, but the Liberal party still retains the political loyalties of many Jewish voters who were formerly garment workers, as well as those of Jews—now mostly in supervisory positions—who have remained in the garment industry.

low the median in Democratic registration but have very few
CDC members (in one case, none).[9] They are thus exceptions
to the general pattern that districts below the middle in Democratic registration have sizable numbers of CDC members.

A possible reason for this is that these three districts are inhabited, to a great extent, by lower and lower-middle income
persons (wage-earners, retired pensioners, lower-middle-class
shopkeepers) who tend to be conservative Democrats. These
are the areas of the lower-income conservatives, and they re-

TABLE 7

CHARACTERISTICS OF THE JEWISH POPULATION OF FIVE
MANHATTAN NEIGHBORHOODS, 1957*

| Community Area | 1957 Jewish Population as Percentage of Total (Est.) | Percentage in Professional or Managerial Occupations (Est.) | Percentage with Incomes $10,000 a Year or More (Est.) |
|---|---|---|---|
| Lower East Side..... | 33.7 | 13.8 | 0.6 |
| Park West.......... | 28.8 | 33.9 | 8.5 |
| East Central Park– Yorkville.......... | 19.8 | 28.5 | 11.0 |
| Washington Heights.. | 34.5 | 26.0 | 3.5 |
| Times Square....... | 18.3 | 40.9 | 18.8 |

* These data are from C. Morris Horowitz and Lawrence J. Kaplan, *The Jewish Population of the New York Area, 1900–1975* (New York: Federation of Jewish Philanthropies, 1959), pp. 125–67. The population estimates are based on what is known (believe it or not) as the "Yom Kippur Method" in which the drop-off in school attendance on Yom Kippur is noted, weighted for various neighborhood factors, and then inflated by a predetermined coefficient to arrive at the total Jewish population.

spond differently from the areas of the upper-income conservatives. There are neither enough upper-middle-class persons to
provide club leadership even if the area remained Republican
indefinitely nor enough lower-income persons of the kind who
vote Democratic without club influence.

In the Seventieth Assembly District, for example, an em-

[9] California politics is such that a district which is 55 or 56 per cent
Democratic in registration is regarded as "marginal." Of the seven assembly districts in Los Angeles County which had, in 1960, a Democratic registration of 50 to 56.5 per cent, five were held by Republican
incumbents. No one considers a district Democratic unless it has at least
a 56 per cent Democratic registration, and not safely so unless it is
58 per cent or more Democratic.

bryonic club movement began to evaporate after 1958 and virtually disappeared after 1960 when it found itself unable to elect a Democrat even though the district had a Democratic registration of over 56 per cent. Club leaders told an interviewer that they discovered that these people were, in large measure, only nominally Democratic (perhaps because of a Southern background) and usually voted Republican for almost all offices. The inability to win in a district which "ought" to have had a Democratic incumbent, and the shortage of club-type people in a district with moderate incomes and few Jews, led to a sense of frustration and defeatism which destroyed some of the clubs. Similar factors have been at work in the fiftieth and to some extent in the fifty-third. In addition, the situation is compounded by the fact that in these areas, remote from the center of political life in Los Angeles, such clubs as existed had been part of an independent district council for nearly six years before the formation of CDC. There was, thus, less of a vacuum for CDC to fill, and many of the leaders of the old clubs and councils preferred to stay aloof from CDC and its politics.

Some indirect but suggestive evidence for this interpretation can be found in the fact that these "deviant" districts (50, 53, and 70) were all in the first quartile (upper 25 per cent) of those Los Angeles County assembly districts which gave, in the 1960 Democratic presidential primary, the largest vote to George McLain, a pension promoter and leader of an organization of old folks. These are people on small, fixed incomes who tend to be politically conservative. The McLain vote tends to support the distinction made earlier on the basis of the level of CDC club activity, to wit: there are two kinds of Republican districts—those whose Democratic voters are upper-income liberals and those whose Democratic voters are lower-income conservatives.[10]

[10] The data gathered for this book were not of a kind that would permit the testing of this hypothesis. My interpretation, however, is widely shared by many politicians active in these areas. The districts in question should provide an excellent place to examine further what Professor Lipset and others call "status politics." Low or moderate

In summary, then, club strength appears to be closely related to income modified by ethnicity and status. Areas with upper-income professional and business people provide amateur Democrats who are not discouraged by their minority status, who realize that there is virtually nothing they can do to elect a Democratic incumbent and hence are not disappointed by frustrated ambitions, and who turn their attention and energies to the internal politics of the Democraic party and the club movement. If such upper-income areas are also heavily Jewish, the district is likely to be Democratic as well as deeply involved in club activity. Lower-income Jewish areas are much less likely to have club activity. If districts are Republican or only marginally Democratic as a result not of class (i.e., income) but of status, the CDC does not fare well. Finally, in areas which are heavily Democratic as a result of being low-income Negro, Puerto Rican, or Mexican-American, the club movement is weak.

## The Excluded Majority

In general, there are six major groups within the Democratic party which, for a variety of reasons, are not attracted to or enthusiastic participants in the club movement. These are the Negroes, Mexican-Americans, Puerto Ricans, organized labor, big financial contributors, and professional politicians. The tension between the amateur and the professional will be discussed at length in the next chapter, since it is the principal focus of the struggle for political power within the party. The absence from the club movement of the other five groups is less a struggle for power than a product of alienation. The amateur clubs pride themselves on being "open" organizations —open at the top for new leadership, democratically elected,

---

incomes, combined with rural backgrounds and old age, may produce a kind of conservatism and even, in some cases, nativism. Cf. Seymour Martin Lipset, *Political Man* (Garden City, N.Y.: Doubleday & Co., 1960), pp. 238–48, and Daniel Bell, ed., *The New American Right* (New York: Criterion Books, 1955).

and open at the bottom for new members, freely admitted. In fact, however, the orientation of the clubs to the intellectual middle class means that the political style and rhetoric of the organization are not felt to be congenial by groups which, in total, represent the bulk of the electoral and financial support of the Democratic party. Many club leaders realize this. CDC President Joseph Wyatt found himself agreeing with Assemblyman Jesse Unruh's criticism of the CDC for not being genuinely representative of the party's rank and file when Unruh's views were under attack at a Sacramento meeting of club leaders:

> No, the clubs aren't really open. We have to be . . . open at the top and the bottom, but . . . there are many people who are organizationally unsophisticated, who feel socially and educationally inferior in a club situation. People don't go, you know, where they don't feel welcome, and many people don't feel at home in the clubs. They don't understand parliamentary procedure. There's quite a technique . . . to being active in the CDC. A lot of people don't have this. Many clubs, as a result, price themselves out of the market—in money or in the kind of activities they undertake.

The absence of Negroes, Mexicans, Puerto Ricans, and laborers from the amateur clubs is probably only a special case of the general failure of lower-status groups to participate in voluntary associations, a phenomenon which has been widely documented.[11] Lower-income persons have less leisure time and less money to give to community-regarding endeavors; their work time is not flexible and they can rarely attend that fundamental institution for the transaction of civic business, the conference-luncheon; they often lack the educational back-

---

11 See, for example, Mirra Komarovsky, "The Voluntary Associations of Urban Dwellers," *American Sociological Review*, XI (1946), 686–98; Floyd Dotson, "Patterns of Voluntary Association Membership among Urban Working-Class Families," *American Sociological Review*, XVI (1951), 687–93; Genevieve Knupfer, "Portrait of the Underdog," *Public Opinion Quarterly*, XI (1947), 114; Charles L. Wright and Herbert Hyman, "Voluntary Association Memberships of American Adults: Evidence from the National Sample Surveys," *American Sociological Review*, XXIII (1958), 284–94.

ground and particularly the verbal skills to feel at ease in organizational situations; they are aware of and made uncomfortable by differences in style of life and manner of speech; they are often suspicious of motives and less willing to play what they regard as the other fellow's game; and they are often put off by what they feel is pointless parliamentary maneuvering and bickering, particularly over questions of only remote or theoretical significance. Of these, the felt differences in style of life are probably most important. One laborer, who quit a CDC club and sought to organize a club composed of his kind of men, explained in disgust that "the CDC was run by the kind of people who want to raise money through a wine-tasting contest."

Even when clubs are successfully formed in lower-income areas, they function in a significantly different fashion. One small but particularly vigorous example was the Harry S. Truman Democratic Club in Los Angeles. It came into being just before the elections because a few friends were concerned over unemployment in the aircraft plants where they all worked. They wanted to "do something" about it by working to defeat the incumbent Republican assemblyman and elect a Democratic president who would deal with a bread-and-butter issue. Because of the ability and energy of two members who spent their evenings on club business, the group was able to raise over $600 for party candidates, stage a registration drive that helped bring in between 900 and 1,000 new voters, canvass their forty-two precincts to produce a turnout that averaged almost 90 per cent, and operate a campaign headquarters. This remarkable performance would do credit to a larger club in a much more affluent neighborhood. But the club was quite unlike a middle-class CDC unit. It never had more than thirty members, only fifteen of whom were active and most of whom quit as soon as the election was over. The club never had regular meetings, never drew up a constitution or bylaws, and operated entirely on the basis of informal understandings about the division of labor. No name speakers were asked to address the club, and the only social event was a pizza dinner to raise money for the campaign. Because of the religious issue, President Kennedy did very poorly in the area, but the Democratic congressman was re-elected overwhelmingly. The headquarters was made possible by the local United Auto Workers union, which gave them a hall for the nominal fee of five dollars a month. With the election over and having held no meetings since election night, the club was uncertain what to do. A sucession of clubs had existed in the area, each with the same name and each called into being for a specific election. The president told an interviewer that he wanted to keep the club going and organize it on a regular basis, but he was afraid the members would get bored with the "long, petty fights" this would require.

In and around Chicago, the relations between middle-class amateur Democrats and the working classes are similar to those in Los Angeles. But in downstate Illinois, the two areas of greatest club strength were Rockford and St. Clair County. These clubs, unlike their Chicago and suburban counterparts, were firmly based in the working class and had done remarkably well. In Rockford the club in 1961 had 320 members and had managed to elect half the precinct committeemen in the county.[12] In 1958 it only narrowly failed to control the Democratic county convention. The leadership of the club has been drawn in great part from union leaders, lesser white collar workers, small shop owners, and workers. Proportionally fewer lawyers have served on the Board of Directors.

In St. Clair County, there were nine DFI clubs, all drawing on workers from the industrial area of East St. Louis and Belleville. Some of these clubs have had several hundred members. The Rockford and St. Clair clubs are as different from the intellectually oriented Chicago clubs as the Harry S. Truman club in Los Angeles is from the club in Beverly Hills. The St. Clair clubs can serve as an illustration. Their leader,

---

[12] In Chicago, precinct captains are appointed by the ward committeemen. Downstate, however, the law provides that the precinct workers be elected by the voters. This provides clubs with an excellent opportunity for challenging the control of the regular organization.

Mike Haas, at fifty-nine was at least twenty years older than most of the middle-class leaders. He smoked cigars and held and sought patronage jobs. The goals of his clubs were clearly local. They sought to unseat the existing Democratic county chairman and to this end had formed an alliance with other professional politicians. Haas told an interviewer he opposed letting the clubs become involved with or concerned in national and international issues which, he felt, were only a distraction. He gave at best lukewarm support to such race relations measures as a proposed fair employment practices act which had excited the enthusiasm of the Chicago clubs. He was contemptuous of the elitist nature of the Chicago clubs and their small memberships. "Maybe in the eyes of Chicago we are a little hay-seedy. . . . But I could never understand why Cook County couldn't organize bigger clubs." Because of the size of his clubs, Haas became a leader in the statewide DFI, was elected executive vice-president in 1959, and eventually succeeded to the presidency when Dan Walker resigned.

The young, middle-class DFI leaders were suspicious of Haas and his clubs, and some were openly hostile. "St. Clair County was just a patronage organization," said one. "It was as if Daley had come in." Another noted that Haas "had a different kind of organization than most of our people. They were union people, working people, willing to follow him blindly. I don't want to give the wrong impression. He is a fine guy . . . but personally ambitious [and] he wants to be a power in his own county."

Relations between reform and working-class groups in Manhattan are indicated by the problems created for the CDV when it had to choose between two competing reform clubs in one district. In the Third Assembly District North, one club, the Park-Hudson Independent Democrats, had a strong working-class base, including many Puerto Ricans; the other, the Ansonia Independent Democrats, was a middle-class club with several lawyers. Both put up candidates for district leader in 1961. It quickly became clear that the reform movement generally found it easier to work with the middle-class

Ansonia club. Some reformers spoke wistfully of the need to attract into the movement the kind of members the Park-Hudson club had, but they felt the club had "bad leadership" and was "unreliable." The Park-Hudson leaders were too concerned with patronage for the militant reformers. "Those people are only interested in personal gain," said one CDV officer. "Now their leaders are all supporting Levitt [the regular organization candidate for mayor in 1961]. We never recognized them [but] we left the door open in hopes they would turn out to be our kind of people. The only reason we worked with them at all is because of their working-class membership, which we felt we needed." The CDV distrust of the Park-Hudson club, like the DFI dismay with the St. Clair County clubs, was probably more than just a dislike for "questionable leaders," but more fundamentally a special case of the general reaction of cosmopolitan amateur Democrats against what are, in all probability, the inevitable attributes of any political organization with a working-class base.

## Labor

The reasons why lower-income groups either do not respond to the appeals of the club movement or respond in a distinctive (and, to club leaders, inadequate) fashion are, of course, well known and widely discussed. What is not so obvious is why organized labor (the leaders of which are, in most cases, above their followers in income, status, and organizational skills) should reject an alliance with the CDC or the CDV and why so many middle-class and even intellectual Negroes and Mexicans should remain aloof from the club movement. The first case, that of the trade unions, can be explained in simplest terms as a conflict between the maintenance requirements of the two organizations. For example, the Los Angeles Central Labor Council, which has represented since 1959 the merged AFL and CIO labor movement, is, like many such county federations, a body concerned in its political relations with bread-and-butter, largely non-ideological issues of interest to mem-

bers and to the organization. The council has a Committee on
Political Education (COPE) with a full-time director, but in
the past labor has played only a small role in campaigns except by making endorsements and contributing funds.[13] This is
probably a function of labor's past weakness in the city as a
whole. Unlike Detroit, there is no single union giant which
dominates the movement, and union membership has been low.
In general, most locals have been "business unions," and even
those unions most deeply involved in government (such as
Local 18 of the International Brotherhood of Electrical Workers, which represents a large and powerful group of city employees in such agencies as the Department of Water and
Power) engage in little political activity at the district level.
Beginning in 1960, however, COPE has attempted to organize
committees in each congressional district with subcommittees
in several assembly districts and in the 1960 general election
was active to some degree in at least seven congressional
districts (17, 18, 19, 21, 22, 23, and 25).

COPE regards the CDC and its clubs as both a rival for political influence and as a source of irrelevant and possibly dangerous ideology. In January, 1961, the County Federation of
Labor gave expression to this view by passing a resolution opposing pre-primary endorsements made by any organization
using the name of a political party.[14] Although stated in general terms, it was clearly aimed at the CDC. The resolution
gave as reasons the view that voters should have a free choice
in primaries and that pre-primary endorsements reduced that
choice by party "interference" which discouraged able potential candidates from entering the contest. In fact, CDC endorsements were opposed because they were often in conflict

[13] Labor in Los Angeles is exhaustively discussed in Richard Baisden,
"Labor Unions in Los Angeles Politics" (Ph.D. thesis, Department of
Political Science, University of Chicago, 1958).

[14] Text in *Los Angeles Citizen* (official publication of the Los Angeles
County Federation of Labor), January 20, 1961, pp. 1, 4. The resolution called upon the state legislature to adopt a law prohibiting pre-
primary endorsements "by any political party or members thereof using
the name of any political party."

with labor endorsements.[15] There were at least five cases of labor and CDC candidates opposing each other in Democratic primaries in 1960 (labor candidates won in three, CDC in two) and several more in which labor candidates, although not challenged by a rival, were not accepted by CDC.[16] The Secretary-Treasurer of the County Federation of Labor supported the anti-CDC resolution because it would "enable organized labor to carry out the COPE program without interference or coercion from political parties or political clubs."[17]

Labor leaders, such as the Director of COPE, are critical of the clubs for many of the same reasons advanced by Democratic legislators: the CDC is preoccupied with "left-wing" issues, has been infiltrated by persons with dubious political backgrounds and radical sentiments, and is ineffective in heavily Democratic low-income areas. Whatever the validity of such views, there is no doubt that, with the possible exception of certain United Auto Workers locals (which have large memberships in the aircraft and auto assembly plants in the country), organized labor and COPE will continue to consider CDC a rival. Labor prefers a weak party for the same reason that many incumbents do: a strong, even unofficial, party organization, such as CDC, which can only be maintained by the use of ideologically significant issues, is a possible source of political contamination.

In New York, the relations between organized labor and the amateur clubs have been characterized more by disinterest than by active hostility. In part this may be because the re-

[15] Needless to say, the federation did not suggest that organized labor should be denied the right to make endorsements in primaries. This omission was explained to an interviewer on the grounds that labor is not an official party organization but a private association making recommendations only to its members.

[16] Labor defeated CDC candidates in the Eighteenth Congressional, Eleventh Senatorial, and Seventh Assembly districts. CDC defeated labor endorsees in the Ninth Congressional and the Eleventh Assembly districts. In the Fifteenth Congressional District, a candidate with strong club backing (although no official endorsement) was strongly opposed by labor.

[17] *Los Angeles Citizen*, January 20, 1961, p. 4.

formers had not pressed any legislative program that would arouse the antagonism of labor and, in any case, had not by 1961 arrived at such a position of power within the Democratic party that labor would have to deal with them. The unions most active in politics at the local level have been those (the ILGWU and the Hatters) which form the backbone of the Liberal party. The Liberals have frequently failed to endorse reform candidates in Manhattan.[18] Most of the other unions have rarely played an important role in the endorsing process and few have engaged in any significant canvassing work. The AFL, dominated by the Building Trades Council, was for many years oriented toward Tammany Hall and the regular organizations, and followed a conservative, apolitical policy of seeking bread-and-butter benefits for its unions.

In 1961, two years after the AFL-CIO merger in New York, the Central Labor Council of the city announced plans to form a new political party for the purpose of strengthening labor's hand in dealing with political leaders. This new organization, which came to be called the Brotherhood party, was led by the chairman of the Central Labor Council, Harry Van Arsdale, and included among its supporters most of the leaders of the major New York unions, including the Teamsters, the Building Trades Council, the Transport Workers Union, the Building Services Employees, the Hotel Trades Council, the Utility Workers Union, the Brotherhood of Sleeping Car Porters, the Retail, Wholesale, and Department Store Union, and others. The first act of the new Brotherhood party was to endorse Mayor Wagner for re-election and to open campaign headquarters in various assembly districts.

The purpose of the new labor party was not to "reform" the Democratic organization or to press for any particular candi-

[18] The Liberal party endorsed Ludwig Teller rather than the reform challenger, William Fitts Ryan, in the 1960 congressional primary. In 1961, they backed Stanley M. Isaacs, the Republican city councilman, rather than his reform Democratic opponent, Richard Zief; Harry Suchman, rather than the reform Council candidate, Theodore Weiss; and Isobel Soto Garcia, rather than the reform Council candidate, Robert A. Low.

date or legislation, but simply to win bargaining power for labor leaders in the same way that the Liberal party unions had won power for themselves. "We are sick and tired of being taken for granted, of being handed candidates we have to take without consultation and of being ignored once the balloting is over," said a union leader. "We are not mad at anybody. . . . What we are against is the notion that we are a bunch of idiots . . . whom the politicians can push around without worrying about the consequences."[19]

The labor leaders of the Brotherhood party were not enthusiastic about the reform movement. "We feel we can't rely on the reformers," a top labor leader said. "As soon as they get in power they will act just like Tammany Hall. The only way to get anything from any politician, regular or reform, is to be able to deliver votes on your own. Then they'll listen." Evidence of this disinterest in the questions that agitated reformers was the support given by Van Arsdale and other top labor leaders to Democratic State Chairman Michael H. Prendergast and Tammany leader Carmine De Sapio just four months before the formation of the Brotherhood party. The support was given at a time when reform attacks on the two Democratic leaders were at a peak.[20] The break with the regular Democratic organization and the support given Wagner by labor were evidence, not of any objection in principle to Tammany, but of a desire to display independent strength and provide some support for a mayor who was personally popular among certain labor leaders.

*Minorities*

Negroes are not prominent in club politics in Chicago, Los Angeles, or New York.[21] In Chicago, where Negroes organized

[19] Quoted in *New York Times*, April 13, 1961.

[20] *New York Times*, January 14, 1961. The CDV General Committee has only two labor members, both elected at large: one from the United Auto Workers, the other from the Textile Workers.

[21] On Negro political and civic leadership, see James Q. Wilson, *Negro Politics: The Search for Leadership* (New York: Free Press of

and led by Representative William L. Dawson are a large and important part of the regular Democratic organization, their absence is understandable. Almost all the rewards of political activity are controlled by the Chicago machine. Although the membership of one unit of the IVI was about 40 per cent Negro, this organization drew almost entirely from two integrated, upper-middle-income, high-rise apartment projects located in the Second Ward and only from a minority of the Negroes living there at that.

In Los Angeles, where there has been no organized political party Negroes could move into and where the opportunities for organizing Negroes seem unlimited, the CDC clubs have made few inroads. In 1961 there was no Negro among the thirty-eight voting members of the CDC board of directors and no Negro who was president of a congressional district council. The absence of any club life in the Fifty-fifth and Sixty-second Assembly districts, which are populated for the most part by low-income Negroes, is understandable. Their absence in the middle-class Negro areas of the Sixty-third and Sixty-fifth districts is not so easy to explain. Although there were eleven CDC clubs in the Sixty-third in 1961, all but two were in the all-white, largely Jewish west side of the district. Negro clubs in the Sixty-fifth and Fifty-eighth districts were, in most cases, small in size and not affiliated with the CDC.

In part, of course, the growth of clubs in their districts is discouraged by Democratic incumbents. This is true of all-Negro areas, even (or particularly) the one represented by the Negro office-holder.[22] For the Negro assemblyman, clubs are of no value in a solidly Democratic area and a possible

Glencoe, 1960). On New York and Chicago Negro politics, see James Q. Wilson, "Two Negro Politicians: An Interpretation," *Midwest Journal of Political Science,* IV (November, 1960), 349–69.

[22] Augustus F. Hawkins was the sole Negro holding elective office from Los Angeles County (Sixty-second Assembly District). He had been in office continuously since 1934. The other solidly Negro district (55) was represented by a white man (Vernon Kilpatrick), as were the other districts where Negroes were a sizable minority (63, 65, and 58).

nuisance in their concern over issues and endorsements. For the white assemblyman, such clubs in Negro areas have the added disadvantage that they might consider agitating to replace the white incumbent with a Negro.

But incumbent hostility is not the only factor, or even the most important one. Lacking any substantial amounts of patronage, there is little an assemblyman could do in any tangible way that would frustrate the efforts of determined club leaders. In fact, there are few such determined leaders. In Los Angeles, there are (unlike Chicago) few rewards available for an ambitious and energetic Negro attorney seeking a place in politics. There is no machine which can "buy off" the restless and thereby co-opt possible sources of political rebellion. And, because of the manner in which district lines are drawn, there have been practically no opportunities for Negroes to win elective office. The able and the ambitious Negroes are, insofar as they are interested in politics, confronted with a frustrating situation in which elective rewards are denied them and patronage rewards are unavailable.[23]

In Manhattan, there were no reform clubs in any Harlem district in 1961 and none in prospect. The politics of Harlem is unstable because politics in New York City generally is unstable; alliances are made and broken with dazzling speed and the rate of insurgency is as high or higher than anywhere else in the city. As a result, Harlem's political life is Florentine in its complexity and subtlety. But reform has not been an issue. Reformers are bent on changing the political system; the Harlem leaders do not want to change it so much as they want to get in on it. In a speech to the Lexington Club in 1960, Harlem politician J. Raymond Jones said, in effect, that Negroes in Manhattan are more interested in winning representation in local politics than in the fight against bossism.[24] Harlem leaders, like Tammany leaders generally, regard the reformers

[23] This is explored in James Q. Wilson, "Negro Civic Leaders," paper read before the 1960 annual meeting of the American Political Science Association, New York City, 1960 (mimeographed).

[24] *New York Times,* June 21, 1960.

as hypocritical, unreliable, and overly ambitious. The reformers, in turn, consider the Negro leaders mere opportunists anxious for the spoils of politics and willing to make any deal with De Sapio that is to their advantage. One reform leader said in public that "they are not our kind of reformers."

In all three cities, amateur club leaders have been disheartened by their attempts to bring Negroes into the movement. Except for a handful with an intellectual orientation or a professional background, most potential Negro leaders seem (to the amateur Democrat) to be primarily interested either in the conventional rewards of the professional politician or in "racist" slogans and extreme positions. Few seem to share the white liberal's concern for "integration" and "equal opportunity" or the white reformer's desire to "democratize" the party. Adam Clayton Powell, Jr., the mercurial Harlem congressman, arouses the profound distrust of almost all Manhattan reformers. Powell himself was an insurgent who broke with Tammany in 1958 after De Sapio had attempted to "purge" him in the congressional primary.[25] Easily defeating his opponent, Powell went on in 1959 to lead a group of Negro politicians who won the leaderships in three Harlem districts formerly ruled by De Sapio allies. This new group, which termed itself the "Unified Democratic Leadership Team," was lead by Representative Powell and his chief political strategist and fellow district leader, J. Raymond Jones. The Harlem group, which soon increased to five district leaders, opposed De Sapio on several issues. One was Negro dissatisfaction over the allocation of patronage to Harlem leaders. Another was the embryonic contest between De Sapio and Harlem over the Democratic nomination for Manhattan borough president, a post then held by a Negro, Hulan Jack. When Jack was convicted on charges of improper conduct in office, it was evident he would not be a candidate again. During the summer of 1960, the Harlem team waged a frankly nationalistic campaign urg-

[25] David Hapgood, *The Purge That Failed: Tammany v. Powell* ("Case Studies in Practical Politics" [New York: Henry Holt & Co., 1959]).

ing Negroes to support their local leaders in order to compel concessions from De Sapio. Posters urged: "Negroes! Don't You Be Responsible for Our Losing the Borough Presidency. Register and Vote!"

Within two years, however, this "Unified Team" fell apart. Jones and Powell fought each other over a nomination for a City Council seat being vacated. Both leaders advanced candidates for the post and no compromise proved possible. Further, Jones had been brought into alliance with Mayor Wagner after the latter had supported Jones's nominee for borough president. Indeed, Jones quickly became one of the chief strategists for the Mayor's re-election campaign, running the petition-gathering operation and organizing the Harlem workers. Powell, in the meantime, announced his support of Wagner's opponent, Arthur Levitt, and thereby re-established his alliance with De Sapio that had been broken three years before.

Such maneuvers, needless to say, left the reformers perplexed and disdainful. One reform club which shared a City Council district with Jones's club entered into a temporary alliance with him to support a common candidate, but there was a certain uneasiness on the side of the reformers about how much stock to place in their ally's good faith. Moderate reform leaders were willing to consider an alliance with Harlem forces for the purpose of deposing De Sapio, but militant reformers, with a less instrumental view of strategy, rejected such bargains with politicians who, in their eyes, were no better than De Sapio himself. They reverted to a central theme in the reform philosophy—ethnic recognition has no place in a democratic political system (where the "best man" should be supported regardless of his racial background) or in a democratic society (where racial justice means equality of opportunity but not special concessions). Thus, one reform district leader was hopeful of electing a reformer to the post of borough president in 1961. "I don't think it ought to be labelled as a 'Negro job.' . . . This will be a real fight, but I think by then we will have the votes, and Harlem will have to come to us." Reformers look forward to the day when "real leadership" emerges in Harlem (i.e., leadership similar in status and views to themselves) in place of the "bad" leadership that exists there today.

For his part, Jones had "a suggestion for all these dedicated idealists. They can join the Peace Corps." Powell, from the time he became district leader, announced that his primary concern was to see to it that Negroes were appointed to their share of patronage jobs in the city. He charged that Negroes, who he claimed cast 21 per cent of Manhattan's vote, received only 6 per cent of the political jobs. Instead, he argued, they should receive 21 per cent or more.[26] He also attacked New York police for driving Negro "bankers" out of the numbers racket in favor of Italians.[27]

The only reform club to have made significant inroads in the Puerto Rican and Negro areas of East Harlem has been the East Harlem Reform Democratic Club. The club's president is a Puerto Rican, Carlos Rios, who managed, in 1961, to be elected district leader, supplanting City Councilman John J. Merli, until then one of the most powerful of the Italian district leaders. The year before, this club, in alliance with the Yorkville Democratic Club in the south end of the district (an area of lower-income, often foreign-born whites), won the post of assemblyman for a young Jewish lawyer, Mark Lane. But because of the area, these reform clubs function in a way quite dissimilar to the conventional reform model and, indeed, many CDV leaders are not certain that Lane, Rios, and the others in the Tenth Assembly District should be considered reformers at all. With an incredibly congested, polyglot, lower-income constituency, these clubs are frankly interested in jobs for their members and material services for their constituents. Campaigns in this area, often called by both sides "the jungle," tend to be rough and raucous, with no holds barred. Lane entered politics first as an insurgent, not a reformer, after having served as an administrative assistant to the local regular-organization congressman; he moved into the reform camp

[26] *New York Times,* January 10, March 24, and April 5, 1960.

[27] *Ibid.,* January 10, 1960.

later. The East Harlem Reform Club from the first was different from the middle-class reform clubs with its loose structure, the concentration of authority in the hands of its leadership, and the absence of a strong emphasis on correct club procedures.

Similarly in Los Angeles, the active Negro political leaders have goals which the CDC club liberals find difficult to accept. Faced with their virtual exclusion from the political life of the community, some Negroes responded with the formation of the Democratic Minority Conference (DMC), a political organization which frankly sought increased political recognition for Negroes.[28] The DMC attempted to serve as a coordinating body for Negro clubs which would press for Negro offices in the Los Angeles County Democratic Central Committee, the City Council, and the state legislature. It was not part of CDC and soon found itself at odds with that group, on both organizational and ideological grounds. A sizable segment of the politically active Negro middle class tends to be nationalistic—i.e., to seek political gains for Negroes because they are Negroes rather than to be content with demanding "equal opportunity." CDC liberals are much more likely to consider the Negro question from the perspective of equal opportunity and integration, and to resent Negro demands for recognition simply on the grounds that they are numerous and entitled to them. There are many thoughtful Negroes who reject the equal-opportunity view as an empty abstraction. One prominent Negro attorney told an interviewer:

> We're beginning to feel that this attitude among white liberals is never going to get us anywhere and what we need is not opportunity but power. The only way we're going to get that is by drawing [the district] lines to give it to us. You're never going to have a Negro elected anywhere from a district that isn't all-Negro. We're just kidding ourselves if we think we can get it on any other basis.

[28] The Democratic Minority Conference is discussed in James Q. Wilson, *Negro Politics: The Search for Leadership,* p. 37.

This view represents, of course, not only an ideological difference with white liberals but an organizational conflict as well. The Negroes who enter clubs, with or without the DMC, are caught in what one Negro called a "paradox." The leadership wants more Negro representation in party and public office, but the rank-and-file Negro voters remain intensely Democratic. In Los Angeles, voting Democratic means, in all cases but one, voting for a white man. The dilemma is heightened by the fact that, since no Republican can win in a Negro area, a Negro can often obtain the Republican nomination by default. Thus, Negroes, by voting Democratic, vote not only for a white man but against a Negro. Negro leaders, who place office over party, find they lack the resources in their own community to overcome the frustration the city's political system forces upon them. The DMC has sought allies to strengthen its resources. Its only possible allies are the CDC and CDC clubs. But joining with the CDC means joining with an organization which, out of political necessity, feels it cannot afford not to endorse the Democratic incumbents in Negro areas and which, out of conviction, believes that the cause of integration is not served by what many refer to as "discrimination in reverse"— putting a Negro on the ticket just to have a Negro there. The price of allies for the DMC is endorsing white men, and this price has often been found too high. As a result, most observers feel the DMC is declining for lack of achievements or prospects.

In 1960, a Negro organization called the Committee for Representative Government was formed in Los Angeles to press on the state legislature a reapportionment plan, called the "two-four" plan, which would draw the new lines so as to create districts for two Negro congressmen and four assemblymen. Such a plan had little prospect for success, although one Negro congressman may be created. It is widely believed that Hawkins is planning to run for this seat.[29] At various CDC

[29] As a result of Hawkins' ambition for higher office, there are some signs of increased club activity in his area. County Committee officials ascribe this activity to his desire to build a wider organization, under his influence, which can further his candidacy.

and party meetings, Negroes advocating the two-four plan appeared to urge its adoption, but there was no sign of CDC support for the move and, indeed, every sign that the Negroes aroused some ill-will. At CDC conventions and conferences, very few Negroes are in evidence, even though the total attendance may number three or four thousand people from every part of the state, and those Negroes present are usually seen keeping to themselves, outside the flow of events of the meeting.

The same problem faced amateur Democrats in Chicago. With the exception of a few Negroes in the IVI and an even smaller number in the DFI, the bulk of the active Negro political leaders were either working within the regular organization, fighting the regular organization over questions of patronage and nominations for elective office, or organizing themselves on the basis of civil rights issues. Few were interested in reforming the Democratic party generally or in helping get "good candidates" (which usually meant white candidates) slated for office. A Negro Voters League was formed in Chicago to fight the regular organization, but the DFI-IVI amateurs quickly decided that its tactics and appeals were "too racist." The League sought to replace white ward committeemen and precinct captains with Negroes on the grounds that, if the area was heavily Negro, the political leadership ought to be Negro. One DFI leader observed that "our people usually found [the League] too race-oriented. Some of our people attended meetings of the League, and were put off because it was so rabid." A similar attitude was expressed by DFI leaders toward a Negro-based (but white-led) organization formed to protest against an urban renewal project. Amateur Democrats are passionately committed to a militant stand on civil rights, but they shy away from militant Negro organizations because they find them "too race-conscious."

The problems which afflict reformers in their stated (but sometimes not serious) desire to obtain minority-group support is not confined to the Negroes. Essentially the same difficulties are evident in their relations with Mexican-American leaders in Los Angeles who, like the Negroes, are not found in large numbers in the CDC. In part this may be because the Mexican middle class is smaller than that found among Negroes. Indeed, a recent voter registration drive conducted in the Mexican community (most of the Fortieth and Forty-fifth and parts of the Fifty-first and Sixty-second Assembly districts) was in great part financed by Negroes acting through the Democratic Minority Conference. Nonetheless, there has been a great deal of organizational activity among Mexicans, much of it with surprising success, and these organizations have in part pre-empted the vacuum which CDC would otherwise occupy.

The Community Service Organization (CSO) was begun after the Second World War in order to mobilize the voting strength of Mexicans. It was built on a base of labor unions and social workers, stimulated by workers from a Chicago organization called the Industrial Areas Foundation headed by Saul Alinsky.[30] A non-partisan organization, the CSO does not endorse candidates but does take positions on issues and particularly emphasizes voter participation. Its voter registration drives have usually been exceptionally successful. Working door-to-door in the Mexican community, it has enrolled, in some years, as many as 25,000 voters. The ability of CSO to turn out the vote is widely believed to have been crucial in the election of Edward Roybal, a Mexican-American social worker, to the Los Angeles City Council. Roybal, like Hawkins among the Negroes, has remained the sole elective official from his ethnic group.

In addition to the CSO, the Mexican community has two or three other, less important community organizations, such as the American G.I. Forum (a veteran's organization) and the Mexican-American Political Association (MAPA). The CSO is remarkable in that it has a solid working-class base, which is

[30] The interesting career and role of Alinsky in Chicago community politics is touched on in Peter H. Rossi and Robert Dentler, *The Politics of Urban Renewal* (New York: Free Press of Glencoe, 1962). Alinsky is the author of *Reveille for Radicals* (Chicago: University of Chicago Press, 1946), a book calling for grass-roots mobilization for civic action.

rare in organizations of this kind. Neither the CDC nor the Negro-led Democratic Minority Conference has been successful in establishing any kind of political alliance with the CSO, although both have sought ways of making inroads in the Mexican community.[31] The few CDC clubs in the Mexican districts are small and relatively ineffectual. Interestingly enough, President Kennedy's campaign organization relied, in 1960, on the CSO to get out the vote in the Mexican areas.

Thus, the politically involved segments of both the Negro and Mexican communities are concerned with the internal politics of their own areas and with certain concrete issues and specific candidates. Minority-group politics is a combination of pressing for "recognition" and pursuing the tactics of a single-interest pressure group. In both cases, the white amateur Democratic clubs are at best only partially satisfactory allies. Their political position limits their ability to urge the replacement of white, Anglo-Saxon incumbents with minority challengers, and their ideology makes pure ethnic recognition suspect. Further, these clubs will never, particularly in the eyes of minority group leaders, subordinate all other issues to the questions of minority-group rights. To many Negro and Mexican leaders, a concern over democracy in Tammany Hall, the recognition of Red China, or disarmament negotiations, while laudable, are diversions from the central problems. Finally, the demands placed on an amateur club activist are hard for most minority leaders to meet: there are few politically involved members of these groups who can afford to spend the large sums of money necessary to meet the expenses of a district leadership or a statewide CDC office.[32]

The amateur Democrat, in short, is oriented to a world of

[31] The CDC nominated a Mexican-American, Henry Lopez, for secretary of state in 1958. This move split the Mexican community and did not increase the CDC's appeal for Mexicans. Lopez lost to his Republican opponent in the general election.

[32] I am indebted to Ralph Guzman, Falk Fellow in the Department of Political Science at the University of California at Los Angeles and himself a leader in Mexican community affairs, for making his knowledge and researches available to me on this subject.

ideas but many of these ideas, such as "small-d democracy," "integration," "equal opportunity," "good candidates," and "liberalism" are simply irrelevant to the major preoccupations of both the lower classes and those middle-class representatives of minority groups which are seeking *material* necessities: housing, jobs, better working conditions, welfare benefits, and protection from the police. The traditional political strategy for a leader of a rising ethnic group has been to convert the material needs of his followers into his personal advantage by persuading the voters that their needs can only be met if "one of their kind" is in office. His own ambition is thereby transmuted into "recognition" for his group, and that recognition is then used as a base of power from which, in the ideal case, the leader bargains for houses and jobs for his constituents. The amateur Democrat is not part of this tradition and indeed rejects many of its essential features. He seeks to mobilize intellectual, not material, discontent; to obtain recognition for the cosmopolitan middle-class, not for the disadvantaged lower class; and to press for the rationalization of the social order on the basis of general principles rather than for the distribution of tangible benefits on the basis of personal mediation.

# 10  The Amateur versus the Professional

The hostility between professional politicians and the amateur Democrats is pervasive, but its expression varies with the political environment. In the older, polyglot cities such as Chicago and New York, the amateurs are viewed as Jews and eggheads who want recognition in the party. Here, the advent of reform was seen, at first tolerantly, as simply another example of the timeless pattern of ethnic succession; then, when some amateur leaders seemed dissatisfied with mere recognition and sought greater prizes in violation of the conventional rules of politics, the tolerance vanished and was replaced with a profound sense of outrage. In Los Angeles, on the other hand, a city where (except for the Negroes and Mexicans) ethnic distinctions are neither visible nor important and where no machine based on nationality neighborhoods ever existed, the professional's suspicion of the amateur is not expressed in terms of "recognition." No such explanations are available and thus the cleavage between the two groups is pure—that is to say, unaffected by ascriptive distinctions but based almost entirely on the differences in political style and motivation which divide the amateur from the professional.

When we speak of "professionals," we must be careful to remember that the identity of these men differs in the three cities we are examining. In New York and Illinois, the professional against whom the amateur directs his energies is the party leader—the boss, the district leader, the ward committeeman, the city or county chairman. In Los Angeles, on the other hand, where these party posts are either non-existent or relatively unimportant, the professional with whom the CDC clubs struggle is the elected official, particularly the incumbent state legislator and congressman. This means that the rhetoric of the contest and the strategies of the amateurs will vary from place to place as the identity of the contenders differs. In New York, amateurs may seek to strengthen the position of elective officials against the control of party leaders; in California, by contrast, the amateurs may be more concerned with weakening the elective officials and enhancing the power of the legal or extra-legal party organizations.

Superficially, one might expect that amateur Democrats and incumbent elective officials could work together in harmony. With no party "machine" to reform or overcome, the hostility between amateur and professional, so understandable in New York or Chicago, should be absent. Although there is no organized struggle between regulars and volunteers in Los Angeles, tension exists nonetheless. The conflict between incumbent legislators and amateur club members, particularly CDC members, springs from the different sets of constraints which circumstances force on each group. The actions necessary to win re-election to office are not at all similar to those necessary to maintain an organization of ideologically oriented volunteers. Incumbents ideally would like a party composed of silent but industrious workers who accept without a murmur the nominees selected by incumbent officials and work diligently for them, using whatever voter appeals seem best calculated to produce a victory at the polls, and who, after the victory, confine themselves to fund-raising and social activities. The CDC leadership, on the other hand, ideally would prefer a system in which a mass-based volunteer organization selected nominees, rejecting those incumbents it deemed unsatisfactory, binding them to a clear and outspokenly liberal platform or set of policy statements, working for and electing them on the basis of liberal, issue-oriented appeals to voters, and, following victory, scrutinizing their conduct in office to make certain they were worthy of the trust placed in them.

With the revitalization of the Democratic party in California, the number of Democratic incumbents was increased at the same time the CDC clubs were beginning to feel their power; tension between incumbent and amateur increased because suddenly there were more of both. The resurgence of the party meant the creation of new centers of political power which could effectively challenge the attempt of the CDC to fill the power vacuum. To the extent that the CDC and the clubs were successful in their original goal of electing more Democrats to office by overcoming the debilitating effects of cross-filing, they were also instrumental in creating a group of men who were destined to become their rivals.

Beginning in 1954, the Democratic contingent in the state legislature steadily increased. The first group to take advantage of the requirement that party labels appear on primary ballots was the so-called class of 1954—Democrats elected to office in that year from previously Republican districts. One of the weaknesses of the party in statewide campaigns, such as that for President in 1952, had been the fact that few Democrats survived the primary races for assemblyman. Ordinarily, these local nominees would have provided the core of the local campaign effort by establishing headquarters and acquiring workers. Their absence left almost unlimited scope for such volunteer groups as chose to work on behalf of a presidential nominee at the local level. From 1954 on, as more and more Democrats survived the primaries, local nominees for state office were found in assembly districts who asserted a right to provide the leadership for local campaigns.

In 1958 the Democrats swept all but one state executive office and assumed control of the legislature. This created, for almost the first time in this century, a real center of party strength in Sacramento. Democratic officeholders not only gained control of patronage appointments but, more importantly, assumed responsibility for governing and became concerned, not about getting elected, but about getting re-elected. This meant that the club movement was deprived of one of its enemies—the Republicans who formerly were in office in Sacramento—and acquired a set of allies who were no longer certain of their enthusiasm for the clubs and the CDC. A club organizer referred to those problems when he told an interviewer:

> We used to organize against the Republicans in Sacramento. . . . But in 1958 we won the state for the Democrats and in 1960 we won the nation for the Democrats. Now, we're in power and I'm really worried about what this will mean for our organization. I feel we may diversify so badly we won't be able to get together for the important tasks. We can't be *for* much of anything, of course, because we can't agree on what our purposes are. It's much easier to be against something, but what can you be against after you've won?

The answer obviously was that you can be against each other. The conflict between incumbents and party workers, long latent in the state, became a major preoccupation of the party once there were enough incumbents to assume control of the government.[1]

The California experience suggests that the amateur will always have an opponent within the party regardless of whether or not he defeats the leaders of the party organization. Even if the reformers should dominate Tammany Hall completely, they would quickly discover that the professional politician has not vanished. He remains on the scene in the guise of the elective official. And this would be true *even if* the reformers put their men in office as assemblymen, congressmen, or state senators. Any man who holds such an office and desires to re-

---

[1] Indeed, the end of cross-filing in 1959 meant that the state committee was now, more than ever, the creature of the elective officials and nominees. When the Democrats won both houses in the legislature, it meant that incumbents for the first time outnumbered nominees. And there was no longer any reason for accepting any appointments from county central committees. In the past, when a cross-filed Republican had won the Democratic nomination for a state legislative office, the appropriate county central committee would appoint a Democrat to the state central committee seat which the Democratic nominee would normally occupy. When cross-filing ended, county committees no longer had the opportunity to place appointees on the state committee. (This was not an insignificant power. In 1950, of 162 posts on the Democratic state committee to be occupied by nominees, county central committees appointed 71.) Cf. Dean R. Cresap, *Party Politics in the Golden State* (Los Angeles: Haynes Foundation, 1954), p. 30, and *Elections Code*, secs. 2796, 2797.

tain it begins to acquire the habits and attitudes of the professional and to discover that his relationships with other legislators and with the voters to whom he must turn for re-election inevitably create differences between himself and the club
leaders. And since the amateurs renounce those means—such
as patronage and the centralized control of nominations—used
by regular party leaders to exact obedience from elective officials, the cleavage between public official and club leader may
widen well beyond what it is today. Making elective officials
"responsible" is not simply a matter of putting in office "good"
men in place of "bad," for it is the office itself which shapes
the perspective of the incumbent. The job creates the constraints on the occupant; the character of the occupant is free
only within those constraints.

Manhattan or Chicago reformers may believe that by picking candidates for public office through local reform clubs
they can insure that these men, once in office, will be responsive to the goals of the club. This is true within certain limits.
An incumbent who is dependent on a club will not knowingly
alienate it, at least not over matters which are relatively unimportant to him or his constituents. And able officials from an
amateur club background are usually men and women adroit
at using the rhetoric and slogans of the club and persuasive in
making their case before a college-educated audience. But
these limits are fairly loose. And when the constituency of an
official is larger than that of the club, or when his election was
made possible by support from other sources in addition to the
club, then his relations with the club will become even looser.

The very day after Robert Wagner won the 1961 mayoral
primary with the CDV clubs as his principal grass-roots support, the breach between them opened publicly. Now that he
was the nominee of three parties, including the Democratic,
and soon to be re-elected mayor, Wagner saw his task as
bringing the *whole* party organization under his influence, ex-
tracting funds from conservative donors, and presenting himself to the electorate in a posture which would be acceptable
to independents, middle-of-the-road Democrats, Republicans,

and the newspapers. This could not be done by continuing to brandish the more extreme slogans of the reform movement. As a result of these constraints, the day after his victory "Mayor Wagner appeared to be taking great pains, by various devices, to prevent the Democratic reform faction . . . from being credited with the major responsibility for his victory."[2] The reformers produced two candidates from among their ranks for the key party posts of county leader and county chairman, but the Mayor refused them both. Instead, he had his man elected county chairman[3] and played a "commanding role" in the selection of Edward N. Costikyan as county leader (the post vacated by De Sapio) over the opposition of reformers who were supporting John T. Harrington.[4] Costikyan, although a member of the Reform District Leaders' Caucus, was not affiliated with the CDV and was regarded by many Harrington backers as so "moderate" as not to be a "true reformer" at all.

One of the two politicians elected to office in Chicago as a result of amateur backing soon began to drift away from the amateur organization. His "long-range" goals continued to be reform-oriented—reducing patronage and formulating liberal issues—but on day-to-day affairs he found himself closer to the regular organization and the professionals. He told an interviewer:

[2] *New York Times*, September 9, 1961, p. 10. The story continued by observing that "the Mayor is reported to feel that he was more responsible for the success the reform faction scored in [City] Council and district leadership contests than the reform faction was for his success."

[3] *New York Times*, September 22, 24, and 28 and October 1, 1961. The mayor's candidate for county chairman, Edward Cavanaugh, had been his campaign manager and was also vice-president of an old-line Tammany club which a reform club had just defeated.

[4] *New York Times*, March 3, 1962. The vote in the Democratic executive committee ("Tammany") was 9½ for Costikyan, 6½ for Harrington. The losing reform faction tried to find alternative candidates, but neither of their second choices—James S. Lanigan and Alan Finberg—was acceptable to the old-line leaders who held a slim majority. Wagner was either unable or unwilling to use his influence to destroy this majority by forcing a militant reform candidate on the regulars.

> By philosophy, goals to be attained, the issues that the Democratic party should be based on, I am much more in sympathy with the out-and-out independents than with the regulars. . . . I agree about everything with [them], but I have now spent six years in active politics in Chicago and . . . they have made me aware of what the problems are. I hope they haven't made me cynical.

Further, the six state representatives in the Illinois legislature who had DFI backing all realized that their constituencies were larger than the membership of the clubs, and on crucial issues divided amongst themselves. When a critical vote was taken on electing a speaker of the lower house, downstate DFI members voted against Mayor Daley's choice, while Chicago DFI representatives voted for him. This split the legislators and some Chicago officials dropped out of the DFI because it seemed to be in danger of becoming too anti-Daley while the downstate representatives became inactive because the DFI was not sufficiently anti-Daley.

## Role Conflict: The Case of California

The absence of a machine and ethnic considerations makes California a pure example of the cleavage between amateur party leaders and incumbent elective officials. The latter are far more willing to express to an interviewer their annoyance at the CDC role in local pre-primary endorsements than their gratitude for whatever help the CDC may have given them in winning office. The need to resubmit their candidacy to the vote of a club or local endorsing convention is annoying in the extreme, particularly if it becomes the occasion for attacks and criticisms from club members who dislike some aspect of the incumbent's career. An assemblyman, a liberal who was particularly well regarded by the CDC, addressed a meeting of CDC leaders in Sacramento in these terms:

> What we are most likely to be afraid of as incumbents is some irresponsible group which springs up to make endorsements purporting to be the endorsements of the

> Democratic party. We must ease the fear of incumbents about the threat which can arise from greater party activity in their own district.

In 1960, only one Democratic incumbent was opposed in the primary by a CDC endorsee,[5] but the latent threat of such opposition and the need to be "approved" by some group other than the electorate is distasteful to many, perhaps most, officials. The endorsement which was welcomed by a nominee when he was first seeking office is seen, now that he is concerned with re-election, as an obstacle.

This has led certain California legislators either to oppose pre-primary endorsements or to demand greater representation in these conventions. Many incumbents would prefer to see such proceedings entirely under their own control. This is justified by the argument that as elective officials they have the ultimate responsibility for their actions. They lose office if the voters are dissatisfied, not the CDC leaders. "We are in charge with the responsibility to the electorate," a legislator said. "We reflect the party image. We should have some larger voice in determining what that image is and who the candidates will be." Assemblyman Jesse Unruh told a meeting of CDC leaders that because the incumbents have the most at stake, and because CDC is concerned primarily with issues, it should stay out of the endorsing business.

> The group which is concerned with agitating, with being the gadfly, with being out in left field . . . should not also be the group which makes the selection of men to run with the Democratic party label. This group has no responsibility and dreads responsibility.

The CDC and the clubs create in the districts what such officials regard as a "dual constituency." The incumbent must pay heed to what he regards as a Democratic party faction even if the demands of that faction run contrary to what he considers the views of the voters and the interests of the com-

[5] State Senator Luther E. Gibson, Fifteenth Senatorial District (Solano County), was opposed by William Beeman. Gibson won easily, 13,591 to 9,799.

munity. The clubs usurp the incumbent's judgment of what is in the best interest of his district. "I can tell you this," said one regular, "the big contributors . . . never have been as demanding of our incumbents as some of these people in the clubs and councils try to be. . . . The representative has an obligation to all the people of his district, and not just to the members of a Democratic club in the district." The clubs should help these incumbents and thus earn the right to express views on policy. Campaign work is a better test of "the validity of a person's Democratic credentials" than "how many resolutions favoring the recognition of the Chinese Communists he has happened to sign."[6]

To the amateurs in the clubs, these arguments by incumbents are but special pleading intended to justify an assault on the club movement as a whole. In the eyes of the amateur, the conflict with the elective officials is but another case of the general conflict between power and principle. "Here in the County Committee," said one club organizer, "you could say there are some people more interested in power and other people more interested in ideals. . . . It [the conflict] is between one group which feels that power should be used to beat your opponent because he is an opponent and that you should always try to maximize your power . . . and the other group which feels that the substantive purposes of the organization are more important." A CDC officer agreed with this assessment. He admitted that many incumbents are liberals. Speaking of Assemblyman Unruh, he said:

> There's very little divergence between us on substantive issues. By and large he tends to be on the liberal side of things . . . but he is basically a power-seeker. He is compatible with the CDC insofar as the CDC is useful to him in attaining his own goals and his goals seem to be enlarging his own power. He opposes us only to the extent that our organization's power seems to thwart his ambitions.

[6] Quoted in Francis Carney, *The Rise of the Democratic Clubs in California* (New York: Henry Holt & Co., 1958), p. 10.

By being more concerned with principle, the CDC can describe itself as the "conscience of the party." One CDC leader
could understand why a liberal congressman would resent
being criticized for one bad vote out of a hundred when he
has cast ninety-nine good votes. "But could we have it any
other way? I don't think so. After all, we have to prick their
consciences. What does he expect us to do? Sit around and
say nothing when he casts a vote we can't agree with?" Those
CDC leaders who see any force at all to the incumbent's objection to the creation of a "dual constituency" counter by
pointing out that there are many forces in any district and
that the CDC is only one of these. To the extent that the CDC
represents a liberal cause based on mass-membership clubs
which are internally democratic, then the pressure CDC exerts
on elective officials is a desirable counterweight to the pressures brought to bear by well-organized special-interest groups
which may be seeking selfish goals inimical to more general
ends.[7] Stating the case more strongly, another CDC officer
called talk of a dual constituency "a lot of cock and bull." He
asserted that "we have a right to make our views known" and
that this is not harmful because "we're not in control of the
party . . . all we are is one important source of influence. If
we were in control of the party and if we controlled the selection of candidates, then we might have usurped the electorate's
functions."

A militant stand on issues is essential for a variety of reasons,
in the opinion of the amateurs. An editorial in *The Liberal
Democrat* summarized some of these.[8] Outspoken liberalism is
necessary to "attract the largest number of new recruits" to
the CDC, and, given the turnover, the CDC needs new recruits "just to stay even." Further, the party leadership—Gov-

[7] Carney, *op. cit.*, p. 10, cites remarks of CDC President Wyatt to this
effect.

[8] *The Liberal Democrat* is an independent monthly journal of liberal
opinion, published in Berkeley, California, by two young intellectuals,
one of whom, Tom Winnett, was a CDC vice-president. It has no official
connection with the CDC and is not a recognized organ of CDC views,
but it has strongly supported the California club movement and endorsed
its aims. The editorial appeared in the March, 1961, issue.

ernor Brown and President Kennedy—are "moderates" who stand near the center, ideologically. Unless organizations like the CDC "occupy ground to the left of Kennedy and Brown, the natural requirements of political compromise will force the Democratic party into greater conservatism." The CDC is thus a counterweight to the right-wing position of Senator Barry Goldwater. In addition, there are a number of Democratic incumbents who are on the left, and CDC, by standing behind them, enables them to speak out more willingly. Without the CDC, they might refrain from issuing statements which, for example, attack the House Un-American Activities Committee. In any case, the CDC cannot "play tame in the hope of appeasing these people" who are "the organization's enemies" by showing signs of weakness which would encourage these enemies to "move in for the kill." In politics, "you cannot win over your enemies by placating them."

The club leaders believe that the incumbents, in attacking the clubs and the CDC, are only seeking their own ends. Whatever their verbal objections, the real cause of their animosity is that they dislike and fear any kind of party activity in their districts which they cannot control. Independent clubs are a threat and the incumbents will, in the opinion of the amateurs, act either to eliminate or to subordinate them. The 1951 reapportionment of assembly and congressional districts in California, performed by a Republican legislature, exacerbated this problem by creating a small number of districts with very high Democratic registration and a large number of districts which Republicans could carry by safe but not large majorities.[9] With absolutely safe districts, these incumbents saw no need for party activity of any kind. A high party official said to an interviewer:

> These Congressmen didn't . . . want the Democrats in their district to organize. They could win regardless of whether their areas were organized or not, simply because the

[9] Four of the twelve congressional districts in Los Angeles County have Democratic registrations in excess of 61 per cent, and one is nearly 75 per cent Democratic (districts 17, 19, 23, and 26). In 1950, these were the only districts held by Democratic congressmen.

Democrats so thoroughly outnumbered the Republicans. Indeed, they opposed party activity because party activity might give rise to primary contests. Any kind of activity would be seen as a threat by these men. Therefore they went to great lengths to keep down the club movement in their districts.

The reapportionment being carried out in 1961, this time by a Democratic legislature, presented, in the eyes of the amateur, many of the same questions. They see the incumbents preferring safe districts where party activity and its threats will be unnecessary, while the amateurs prefer the creation of marginal districts where the clubs will be essential for keeping Democrats in office. Given safe districts, the volunteers fear that the incumbents will continue to attempt to block the formation of new clubs and hold down club activity in their areas. They are convinced that there are relatively few clubs in heavily Democratic districts, not simply because lower-income and minority groups are harder to organize, but also because Democratic incumbents discourage or co-opt club leaders. A club organizer in Los Angeles, with experience in all parts of the county, had no doubts on this score:

> The Democratic incumbents tend to fight you. [They are] a little leery of having many clubs organized in their areas. They fight me. When I was hired, my job description said that my principal obligation was to go out and charter clubs. I went out and started doing this and then I discovered that I not only had to fight people in the districts, I had to fight some of my own bosses. A lot of these people take the attitude that the club movement is fine, but organize clubs in somebody else's district—don't organize them in mine.

When there are several incumbents in a district, there is often a struggle to control the local Democratic councils and endorsing procedures. Although the incumbents have little power in statewide CDC endorsing conventions, they often have much more representation in some local conventions and councils. In both the Fifteenth and Twenty-fourth Congressional districts in Los Angeles, the bitter fights in 1960 over congressional endorsements were, in part at least, a fight between incumbents and party professionals on the one hand and club leaders on the other. Since the incumbents are usually entitled to representation on assembly district councils, and since these councils are often small, incumbents can here wield some influence. As a result, clubs and the CDC continuously press for stricter rules governing local endorsing procedures which will increase club representation and thus weaken incumbent influence.[10]

At the same time, the shortage of new elective offices to win, the absence of a formal local party structure to capture, and the example of the Manhattan reformers have transformed, for many CDC leaders, incumbent opposition from a liability into an asset. They have begun to identify certain of these incumbents as "bosses" who must be defeated in order to "reform" the party. In fact, of course, men such as Assemblyman Jesse Unruh, most often mentioned as a "boss," is by Eastern standards nothing of the kind. But if Unruh or someone else with influence and a heavy-handed manner can be identified to California amateurs as a "boss," then a new source of incentives for club work can be tapped.

## Tribal Conflict: The Case of New York

The tension in California between incumbent and amateur Democrat illustrates the essence of the contrast between the professional and the amateur: the goals of each are different. When, as in Manhattan or Chicago, this essential conflict is inextricably bound up with matters of party control, ethnicity, religion, and style of life, the struggle becomes, if not more profound, then certainly more complex. The nature of this struggle can be seen by looking at it through the eyes of the professional politician. To understand why these politicians

---

[10] The CDC bylaws were amended in 1960, effective in 1962, to require that local councils be composed only of CDC-affiliated clubs and grant club representation on the basis of at least one delegate for every twenty club members. The intent of these amendments was clearly to outnumber the anti-CDC forces in the districts.

react as they do to the amateur, we must put ourselves in their shoes.

To the regular organization politician, the reformers are simply a group of ambitious young men seeking political office and power by attacking the status quo. To most Tammany and Chicago machine leaders, it was just another case of outsiders wanting to break into the system and displace existing leaders, using as weapons conventional cries of "reform" and "bossism" which had been the stock-in-trade of the ambitious since the earliest days. Some younger members of an ethnic group were struggling to gain recognition, but using hypocritical and unfair charges to aid their cause. Said one powerful Tammany district leader:

> The reformers in this city are a sham. . . . [They] are young Jewish people who are trying to make a place for themselves in the sun, who are trying to break into politics. The old pattern, of course, was for one ethnic group or one nationality group to replace another. . . . In the past they have all used a racial appeal—Italians against Irish, Negroes against Italians. Now there are these young Jewish lawyers, bright, able people, who want to break in. The difficulty for them is that it's hard for them to use the race issue. In many areas they are running against older Jewish leaders. The difference between them is age, not nationality. But they don't have to use the race issue in the way other people have had to, because Eleanor Roosevelt and Herbert Lehman have given them the issue of Adlai Stevenson and Carmine De Sapio and the whole question of bossism. It's an old story. The history of Manhattan politics is the history of insurgency.

This ingenious explanation of reformism undoubtedly has substantial elements of truth in it. There unquestionably are ambitious young lawyers trying to break into the system who, unable for a variety of reasons to make an effective appeal for votes based simply on the claims of ethnic recognition, have developed the issue of bossism instead. Variations of this explanation command wide agreement among Tammany leaders. Another, himself a Jew from the lower East Side and regarded as a liberal, felt that reformism was "simply a case of another group wanting to start at the top."

> I keep telling these reformers, "You should never win. Once you win somebody will come in and try to reform you." They'll reform the reformers. It's the old story of the ins and outs again. I was a reformer, myself. Me and my followers took over our club. We were insurgent. We were called the reformers and we beat the regular organization. Now we're on the inside. Now, I suppose someday somebody's going to come along and try to reform us. The same thing happens all over Manhattan and it's been happening for years.

The reason, in the eyes of the regulars, why some Tammany leaders are defeated by reformers is partly the change in the ethnic composition of the districts and partly the failure of older leaders to adapt to new times. "They had grown old and fat and failed to change," said one Tammany district leader. "It's not just ethnic succession alone."

> I know that Denny Mahon is alleged to have lost on the West Side because he was an Irishman in a district that had become Jewish, but other Irishmen have held on to their districts which have become Jewish. Take Joe Whitty of Brooklyn. He's an old man in his seventies and an Irishman, but he still controls a Jewish assembly district. He does this by adapting himself to the times. Denny Mahon didn't.

There are obviously grounds for such beliefs. After all, of the sixty-two Democratic county chairmen in New York state in 1961, only two were Jewish and neither of these was from New York City. All five county leaders in the city were Catholic, and there were no white Anglo-Saxon Protestants in the New York City Democratic delegation to the state legislature or congress.[11] In such a situation, and given the pattern of insurgency with which most regular politicians are familiar, it

[11] Daniel P. Moynihan, " 'Bosses' and 'Reformers,' " *Commentary*, June, 1961, pp. 46–64. Nassau County, a suburb of New York City, offers an interesting contrast. There, 50 per cent of the Democratic county committeemen are Jewish, 10 per cent are white Anglo-Saxon Protestants, and the remainder are Catholic. *Ibid.*, p. 469.

is only natural that the professional would assume that Jews and Anglo-Saxon Protestants are seeking a place in the political sun. To make such a view even more convincing is the historical fact that one of the few permanent effects of the various reform and fusion movements in the past has been the appointment to high office of a sizable number of just such people.

Theodore Lowi has shown that reform in New York City has always meant a change in the class and ethnic background of top appointees. The three "reform" mayors preceding Wagner favored upper-middle-class Yankee Protestants six to one over the Irish as appointees. Almost 40 per cent of the appointees of Seth Low were listed in the Social Register. Further, all four reform mayors—Low, Mitchell, La Guardia, and Wagner —have appointed a much larger percentage of Jews to their cabinets than their regular organization predecessors.[12]

In fact, of course, the problem posed by the amateur Democrats is not simply one of ethnic succession. Militant reform leaders in Manhattan get angry when they hear this "explanation" of their motives, for they reject the idea that ethnicity or religion ought to be considered at all in politics. Although most amateur Democrats are either Jewish or Anglo-Saxon and practically none are Catholic, it is not their desire for ethnic "recognition" which prompts their entry into politics so much as it is their desire to see a certain political ethic (which middle-class Jews and Yankees happen to share) implemented in local politics.

Intuitively, many professional politicians realize that the amateurs are different from the traditional insurgents who sought recognition or a share of the patronage pie. Their sense of this fundamental difference is expressed when they charge the amateurs with being "unfair," "unreasonable," and "ineffective."

At the close of the uneasy truce between Tammany and

[12] Theodore J. Lowi, *At the Pleasure of the Mayor* (New York: Columbia University Press, forthcoming), pp. 224–32. La Guardia doubled the number of Jews in the cabinet, and Wagner increased it by another 25 per cent.

reform leaders during the 1960 Presidential campaign, De Sapio issued a statement attacking the reform element as a "small group of self-proclaimed prophets who, themselves, want nothing less than to be bosses." He termed as "fantastic" and "hypocrisy" the claim by reformers that they deserved a major share of the credit for the victory of President John F. Kennedy, stating that "the time has come to stop coddling those who . . . resort to deceit and demagoguery as they permit themselves to be used by opportunists who desire to ruin the Democratic party."[13]

Most regular Tammany leaders regard the reformers as untrustworthy and unscrupulous. "I don't like the dirty, unprincipled campaign tactics they've been using. A good hard fight is all right, but some of them have been going into the gutter." Such behavior is explained by the fact that the reform leaders cannot or will not negotiate with regular leaders but insist on an all-out campaign of unrelenting attack. "You can't compromise with reformers in New York City. You can't even deal with them. They won't sit down and talk with you." Another Tammany leader observed, "The thing that's wrong with the reformers at present, in my estimation, is that the reform clubs take candidates solely on the basis of whether they're pro- or anti-De Sapio, and that's too narrow a viewpoint."

The Tammany leaders are shrewd enough to see some of the reasons for the behavior of reformers. Said one:

> The reform leaders don't compromise. I think the reason is that they're not strong enough to go back to their clubs and sell them. They realize that if they tried to appease on the outside or compromise, then when they went back to their clubs, they'd be murdered.

Said another:

> The reform leaders, so-called, don't decide or act on anything. Therefore, they don't seem to be leaders to me. I don't think they should be responsible to 40 or 50 club members who take an active interest in their club. I think it is wrong. I think they should be in a position to act on their own initiative.

[13] Text of statement in *New York Times*, November 10, 1960, p. 43.

These comments by regular organization men—that the reformers are uncompromising, unprincipled, and preoccupied with defeating De Sapio himself—suggest that there are factors which distinguish the present group of reformers from their predecessors. If the contemporary insurgent forces were simply outsiders wanting to get in, the Tammany leaders would presumably know how to deal with them. After the insurgents had proved their strength, arrangements would be worked out to give them some of the advantages of recognition. What is baffling about the present group is that they seem to reject recognition except on their own terms. They are "unreasonable." This implicit contradiction in the judgment of the Tammany leaders—writing off the reformers as simply outsiders seeking to get into the political game but at the same time criticizing the reformers for being unwilling to observe the rules and conventions of that game—indicates the distinctive feature of these challengers. That feature is the extent to which they have found it either desirable or expedient to urge the destruction of the existing party mechanism. The reformers do not want simply to get into the system, they want to change it permanently, and it is this promise which is both the basis of their strength and the source of the constraints on them. Some intellectual members of the Tammany organization realized that the essence of the movement was not so much the ethnicity of the reformers as the ideas and beliefs to which they adhered. One young Jewish lawyer who had once belonged to the reform Lexington Club before he joined a regular Tammany club understood better than most of his political colleagues the crucial difference between the regular and the reformer. He wrote of the newcomers to his district who supported an insurgent reform club: "When the vote is at the disposal of a stranger to a community, it cannot be cast for old ties and old loyalties. It can only reflect generalized attitudes, fears and prejudices or be used to settle real or imagined wounds suffered there or elsewhere." Less reflective Tammany leaders were keenly aware that the amateur is a newcomer, an outsider, alien and thus a threat, but they did not understand the ethic which he brings to politics. Carmine De Sapio's campaign slogan in his fight to retain control of his own Greenwich Village district was, "Don't Surrender Your Community to Outside Forces," meaning, of course, the "new Villagers" who were displacing the old Sicilian and Neapolitan families in the community.[14]

The ordinary professional politician may not be able to speak in abstract terms about the cause of the amateur mentality, but he is quick to recognize the effects. Tammany leaders never fail to point out that most reform leaders are relative newcomers to their community, while the Tammany leader often has lived his whole life in the same district in which he was born. "I have lived for over fifty-seven years in the same house I was born in," said one Italian leader. "I'm a member of every community organization in the district. I'm a trustee of my church. Who are these young kids, they should come in here and try to tell me they want to take over now?" His opponents were a Puerto Rican and a Jew in an area which had long since lost the bulk of its Italian population. Similar remarks are heard whenever the cosmopolitan invades the territory of the local.

But even in Los Angeles, where practically nobody can boast of ancient ties to his neighborhood, the difference between the local professional and the cosmopolitan amateur is clear enough, at least to the former. Professionals in California feel that the CDC is more likely to endorse the "club type," whose only experience is within the CDC, than a person with wider community experience but less activity in a club. A former assemblyman made this point to an audience of CDC leaders:

> A man who works his tail off for the Chamber of Commerce, for the United Crusade, who heads up the Boy

[14] The reform insurgent candidate opposing De Sapio in Greenwich Village in 1961 moved into the area only a few weeks before the campaign. When asked for his reaction to this Tammany criticism, he replied that it was "irrelevant," for it was the *ideas* in which you believed rather than the *neighborhood* in which you lived that should determine your "qualifications."

> Scouts and does everything he can for the widows and
> orphans, who's a real community leader, has difficulty in
> getting a CDC endorsement. This man may be the best
> qualified person who has done the most for the community,
> but who gets the endorsement? Some guy who has only
> been the vice-president of a local CDC council.

These councils are susceptible, in the eyes of one party
regular, to a certain technique for obtaining endorsements.
This involves "going before them and taking the most liberal
possible stand on every and all issues, and, most of all, telling
them that they are the greatest thing that ever happened to
the Democratic party and that anyone who says they are not
is either a crypto-Republican or a lousy party boss."[15]

If it is true that the cosmopolitan amateur feels unwelcome
and ill at ease in a regular Tammany club, it is equally true
that the professional feels uncomfortable and alien in the
midst of his reform opponents. To the professional, the atmosphere of an amateur club is either incomprehensible or
absurd or both. The reform club seems to violate every rule
of what a political organization ought to be. "No one characteristic," writes Daniel Moynihan, "divides the 'regular'
party men in New York from the 'reform' group more than
the matter of taking pride in following the chain of command."
The reformers seem not to believe in organization at all, while
the professional has, at the very center of his personal loyalties,
a commitment to "the organization" and a firm belief in the
rightness of the rules which require and define such fealty. A
middle-class, well-educated amateur regards waiting in line
to see one's leader as slavish, unmanly, and undemocratic,
"the kind of conduct that could only be imposed by a boss."
By contrast, "the organization regulars regard it as proper and
well-behaved conduct. The reformers, who have a tendency
to feel superior, would be surprised, perhaps, to learn that
among the regulars they are widely regarded as rude, unethi-
cal people."[16]

[15] Mrs. Elizabeth Snyder, quoted in Carney, *op. cit.* p. 9.

[16] Daniel P. Moynihan, "The Irish," in Nathan Glazer, *The Ethnic
Groups of New York City* (forthcoming).

To the professional, one sign of the disregard for organizational loyalties is the unwillingness of the reformer to follow those rules which professionals regard as essential for maintaining the party. This is not to say that all professionals are fraternity brothers with a sentimental attachment to their common clubhouse (indeed, the tension between Irish and Italian leaders in New York and Chicago is almost as great as that between professionals and amateurs); rather, whatever else their differences, the professionals feel the party organization must be protected. Thus, they take as a sign of the amateurs' unfitness for party leadership the way in which they go about making up a slate of candidates for public office.

Amateur clubs are committed to supporting the party, but the enthusiasm with which their volunteer members work at getting out the vote is directly proportional to the perceived virtues of the candidates themselves. The regular organization, on the other hand, nominates candidates for a variety of reasons, and quality is only one of these (although one not neglected as frequently as some suggest). Making up the party ticket is a crucial factor in maintaining the regular organization, just as the quality of the candidates is crucial for maintaining the amateur organization. To the regulars, however, the importance of the ticket lies not in its power to inspire volunteer enthusiasm but in its value for discharging party obligations, satisfying demands on the leadership, recognizing powerful groups within the party, and resolving intraparty conflicts. Tammany leaders cannot understand why the reformers do not grasp this essential fact. To the Tammany leadership (as to the leadership of any regular party), nominating all men on the basis of ability alone would be destructive of the organization itself, and since the organization must endure while candidates come and go, the organizational-maintenance aspects of ticket-making must come first.

When the amateurs show no hesitation in attacking the party which has supported many of their liberal heroes, the professionals feel it is a sign of the worst kind of hypocrisy. The amateurs, of course, defend their attacks on the grounds that the principles and the quality of candidates are more important than the party organization. Professionals retaliate by pointing to the number of times present-day reformers were willing to accept organization backing without displaying any qualms about the virtues of that organization. Carmine De Sapio charged that Senator Lehman had been kept in office, without any complaints from him, by the regular organization in New York and that both his brother and his nephew had been elevated to high judicial offices in the state on the organization slate. Wagner had become mayor as the candidate of De Sapio and had accepted that support for seven and a half years with scarcely a public murmur; indeed, on the eve of his alliance with the reformers, he was reported to have been engaged in negotiations with regular party leaders in hopes of retaining their support.[17]

Equally with the ingratitude of amateurs in turning on the party which had supported their candidates, the professionals criticize the amateurs' unwillingness to give credit to the organization for those measures it has supported. Legislators in California feel that the CDC, for example, fails to give proper recognition to the liberal achievements of those legislators who are not club types. "What really irks me," said a party professional, "is the fact that no one recognizes the really solid liberal accomplishments that Unruh has got through the legislature. He has more bills to his credit than any of the CDC people, but they never give him credit for it." He mentioned the Unruh Retail Credit Installment Act and the Unruh Civil Rights Act. "As far as I know, the CDC has never even passed a resolution thanking him for his efforts." This professional contrasted Unruh's performance with that of a CDC favorite, State Senator Richard Richards of Los Angeles. "Dick Richards could introduce a Mother's Day resolution and he wouldn't get it out of the Rules Committee," he claimed.

Just as California Democratic legislators dislike having their

[17] The late Irving Lehman was Chief Judge of the New York Court of Appeals and J. Howard Rossbach, Herbert Lehman's nephew, was a judge of the Court of Special Sessions. *New York Times,* February 6, 1961. On Wagner's negotiations with party leaders, see *New York Times,* June 18, 19, and 23, 1961.

liberalism questioned, so certain Tammany leaders felt chagrined at not receiving credit for having instituted a series of procedural reforms within Tammany Hall. These changes, supported by De Sapio, took place between 1953 and 1959 and were intended to demonstrate the willingness of the regular organization to "reform" itself. In part at the behest of reform leaders, and in part on their own initiative, Tammany leaders adopted simplified primary election procedures, including the direct election of district leaders. Until then (1953), district leaders were chosen indirectly by the county committeemen from each district. These county committeemen are elected from each election district (at least two, and frequently many more, from each election district). In the past they, in turn, selected the district leader. Each candidate for district leader, thus, ran his slate of county committeemen in the party contests. The winning district leader was the man who carried the most election districts. Under the direct election system approved by Tammany, the district leader runs as an individual, with his name on the ballot. In 1957, a law was passed authorizing a system of permanent personal registration of voters in place of the older system in which a voter was required to register each year in order to participate in the election. In 1959, Tammany approved more democratic methods for designating party candidates and the use of voting machines in contested primaries.

All of these procedural reforms had the effect of aiding the reform movement. Direct election of district leaders meant it became easier to wage a personal campaign for that office, with less chance of being defeated by political maneuvering and the manipulation of votes in the county committee. Permanent personal registration (PPR) reduced the advantage held by the party best organized to perform the laborious task of registering voters each year. Now, reform-minded people, once they were registered (say, in a presidential election) would stay on the rolls so long as they did not move and continued to vote regularly. The use of voting machines reduced the possibility of tampering with or miscounting the vote in primary elections.

Some of these changes were instituted by De Sapio over the objections of other Tammany leaders who felt it unwise to make any procedural concessions at all to reform forces. To his chagrin, De Sapio then discovered that not only did these reforms aid his opponents who were sworn to defeat him, but in addition he got little or no credit for having brought them about.[18]

### The Problems of the Professional

The animosity of the regular organization leader toward the amateur reformer cannot completely conceal the very real problems which the regular faces and which he knows, although rarely admits, may end by defeating him. Some regular organizations have simply failed to adapt to changing times. This is most true in Tammany. In Manhattan, unlike Chicago, neighborhood change has not always meant the entry of a lower class into an older neighborhood being vacated by a higher income group now able to purchase newer housing elsewhere. On the contrary, neighborhood change—on the East Side, parts of the West Side, and in Greenwich Village—has often meant the raising of the class level of the community. Chicago ward organizations adapt easily to changes that "downgrade" an area, for the newly arrived lower-income groups rarely offer a serious immediate challenge to existing political leadership. When, as in Manhattan, the new arrivals "upgrade" the community because they possess a higher degree of organizational and verbal skills than the old residents, a challenge is almost inevitable.

Tammany has, in a few instances, attempted to deal with

[18] One of these reforms, however, helped De Sapio himself—indeed, it probably saved him from defeat. In the 1959 leadership fight in De Sapio's own district in Greenwich Village, his insurgent opponents carried more election districts than he. (De Sapio won in 18 districts, the VID in 22.) Had not direct election been instituted, De Sapio would probably have been defeated by an adverse vote of the county committeemen. By 1961, of course, nothing could save him.

the problem of the "upgraded" neighborhood. In 1954, Ludwig Teller, a professor of law at New York University and a state assemblyman, took over, with De Sapio's backing, as district leader in the Fifth Assembly District South in order to improve the quality of local leadership and deter an insurgent fight. Teller's arrival was interpreted as a Tammany-approved "face-lifting operation."[19] Teller soon announced that the clubhouse in its old form had no future but in its new form it would be an "effective instrument for community action"—a phrase which could have been heard a few years later in any reform club. The new Teller club, which De Sapio described as a "model" for other Tammany organizations, started to set up community service and public affairs committees and organize conferences and seminars.[20] But it was already too late. Within a short time, Teller was under fire from reform clubs for being allied with De Sapio, and in 1960 he lost his congressional seat to a reformer. The following year he announced that he was resigning his district leadership without bothering to defend it against the inevitable reform insurgents.

The Teller case was the exception. Few other Tammany clubs were able to change sufficiently to meet the challenge posed by an upgraded neighborhood. And such changes cannot easily be dictated from the top. The Tammany organization, and even the Chicago organization of Mayor Daley, are less hierarchical and centralized than they appear. The boss is dependent on his district leaders and ward committeemen for whatever power he has. He needs them just as they need him. No fiat from county headquarters can change the political habits of a lifetime or alter in any fundamental way the style of life of an old-line clubhouse.

The Irish leaders have suffered more than any other group from an inability to adapt. This may be because, although they have been in power longer than any other leaders, their areas have changed the most. Most reform victories in Manhattan before 1961 were won against Irish leaders; very few

19 See *New York Times*, November 24, 1954.
20 *New York Times*, January 16, 1955.

Jewish leaders and practically no Italian leaders were defeated until reformers had Wagner at the top of their ticket. The Jewish and Italian leaders are in power mostly in the areas which have not been "upgraded." The lower East Side and lower Manhattan are still areas of tenements—not nice houses converted into slum units (and which could be reconverted to nice houses), but buildings built from the first as tenements. The land clearance projects have brought in lower-income public housing, not middle- or upper-income luxury units. In these areas the clubhouse still can play its conventional role, and the Jewish and Italian leaders are by and large younger men, energetic and ambitious.

The older Irish leaders could not adapt to the arrival of young Jewish lawyers or the hordes of Puerto Ricans. The leader, surrounded by men who had been election district captains for twenty to forty years and whose whole lives had been spent in the clubhouse, found himself with no one who could canvas in the forbidding new high-rise apartment buildings guarded by doormen and populated with young college graduates or in the crowded buildings filled with Spanish-speaking immigrants. One old Tammany leader shook his head sadly and said, "What can I do? I can't just get rid of my old captains. Some of them have been with me from the first. What kind of reward is that, that I should replace them now with young kids who maybe can do the job but who don't deserve it?"

Chicago and Manhattan offer an interesting contrast in leadership control over party workers. In the former city, the organization has sizable patronage resources—enough so that the Democratic machine can be in its entirety an organization relying on these material incentives. When almost everyone receives a money income from political participation, hiring, firing, promoting, and demoting precinct captains is a relatively simple matter. But when, as in Manhattan, there are not enough jobs to go around, other rewards must be relied on—rewards which give much less discretion to the leader. In old-line Irish Tammany clubs the amount of patronage is even smaller than usual because the leadership has been unable to compete with the newer Jewish and Italian leaders in the scramble for jobs. Thus, the local organization comes to rely more and more on the solidary rewards the clubhouse can provide—friendship, card-playing, and being near the *pater familias,* the district leader. An organization based on these solidary incentives cannot easily be reorganized, shaken up, or modernized; change itself destroys the value of the rewards on which all depends. The Tammany workers see in their club a comfortable social organization and a lenient employer. The jobs are neither so plentiful nor so lucrative as to justify strenuous efforts in campaigning and the exhilaration of fighting for the cause of ethnic recognition (e.g., Italians fighting the entrenched Irish) is a thing of the past. Robert Heilbroner notes the decay that has afflicted many older clubs in Manhattan:

> The people who make [machine] politics their occupation do not tend to thrive on ideas and ideals, and the Tammany clubs—indeed, machine clubs everywhere—tend to become pleasant fraternities where "the boys" can sit around and play poker, gossip, and get away from their wives and relax.[21]

When we describe the clash between the amateur and the professional in cities such as Chicago and New York, we are providing data for a theoretical distinction among three kinds of political organizations. The strong, patronage-based local club is a *utilitarian* organization. The motivation for vigorous political activity is relatively high because one's job depends on doing the work. The leader's control over his workers is precise and flexible because a material reward, such as a job, is a divisible benefit which can be given to or withheld from an individual and thus used to govern his behavior regardless of the behavior of others. Such an organization is usually a match for an amateur club which is a *purposive* organization. Here the motivation for political activity is high because the amateurs are part of a "cause" with a moral rationale and a powerful slogan. Control over any given individual's behavior is rather low, however, for the purposes of the organization are indivisible benefits—rewards which all can share in regardless of the amount of work each does. Purposive rewards are strong sources of stimulation but weak devices for control, for they cannot be withheld, in the way a salary can be withheld, to punish disobedience. In between these two types, however, is the *solidary* organization—the old-line, decaying regular club —in which the rewards of politics come neither from the jobs it offers nor the purposes of the movement, but simply from the act of associating together. Such solidary incentives provide neither much stimulation for hard work nor much opportunity for the precise control of the behavior of the workers. Any attempt to punish a slack worker in a solidary organization runs afoul of the fact that solidary incentives are indivisible and fragile. Demoting a poor worker upsets crucial social relationships, disrupts the harmonious atmosphere of the club, and weakens or destroys the value of the rewards used to hold the allegiance of other workers. A utilitarian and a purposive political club may be fairly matched, but a contest between a purposive and a solidary organization—what, in most cases, is a contest between Jewish amateurs and Irish professionals—is often a very one-sided affair.

# 11 The Power of the Clubs

Although many claims are made by both the amateur Democrats and their opponents about the power (or lack of power) of the clubs, very little can be said on this subject with any certainty. In New York, where the clubs have been fighting an intraparty enemy in Democratic primaries for control of certain specific party positions and certain specific nominations for public office, the achievements of the reformers are (up to a point) fairly easy to determine. Running in individual contests without the aid of any citywide "ticket" headed by a prominent nominee for important citywide office, the reformers were able, by 1960, to win control of eight district leadership posts in Manhattan solely through their own efforts.[1] In 1960, they nominated six candidates for public office and elected four, all to posts formerly held by regular organization men. In addition, they elected candidates to various minor party offices, such as the state committee and the judicial convention. Through 1960, the reform record was clear.

## The Ambiguity of "Power"

The mayoralty election of 1961, however, muddied the record considerably. In that contest, the reformers increased their district leaderships in Manhattan from eight to fifteen. But for the first time they did this as part of a citywide "reform ticket"

[1] At least three of these clubs first won the leadership without real opposition from De Sapio. De Sapio did not actively back the opponents of the West Side Democrats in 1951, the Tilden Club in 1953, or the Murray Hill Citizens Club in 1959. In 1961 they were all opposed by De Sapio candidates.

headed by Robert Wagner, the candidate for mayor. There is no simple way to demonstrate whether this victory—the largest single gain the reformers had ever won—was the result of their grass-roots organization, Wagner's personal standing and campaign, or some combination of both. Indeed, no sooner was the election over than the Mayor and his erstwhile allies fell to arguing over the proper allocation of credit. The argument will not be resolved, because there is no way to demonstrate conclusively that one or the other factor was most important.

TABLE 8

WAGNER VOTE IN 1961 PRIMARY, NEW YORK

| Borough | Total Vote | Wagner Vote as Per Cent of Total |
|---|---|---|
| Manhattan...... | 189,121 | 64.5 |
| Bronx.......... | 121,154 | 61.8 |
| Queens......... | 167,523 | 61.5 |
| Staten Island.... | 25,913 | 59.7 |
| Brooklyn....... | 239,419 | 56.8 |
| Total....... | 743,130 | 60.8 |

However, there is a strong presumption that the Mayor was the most important single factor. Two pieces of evidence give some credence to this. First, although Wagner ran best in Manhattan, where the reformers are numerous, well-organized, and active, he ran almost as well in the other four boroughs where they are almost non-existent (Table 8).

Second, within Manhattan, there was apparently a good deal of straight-ticket voting. As Table 9 shows, there was very little discrepancy between the percentage of the primary vote won by Wagner and the percentage won by reform candidates for district leader whose names appeared on the voting machine on the same line as Wagner's.

This presumption in favor of Wagner's contribution to the 1961 victory can, of course, be challenged on two grounds. First, some reformers might argue that he would not have done as well in reform-controlled districts without reform support. Second, the issue of "bossism" on which Wagner based his entire campaign was in great part an issue created by the reform movement; it provided him with the vital slogan, if not the vital manpower. There is no way to assess these rejoinders and thus the issue must remain moot.

But these problems are minor compared to those which confront anyone attempting to judge the power of the amateur Democratic clubs in Illinois or California. In these states the clubs have not, by and large, been engaged in a clear-cut con-

TABLE 9

WAGNER AND REFORM VOTE, MANHATTAN
ASSEMBLY DISTRICTS, 1961 PRIMARY

| Assembly District* | Wagner Vote as Percentage of Total | Reform Leader Vote as Percentage of Total |
|---|---|---|
| 1............. | 59.1 | 60.3 |
| 5............. | 73.8 | 74.8 |
| 7............. | 79.8 | 79.6 |
| 8............. | 67.4 | 64.9 |
| 10............. | 64.9 | 61.5 |

* Vote given only for whole assembly districts; reformers also won in parts of other districts (3 and 6). Reformers also control the 9th, but there was no leadership contest there in 1961.

test with an organized intraparty opposition for control of specific party posts. In such cases, power can only be inferred from the clubs' record in winning nominations for public offices and in contributing votes to the defeat of the Republican opposition. Since the clubs in these states are not involved in a struggle for votes in or seats on a single, powerful party committee, there is no obvious scoreboard on which political power can be calculated. Outside the party, in the battle against the Republicans, other forces besides the clubs are always at work and thus it becomes almost impossible to demonstrate the effect of the clubs alone.

Of course, to a club worker who has had the experience of personally registering voters he knows would not have registered without his urging and of dragging to the polls people he knows would not have voted without his insistence, the question is academic. He is certain of the impact of the club movement. But to those concerned with establishing beyond reasonable doubt the significance of these activities at the district and state level, the question is far from academic. It is, after all, entirely possible that voters who must be coaxed into registering and voting are not the voters most likely to support out of conviction a full slate of outspokenly liberal candidates.

The CDC has never lost a statewide nomination, but there

TABLE 10

NUMBER OF CALIFORNIA DEMOCRATIC INCUMBENTS, 1952–60

| Office | Total | 1952 | 1954 | 1956 | 1958 | 1960 |
|---|---|---|---|---|---|---|
| Statewide executive*........... | 6 | 0 | I | 1 | 5 | 5 |
| Board of Equalization........... | 4 | 2 | 2 | 2 | 4 | 4 |
| U.S. Senate................... | 2 | 0 | 0 | 0 | 1 | 1 |
| U.S. House of Representatives.... | 30 | 11 | 11 | 13 | 16 | 16 |
| State senate.................. | 40 | 11 | 16 | 20 | 28 | 30 |
| State assembly................ | 80 | 26 | 32 | 38 | 47 | 47 |
| Total..................... | 162 | 50 | 62 | 74 | 101 | 103 |

* Governor, lieutenant-governor, attorney-general, controller, secretary of state, and treasurer.

have been only two cases of a CDC state endorsee being challenged in the primary: the Richards-Yorty fight in 1956 and the contest between Stanley Mosk and Robert McCarthy for attorney-general in 1958. There is no doubt that the number of Democrats in partisan office has risen dramatically since 1954, as Table 10 shows. But most of the gains in the state senate have been made in largely rural counties where there are few clubs with few members. In the assembly, of those districts which are predominantly rural and which have few clubs, the Democrats hold twice as many as the Republicans. In short, part, but certainly not all, of the Democratic revitalization has been due to its renewed strength in rural and agricultural areas of the state.

Many incumbent legislators in California believe that the effectiveness of the CDC clubs has been greatly overrated except, perhaps, in a few heavily Republican areas. These men ascribe the resurgence of the California Democratic party more to the modification and then the abolition of cross-filing. Assemblyman Jesse Unruh, the man who comes as close to anyone to meeting the CDC's need for a "boss" against whom to work, told a meeting of CDC leaders that although he was opposed to prohibiting the CDC from making pre-primary endorsements, he felt such endorsements were not the major cause of the improvement in the party's fortunes: "I think most reasonable people will agree that the DEM on the ballot was probably far more reason for our success than the DEMOCRAT in the district." Further, he felt that Governor Brown's victory in 1958 resulted, not from the undiluted liberal appeal of the clubs, but from the fact that the Republicans were divided (former Governor Goodwin J. Knight was fighting former Senator William F. Knowland) and that Brown was "the first Democrat in years who could successfully appeal to conservative and moderate party members."[2]

There is no simple statistical method by which such charges can be refuted. For this study, three aspects of party strength were examined to discover if there were any obvious relationships between them and the concentration of CDC club members. These measures of party strength were turnout of registered Democrats, increase in Democratic registration, and the size of the "swing" in favor of the party from one election to the next. All three measures, far from demonstrating the relevance of club activities, are at best inconclusive.

If all the Los Angeles County assembly districts are ranked in terms of the vote cast in 1960 for the Democratic candidate for assemblyman as a percentage of each district's Democratic registration, the six districts with the highest voter turnout include three (59, 61, and 63) which have a high level of club

[2] Unruh's speech reprinted in the *Liberal Democrat*, March, 1961, p. 5.

activity but two (67 and 68) which are among those with the smallest number of club members.[3]

Before the 1960 presidential election, many clubs carried on active voter registration drives. There is no doubt that many clubs registered large numbers of people. One club reported registering over two thousand. But these efforts were not readily evident when the over-all registration pattern was considered. If all assembly districts in Los Angeles County are ranked on the basis of the percentage increase between 1958 and 1960 in Democratic registration (expressed as the Democratic percentage of the total registration) four districts are discovered which increased by 2 per cent or more. Of these, only one (63) has any significant club activity, while the other three were largely Negro. Of the six districts with the *smallest* registration increase, three (48, 49, and 61) had a high level of club activity.

Finally, the increase in the Democratic vote for President between 1956 and 1960 was greatest in non-CDC districts in Los Angeles. The Democrats improved their vote in the county from 44.3 per cent in 1956 to 49.7 per cent in 1960, making a total "swing" of 5.4 per cent. The eight districts with ten CDC club members per thousand Democrats or more had an average "swing" of *less* than this amount; the ten districts with the smallest number of CDC members had an average swing which was *greater* than the county total.[4]

[3] The exact figures are given here:

| Assembly District | Dem. Vote as Percentage of Democratic Registration | CDC Club Members per 1,000 Registered Democrats |
|---|---|---|
| 42......... | 91.1 | 5.9 |
| 59......... | 90.2 | 36.0 |
| 68......... | 86.3 | 1.5 |
| 63......... | 85.8 | 11.8 |
| 67......... | 82.9 | 1.4 |
| 61......... | 82.2 | 10.0 |

[4] The eight CDC districts had a swing of 4.7 per cent; the ten non-CDC districts a swing of 6.4 per cent. If the Negro districts are dropped from this list, the non-CDC districts still lead with a swing of 6.1 per cent.

Figures which seem either to deny or exaggerate the importance of the clubs must be qualified, however. It can be argued that the increase in registration, the size of the turnout, and the increase in the Democratic vote would have been even less in districts which have many clubs if these clubs had not been in existence. There is no way to refute this rejoinder. The better showing the Democrats made in registration, turnout, and size of vote in non-club districts may be due to the social and economic character of those areas. The problem that confronts the analyst is that virtually all upper-income areas have a sizable club movement, and hence no comparisons may be made among these areas. In short, the existence or non-existence of clubs is only one factor affecting the political behavior of an area. When two districts differ in one characteristic (such as the level of club activity), they invariably differ in other characteristics as well (such as income, ethnicity, etc.), and thus no control is available.

An analysis of primary contest elections therefore becomes almost the only way in which the clubs can be assessed. When a CDC-endorsed candidate opposes another candidate who is backed by other powerful, non-CDC forces (such as organized labor, special-interest groups, party regulars, or the press) in a primary election, the chips are down and an unambiguous result is available with which to measure the power of the clubs. Even here, of course, the character of the candidates blurs the issue.

To begin with, it must be noted that CDC clubs, acting through a local endorsing council, have opposed but never defeated a Democratic incumbent. But a fairer test of strength occurs when a primary is held to select a Democratic nominee for a seat which is either vacant or held by a Republican, and thus the lure that incumbents seem to have for the voter is eliminated. In the June, 1960, primaries, 150 partisan offices were at stake and of these, 50, or one-third, were contested by two or more candidates. CDC clubs and councils made endorsements in 43 of the 50 contested elections, and won in 36 of the 43, for a record of 83.7 per cent. However, many of the CDC endorsements went to Democratic incumbents who would probably have won without that endorsement. Of the 50 contested primaries, 16 were entered by Democratic incumbents, leaving 34 "open" contests in which there could be a free-for-all among all Democratic aspirants. Of these 34 open races, CDC made endorsements in 30 and their candidates won in 22. These facts are summarized in Table 11.

This table indicates that CDC was less successful in congressional than in state races, losing half of its primaries to non-CDC candidates in the congressional districts with open contests. Nonetheless, the record is impressive in senatorial

TABLE 11

THE CDC IN CONTESTED PRIMARIES, 1960

| Contest | Total Contests | Democratic Incumbents | "Open" Contests | CDC Endorsements | CDC Victories | CDC General Election Victories |
|---|---|---|---|---|---|---|
| Congress....... | 10 | 2 | 8 | 6 | 3 | 0 |
| State senate ... | 10 | 4 | 6 | 5 | 4 | 0 |
| Assembly...... | 30 | 10 | 20 | 17 | 15 | 3 |
| Total...... | 50 | 16 | 34 | 30 | 22 | 3 |

and assembly districts. One reason for this becomes clear when one considers what became of the CDC-endorsed primary winners in the general election. All but three were defeated by their Republican opponents. Apparently a sizable number of CDC victories were in districts which, in a Democratic year, were won by Republicans. Some of these districts are heavily Republican in registration, and no Democrat has a chance. Thus, few, if any, serious Democratic candidates were willing to spend time and money on a hopeless cause, and a CDC-endorsed candidate could have the nomination by default. This raised the question of whether non-CDC candidates fare any better in the general election. In Table 12 are shown the results in the 1960 general election of the 22 CDC and 12 non-CDC candidates. (By "non-CDC" is meant a candidate who

won a Democratic primary in which either no CDC endorsement was made or in which the CDC candidate was defeated.)

This table suggests that non-CDC candidates have done
slightly better than CDC candidates in defeating their Republican opponents after winning an open primary in which no
Democratic incumbent was running. While non-CDC candidates won one-third of their contests against Republicans,
CDC candidates won only one-seventh. But the advantage is
not decisive, and may vary from election to election.

Chicago, like Los Angeles, provides few clues to club
strength. And since the DFI neither endured nor played a con-

TABLE 12

CDC AND NON-CDC CANDIDATES COMPARED, 1960

| CONTEST | TOTAL OPEN CONTESTS | CDC | | NON-CDC | |
|---|---|---|---|---|---|
| | | Primary Wins | General Wins | Primary Wins | General Wins |
| Congress......... | 8 | 3 | 0 | 5 | 0 |
| State senate...... | 6 | 4 | 0 | 2 | 2 |
| Assembly......... | 20 | 15 | 3 | 5 | 2 |
| Total........ | 34 | 22 | 3 | 12 | 4 |

spicuous role in local politics, not even its most ardent supporters can claim much electoral impact for it. But the IVI, as
an independent rather than Democratic organization, offers
one unique opportunity for assessing club power. It backs
split tickets, endorsing both Democrats and Republicans. Presumably, therefore, the extent to which voters follow IVI recommendations on splitting their ballots may be a fair measure
of its organizational strength. In the Fifth Ward, where the
IVI is strongest, it was able in 1960 to carry almost all the
forty precincts it worked for its major candidates: John F.
Kennedy and Benjamin Adamowski, the Republican candidate
for state's attorney. In the parts of the Second Ward which the
IVI worked, four precincts voted for the Democratic President–Republican state's attorney ticket.

But even this measure is open to question. The vote in favor of the split ticket could be explained by the character of the precincts as well as by the efforts of the organization. Adamowski was backed by other groups besides the IVI, and many people may have voted for him and Kennedy whether or not the IVI asked them to. That this may be the case is suggested by another instance of ticket-splitting which occurred in Chicago's Twelfth Congressional District. There, the IVI backed in 1960 a Republican candidate for Congress along with the Democratic presidential nominee. The IVI has members living in two parts of this congressional district—the Forty-ninth and Fiftieth wards. Although its members were in both wards, the IVI decided to canvass only in the Forty-ninth Ward on the grounds that the regular Republican organization was weak there. The results indicate that the Forty-ninth Ward made, by IVI standards, only a slightly better showing than the Fiftieth. If we calculate the vote of the IVI-backed Republicans, we find that in the Forty-ninth Ward, the Republican got 81.1 per cent of Kennedy's vote, while in the Fiftieth he got 76.0 per cent. IVI *canvassing*, as distinct from the existence of the IVI as an *endorsing* organization, may have accounted for a gain of no more than five percentage points in the vote of the Republican.

All of the questions which have been raised in this section are, of course, but special cases of the general difficulty of assessing the consequences of party organization of any kind. Precisely the same kinds of difficulties confront someone who hopes to evaluate the impact of the Chicago machine, the regular Bronx organization, or the League of Women Voters. Very few studies have been made which illuminate this general problem; those by Professor Peter H. Rossi and associates have perhaps been the most sophisticated.[5] At least one study

[5] Peter H. Rossi and Phillips Cutright, "The Impact of Party Organization in an Industrial Setting," Morris Janowitz, ed., *Community Political Systems* (New York: Free Press of Glencoe, 1961), pp. 81–116; Cutright and Rossi, "Grass Roots Politicians and the Vote," *American Sociological Review*, XXIII (April, 1958), 171–79; and Cutright and Rossi, "Party Organization in Primary Elections," *American Journal of Sociology*, LXIV (November, 1958), 262–69.

of a volunteer campaign effort in Manhattan has been made. In an analysis of two amateur clubs in the 1956 presidential election, it was found that there was at best only a very slight correlation between the extent of club contact with voters and the increase in the Democratic vote over the 1952 election.[6]

The lack of a definitive measure of the power of the amateur clubs in all cases except the Manhattan intraparty fight places the clubs in a situation in which their claims to a share in party leadership and legislative influence can be rejected by professional politicians and incumbent legislators on the grounds that the clubs cannot be shown to have "muscle." The absence of a party structure, as in California, not only deprives would-be amateur party leaders of positions in which they can influence party policy and candidates, it also (and more importantly) deprives them of any means of demonstrating in a convincing way their power to capture such offices. This has serious implications for the CDC's effort to become a source of party platforms and thus a major force in determining the ends of government. The liberalism of the CDC is hard to convert into the liberalism of the Democratic party or the liberalism of the state government because the consequences of ignoring CDC imperatives are by no means obvious.

It is doubtful that the CDC has been able to influence state legislation in the direction of its liberal goals. Although CDC clubs and councils regularly send resolutions and letters to legislators and state officials, as well as participate in the annual Issues Conference, very few of these views are advanced in a way that would carry weight with assemblymen and state senators. Although most of its leaders believe that the concern for issues is the most important aspect of the CDC's life, the CDC is not organized for or equipped with the resources to lobby effectively for these ends. Instead, the CDC hopes to

[6] Shirley Jacobson, "Activities of Local Party Organizations as a Determinant of Voting Behavior" (M.A. thesis, Department of Government, New York University, 1958), p. 51. Voter contact was measured by dividing the number of voters contacted in each election district by the total Democratic registration in that district. The correlation between this index and the increase in the Democratic vote was .21.

achieve these goals through the institutionalization of intra-party democracy in a way that will commit candidates, at least to some extent, to the liberal platform of the CDC *before* they are elected and make them responsive to its views in hopes of re-election. There is little evidence to suggest that this approach has directly affected the attainment of liberal ends. Paradoxically, the Democratic legislators may well have been more "liberal" when they were in the minority in Sacramento at a time when the CDC was weak than they are today when the CDC is much stronger and they are in the majority. Whatever success the CDC had in winning a Democratic majority in the assembly and senate may have been purchased at the price of decreasing the liberalism of the legislators by giving them the responsibility for governing.

No precise statement can be made of the impact of CDC on legislators for the same reason that no accurate assessment can be made of most of the influences at work on the legislative process. But several liberal pressure groups, concerned with goals which the CDC shares, reject any possibility of an alliance with CDC and express doubt over its influence. One such organization is a statewide committee created to press for a fair employment practices act in the 1959 legislative session and which continued in existence in the 1961 session to lobby for anti-discrimination measures in the field of housing. One of the officials of that organization, an active worker on behalf of many liberal causes, explained his attitude toward CDC:

> We want the CDC president to be on our letterhead. But that's all. We would never get involved with the CDC in any legislative campaign. First of all, they are a political party, and we are a non-partisan group trying to find votes wherever we can for a cause we believe in. The CDC may want the same liberal things we do, but they have to fight Republicans, and there are some Republicans who will vote our way. . . . Furthermore, they [the CDC] have a problem with Communist infiltration. We wouldn't go to them for help. Besides being infiltrated, they have no real impact. I would say they are ineffective in the legislature.

These remarks about infiltration are possibly exaggerated, but the liberal lobbyists, such as this one, have been extremely cautious about such matters in recent years. In any case, what is important in this connection is not what is true, but what this person (and others like him) believe is true.

Further, the ambiguity of the CDC's power works against its ability to win certain political rewards for itself. When, for example, the California delegation to the 1960 Democratic National Convention was being assembled, there were only eight CDC leaders among its 162 members, despite the CDC's claim that it was the only grass-roots, doorbell-ringing organization the party had. Legislators, labor union leaders, representatives of minority groups, and big financial contributors filled most of the spots on the delegation. And when a fight over the selection of a new national committeeman broke out, Paul Ziffren, who had strong CDC backing, lost to Stanley Mosk by a vote of 115 to 37.[7]

After Kennedy's election to the presidency, the bulk of the federal patronage in California went to non-CDC politicians. No prominent CDC official received a federal appointment. The two most important jobs went to men who had been heavy financial contributors to the party.[8]

Despite all these doubts and limitations, however, probably the most significant piece of evidence on the influence of the CDC is the fact that a large number of legislators and party professionals, as well as organized labor, would like to strip CDC of the right to make pre-primary endorsements. CDC's influence, although it is difficult to establish statistically, must

[7] *New York Times,* June 19, 1960, p. 38. A detailed and knowledgeable case study of the California delegation is John H. Bunzel and Eugene C. Lee, "The California Democratic Delegation of 1960," a manuscript prepared for the Inter-University Case Program, New York City, 1961.

[8] J. Edward Day, who became postmaster-general, and Clarence Martin, who became assistant secretary of commerce. Day was chairman of Democratic Associates, Inc., a fund-raising organization. Martin was a member of the Finance Committee of the State Central Committee. A list of thirteen federal appointments given to Californians during the first month of the Kennedy administration is found in the *Sacramento Bee,* January 28, 1960, p. 6.

be sufficient to concern those who are not in favor of the endorsing process. It is probably fair to say that the label provided candidates by the endorsing process is sufficiently valuable to be worth seeking if you are not an incumbent and sufficiently troublesome to be concerned about if you are an incumbent.

## The Resources of the Clubs

The principal resources which the amateur Democrat brings to the club are his enthusiasm and his personal skills. This is essential, for in nearly every other respect, the amateurs are seriously lacking in the conventional resources of politics.

The amateur, if he is up against a regular organization that has failed to adapt and whose level of discipline is low—an organization, in short, which relies on what have been called "solidary" rather than "material" rewards—is usually more interested and more energetic in political contests than his rivals. If he is up against a well-drilled professional club or ward organization, his advantage disappears *unless* the voters in the district are similar to the amateur in class, status, and education. In any case, the amateur, by deciding to enter the party at the local level rather than attempting to "reform" it from a position outside and above it, has been forced to develop a considerable set of politically valuable skills and a sophistication in the realities of campaign work.

Indeed, the amateurs pride themselves on the extent to which they are "tough-minded" about politics. They are very conscious of their realistic engagement in grass-roots politics. Unlike gentlemen reformers of an earlier era, this group feels it "knows the score." They pride themselves on being able to beat the professionals at their own game, asking no quarter and giving none. The larger clubs, with their high proportion of lawyers, public-relations experts, advertising men, and young executives, are able to utilize a wide range of professional skills which regular clubs often do not have or which, because of a commitment to a traditional style of politics, they are unwilling to use. A reform club in Manhattan's First Assembly District was able in a 1953 court race to have its opponent taken off the ballot in a court action which attacked his petitions as fraudulent. Similarly, Edward Costikyan became the reform leader in the Eighth Assembly District South when he was able to have his opponent's petitions thrown out on a technicality. In a court action, he established that the Tammany leader had not complied with the law in drawing his petitions. He was stricken from the ballot and compelled as a result to run as a write-in candidate.[9] In East Harlem, a reform candidate for assemblyman was able to prove that many Italian voters whose names appeared on the election rolls of the district no longer lived in the area. He developed a clever stratagem for the purpose of gathering this evidence:

> My secretary is working on her Ph.D. at Columbia. She and some other Columbia graduate students went around from door to door pretending to be taking a survey on TV audiences to find out how many people had a set and what programs they listened to. Actually, of course, the purpose was to find out how many adults lived there. There was one building in which 13 Italian names were registered but there were only 2 people living there. On election day, all 13 showed up. We began challenging them right and left. They protested vehemently, but we had the proof on them.

Considering the fact that Tammany has controlled the Board of Elections in New York, surprisingly few reformers have been thrown off the ballot by challenges brought against their petitions or for failing to meet the complex requirements of the elections code. In the 1961 primary, for example, they had no difficulty obtaining enough signatures to qualify all their local candidates except one.

The utility of the skills of the amateur vary with the character of his constituency. There are at least three different kinds of assembly districts in which amateur clubs have been

---

[9] On this campaign, see Gerald Pomper, "Revolt in the Eighth Assembly District South," in Richard T. Frost, ed., *Cases in State and Local Government* (Englewood Cliffs, N.J.: Prentice-Hall, 1961), pp. 95–108.

successful. Because of important differences in class among these districts, different campaign tactics must be used. On Chicago's Gold Coast or in the silk-stocking Ninth Assembly District on Manhattan's East Side, the level of both income and education is high. Many voters live in expensive apartments, most of them carefully guarded by doormen and building superintendents. The inhabitants, who lead professional careers, often keep erratic hours, with many nights spent away from home. Under these circumstances, door-to-door canvassing is difficult. Not only is it often hard to get past doormen who are paid to keep building occupants from being disturbed, but it is difficult to say anything in a two- or three-minute interview with an educated voter at his front door that will make a deep impression on him. In order to reach these voters, therefore, such clubs as the Lexington or the Schiller Banks rely heavily on cocktail parties, given by friends of the candidate, in which the undecided voter may rub elbows with prominent men and women, meet the candidate in a familiar social setting, and participate in the well-understood ritual of cocktail-party conversation. A Lexington club candidate described her campaign methods in a way that illustrates the nature of the district:

> The campaign tactics . . . involve the use of cocktail parties. We don't try to use *kaffeklatsches*, as they do in other areas, and we certainly reject sound trucks. It's very hard to get people together on Park Avenue or Fifth Avenue. The candidates have some cocktail parties, and other people give cocktail parties in their behalf. This is the best way to reach them. The other good way to reach them, of course, is with personal canvassing, even though you reach only a very few. It is difficult, but not impossible, to canvass in buildings which are guarded by doormen and which have elevators. . . . I will work one to one-and-a-half hours a night. During that time I will be lucky to see 10 or 12 voters. . . . During the time I have available to me in the campaign I will reach perhaps 1,000 to 1,500 registered voters. That would be tops.

On Manhattan's West Side or in Chicago's Fifth Ward, the constituents of the amateur clubs are comparably high in education but not so high in income. In addition, they are more heterogeneous in class and status. Here, great reliance is placed on door-to-door canvassing and *kaffeeklatsches*. Few of the buildings have doormen, and there are more walk-up apartments. Cocktail parties are expensive, but almost any family can afford coffee and tea. A great value is placed on finding candidates who can perform well in the intimacy of a small, front-room gathering of educated voters who consider themselves (rightly or wrongly) well-informed on current affairs. In a typical reform-Tammany contest in such an area, the reform candidate will appear at as many as 5 or 6 coffee parties a night, invariably speaking about issues and programs, while the Tammany candidate will address larger gatherings and rely on the work of his election district captains.

Finally, there are some districts, such as those around East Harlem in Manhattan, where neither of these approaches is fruitful. In these areas of low incomes and low education, overcrowded and disorderly, the sound truck is the principal campaign weapon. A reform leader there describes his tactics:

> I used strictly a sound-truck operation. I once tried the *kaffeklatsche* technique, but it was a dismal failure. The people wouldn't come, they were embarrased, they wouldn't talk—it was horrible. We quickly discontinued it and went back on the sound trucks. Here the people are very poor and can't afford to go to movies in the evening, but they stay awake rather late at night. They're always interested. If a dog gets run over, 30 people are on the street immediately. The sound truck for them is a form of entertainment. They like to see what's going on, so you stop in front of every corner block and give your speech. This, I think, was our vital strategy. I spent 6 weeks, every day from 3 p.m. to 10 p.m., on that truck. On Saturday I worked from 10 a.m. to 10 p.m. on that truck.

The nature of club campaigning in Los Angeles is far different from in Manhattan. In the latter city, the clubs are almost all in areas which are so heterogeneous that the middle-class intelligentsia who make up the bulk of the club activities are forced to work in many election districts which are not inhabited by club types but by persons quite dissimilar in class and status.[10] In Los Angeles, by contrast, the greater homogeneity of the communities, and hence of the areas served by most clubs, means that precinct work is much less arduous. One club president described this task in revealing terms:

> Our precinct work is done on Sunday morning. We found this is the best time. We start out at about 10:30 and work for two hours and then we come back to somebody's home and have a brunch and if there's a swimming pool around we have a swim. We try to make it a social affair. We do this every Sunday. I suppose we have between twenty and fifty people working every Sunday morning. The same people, of course, don't come out every Sunday, so you get a little turnover. Voters in the precincts are easy to talk to. They are pretty much like us, although some are a bit wealthier. They stay home on Sunday mornings.

The picnic aspects of precinct work are not, of course, found in all clubs. In this, as in everything, there is a wide range of variation. But the club whose activities are described above is one of the largest and located in a district, composed of similar clubs, which has more CDC members than any other district in the county.

Club organization in such assembly districts as the Fifty-ninth, the Sixtieth, the Sixty-first, and the Fifty-seventh in Los Angeles is extensive enough to be an important factor in registration and elections. But the coverage is incomplete. The Beverly Hills Democratic Club, the largest in California with over 720 members, is responsible for the 78 precincts in the city of Beverly Hills (which is part of the Fifty-ninth Assembly District) during the campaigns. This club, and others in the area, have no trouble in manning all their precincts during a presidential election. In 1960, all but 46 of the 633 precincts in the Sixteenth Congressional District (which is made up of the Fifty-ninth and Sixtieth Assembly districts) were canvassed to some extent by workers in the two weeks before

[10] For a vivid although naïve account, see David L. Hurwood, "Grass-Roots Politics in Manhattan," *Atlantic*, October, 1960, pp. 65–70.

the election, and on election day all were checked by workers to ascertain who had not voted. But in local and primary contests, even the biggest club has some difficulty. In the June, 1960, primary, the Beverly Hills Club managed to cover only two-thirds of its 78 precincts, despite its large membership. In districts with far smaller concentrations of club workers, far fewer precincts are manned by CDC members. (They may, of course, be partially manned by non-CDC workers, such as COPE workers, personal supporters of certain candidates, and members of non-CDC clubs. There is little or no attempt to provide a systematic division of labor among these competing and often hostile groups, however.) There is little doubt that many of the more than eleven thousand precincts in Los Angeles County are not worked at all.

CDC leaders are aware of this and frequently urge CDC meetings to find ways of providing more "campaign muscle" so that CDC endorsements will be more "meaningful" and the power of the CDC more evident. This is tantamount to urging the organization to find ways of organizing lower-income and minority groups, and, as we have seen, the club style of politics is probably not adaptable to this end.

In the other resources of politics—money, publicity, and prestigious names—the New York reformers have enjoyed a considerable advantage over their counterparts elsewhere. In 1960, the CDV raised and spent over one hundred thousand dollars, of which nearly forty thousand was given directly to reform clubs to further their growth.[11] Next to these grants, the largest sum (over twenty-eight thousand dollars) went for salaries for the CDV staff. Some reform clubs, of course, express their suspicion of the CDV by referring to its "excessive" expenditures for staff; the "CDV is a reform boondoggle," said one. Nonetheless, insurgent reform clubs have obtained as much as half their campaign funds from CDV sources; the CDV, in turn, has been able to raise such sums because of the

[11] Data from the tentative statement of expenses, issued by the CDV in February, 1961.

prestige of its elder statesmen and their contacts among liberal donors in Manhattan.

The CDV assembles and distributes not only money but status. Lehman, Roosevelt, Finletter, and the other CDV "advisors" are well-known names in New York politics. Their identification with the reform cause has probably been crucial to its success. The CDV can stimulate and co-ordinate the endorsements and campaigning of these prestigious people. Most active reformers are young and generally unknown in their communities and in the city. Indeed, the reform movement as a whole seems to consist of a large number of vigorous, intelligent, and ambitious—but unknown—young men and women, and a handful of aging, but prominent, elder statesmen.[12] Few people of middle age or moderate prominence seem to be involved. As one reformer phrased it, "I've had the feeling that there are about nine rungs of the status ladder missing between Herbert Lehman and Eleanor Roosevelt at the top and the rest of us at the bottom."

The battles between reformers and Tammany were, at least before 1962, waged almost entirely against Carmine De Sapio personally. Although there have been local issues used in various districts, such as the Manhattantown urban renewal scandal,[13] most reformers are convinced that the payoff issue was De Sapio. Posed against De Sapio, the symbol of evil, was the reform clubs' symbol of liberal goodness—Herbert Lehman. A leading Riverside Democrat observed after their 1960 campaign:

> I don't think he [Ryan] would have won unless we had Lehman's backing in the campaign and unless we had the big issue of De Sapio influence. We turned the fight into a Lehman versus De Sapio fight instead of a Ryan versus Teller fight. That was the clincher.

[12] Cf. Joseph Kraft, "The Decline of the New York Democrats," *Commentary*, July 1960, pp. 17–21.

[13] A history of the so-called "Title I" scandal in New York City is provided by Donald B. Rosenthal, "Issue Politics in New York City" (M.A. thesis, Department of Political Science, University of Chicago, 1960).

The central theme in all recent campaigns, repeated a thousand times in posters, speeches, and pamphlets, was the issue of bossism. Every reformer who campaigned ran nominally against his local opponent but in fact against Carmine De Sapio. When the reformers backed a young Jewish lawyer in a primary fight against an incumbent Irish state senator, reform workers moved throughout the district pasting large stickers across the posters of their Irish foe which read "De Sapio's Choice." On many of their own posters, the name of the reform candidate was almost overshadowed by the name and picture of Herbert Lehman, urging voters to support his young friend. Herbert Lehman is a proven vote-getter in New York City, particularly among Jewish voters, and De Sapio came to be a proven vote-loser. This in part accounted for the fact that a young, virtually unknown Irishman was able to defeat an older, much better-known Jewish incumbent in a race for the Democratic nomination for Congress in a district that is heavily Jewish. William Fitts Ryan appeared frequently in the company of Lehman, who endorsed him strongly; Ludwig Teller, although probably the best Congressman from Manhattan at the time, was made to appear the hand-picked satellite of De Sapio. In the final returns, it appeared as if an Irishman had beaten a Jew in a Jewish district; in fact, a Jewish elder statesman had beaten an Italian boss.

The money and the status which the CDV was able to organize on behalf of reform were of critical importance, not only in winning elections, but in providing most of whatever imperfect unity the reform "movement" exhibited. The demand for Lehman's endorsement and for Lehman's money was such that even the militant reformers were reluctant to oppose him openly (although many opposed him privately).

Added to these resources was the favorable treatment the reformers received at the hands of the "good government" press in New York City. The *Times,* the *Herald Tribune,* and the *Post* gave considerable coverage to the anti-De Sapio struggle waged by the reformers and gave currency to the epithet, "bossism," which enabled the reformers to extend their appeal beyond the territories of their clubs.[14] De Sapio became an electoral liability because bossism became such a familiar charge and one he was never able to overcome. New York is one of the few major cities with a large "liberal" press. It has, of course, an even larger tabloid and conservative press, such as the *Daily News*, the *Daily Mirror*, and the *Journal-American*, but these papers circulate mostly in the Bronx and Brooklyn, whereas the others circulate most heavily in Manhattan.[15] New York's "low-brow" press has more or less consistently opposed the reformers, often describing them as self-serving radicals.

All these resources have been conspicuously lacking in other club movements. The DFI failed in part through lack of money (although more through lack of purpose or achievements) and had to "import" from outside Illinois almost all its well-known speakers. Stephen Mitchell was the best-known local DFI member, and he was hardly an "elder statesman."

In California, the CDC had, for 1960, a total income of only $47,532 for its entire state organization, the bulk of which ($27,000) came, not from large donors, but from club dues. In fact, there were virtually no large donors at all, the rest of the money being earned through sales of a souvenir program at the CDC convention and of a bloc of tickets at the Democratic National Convention and from registration fees col-

---

[14] This will be denied by many reformers who feel the New York press neglected them. The only answer to this is to suggest that they don't know what neglect is. They would feel differently if they had experienced the lofty indifference of the *Los Angeles Times* or the *Chicago Tribune*.

[15] The Audit Bureau of Circulation has kindly provided the following breakdown of the circulation by borough of the four major New York City morning daily newspapers, as of March 22, 1960.

| PAPER | TOTAL NYC CIRCULATION | PER CENT OF TOTAL CIRCULATION BY BOROUGH | | | | |
|---|---|---|---|---|---|---|
| | | Bronx | Brooklyn | Manhattan | Staten Island | Queens |
| Times | 380,420 | 14.5 | 21.5 | 42.5 | 1.4 | 20.1 |
| Herald Tribune | 164,794 | 11.2 | 19.9 | 45.4 | 3.2 | 20.3 |
| News | 1,248,259 | 16.6 | 30.2 | 29.8 | 2.8 | 20.4 |
| Mirror | 550,134 | 14.2 | 34.8 | 28.1 | 2.2 | 20.7 |

lected at its conferences. Although statewide in scope, it paid out in 1960 only $17,000 in staff salaries. Only a loan from certain well-endowed member clubs kept the CDC out of debt. Although there are many organizations for fund-raising in the California Democratic party at the county and state level, there are few CDC leaders who are members of these bodies and none of the money finds its way into CDC coffers.

A liberal member of the Finance Committee sympathized with the plight of CDC but felt that nothing could be done so long as the president of that organization was a person who was both politically unknown and outspokenly liberal. There is no one in Los Angeles who is financially affluent, politically secure, and temperamentally liberal comparable to Herbert H. Lehman in New York, and thus no one who can provide CDC with the kind of status and money that is given to the Manhattan reform clubs by Lehman and his associates in the New York Committee for Democratic Voters. "CDC needs a president with stature before it can raise money," he told an interviewer. "Nobody I know will give to it now, even though I think the CDC president is a brilliant fellow, very clever and intelligent, witty, very good at presiding over debates within the CDC. But he can't raise five dollars."

# 12 The New Party Politics An Appraisal

The changes which the amateur Democrat proposes to make in the structure and functions of American political parties are not trivial; they are fundamental. Even the pseudo-amateur who seeks only power and office is compelled, by his position of leadership in an amateur club, to play his part in a major effort to alter radically the local organizations of American political parties. Although the successes of the amateurs will probably be limited to a few localities, their proposals for a new party politics deserve serious attention.

Most generally, the amateur believes that political parties ought to be programmatic, internally democratic, and largely or entirely free of a reliance on material incentives such as patronage. A programmatic party would offer a real policy alternative to the opposition party. A vote for the party would be as much, or more, a deliberate vote for a set of clear and specific proposals, linked by a common point of view or philosophy of government, as it would be a vote for a set of leaders. The programmatic basis of one party would, to some extent, compel an expression of purpose by the opposing party and thus lead toward the realignment of both parties national- ly, with liberals in one and conservatives in the other. Elective officials would be bound by their party to put into effect at least the more important of the policies of the party and would be held responsible for failure to do so. Otherwise, programs and platforms of the new party politics would be as meaningless as those of the traditional parties—i.e., designed to win votes but not to influence government. Thus, a com- mitment to a programmatic party implies a commitment to a disciplined party. In order to insure that party leaders are responsive to the rank and file, the parties would be internally democratic, with party members choosing party leaders and holding them accountable. Candidates for public office and platforms would be ratified, after some meaningful debate and with real opportunities for choice, by the membership. Although the possibilities of material gain would not necessarily be foreclosed, the strength of the party would not rest on patronage and favoritism but on the freely given consent of the members and their voluntary contributions of time, effort, and money. Party leaders might legitimately aspire to high appointive office (for here policy can be made and it is important to have good men in office, committed to programs in which you believe) but not to lesser appointive posts which exist not to make policy but to reward workers for service and to compel their loyalties.

The value of this conception of a new party politics is rarely discussed by the amateur Democrats; instead, it is largely taken for granted. Despite the conspicuous parallels between the amateurs' proposals and the recommendations of certain scholars who are also critical of traditional political practices, no amateur interviewed ever referred to these writings and no one ever called attention to any systematic defense of the goals of the club movement.[1] And yet these goals, insofar as they refer to party structure and function, can be questioned at almost every point. Many theoretical criticisms have been made of the abstract proposals for party reform; the amateur clubs offer an opportunity to evaluate such proposals on the basis of the actual experience of party organization.[2]

[1] Proposals for party reform include E. E. Schattschneider, *Party Government* (New York: Farrar & Rinehart, 1942); Committee on Political Parties of the American Political Science Association, *Toward a More Responsible Two-Party System* (New York: Rinehart, 1950); Stephen K. Bailey, *The Condition of Our National Political Parties* (New York: Fund for the Republic, 1959); Thomas K. Finletter, *Can Representative Government Do the Job?* (New York: Reynal & Hitchcock, 1945).

[2] Criticisms of party reforms include Pendleton Herring, *The Politics of Democracy* (New York: W. W. Norton, 1940); Herbert Agar, *The*

The two crucial proposals of the amateurs are that parties be internally democratic and that they be committed to certain substantive goals. The analysis presented in this book of the workings of amateur Democratic clubs in three major American cities suggests that there is a serious question whether it is either desirable or feasible for American parties to be either internally democratic or the source of programs and issues.

The answers to these questions depend on one's conception of the nature of democracy generally. The view held by the amateurs implies that in a large and heterogeneous society the probability of government being "democratic" is increased significantly by political arrangements which broaden popular participation in the making of political decisions. Democracy, in this view, is the method for realizing the common good by allowing the people to decide issues through the election of individuals who assemble to carry out the popular will. If this is the case, then clearly the selection of elective officials ideally must be as democratic as possible from the very first— i.e., the selection of candidates by political parties must be as democratic as the election of officeholders by the voters. And the formulation of the popular will ideally must begin as soon as possible in the political process—i.e., policies must be stated explicitly by the rank-and-file members of the parties and not merely inferred from the vague "mandate" of the electorate when it has chosen a president or governor. In a general election, the choice of the electorate is limited, in the typical case, to two candidates and two party platforms. Government will be more democratic if as many people as possible can participate in the choice of those candidates and the writing of those platforms.

An alternative theory of democracy rejects this view as unrealistic. This second theory takes into account the fact that

---

Price of Union (Boston: Houghton Mifflin, 1950); Austin Ranney, "Toward a More Responsible Two-Party System: A Commentary." American Political Science Review, XLV (June, 1951), 488 ff.; Edward C. Banfield, "In Defense of the American Party System," paper prepared for the Public Affairs Conference Center, University of Chicago, 1961 (mimeographed).

people have many fundamental disagreements which cannot be reduced to two simple choices no matter how elaborate the party system may be; that these people are by and large uninformed on all but the most dramatic and fundamental issues; that many of the politically relevant views of people are emotional and even irrational; and that therefore there is no way—and there *should not* be any way—to arrive at decisions on all important matters or at some conception of the common good by algebraically adding the likes and dislikes of the voters. The implication of this view is that, far from increasing public participation in the choice of candidates and issues, democracy is best served by reducing and simplifying those choices to a single elemental choice—that of the principal elective officials. The democratic system is defined, in this theory, not as some method by which "the people rule," but as "that institutional arrangement for arriving at political decisions in which individuals acquire the power to decide by means of a competitive struggle for the people's vote."[3] A political party, therefore, is a group "whose members propose to act in concert in the competitive struggle for political power."[4]

The amateur Democrats hold a view of democracy which implies that many—if not most—people are similar in character to the amateurs themselves and thus equipped to operate issue-oriented parties by democratic means in the interests of the common good. The alternative view of democracy implies that most voters are radically unlike the amateurs, and that their interests will be better served by a party system which asks them to make a single fundamental choice rather than to participate in a kind of party town meeting. The amateurs believe that America's governing institutions are best served if there is democracy within the political parties as well as between them; the adherents of the alternative view argue that while *inter*party democracy is essential, *intra*party democracy

[3] The phrase and, of course, the theory, are from Joseph A. Schumpeter, *Capitalism, Socialism, and Democracy* (London: George Allen & Unwin Ltd., 1954), p. 269.

[4] *Ibid.*, p. 283.

is not and, indeed, that the success of the former is reduced by the extent of the latter.

Although they are not given to theorizing or even to disinterested reflection, professional politicians by and large act as if they subscribed to this second view of democracy. Its advantage for their purposes is manifest: if a popular choice between competing leaders is all that we can or should reasonably expect of the voters, then a democratic society (and perhaps the public interest) can be served by men who act selfishly. The ends of government (public policies) need not provide the motives for undertaking political action. Further, the party can attempt to give the voters whatever they seem to want without concerning itself with whether what is offered conforms to some particular ideology or was shaped by the votes of party members. Internal democracy and a commitment to substantive programs would be as irrelevant to the selection of candidates and issues by a party as they would be to the choice of merchandise and sales programs by department stores.[5]

An amateur politician, on the other hand, is threatened by a fundamental problem on which his attitude is generally ambiguous. That problem is this: If the voters reject the substantive ends of the amateur Democrats, on what grounds can the amateurs claim the right to control the party? If, as seems likely, most voters are not as liberal as the amateurs in New York, Chicago, or Los Angeles, will the amateurs insist on committing the party to liberal programs defined through democratic means? Stated more briefly, is liberalism compatible with democracy if democracy involves the procedures upon which amateur politicians insist? An article discussed among California club leaders raised but did not settle these questions. After the 1960 presidential election, the author wrote that "mass ignorance sets the tone of political discourse." Because the American public is poorly informed and the

[5] E. E. Schattschneider, who advocates more programmatic political parties but opposes making them internally democratic, has used the same metaphor. *Op. cit.*, p. 60.

parties do little to remedy this, the election "cast serious doubt upon the reliability of the American form of government." The author quoted approvingly from Walter Lippmann's book, *The Public Philosophy*, the passage which states the "unhappy truth" that "the prevailing public opinion has been destructively wrong at the critical junctures. The people have imposed a veto upon the judgments of informed and responsible officials." The author goes on to note that "Congress as a whole is even more ignorant and hostile to new ideas than the general public" and then faces up to the choice which must be made:

> I think the U.S. is faced with two rather clear-cut alternatives if it hopes to compete with expanding Communism. Either it must deprive mass opinion of its power by abandoning democracy and turning to elitism or it must undertake the difficult task of improving the quality of mass opinion. Obviously, liberal democrats must prefer the latter alternative, and it is therefore our responsibility to suggest methods whereby this task might be accomplished.[6]

Fortunately, this may not be the choice at all, for if it were, the "obvious" alternative would probably be doomed to failure, and the amateur Democrats would be faced with the unchangeable fact that the people may be wrong. The inability of the clubs to organize the mass of the electorate or even to establish a working alliance with those labor and minority-group organizations which do have a mass base suggests that the reformation of public opinion, which is described as the only alternative to "elitism," is a vain hope.

The conventional political parties seek neither to abandon democracy nor to improve the quality of mass opinion. Instead, they organize the electorate so that it is confronted with a choice between leaders rather than between policies. Then they endeavor to insulate, to the extent possible, the elected leaders from the pressures of local opinion so that, to revert to Lippmann's phrase, erroneous public opinion cannot

[6] Marshall Windmiller, "Prescription for a New Style of Politics," *The Liberal Democrat*, December, 1960, p. 34.

"impose what amounts to a veto" upon the informed judgment of those responsible for governing.[7] To be sure, parties succeed only imperfectly in this task, in part because they have been steadily stripped of the resources with which to mobilize voters without appeals to divisive issues and in part because in certain sections of the country they are not strong enough to assure political support for elective officials who are threatened with reprisals by special-interest groups with large constituencies or pocketbooks.

If democracy involves the choice of leaders rather than policies, then the possibilities of statesmanship free from the vetoes of uninformed opinion are greater. Votes for leaders can be won with a variety of appeals, including personality, sectional and ethnic loyalties, traditional party allegiances, patronage, and the inculcation of a general belief that the candidate "will do a good job." Votes for policies, on the other hand, can only be won by persuading people to agree to those policies, and for this the old issueless appeals are of little value. Further, obtaining agreement on anything but the most general (and most vague) issues is usually impossible. To the extent that amateur politicians have as their model a political party which concerns itself entirely with appeals to issues, they are working for the creation of a system which will have enlarged powers for imposing vetoes on the judgment of elected officials. And, even with the most optimistic allowances for the ability of the new party to inform its workers and followers and generate thoughtful proposals, there can be little doubt that, with the inherently superior sources of information at the disposal of the officials and their inherently greater sense of the realities of the situation within which they must act, these officials will find a programmatic party a burdensome constraint. If a weakness of democratic government is that its crucial decisions are subject to uninformed popular vetoes, then the problem will be made worse by converting

[7] Walter Lippmann, *The Public Philosophy* (Boston: Little, Brown & Co., 1955), pp. 19–20.

parties into plebiscitiary mechanisms for taking those decisions into the market place.

Having set forth these general considerations, let us now turn our attention to a more detailed examination of the two principal innovations of the amateur Democrats.

*Intraparty Democracy*

If one's theory of government stipulates that the electoral choice between candidates in the general election is an insufficient guarantee of democracy, then the demand for democracy within the political parties is understandable. But if one's theory of government holds that the essence of democracy is and can only be offering the voters a single meaningful choice in the general election, then intraparty democracy may well be a serious disadvantage.

If the party is to be a competitor for votes, then the requirements of that competition will be, in most cases, the opposite of party democracy. The party is an agent of conflict, an instrument of political warfare, for which internal democracy is about as useful as it would be for an army. The ultimate decision of the voters is the test, and it is folly to give the advantage to the enemy by being preoccupied with the votes necessary to settle who shall be officers and what shall be the strategy. Internal democracy is harmless—and meaningless—when the interparty contest is hopeless. The selection of candidates and issues is irrelevant for a Democratic club in an overwhelmingly Republican district, for the good Democrat will be defeated almost as easily as the bad. But in the districts where victory is possible or even assured, internal democracy is neither meaningless nor harmless. The struggle for leadership and for nominations among amateur Democrats constrains the ambitious to outbid one another in the effort to prove their ideological purity and establish their liberal credentials; this, in turn, drives the clubs further from that middle ground on which all parties must stand if they are to appeal successfully for those crucial votes which are not committed to either extreme.

Further, the publicity which inevitably attends organizations concerned with internal democracy can deprive such organizations of essential resources. The requirement of public financial records, if it is to be meaningful at all, would require that contributors to the party identify themselves. This would, in all likelihood, deter not only the corrupt and self-seeking contributor, but the honest and disinterested as well, for in politics, purity is hard to prove. The CDC in California has received little money, not simply because it has found it hard to establish the extent of its power, but also because contributions to incumbent legislators are less likely to be publicly disclosed. Secrecy in finance protects the innocent along with the guilty, and if the ends of political activity are praiseworthy, on what grounds can one justify deliberately reducing the resources available to attain those ends? It is easy to criticize the notion that "the ends justify the means," but if the *ends* do not justify the means, it is difficult to imagine what else can.

The same argument can be made about patronage. In those areas where potential recipients value it at all, its utility ought to depend, not on whether its acceptance entails no obligations to party leaders, but precisely on the fact that it *is* a means of exercising control. If the test of a democracy is its ability to offer simple but meaningful choices to the general electorate, that test may be best met if both parties are in a position to field strong organizations backing their candidates, and the strength of the organizations is often (but not always) proportional to the ability of party leaders to discipline the party rank and file. Only if intraparty democracy is an end in itself can an argument against intraparty discipline be made. Reformers tend to assume that it is such an end, but they offer little justification for the view, and certainly no justification that links the level of democracy within the party with the health of the polity as a whole. In any case, a political party is not in the same position as a labor union under a closed shop agreement: no one is forced to join the party in order to earn a living.

Even more important, however, is the fact that to offer a meaningful choice to the general electorate, the party must be held responsible for the actions of its members. If most voters form judgments about parties *as a whole,* it is unfair to penalize parties for the actions of members who have no obligation to the party and who can defy it at will.

A party which is internally democratic and lacking in such resources as patronage is not equipped with those sanctions necessary to enforce the party mandate—i.e., its program—on those whom it elects to office. Program implies discipline, but discipline, as the history of West European socialist parties abundantly suggests, is the enemy of intraparty democracy.[8] In parliamentary governments, such as Great Britain, the party leadership in Parliament exercises a tight discipline over back-bench members in order to implement the programs of the leaders (which, it should be pointed out, are not necessarily the programs of the party workers in the constituencies). The Conservative party in the House of Commons makes little pretense at internal democracy; the Parliamentary Labour party does make that pretense, usually when it is in opposition but rarely when it has the responsibility for governing.[9]

The problem of obtaining unity among elective officials sufficient to implement party program is multiplied manyfold when, as in the United States, the formal governing institutions are fragmented and decentralized such that almost every elective official is legally independent and equipped with the power to obstruct or veto the proposals of others. To the extent that British political parties, so often taken as a model by American critics of our traditional political arrangements, are able to offer clear programmatic alternatives to the voters, it is precisely because they are *not* internally democratic but

[8] Robert Michels, *Political Parties* (Glencoe: Free Press, 1958), pp. 145–48, 192–93; Maurice Duverger, *Political Parties,* trans. Barbara and Robert North (2d ed.; London: Methuen & Co., 1959), pp. 168–82.

[9] R. T. McKenzie, *British Political Parties* (London: Wm. Heinemann, 1955), pp. 581–91.

rather are led by men with considerable disciplinary powers over back-bench members. Although recent research has suggested that British parties are less programmatic than their admirers claim and less disciplined than their critics charge, it remains generally true that the opportunities for the average member to act independently by crossing the aisle or challenging the leadership are both rare and costly.[10]

American parties have attempted to overcome the fragmentation of government at the state and local level by various devices. Essentially, these devices involve attempts to compel acceptance of leadership programs without having to win that acceptance by compromising or modifying the substantive issues. This is true even for corrupt parties, for discipline is as necessary to put through a fragmented governing apparatus a program for enriching the bosses as it is to enact a program for realizing the public interest. Agreement on programs can be won without modifying the program if the party leaders have non-programmatic resources with which they can bargain. These resources are principally two: control over party nominations for office and control over the patronage resources of the government. The direct primary has weakened the former and the merit system the latter. If candidates are picked by a direct primary rather than a party convention, and if the party is not (as it is in Chicago) powerful enough to control that primary, then candidates can win on the basis of personal appeals and independent campaigns and thereby owe little or nothing to the party leaders. The power of British party constituency associations over M.P.s is due in large measure to the fact that there is no direct primary in Britain; only the associations can adopt candidates and thus can refuse to readopt them.[11] Similarly, the reduction in patronage avail-

[10] Peter G. Richards, *Honourable Members* (London: Faber & Faber, 1959), chap. xiv. Among the recent writers who have questioned the extent to which British parties are "programmatic" is Sir W. Ivor Jennings, *Party Politics*, II (*The Growth of Parties*) (Cambridge: Cambridge University Press, 1961), 327–43.

[11] Leon D. Epstein, "British M.P.s and Their Local Parties: The Suez Case," *American Political Science Review*, LIV (June, 1960), 389.

able to party leaders through the extension of various good government measures combined with the entry into politics of people for whom minor forms of patronage have no attraction reduces the resources available to party leaders for overcoming the centrifugal tendencies in parties and elective officials without making policy concessions.

If a party interested in substantive issues could be completely instrumental in its choice of the means to realize those objectives, it would select candidates at party conventions rather than in primaries, seek to increase the amount of patronage available with which to buy agreement from elective officials, place in such offices men who would be responsive to such inducements and thereby amenable to outside direction, and eliminate intraparty democracy. With some modifications, this, of course, is precisely what the Communist party does. It is able to do so because its extreme ideology and the crucial role it plays in the lives of its members permits it to dispense with intraparty democracy as an incentive and otherwise be completely flexible in tactics without sacrificing goals.[12] The amateur club movement cannot act like the Communist party, because it does not have an extreme ideology nor does it play a deep role in the personal lives of its members; it must be internally democratic to survive. Because of the way organizations such as the CDC or the Manhattan reform clubs must be maintained, they can (and must) generate a concern for issues without being able to assemble the power to realize them. So long as the club movement is but one part of a diverse party, raising issues it cannot implement may result in a useful counterpressure to other special-interest groups; should the club movement *become* the party, then programmatic appeals used in a political context that renders discipline of officials impossible but constraints on officials inevitable may

[12] See Phillip Selznick, *The Organizational Weapon* (Glencoe: Free Press, 1960), pp. 17–73. The Communist party relies on its ideology as an incentive and involves its members in numerous activities in order to indoctrinate them. Amateur Democratic clubs have much vaguer goals to use as incentives and, therefore, must rely on the opportunity they offer members to *define* the goals—in short, on internal democracy.

well be less in the public interest than the more traditional party mechanisms.

In California, where the CDC has had experience in attempting to influence legislation, the clubs have discovered that intraparty democracy has not, except in a few cases, made incumbent officials responsible to party policies. On the contrary, the "club types" who rise above the CDC to win public office are often successful precisely because they have a strong personal hold over the membership and a considerable ability to capture their enthusiasm with speeches at conventions and club meetings. This has been clearly shown whenever men such as State Senator Richard Richards or State Controller Alan Cranston take the floor to urge a policy on club members (as they did when they persuaded, in a few minutes, the 1961 Issues Conference to delete a policy statement urging the diplomatic recognition of Red China after a sizable majority the night before had indicated their approval of such a measure). Intraparty democracy in reality places few real checks on incumbents and, instead, gives them an opportunity to modify policy to suit their needs and views. In short, a programmatic orientation and internal democracy may frustrate, rather than further, the possibility of binding elective officials to party program, for program itself provides no basis for discipline but every basis for dissension. The experiences of the CDC in this regard are little different from the experiences of European liberal and socialist parties which find it difficult in the extreme to control the behavior of their parliamentary delegates.

In Wisconsin, the state with the longest experience with volunteer clubs, neither the Republicans nor the Democrats have been able to formulate "party programs" which the party's legislators then support and for which they take responsibility. On the contrary, the legislators do not feel bound by the party platform and tend to resent "outside dictation" of what, for them, should be a matter of "conscience."[13] Both parties' legis-

[13] Frank J. Sorauf, "The Voluntary Committee System in Wisconsin," (Ph.D. thesis, Department of Political Science, University of Wisconsin, 1953), pp. 211–12, 220–23.

lative delegations are split into various factions. The attempt to use the endorsing process to control the behavior of candidates and elective officials has not met with great success. Incumbents are rarely challenged, in part because they have, as successful campaigners who have won in an open primary, political strength of their own which the clubs cannot take away from them. Further, the voluntary committees lack patronage and large campaign resources and thus incumbents are free from sanctions. The parties in Wisconsin, Professor Sorauf concludes, "seem unable to state a consistent party creed and enact a consistent program of legislation, and the classic reasons for party weakness—the need for compromise and decentralization—offer the explanation."[14]

Finally, the insistence on internal democracy, with all that this implies in terms of elaborate procedures, lengthy debates, attention to detail, the need for rhetorical skills, and the absence of patronage controls, incapacitates the clubs from organizing and leading the traditional sources of Democratic party strength—the lower classes and minority groups. It is one thing for the middle-class intelligentsia to compel the party leaders to accord them recognition within the organization and to elect officials in their districts by whom they can feel represented; it is quite another, and far more serious, thing to insist that the party govern itself *entirely* in accord with the dispositions of the amateurs. The only clubs which have been successful in lower-class and minority-group areas have been those which have abandoned the "democratic mold" on which middle-class amateurs insist.

In elections for President, the failure to organize the lower classes might be, at least in the short run, of little significance, for the habits of a lifetime are not easily broken. But in the long run, and particularly in elections for local offices, the consequences of amateurism may be more serious. It is absurd to expect that there will ever be many lower-income Negroes who will feel at ease in an amateur Democratic club. Rather, if they are organized at all, they will be organized on their own

[14] Frank J. Sorauf, "Extra-Legal Political Parties in Wisconsin," *American Political Science Review*, XLVIII (September, 1954), 703.

terms by leaders of their own choosing, and these leaders are likely to be either professional politicians who will demand jobs and favors from the citywide party or clever adventurers who rely on racial, nationalistic, or charismatic appeals that the amateurs will find repellent.

The change in party function sought by the club volunteers goes beyond the tangible matter of patronage. If the center of gravity in the Democratic party moves toward the middle-class, intellectual clubs, then the party will, to a great extent, cease to be a device for the socialization of the lower classes and the excluded minority groups. One party or the other (and, in the past, the Democrats have had no monopoly on this role) has always served as an avenue of upward social mobility for those with limited access to more conventional routes in business, skilled occupations, or the professions. The club movement seeks to alter the parties from an organization which has as a latent function the socialization of the disadvantaged to an organization which serves as a vehicle for the political expression of the already socialized members of the middle-class intelligentsia. Thus, it is not simply the lack of patronage that weakens the clubs' ability to organize the lower classes; it is also the fact that, in reality if not in theory, the clubs do not offer many opportunities for leadership positions to persons who do not share the style of life of the intelligentsia. The clubs lack the intangible as well as the tangible means for harnessing the ambitions of the disadvantaged to a political party.

Running an internally democratic club is a diverting luxury in which only the relatively affluent and secure can indulge, and *being* an internally democratic organization is something relatively few groups can afford.[15] This, of course, is not an argument against entering party politics, contesting primaries, or

[15] Compare the account by Lipset and others of the single major example of a democratic trade union in the United States. S. M. Lipset, Martin Trow, and James S. Coleman, *Union Democracy* (Glencoe: Free Press, 1956). The affluence, status, and education of the members and the high level of their after-work interaction were among the factors which accounted for the two-party system in the ITU.

challenging established leaders. Such ferment is essential if the parties are to get from time to time the necessary infusions of new, vigorous leadership. These infusions are particularly necessary in such one-party cities as New York and Chicago. The argument being made here is not against intraparty competition, as in contests for district leaderships or nominations for public office, but against intraparty democracy—i.e., against institutionalized controls by party members over party leaders. The struggle for party office and partisan nominations is ceaseless and valuable, but the party should not be made to pay an excessively high price for this new leadership by compelling it to alter fundamentally its structure and thus its ability to maintain itself in the interparty contest. This is particularly true when such structural changes have as their result, not genuine intraparty democracy, but only a transfer of power to that segment of the middle-class intelligentsia which is able to operate complex parliamentary procedures. To be sure, some cities and some states are undemocratic in the sense that there is no meaningful two-party competition for office. It is doubtful, however, whether these areas will become significantly more democratic if the leadership of the dominant party is placed in the hands of a group of young leaders responsive to the requirements of Robert's Rules of Order. Rather, such a change will probably mean that the party will serve the ends of these people rather than the ends of those less adept at this style of politics. In no other major democratic nation have the principal political parties of the left or the right found it possible (or, I would add, desirable) to become internally democratic. This is a lesson well worth pondering.

## The Commitment to Issues

Amateur politicians are faced with the same fundamental problem which confronts all party organizations, including political machines: the party leadership must attract and hold the support of two different constituencies, the party workers and the party voters, and the incentives available to induce the support of one group may not be useful to gain the support of the other. The essential problem in maintaining a political organization is that the expectations of the two constituencies are not only different, but are usually in conflict. In a big-city political machine which relies on patronage to reward party workers, the allocation of resources to these workers must be balanced against the need to appeal on a conspicuously non-material basis to middle-class voters in the "newspaper wards." The support of an army of ward leaders and precinct captains who are uninterested in substantive issues weakens the ability of the organization to win votes from those areas which believe that the mere existence of such a patronage-fed army is a violation of a public trust. But using resources to satisfy these voters, by sponsoring civic projects and endorsing prestigious blue-ribbon candidates, lessens the resources available for rewarding the precinct workers who are adept at winning votes in lower-income areas.[16]

A logically identical conflict confronts a party run by club-based amateurs. In this case the resources available to reward party workers are a commitment to issues and to candidates who support these issues. The most active workers are often those most interested in issues. Although many workers remain active in the clubs because of supplementary rewards (such as the fun of the game, the desire to win, or personal ambition), the turnover in the personnel of the club movement is so high that the organization is perpetually faced with the problem of attracting into the organization *new* members and firing the enthusiasm of the apathetic or mildly interested member. Amateur politics must necessarily be inefficient in its use of human resources because it must constantly recruit more workers merely to stay even. Thus, even though many inner-core leaders can be held without extensive and continuing commitments on issues, the need to attract new members (for whom liberalism and candidate personality is usually the primary initial

[16] This argument is made in detail in James Q. Wilson, "The Economy of Patronage," *Journal of Political Economy,* LXIX (August, 1961), 369–80.

inducement) and to stimulate periodic bursts of energy from the rank and file means that the elaboration of policy positions and the search for charismatic leaders must be the clubs' first concern.

To the extent that the clubs can identify themselves with precise policy positions on a whole range of issues and find candidates who embody these beliefs in their manner and speech, they reduce their ability to appeal to voters on the basis of other, non-programmatic incentives, such as simple party allegiance, sectional loyalties, ethnic recognition, and personal favors. To the amateur politician, such appeals are irrational and immoral. In one sense, of course, this is true, for they are largely irrelevant to the ends of government. But a strong case can be made that the function of political parties in the United States (and probably in most Western democracies) has been to convert "irrational" loyalties into political power so that leaders could govern without having to persuade 51 per cent of the electorate to agree on all important issues.

Such persuasion in a country of any size and diversity would be, of course, impossible; parties can be regarded as mechanisms for resolving disagreements in ways which reduce to a minimum the number of commitments elective officials must make to policy positions, many of which perforce would be unattainable, unwise, or contradictory. Of these irrational appeals upon which parties rely, that to traditional loyalties is the most important. Only a relatively small percentage of voters switch from one party to another between any two elections; the bulk of the voters can be taken for granted by the parties. The ignorance of voters is what makes party government possible. If all had to be persuaded at every election on a range of issues about which they had strong feelings, it is unlikely that any party could ever win a clear majority. But a party organization which holds its workers by explicit appeals to issues is, in effect, acting to reduce the ignorance of the voters. A purely opportunistic club leader could argue that worker incentives should be kept from the public (by, for example, having "issues conferences" in secret session) so that good leaders (i.e., those selected by the clubs) could be elected by mobilizing blind partisan loyalties among voters. But few club leaders are so opportunistic, and those who are dare not admit it; the openness and publicity of the issues conferences are hailed as among their greatest virtues.

The need to employ issues as incentives and to distinguish one's party from the opposition along policy lines will mean that political conflict will be intensified, social cleavages will be exaggerated, party leaders will tend to be men skilled in the rhetorical arts, and the party's ability to produce agreement by trading issue-free resources will be reduced. In those eastern cities where reformers are attacking weakened machines, the emergence of the pattern now revealed by the CDC will be deferred while the overriding issue is reform versus bossism, but in time, as reformism lessens in value as a goal and slogan, the programmatic emphasis of the CDC will be cultivated.

It may be wondered whether these consequences of attempting to act in a public-spirited, disinterested way indicate a defect in democratic government. They are only defects if one believes that all aspects of society should be rationalized. In fact, no society, certainly no one as complex and dynamic as ours, can cope with its problems or even cohere *solely* on the basis of reason and concern for the public welfare: elements that are not reasonable and public-spirited must somehow help to hold it together and make it "work." A society must, in other words, depend to some extent upon essential social functions being performed by accident or, at least, without being intended, on the chance that motives that are not public-regarding will give rise to long-run, indirect benefits that will help maintain the society. To destroy in the name of reason and morality the mechanisms, the remote and indirect consequences of which may be indispensable to the maintenance of social order, might be disastrous.

The American party system, there is some reason to think, may be such a mechanism. As Schumpeter and others have observed, the very basis of it is a competitive struggle for people's votes, not a reasonable discussion of the common good. American political parties have by and large been a source of social integration rather than of political cleavage (or even on occasion of political choice); some students have found this their greatest virtue; others have seen it as their principal vice.[17] The thrust of the amateur's involvement has been to attempt to convert the two-party sysem from an integrative to a divisive agency.

If American parties have traditionally been sources of social coherence, this has in part been due to the fact that occasionally, and for very fundamental reasons, they have become identified with the opposite sides of crucial issues. Traditional party allegiances exist today because in the past certain traumatic events precipitated a debate and a meaningful choice. In a real sense, American parties can function today to maintain consensus because the Civil War destroyed that consensus and endowed the names of the parties with a meaning which has persisted and which has not, with certain exceptions, been fundamentally re-examined. To a lesser extent the Bryan candidacy in 1896 and the Smith candidacy in 1928 performed the same function. What is important is that these issues and the resulting polarization of political sentiments were forced upon the parties; they were not generated internally through institutionalized intraparty democracy. In short, a politics of interest is made possible by the fact that the American party system occasionally collapses under the onslaught of a politics of principle. The former is the desirable norm and the latter the undesirable but perhaps necessary exception. If

[17] In addition to the references given in the second footnote to this chapter, we may note some of the historians who have interpreted American politics in part in terms of the role of parties in promoting consensus. These include Daniel J. Boorstin, *The Genius of American Politics* (Chicago: University of Chicago Press, 1953), Louis Hartz, *The Liberal Tradition in America* (Boston: Houghton Mifflin, 1955), and David M. Potter, *People of Plenty* (Chicago: University of Chicago Press, 1954). The older historians who saw American politics in terms of conflict rather than consensus included Vernon Parrington and Charles Beard. A critical review of the "consensus" school is John Higham, "The Cult of the 'American Consensus,'" *Commentary*, XXVII (February, 1959), 93–100.

a matter of vital principle is at stake, the parties will be compelled to face it; if it is not, equipping them with principles through contrivances not only is unlikely, but it reflects a profound misconception of the nature of our political system.

But the amateur is not only interested in reducing the center-seeking, consensus-building tendency of parties. He is also concerned over the constitutional arrangements which govern local political life. Particularly in New York, but to some extent everywhere, he has realized that the extreme decentralization and fragmentation of the formal government makes programmatic discipline extremely difficult and perhaps impossible. Many officeholders have some power; none have enough to impose a policy, but all have enough to block policies. Further, since many have a little power, many are susceptible to the pressures of special interests who seek only to block the proposals of others at minimum cost. The answer to this situation would seem to lie in increasing drastically the formal centralization of power in the government. If all elective executive offices but one (the mayor or governor) were abolished, and if the powers of the legislature, city council, or Board of Estimate were reduced, then the possibilities of strong leadership would be enhanced. Such a centralization of power would have two chief advantages: first, it would make programmatic discipline possible by simply eliminating all but a few (ideally, all but one) elective officials; no one would be left to dispute him. Second, it would protect this single executive from the pressures of special-interest groups by making him so powerful and so visible that, in effect, his price would be too high for any group to pay.

The club movement in New York has, in fact, looked favorably on just such proposals.[18] The charter reform suggested for New York City has received support from the reform clubs on the grounds that it would weaken the hold of the party (i.e., Tammany Hall) over the government by downgrading

[18] Spokesmen for the CDV, the ADA, and the Lexington Club endorsed charter reform in testimony before the Charter Revision Commission. *New York Times*, May 12, 1961.

the legislature (particularly the powerful Board of Estimate which, by and large, is the creature of the borough presidents and the county leaders who stand behind them) and enhance the power of the mayor. Since the reform movement, at least for the foreseeable future, will probably lack significant strength in any borough except Manhattan, the prospects of reform control of the City Council and the Board of Estimate are slim. But the reform movement is much more advantageously placed to influence the choice of citywide officials, particularly the mayor. As the 1961 election suggests (but does not prove), the politically potent slogans (such as anti-bossism), taken together with the sympathetic support reformers are likely to get from other organizations which play a role in the choice of a mayor (such as the press, good-government groups, and civic associations), give them greater power in citywide than in district contests. This has the paradoxical consequence of placing the liberal Manhattan reformers in tacit alliance with the Republicans who, because of their financial and publicity resources, likewise feel that their prospects are best at the citywide level. Even if they cannot elect a Republican mayor, they can at least influence the Democratic party choice by making it costly, in terms of votes, to nominate a candidate who is not at least apparently free from party domination.

The result of such charter reforms would, of course, be to weaken further the Democratic organization while strengthening the formal government. The power and resources of a legislator or borough president would be further reduced in order to enhance the power of the mayor, and this would in turn deprive the party of its patronage and capacity for political intervention in the city administration. Maintaining conrol of the party would become more difficult, and factionalism and increased insurgency would likely result. And, in addition, it would weaken the party's ability to organize and turn out voters in disadvantaged neighborhoods. In short, formal government would be strengthened and informal (or party) government would be weakened. The insurgents struggling for party posts are also struggling to lessen the value of these posts.

Mayor Wagner said as much to the reformers less than a month after his re-election. In a speech to the Lexington Club, he argued that control of the party must now be shifted from party leaders to elective public officials. The party leaders would be "in charge of the technical components of the party mechanism," such as circulating petitions, poll-watching, and canvassing, but "they must never again determine the directions in which the party goes . . . [or the] individuals who are to be offered to the people as the leaders of the government."[19] Presumably Wagner interpreted the 1961 election as meaning that mayors would not only be free of a Tammany-controlled party but of a reform-controlled party as well.

In California, where the political situation is, in effect, the opposite of that found in New York, an opposite reform strategy is emerging. Liberal successes have been made possible in part by the political vacuum which the clubs and the CDC filled. Their influence has probably been greatest on the more prestigious, statewide offices. Not only did the CDC defeat the two candidates who opposed their endorsed nominees, but several statewide offices (such as lieutenant-governor, controller, and treasurer) are filled by men who entered politics in great part through the clubs and who probably would not have had an opportunity to obtain the nomination had the CDC not existed. In California the principal opponents of the clubs are certain incumbent legislators. The weakness of the legal party means that there are few party checks on these officeholders. Thus, the CDC—in contrast to the Manhattan reformers—is desirous of enhancing the powers of the party rather than of the formal government. Strong party officials,

---

[19] *New York Times*, December 2, 1961, p. 1. Wagner had become the *de facto* head of his party in the city. Federal patronage was being cleared through him, Tammany was deferring to him in the selection of a new county leader, and he was using his local patronage powers to attack the old-line leaders in Brooklyn and the Bronx. Apparently, when an elective official enforces his will on the party, that is not "bossism."

if under the control of the "grass-roots," would be desirable as a check on the incumbents.

In one place, a strong party compels reformers to seek stronger elective officials; in another place, strong incumbents compel reformers to seek a strengthened party. In the long run, however, neither strategy may realize the goals of the amateurs. Strengthening the executive and weakening the party converts the problem of creating the conditions for the exercise of power into the problem of controlling the use of that power. A strong executive may be not only more powerful than special-interest groups and a party machine but more powerful than a club-based party as well. The British experience suggests that the formal centralization of power in the hands of one or a few men (the prime minister and his cabinet) produces a situation in which programs may be enacted without serious compromises (and, of course, compromises can be useful as well as debilitating), but the leaders are not, in any except the most general sense, "responsible" to party members and workers. On the contrary, the formal structure of the parties is not, except in the most extreme cases, an important check on party leaders; even Labour leader Hugh Gaitskell has been able to withstand and even ignore much of the severe pressure placed on him by constituency associations and certain trade unions. The checks on executive power are found in other places: an electoral consensus which could not be violated without risking defeat at the polls, economic and international realities, and bureaucratic constraints deriving from the control of information by civil servants.

The alternative strategy—that of strengthening the party at the expense of the legislators—runs the risk of creating a party organization which has a set of maintenance needs which place it in opposition to the clubs and beyond their control. If party leaders can be established and equipped with sufficient power to check effectively public officials, they will in all likelihood be equipped with enough power to resist the demands of the party rank and file.

In short, the "good government" aim of enhancing executive

at the expense of legislative authority in local government is a measure which may strengthen the Republicans (who fare best in citywide and statewide contests) and incumbent officials. The amateur Democrats might usefully recall the fact that such measures have in the past been adopted in great part in order to place political power in the hands of Republicans who had moved out of the central city.

## Partial Success

The foregoing comments apply in their full force only if the amateurs attain relatively complete control over their party organizations. In fact, of course, their achievements have been thus far very limited. It then becomes necessary to ask what significance the amateur Democrats have for party politics under conditions of partial success.

The amateur clubs have appeared in only a relatively small number of communities. Generally speaking, the possibility of a liberal or reform club movement with an intellectual orientation exists only where the traditional party resources are absent or being eliminated, where lower-income and minority groups have not established themselves in positions of political power, and where "cosmopolitan" members of the middle class are found in large numbers. There are relatively few places where all these circumstances exist in combination, and thus relatively few places where a sizable number of amateur Democrats are likely to emerge.

The possibility of volunteers significantly affecting politics depends upon the extent to which they are attracted by the prospects of residing in communities which are in the area's political center of gravity. In the Democratic party of the industrial states of the northeast, this center of gravity is found in the large cities where, for generations, organizations based on the mobilization of lower-income immigrant voters have dominated the state party. In the more recently settled states of the west, where immigrants are a much smaller portion of the whole and where the larger cities are often governed under non-partisan arrangements, the locus of power within the party may be, not in city organizations, but elsewhere.

If few central cities fascinate in the way that Manhattan does, one would expect to find club politics stronger in the suburbs. But in only a few states do the suburbs play a crucial role in the internal affairs of the party. Typically, control of the state party is in the hands of city leaders and, although the suburban vote may be important in determining the outcome of general elections, it rarely carries great weight in the councils of the party. Representation in the Democratic State Convention in New York, for example, is prorated according to votes cast for the party ticket, and thus the areas with the largest number of Democratic votes are assured predominance in the convention. Further, the New York Democratic State Committee allocates its membership on the basis of representation in the state assembly.[20] In the 1958 election for governor, New York City cast 51.8 per cent of the total Democratic vote, while the four suburban counties around the city cast only 14.2 per cent. The vast majority of Democratic state legislators and congressmen are from the city. Thus, both the State Convention and the State Committee are controlled by urban leaders, and although the Democratic vote in the suburbs has been increasing at least since 1946, that increase has not been such as to threaten city dominance.[21] A similar situation prevails in Illinois.

In Connecticut, the counties and small towns which are heavily populated with New York City commuters often have very liberal, intellectually oriented local party organizations, but the structure of the Democratic party in the state places power firmly in the hands of the leaders of the city organizations in Hartford, New Haven, Bridgeport, and elsewhere.[22]

[20] Frank J. Munger and Ralph A. Straetz, *New York Politics* (New York: New York University Press, 1960), p. 65.

[21] *Ibid.*, p. 45. The city's share of the total vote cast in the state has fallen in the last twenty years, but not greatly. In 1938, it cast 47.9 per cent of the total; in 1958, 41.3 per cent.

[22] Duane Lockard, *New England State Politics* (Princeton: Princeton University Press, 1959), pp. 258–59.

In Illinois, the DFI has been able to organize clubs in some suburban areas, but there is little chance that they will ever carry much weight in party councils dominated by the Cook County machine.

In these areas, amateur political activity becomes confined, for all practical purposes, to the local communities. Suburban political activity by Democrats, particularly when it occurs in areas likely to return Republican majorities, rarely creates opportunities for the club leaders to rise above the suburban level, and thus the energies of these people must be focused, if they are to have an outlet at all, on either simply turning out the sparse Democratic vote in general elections or on influencing school and village politics.

The movement to the suburbs has had as one of its important political consequences the insulation of large numbers of potential activists from partisan politics. These would-be leaders place themselves outside the channels of party recruitment. They are voters who must be won but not insurgents who must be accommodated (except insofar as they can capture newspaper headlines with a dramatic cause).

In these small towns, the amateurs may do very well as sources of the local political elite, for such communities are often filled with people who accept the ethic of the amateur even if they do not agree with all his substantive goals. In many such towns, however, the population is divided between the metropolis-oriented "cosmopolitan," many of whom are commuters, and the village-oriented "local," and the conflict between the two can be as intense as between a reformer and a big-city boss.[23]

Given the minority status of the amateur club movement in the parties of the cities and states we have considered, the amateur's concern for issues becomes simply one additional source of pressure in a vast system of pressures. And, to the extent that parties are unable to protect elected officials from

[23] See Mark K. Adams, *A Report on Politics in New Castle, New York* (Cambridge: Joint Center for Urban Studies, 1961), pp. II–12 to II–16, for a case of suburban amateur politics in which this conflict has been avoided.

uninformed opinion, something can be said for having pressures from the liberal left to offset pressures from the right, if only to permit elective officials to take advantage of this balance of forces in order to escape from pressure altogether.

In the areas where the amateur is strong, the possibilities of continued expansion are limited. When a neighborhood "boss" has been defeated, the local elective offices filled with amateur Democrats, and the outer limits of club growth reached, it is plausible to expect that amateur enthusiasm will decline somewhat from the fever pitch of its early days. The amateurs who require the highest level of issue commitment, electoral conflict, and emotional appeal will drift away at first; those who have developed what one reformer called an "instinctive pragmatism" will remain active longer. But those who will remain active the longest will be the ambitious young lawyers —the former assistant district attorneys—who are in small or private practices and eager for public office. And these men will provide representation in the government for their constituents. The Jewish lawyer who won office on a wave of reform or liberalism will remain, a permanent reminder that his Jewish constituents were not satisfied with the Irish politician who had been their representative before, but also an ex-amateur who has acquired the habits of the professional as he has been freed from the constraints of his amateur club.

There are some realistic amateur leaders who acknowledge that the club movement will never *become* the Democratic party and that its initial vigor cannot endure, even though it succeeds in capturing many party offices. They will nonetheless defend the amateur Democrats because they form a needed countervailing power against the excesses of professional party leaders in one-party cities and because they can keep open the channels of party recruitment and thus preserve the party from its inevitable tendency toward ossification. Such arguments have some plausibility.

In this view, the pressure on behalf of liberalism generated by the clubs is valuable even if a party composed solely of clubs would be disadvantageous. The amateur club movement, it is argued, is an effort to defend principles and interests which are undefended and perhaps even unrepresented in the conventional political system. This view is akin to that of some city planners who, realizing the theoretical and practical problems which prevent them from engaging in "comprehensive" planning, defend their profession by asserting that planners specialize in protecting values which are not guarded by other specialist agencies and which deserve to take precedence.[24]

This position can be raised to an even higher level of generality. In effect, a defense of an amateur politics of principle can be based, not on the presumed compatibility between the amateur club system and the procedural requirements of democracy, but on the substantive ends the club system seeks. Generally, club leaders, and particularly reform club leaders in New York, defend themselves on the grounds that only their kind of political party is consistent with "democracy." In this concluding chapter some reasons have been given why this may not be so. But a small number of club leaders will argue that amateur clubs are valuable because they seek and defend ends which have few other defenders. This is a view which is implicit in much of the academic and polemical writing on the desirability of party government. It is not accidental that the overwhelming majority of "party government" advocates are liberal democrats.[25] Only rarely do conservatives advocate these kinds of structural changes. What advocates of party government seem to want are not just strong, programmatic parties, but the creation of a strong programmatic, *liberal* party. In the extreme case, as Epstein has noted, a writer like Duverger wants not just "responsible" parties but a class-conscious Socialist party with a dues-paying mass membership.[26]

[24] Cf. Alan Altschuler, "The Process of Planning in Two American Cities" (Ph.D. thesis, Department of Political Science, University of Chicago, 1961).

[25] For example, Stephen K. Bailey, Thomas K. Finletter, Charles M. Hardin, Maurice Duverger, Fritz Morstein Marx, James MacGregor Burns, etc.

[26] Leon D. Epstein, "British Mass Parties in Comparison with American Parties," *Political Science Quarterly*, LXXI (March, 1956), 123–25.

Politics is, in this view, a struggle between "haves" and "have-nots," and the former group, which is usually dominant by virtue of its possession of other sources of power (wealth, propaganda, social position, military strength) is interested only in blocking change and consolidating the status quo. For the have-nots, who seek change, only political power is available. Organization is essential to mobilize that power, and a programmatic party is the best kind of organization.

In this respect, progressive thinking about party government in the United States has passed through several phases. In the nineteenth century, before the first major reform movement, party government was seen as possible (the big-city machines were obviously effective) but undesirable (because machine bosses were corrupt and inefficient). After the reform wave in the first decades of the twentieth century, party government became neither possible (some, but not all, machines had been weakened) nor desirable (direct democracy would, at least for the Populists, replace party organization). Today, party government is once again looked upon as desirable (it is an alternative to government by pressure groups), but it is probably no longer possible without fundamental constitutional changes.

The insistence on intraparty democracy may make this kind of party government even less possible by weakening the power of the party's leaders. It is instructive to note that an influence perhaps more powerful than the reform movement in affecting the kinds of candidates chosen in New York has been the Liberal party. It has usually enrolled only between sixty and seventy thousand voters in recent years, but it has polled between two and three hundred thousand votes, often the difference between victory and defeat for a Democrat who wins the Liberal nomination. But reformers do not participate in the Liberal party, not because it is ineffectual, but because it is internally undemocratic and has no place for a participating mass membership.

If the final defense of amateur club politics is its ability to generate pressure on behalf of liberal ends which would otherwise be overcome by conservative pressures, it becomes difficult to admit this without destroying one of the incentives for amateur membership and effort. It would be tantamount to conceding that an internally democratic programmatic party generally is unattainable. Thus, to generate liberal pressure of this sort, it may be necessary for club leaders to persuade members that the ultimate goal of a programmatic, internally democratic party is attainable, although in fact it is not. In short, to obtain action at all for liberal causes within the framework of a party, people must act *as if* their plans could be realized. This requires ignorance of the true state of affairs.

But political action based on this kind of ignorance entails risks. Most club leaders are neither so sophisticated as to realize that political parties cannot function and never have functioned, except with disastrous consequences, in the manner they envisage, nor are they so unenlightened as to believe that the present parties are all that conventional party leaders claim them to be. This state of partial knowledge creates a fundamental problem: a concern for issues, by making it difficult for candidates saddled with these issues to win elections, reduces the likelihood of attaining the ostensible goals of the club movement and makes these goals instead simply incentives useful for the maintenance of a volunteer organization. The debate over issues becomes, in a strict sense, a spurious debate, because it is not a responsible discussion of real policy alternatives but a device for generating incentives for party activists.[27]

[27] Sorauf comes to the same conclusion about the Wisconsin parties. He writes that a "strong ideological orientation" has as its function "not to present clear-cut, unequivocal policy programs to the voters" but to serve as "an internal, intra-party cohesive, binding the various levels of the party together in a common bond." "Voluntary Committees . . . ," p. 257. Sorauf seems to be less pessimistic than I about the implications of this.

# Index

Abner, Willoughby, 79, 80, 84
Adamowski, Benjamin, 80, 235–36
Adams, Frank, 254
Adams, Mark K., 366 n.
Adrian, Charles R., 162 n.
Agar, Herbert, 341 n.
Akers, Anthony, 208 n.
Alinsky, Saul, 286
Altschuler, Alan, 368 n.
Amateur: concept of party function, 18–21; definition of, 2–3; general description, 2–16; social characteristics, 13–15
American G.I. Forum, 286
American Labor Party, 39
Americans for Democratic Action (ADA), 1, 44, 77, 78, 160 n., 172, 360 n.
Anderson, Glenn, 147
Ansonia Club, 273
Arvey, Jacob, 70

Bailey, Stephen K., 341 n., 368 n.
Baisden, Richard, 274 n.
Baldwin Hills Club, 189
Baltzell, Jack, 130 n., 230
Bancroft, Mary, 174 n.
Banfield, Edward C., 19, 67 n., 342 n.
Barasch, Mal, 231 n.
Barnard, Chester I., 29 n., 170
Beard, Charles, 359 n.
Beeman, William, 296 n.
Bell, Charles G., 107 n.
Bell, Daniel, 159 n., 268 n.
Bendiner, Robert, 58 n., 140 n.
Beverly Hills Democratic Club: activities, 166, 167–68, 180, 189; attitudes toward affluence of, 214, 215; campaign tactics, 334–35; membership, 118, 230, 263 n.
Boorstin, Daniel, 359 n.

Bragdon, Paul, 231 n.
Brotherhood party, 276–77
Brown, Edmund G. "Pat," 101, 112, 203, 205 n., 299, 321; criticism of by party members, 103; endorsed by CDC for governor, 116
Brown, Seyom, 167 n.
Buckley, Charles, 50 n., 51 n., 56
Buffalo convention, 47, 51; and CDV, 58–59
Bunzel, John H., 329 n.
Burns, James MacGregor, 368 n.

California Democratic Council (CDC), 1, 108, 160, 171, 181 ff., 224, 335, 358, 362; alienation from organized labor, 273–75; class basis, 258 ff.; conflict with County Committee, 118; conflict with professionals, 295–301, 307–8, 310; co-ordination problems, 251–52, 256–57; distribution of power in, 120–21; endorsements, 115–17, 247–51, 324; goals, 126, 129, 141–52, 290, 327; intraparty democracy, 352; lack of local focus, 162–63; as model for DFI, 88–89; from Negroes, 278–79, 283–85; north-south differences, 121–25; organization of, 114–15; power of, 321–25, 327–30; requirements of clubs, 117–18; resources, 338–39, 348; and resurgence of California Democratic Party, 110–14; turnover, 229–30
California Republican Assembly, 187
Calkins, Fay, 79 n.
Campaign tactics, 330–35; in N.Y.C., 331–32; in L.A., 334–35
Canavan, Francis P., 23 n.

*371*

Mattura, Elsie Gleason, 236 n.
Mayer, Martin, 219 n.
Mead, George H., 11, 11 n.
Medow, Florence, 78 n.
Merli, John, 134, 282
Merriam, Robert, 71, 80, 231
Merton, Robert K., 10
Mexican-American Political Association (MAPA), 286
Mexican-Americans: Community Service Organization, 286–87; scarcity among amateurs, 268, 273, 285–87
Meyerson, Martin, 67 n.
Michels, Robert, 349 n.
Mid-City Club, 189
Middle-class: basis of amateur club movement, 258–88; basis of N.Y.C. reformism, 61–64, 135, 258 ff.; basis of progressives' movement, 25; dwindling numbers in Manhattan, 42; Jewish membership and club movement, 263, 265–66
Midonick, Millard, 130 n., 213 n., 230
Mikva, Abner, 82 ff., 231
Miller, George, Jr., 112, 113, 115 ff., 124
Mitchell, John Purroy, 38, 39, 304
Mitchell, Stephen A., 22 n.; and DFI, 92–93, 94 n., 338
Morse, Arthur D., 45
Mosk, Stanley, 116, 320, 329
Motivation; *see* Incentives
Moynihan, Daniel P., 303 n., 308
Munger, Frank J., 365 n.
Munnell, William, 123
Murphy, Frank, 69 n.
Murray Hill Citizens Club, 196, 198, 246, 253 n., 254, 317 n.
Murray, Thomas E., 58
Myers, Helen, 113–14, 116, 117, 122

Negro Voters League, 282
Negroes, 41, 42, 76, 189; in Chicago, 68, 154, 285; in garment unions, 265 n.; insurgent victories, 48; in Los Angeles, 278–79, 283–85; in New York City, 279–83; scarcity among amateurs, 259, 260, 268, 273, 277

New Chelsea Club for Democrats, 50 n., 193 n.
New Democratic Club, 196, 254 n., 259 n.
New York Committee for Democratic Voters; *see* Committee for Democratic Voters
Nichols, Mary Peret, 134 n.
Nixon, Richard, 55, 117, 172
Non-partisanship, 23, 96, 110; in Chicago, 82

Odegard, Peter, 115, 116, 183 n.
O'Dwyer, William, 43 ff.
Ohrenstein, Manfred, 218 n., 242 n.
Organization, theory of, 29–30
Organizational maintenance, 30, 160, 226–57, 351; authority problems, 232–39; co-ordination problems, 251–57; endorsement problems, 239–51; turnover problems, 226–32
Ottenberg, James S., 128 n., 133 n.

Pacific Palisades Club, 189
Palmer, Kyle, 149 n.
Parker, Alan, 204 n.
Park-Hudson Independent Democrats, 272–73
Parkhurst, Charles, 38
Parrington, Vernon, 359 n.
Parsons, Talcott, 27 n.
Patronage, 24, 128, 130, 200–225, 293, 348–49, 354, 356; in California, 101–3, 203, 329; in Illinois, 201–5; in N.Y., 40; in N.Y.C., 135–36, 197, 201 n., 205–16; and reform, 205–16
Pauley, Edwin W., 112
Peel, Roy V., 35 n., 36
Pitchell, Robert J., 103 n., 111 n.
Political ethic, 8–9; Yankee, 28
Political parties, function of, 16–20, 344, 349
Politics of interest, 19
Politics of principle, 19
Pomper, Gerald, 331 n.
Populism, 25 ff., 182 n.
Potter, David M., 359 n.
Powell, Adam Clayton, Jr., 34 n., 47–48; conflicts with reformers, 280–82
Powell, Paul, 76–77

# PHOENIX BOOKS
## *in Political Science*

# PHOENIX BOOKS
## *in Sociology*